Kennan and the Art of Foreign Policy

Kennan and the Art of Foreign Policy

ANDERS STEPHANSON

Harvard University Press
Cambridge, Massachusetts
London, England
1989

Library of Congress Cataloging-in-Publication Data
Stephanson, Anders.
  Kennan and the art of foreign policy / Anders Stephanson.
    p.   cm.
  Bibliography: p.
  Includes index.
  ISBN 0-674-50265-5 (alk. paper)
  1. Kennan, George, 1904–   . 2. United States—Foreign
relations—1945–   —Philosophy. 3. United States—Foreign relations—
Soviet Union—Philosophy. 4. Soviet Union—Foreign relations—
United States—Philosophy. I. Title.
E748.K374S73 1989
327.2′092′4—dc19

88-21810
CIP

For Torsten and Inger Stephanson

Preface

In the annals of American diplomacy, George F. Kennan stands tall and daunting, a figure of articulate intelligence who thought about the action but also beyond it. He was not always a great diplomat, for his imagination was lively, and he lacked the self-effacing patience which is so essential to the profession at its most mundane; but he was a great analyst and policymaker, one of the very few this country has produced in foreign affairs, perhaps the finest since John Quincy Adams.

Kennan's fame, or notoriety, rests chiefly on his role in the events of the immediate postwar era, associated as he commonly (and dubiously) is with the so-called containment policy. This centrality was, however, coupled with a certain marginality. The short but critical period (1946–1948) when he played a decisive part in articulating American policy should indeed not serve to conceal the very basic differences of political perspective that set him apart from much of his professional surroundings. As a conservative of organicist orientation, he was in fact largely outside the political and cultural mainstream of the United States.

This quality of being both inside and outside, at once representative and not representative, was one reason I chose Kennan as my object of inquiry. I wanted originally to illuminate the discursive boundaries of American foreign policy during that crucial postwar time when our present system of world politics was formed but things were still fairly fluid. The idea was to see how the underlying character of American analysis limited perceived policy options, an inquiry given added immediacy by the recent unexpected reappearance in the United States of a political language very similar in tone and nature to that of the late 1940s and early 1950s. One could have proceeded to study a variety of anonymous documents in order to reveal the epistemic nature of the discursive formation within which policy was formulated, but preliminary research along these Foucauldian lines proved unrewarding. I found it more congenial to arrive at the intended limits by following Kennan's trajectory toward and, eventually, past them. No other policymaker in the period showed comparable analytical powers and facility of language; no other policymaker espoused the same political ambivalences toward his given tasks. In order to get a proper sense for this new and individual subject matter, it became practical to expand the time span under consideration while preserving a focus on the constitutive postwar developments.

There is now a vast library concerning the early cold war, but the type of project I had in mind seemed mostly to fall outside the range of relevant disciplines and subdisciplines. The history of ideas generally deals with theories and concepts other than those employed in the making of foreign policy; political science usually centers on more contemporary sources and typically engages in either functional description or construction of models; and diplomatic history, the most obvious province, tends to subordinate the explicitly analytical element to the demands of narrative. My aim, by contrast, was to subject Kennan's historical texts to serious theoretical examination, drawing intermittently upon sources that may seem somewhat odd in a diplomatic history proper, such as theories of ethics, aesthetics, and ideology.

If the result is a bit eclectic, there is actually a good deal less theory here than was intended. The reason is quite simple. Historians, because of the very nature of their discipline, spend a lot of time finding appropriate sources (and sometimes even more making sure that none have been overlooked). Equipped with what is often a wealth of artifacts, they must then evaluate the status of their documents and arrange them into some sort of order. Finally, they have to write something readable about all of this. In such circumstances it is not surprising that allowances for analytical contemplation diminish, or that one is occasionally wont to think that colleagues in literary criticism lead a comparatively charmed life.

This, then, is ultimately a work of history, replete with the apparatus that normally attaches to such a product. The emphasis on text over context will nevertheless make some readers wonder about its methodological relationship to that amorphous group of theories now referred to as poststructuralism. A comment is required. History often reduces method to a question of source criticism and its auxiliary rules and regulations: establishing the status of the evidence by ascribing authenticity and authorship to a set of documents and then arguing their relevance to problems posed. To the extent that these procedures are based on a correspondence theory of truth, they are certainly deserving of criticism; plain adequation of concept and externality as a measure of truth has after all long been undermined from a variety of philosophical standpoints. Furthermore, twenty years after the advent of poststructuralism it has become impossible to regard the text as a fixed entity with inviolable boundaries and unequivocal meaning. The very sanctity of the document is in doubt. But if source criticism in itself therefore cannot *exhaust* the problem of method, one would be equally wrong to dismiss it as some mere outdated residue of identity thinking. History is centrally concerned with the collation of massive amounts of basic evidence, while much of poststructuralism is centrally concerned with the fragment, the isolated incident, that which escapes the normal grid of perception. Although Michel Foucault showed that the two are not necessarily incompatible, we are on the whole dealing here with different kinds of research projects, resulting in different kinds of knowledge. Whatever their respective merits, this much seems clear: to abandon on purely theoretical grounds the field of history in favor of some ahistorical fascination with the fragment is also to abandon the field of politics. It is to renounce any claim to power over the center itself.

Still, one advance we do owe poststructuralism is the substitution of a decentered ego for the indivisible self of old. My critique has consequently not been undertaken on the assumption that "George F. Kennan" is a unified consciousness which, all things being equal, ought to be producing unified statements. Though I have looked for internal incoherences, these have been seen as inevitable products of a subjectivity constituted through contradictory practices and impulses. Relatedly, I have not on the whole been concerned with the phenomenological quest to learn what Kennan thought he meant by what he said at any given time; nor have I attempted to write history "as it really was." I do not consider such projects either uninteresting or indefensible. They are merely not mine. Kennan as a historical subject has been accessible to me only as a series of texts read in the 1980s and has been dealt with from that vantage point alone.

There are three connected but distinct parts, or problematics, outlined at some length in the introduction to each and thus given only the briefest mention here. The first part analyzes Kennan's view of the Soviet Union from the 1930s to 1950. He was trained as a Soviet expert and his entire adult life has been indelibly marked by this experience, as has his analysis of American foreign policy. The second part raises the question of how national interest in that policy might be understood, the historical reference point being, chronologically, the period (1947–1950) during which he served as chief policy planner, as well as, thematically, the issues of Germany, NATO, and the Third World. I also examine his attempt after 1950 to find the basis for a coherent and "realistic" policy in this concept of national interest. The third part is a consideration on Kennan's political and cultural critique of American society, or, more precisely, on the difficulties of being an organicist conservative in a society that seems inherently unorganic. It is an attempt to render Kennan's domestic marginality more distinct, to pinpoint his subject-position, and may thus be read as a conclusion of sorts. Finally, there are two appendixes relating to the first problematic: a survey of Kennan's view of the Soviet Union after 1950 and my own reflection on the place of ideology in Soviet foreign policy.

I have largely avoided the practice of informing the reader in advance about everything that is to follow, preferring instead to let the logic of the work unfold on its own. There are some leaps in time here and there, but the underlying structure is more diachronic than synchronic. Despite stretches of traditionally conceived diplomatic history, the overall analytical focus on Kennan's texts presupposes a certain acquaintance with the setting. Those, incidentally, who delight in essayistic footnotes will find a kindred spirit here.

Historiography on American foreign policy tends to be a politicized art, and this work is no exception: I write from the viewpoint of a neutralist Swede of socialist conviction. My intention has otherwise been to "go through" Kennan in order to preserve his moment of truth, to be polemical without being captious, moralizing, or censorious. I have tried, perhaps not altogether successfully, to follow Gibbon's apothegm that history should both instruct and amuse.

Acknowledgments

Responsibility for the content of this work rests with me alone, but I should like to thank the following individuals for assisting me in various ways and to varying degrees: Cornel West, Torsten Stephanson, Inger Stephanson, Ron Steel, Daniela Salvioni, the Salvioni family, Andrew Ross, Sir Frank Roberts, Owen Ranta, Robert O. Paxton, Alec Nove, Mark Kesselman, George F. Kennan, Fredric Jameson, Bruce Hoffman, Sir William Hayter, Wendy Graham, Sara Giller, Jean Franco, Eric Foner, Tony Eprile, Michael Brown, Giuseppe Boffa, and Larry Bland.

Certain institutions have been very helpful in material ways: the Department of History at the University of Gothenburg; the Department of History at Columbia University; the Truman Library at Independence, Missouri; the Center for International Study at the University of Southern California, and the Center for International and Strategic Affairs at UCLA.

Personal thanks are owed as well to three teachers and friends. Herbert G. Nicholas, Rhodes Professor of American Government and Institutions at Oxford University (emeritus), had nothing directly to do with this treatise, but it would scarcely have come about had he not once put his money against dubious odds on an unproven Swedish graduate student interested in Americana. I also owe more than a little to Lennart K. Persson, professor of history at the University of Gothenburg. On, I fear, highly questionable grounds, he saw to it that I was given a doctoral grant in absentia from my alma mater. Final and special thanks to James P. Shenton of Columbia University, long-suffering supervisor of the work on which this book is based.

Contents

PART I

The Soviet Problematic

Relations between the United States and the Soviet Union are strained, and so they have been, in the main, ever since the October Revolution itself. Before the Second World War, one might have regarded this situation with a certain detachment, as nothing much followed from it. The war, however, had the effect of making the inherent contradiction between these two powers the dominant one in world politics and eventually something altogether more sinister in scope. For a war would now mean a global and nuclear war, which is to say that everyone on this earth, regrettably, has a stake in how Americans and Russians resolve their conflicts.[1]

As long as the nature of the two parties is what it is, contradiction rather than harmony will be the order of the day. Yet both sides are aware that neither can afford a war, and it is thus in their mutual interest to ensure that the antagonism takes other forms. A reasonable grasp of each other's position would therefore seem imperative. This is hardly a controversial proposition; but when one actually inquires into the nature of the requisite knowledge, what it means to "know," vexatious questions arise.

Such knowledge, as I see it, is the product of political discourses, relatively coherent structures based on two incommensurable conceptions of truth and meaning. By incommensurable I do not mean that these discourses are entirely untranslatable or mutually unintelligible but merely that each has its own conditions of positivity, which at a certain fundamental level do not allow external propositions to be viewed as meaningful.[2] For example, just as the American classification of the Soviet Union as a totalitarian dictatorship is unassimilable to the discursive formation of the Russian observer, so the Soviet analogue of the United States as an imperialist class dictatorship is meaningless within the American frame of reference. It is only internally that the designations make proper sense and can lay claim to truth and knowledge. Yet translation and comprehension between the two discourses is possible on other levels and for several reasons. Most obviously, simple statements having to do with elementary human needs and characteristics are fairly universal. Moreover, there are essential overlaps and affinities since both have roots in Enlightenment thought. Finally, and most important, having entered into a rising number of common spheres with common rules, the antagonists have also acquired an appropriate discourse (for example, "You have many more ICBMs than we do"). To use Wittgenstein's terminology, they have become part of a language game.

In most conflictual games it is necessary to be able to situate oneself within the adversary's cast of thought. Formulation of tactics and strategy is otherwise impossible, unless one happens to be in a position of omnipotence or is so separated from the other side that real engagement almost never takes place. Either case is unusual, though the latter monological condition was indeed characteristic of the cold war at its most glacial. Vigorous leaps of the imagination into foreign space will, however, eventually come back to basic domestic truth, which is why these maneuvers are doomed in the end to a secondary rank. Two discernible projects are therefore involved in understanding the other side. The first is the overarching task of determining the "real" position of the opponent, a task that can be carried out only within one's own given terms of truth. The second is the subordinate problem of understanding how the other party *thinks* he or she thinks and acts.

These considerations form the starting point for the ensuing critique of George F. Kennan's attempt, in roughly the period between 1930 and 1950, to understand Soviet foreign policy and to devise an American response. My intention is to give a decidedly empirical alpha and omega of this trajectory and to clear away some sedimented historical misreadings of his views. A second aim is to take issue with him, on specific points as well as on the nature of his knowledge.

1

The Thirties

Let us first strike a biographical note and give a brief account of George Kennan's background and whereabouts during his early career.[1] He was born in 1904 in Madison, Wisconsin, where his father, fifty-two years old at the time, practiced law. Two years later his mother died, and he was brought up variously by his stepmother, aunt, and sisters. At the age of thirteen he was sent to St. John's Military Academy in Delafield, Wisconsin. Eventually he found his way to Princeton, where, as an inhibited and relatively impoverished student in this most social of Ivy League colleges, he cut a singularly undistinguished figure. After graduating he applied, as a more or less negative choice, to the Foreign Service and was ultimately accepted. Minor posts at Geneva, Hamburg, and Riga were followed in 1929 by his selection for the newly created specialist training for Russianists, in his case taking place at the Seminar für Orientalische Sprachen in Berlin. This Bismarckian institution imbued him with a sense of realpolitik, but his curriculum, in accordance with State Department wishes, focused entirely on the pre-Soviet period. Having lived and socialized with Russian émigrés, he thus emerged with a good background in Russian history while remaining largely ignorant of the revolutionary regime he was presumably meant to analyze. His lifelong inability to grapple with Soviet marxism can be traced partly to that peculiar form of preparation.

He returned to Riga in 1931. The capital of Latvia, then still independent, this Baltic city had become the chief source of American intelligence on the Soviet Union, a regime that the United States had yet to recognize. When diplomatic relations were finally established two years later, Kennan moved on to Moscow, where he remained until 1937. After a stint at the Russian desk in Washington, he was sent to Czechoslovakia in the fateful autumn of 1938. That country soon having been extinguished, he proceeded to the seat of its new master regime, Berlin. This German sojourn ended with his internment when the United States entered the war at the end of 1941; not until six months later was he able to return to Washington. There we may also terminate for the moment this dry *curriculum vitae.*

The Foreign Service he had entered was a social elite of which there were cumulatively no more than eight hundred members between 1924 and 1946—preponderantly WASPs from the Northeast, upper-middle or upper-class males equipped with an Ivy League education.[2] More middle-class members from other colleges came in during the thirties but soon assumed the air of superior apartness that permeated the Foreign Service. The spectrum of attitudes was similarly predictable. Conservative by temperament, the service evinced a good deal of tolerance for Nazi Germany—and a lot less for the Soviet Union. Anti-Semitism was not uncommon. "Uncivilized" parts of the world were held in low esteem. Despite the elite mentality, however, these Eurocentric officials felt unappreciated by politicians and public alike. The depression decade was indeed a bad one for them. Salaries were cut; public respect reached a nadir; and Franklin D. Roosevelt disliked professional diplomats, whom he was to shun till the end. Furthermore, since this was a period of entrenched isolationism, there was little exciting work to perform. Yet the relegation of the service was on the whole condign. Intellectually incurious, these diplomats had slight understanding of the complex developments that marked international relations in the thirties. When the war came, they were inadequately prepared.

Though politically close to the adumbrated image, Kennan differed from it in other important ways. He was probably from a more frugal background. He was a specialist. He was neither a snob nor an anti-Semite. He was certainly no myrmidon of the bureaucracy. Though he was loyal to its Idea, his actual relations with it expressed the impatience of someone extraordinarily ambitious, given not only to writing voluminous and often unrequested analyses of increasing literary aspiration but also periodically to doubts, ulcers, and resignations.[3]

He remained in the period initially under examination an obscure junior officer, albeit one in exceedingly good standing, as evidenced by a plethora of commendations for good work.[4] This subordinate station has something to do with the scarcity of sources. It rarely falls on secondary officers to write expansive interpretations of politics; and if they do, such *opera* must pass through the hierarchical mill before achieving the status of a despatch. No more than half a dozen substantial texts are available from this period, including ordinary diplomatic papers and soliloquies written outside official duty.

When Kennan joined the Foreign Service, the United States had no official relations with the Soviet Union. American forces had in fact participated in the postrevolutionary intervention against the Bolshevik regime, which had itself expected to be only a brief stage in an international sequence of revolution. None of this was conducive to diplomatic relations. However, once it became clear in the 1920s that neither the Soviet government nor its capitalist adversaries were about to crumble, diplomacy and trade gradually resumed. The United States, alone among the powers of size, continued to refuse Moscow recognition on the grounds that it was a revolutionary government which had repudiated its war debts.[5]

Through successive administrations this posture assumed the character of orthodoxy, particularly in the departments of State and Commerce.[6] Profound changes in the nature of the Moscow government were required, amounting in effect to a demand that the Soviet Union cease being the Soviet Union. To adopt such an approach was obviously to declare the project hopeless from the start.[7] Kennan's attitude was if anything more negative:

[It is my belief that] the present system of Soviet Russia is unalterably opposed to our traditional system, that there can be no possible middle ground or compromise between the two, that any attempts to find such a middle ground, by the resumption of diplomatic relations or otherwise, are bound to be unsuccessful, that the two systems cannot even exist together in the same world unless an economic cordon is put around one or the other of them, and that within twenty or thirty years either Russia will be capitalist or we shall become communist.[8]

Coming from a person whose career would probably be tied to the future of Soviet-American relations, this was a remarkably bleak scenario. Roosevelt chose to ignore the orthodox view, however, and moved instead during his first year in office to recognize Moscow.[9]

The main reason for the altered course appears to have been the increasing aggressiveness of Japan, on whose rulers recognition was presumed to have a sobering effect. With this general aim the Soviet Union was entirely in sympathy, and the two powers accordingly patched together a compromise agreement that rendered the act politically acceptable to Roosevelt's home audience.[10]

A dominant theme in the American debate had been not Japan but the nexus between recognition and expanding trade, an issue that on closer inspection seems to have been misconstrued. The background was this. While denying the diplomatic existence of the Soviet Union, the United States had by 1930 become one of its most important trading partners. Two years later the flourishing traffic had suffered a great decline. Thus originated the argument that the ebb had been caused by the absence of diplomatic relations, the establishment of which would once again open greener pastures for American business. Both Russians and prorecognition Americans peddled this thesis unblushingly and to some extent probably believed it; but in truth it was mostly a potent piece of conjury. For this was the depression, and even though trade had been small by American standards, signs of possible improvement were eagerly seized upon.[11]

The issue also inspired Kennan to make his first significant analyses. Marshaling a formidable battery of data, he advanced two essentially empirical arguments against the idea of a connection between recognition and increased trade. In the first place, he pointed out, trade agreements were presumed to follow recognition, but previous experience showed such agreements to have been so constituted as to put Moscow's trading partners at a manifest disadvantage. The strong implication was that future agreements would similarly disappoint expectation.[12] Second, courtesy of the depression, Russian export markets were shrinking, leaving less and less in the currency coffers with which to buy goods abroad, all of which would put a damper on prospects of increased trade, except with countries willing to grant extensive credits on overly generous terms.[13]

These were plausible arguments. Yet the Soviet-American trade agreement that did in fact follow recognition eventually stabilized trade and was generally more profitable to the Americans than expected, this according to Kennan's own estimation a few years later.[14] The predictive value of his second point was much better: the Soviet Union found itself having to curtail trade in the thirties precisely on the grounds that its exports could not finance its imports.[15]

There was also a political aspect to his argument, for he saw in the Soviet trade monopoly, part and parcel as it was of the state, "a weapon of political pressure which has almost infinite possibilities," putting Moscow in the enviable position of being able, unlike other governments, to "turn trade off and on like a water faucet, regardless of all conditions."[16] If recognition brought increased trade, it would thus be the product of a political decision subject to immediate change should the situation so demand.[17]

This was an erroneous image. Having initiated a gigantic process of industrialization, the Russians were in desperate need of all sorts of foreign equipment and had very little money to pay for it, as Kennan himself had detailed. Moscow was therefore hardly in possession of any commanding political weapon in the form of complete freedom to disperse favors among the capitalist nations, though, like any government, it would no doubt have been pleased to wield such power. It was indeed the Soviet Union that, as a developing nation, faced the problem of economic and even political dependence. Despite their needs, the Russians curtailed imports partly because they feared the sort of debt predicament that is now so pervasive in the Third World.[18]

By way of postscript one might add that in 1946 Kennan conceded that Soviet import policy had been based mainly on the "commercial considerations" common to trade: "Since Soviet need for such goods generally outran available funds of foreign exchange and foreign credit, the Foreign Trade Commissariat was logically compelled to sell Soviet products and place orders for foreign products, as a general rule, where this was most economically advantageous."[19] Yet he refused to see this as an indication of future practice, and as recently as 1974 found cause to warn against possible Western dependence.[20] Otherwise his later overall opinion seems to be that moderate trade serves the good purpose of lessening tension and loosening rigidity.[21] And on that note we may lay the matter to rest, while bearing in mind that turning trade off and on like a water faucet for political reasons has been more of an American than a Soviet habit.

These early interventions reveal two qualities of Kennan's attitude toward the Soviet Union that would remain constant for years to come: namely, an ingrained negativism, conveying an impression that nothing whatever could be done with the USSR—coupled with exaggeration of the Russian flexibility of action. To see the wider ramifications of this, we must now turn to international power politics, a dark and lethal field onto which Moscow was poised for entry.

That this debut was made not from free choice but from necessity is to my mind clear. The Soviet regime would have preferred seclusion and stated so succinctly. As Karl Radek told the West at the end of 1933, "The defense of peace and of the neutrality of the Soviet Union against all attempts to drag it into the whirlwind of a world war is the central problem of Soviet foreign policy."[22] That problem was in fact becoming acute, for the simultaneous rise of Japanese expansion to the east and the fledgling Nazi threat on the western flank must have struck the Russian eye as a very alarming pattern indeed. After a vain attempt in 1933 to come to terms with Hitler, the USSR thus initiated a phase of markedly active foreign policy for the purpose of counteracting these hostile powers. The result was semialliance with Czechoslovakia and France, nonaggression pacts with various border countries, and a leading role in the hitherto despised League of Nations.[23] At the same time, Moscow proclaimed unflinchingly that agreements with capitalist nations would be entered into solely for purposes of self-interest. In fact intermittent signals of a desire to repair relations were secretly conveyed to Berlin even during this period of attachment to the principle of collective security against fascism.[24]

For a while the Russians entertained deluded expectations that their concordat with the United States would lead to collaboration against Japan and so be an important strategic advance. In due course American intimations of joint efforts along these lines were recognized for the velleities they had undoubtedly become by that time. The United States, and more specifically the State Department, decided instead to concentrate its Soviet policy on settling the old debt issue and complaining about Russian ties with the Communist International, none of which was resolved to satisfaction.[25] The differences of interest are well illuminated by these plaintive remarks from Kennan: "When he can be found in Moscow, [Soviet foreign minister] Litvinov has frequently shown a reluctance to discuss topics other than those he considers to be major political matters. These seem at present to be the success or failure of efforts to induce other states to take strong measures against Germany, Italy, and Japan. The result is that few of the current problems of Soviet-American relations attract his interest."[26] There was consequently mutual disappointment and a tendency to let relations slide into a state of lifelessness.

Kennan's view of the new Soviet policy varied considerably, sometimes within one and the same analysis. In 1934, for example, he argued that the official Russian concern over Nazi Germany was so much greater than the real danger that there had to be some other explanation for it, perhaps having to do with the Communist International. Yet on the same occasion he also wrote: "Absorbed as it is with the threat of war in the east, and having recently lost its one reliable ally [Germany] in the west, it is no wonder that the Soviet Union should cast around with the greatest energy after some other guarantee of the safety of its western frontiers."[27] Whether this inconsistency resulted from some deference to higher embassy authority or was simply an unaccountable lapse is impossible to tell. Overall, however, his first view dominated. There was real tension in the East, and here Japan, having turned Russia's "sins" into "genuine vices," was mostly to blame; but in the western theater there was no comparable sign of any great threats:

> Insofar as the rulers of Germany are admittedly unsatisfied with their country's present borders and interested in expansion toward the east, professions of nervousness from the Russian side are certainly deserving of consideration. On the other hand, Hitler's policy is outstandingly one of pan-Germanism and implies the extension of the power of the Reich only to territories now or previously controlled or inhabited by Germans. To be sure, this principle—like all political principles—is open to very wide interpretation. It might even conceivably be interpreted to include certain states bordering on Russia. The wildest stretch of the imagination could hardly interpret it to apply to the Ukraine.[28]

What leaps to the eye here in view of subsequent events is the spectacular misreading of Hitler. Kennan certainly shared this with quite a few reasonable people, and the German regime had no precise plans then as to the lebensraum desired.[29] *Mein Kampf*, however, had advertised no "pan-Germanic" limits to the projected eastward expansion. That Kennan, moreover, should have taken proclaimed Nazi intentions more or less at face value and, having done so, ignored the German minority in the Ukraine seems nothing less than a double error. Envisaging the Volga Germans as potential material for "pan-German" extension probably required little stretching of the Russian imagination.

The passage ultimately indicates that Soviet fears should be discounted because Hitler's goals are so obviously of limited ethnic nature. Objectively baseless, these worries must therefore in some sense be artificial. Further along, in fact, Kennan takes the "histrionic vehemence" with which they are expressed as a sign of insincerity, thus again encouraging the impression of myth making. Referring to "the ghost of foreign intervention," he appears to consider the Soviet rationale an instrumental lie made up for domestic consumption.[30] This makes his literal reception of Nazi pan-Germanism, professions of which were lacking in neither histrionics nor vehemence, all the more questionable.

His argument is worth closer scrutiny. The Russian idea of a threat is compared to the "real" situation in which there is no such threat, from which it is inferred that the idea is not only mistaken but disingenuous, a deliberate act of obfuscation. Clearly, the inference does not follow: if, for the sake of argument, one posits a simple reality for everyone to see, one cannot assume that everyone actually does see it or sees it similarly. The question of whether the threat is real is not the same question as whether the Russians actually perceive such a threat.[31] At any rate, to suggest that they were putting on a charade would have required more solid evidence than official German proclamations.

"Ghosts" aside, Kennan did find some substance in the new Russian stance: "The policy of encirclement of Germany would appear to be motivated in Russia's case not only by a fear of German aggression but also by a determination to prevent at any cost the achievement of any real diplomatic settlement and understanding among western-European powers. Moscow considers, and has always considered, that any such settlement would threaten its existence. For this reason it is the unalterable opponent of any effective peace in the west."[32] In brief, Germany is subjected to "encirclement" for the purpose of obstructing a "real diplomatic settlement" and "effective peace in the west." The organizing category of the analysis is the West, a unity that includes Germany and is counterpoised a priori to the (Eastern) USSR. Prospects of peace within this natural compound are then seen to be undermined by the divisive policy of the Eastern power outside.

The perspective expressed here—that of appeasement—was eventually to receive a brief moment of glory at Munich.[33] Conventional wisdom (to which I subscribe in this case) tends to take a dim view of that celebration of Western unity, but it is impossible to fault Kennan on the grounds that he is misrepresenting Soviet objectives. No doubt these did include separation of Germany from the other Western powers. He was quite right in fact that the Soviet regime had always tried to eliminate, in Lenin's formulation, "any possibility of our enemies forming an alliance among themselves for the struggle against us"[34] Yet this was and is a time-honored diplomatic device. "I would count everywhere on the individual hostility of all the Great Powers but would endeavour so to arrange that they were not united against me," as Lord Curzon, that redoubtable paragon of British imperialism, put the matter at the turn of the century.[35] Kennan himself would later express the same principle with admirable clarity, indeed recommending it in 1950 as a realistic approach for the United States in Asia: "Only the very strong can take high and mighty moral positions and ignore the possibilities of balance among the opposing forces. The weak must accept realities and exploit those realities to their advantage as best they can "[36] And again similarly in 1969: "Since governments normally have the interests of their own people primarily at heart, it is only right and natural that each should wish that its most menacing enemies should waste their strength on someone else."[37] This last statement captures as well as any the nature of international relations in the 1930s.

More fundamentally at issue, however, is Kennan's classification of the USSR as a non-Western Other, essentially outside the legitimate range of actors in international relations and thereby automatically unthinkable as a subject of cooperation against any Western power (especially Germany). To sort this out, we must first look at how he grasped the anti-Western essence of Soviet foreign policy.

Kennan appears to have concurred in the dictum that foreign policy can be understood only in relation to the structure and history of the social entity from which it issues. Soviet aggressivity therefore had to be explained with reference to what, so to speak, the country was all about. Here he espoused a variety of arguments, making no attempt to produce any systematic theory of Soviet behavior. By inclination an empiricist, he was suspicious of the sort of abstract reflection needed to achieve such a theory. Nor was it necessarily incumbent on a junior member of the Foreign Service to come up with one. Nonetheless, he did derive various models. They are, in chronological order of development:

1. Soviet aggressivity as a function of communist doctrine: "Life in Soviet Russia is still administered in the interests of a doctrine: the doctrine of the inevitable violent communist revolution in all countries,—the doctrine of the limitless predominance of the class struggle

in every phase of human activity. This doctrine has created and necessitated the continued hostility between Russia and the rest of the world. It has necessitated the maintenance of the Red Army and the entire industrial-military development known as the Five-Year Plan."[38]

2. The Soviet Union as a form of imperialism: "The Soviet Government is, in actuality, nothing more or less than the greatest capitalist group that the world has ever seen. Its imperialism will differ from that of other capitalist interests only because it holds actual political sovereignty in the great territory it controls."[39]

3. The Russian personality as molded by geography and history: This personality, "so deep-seated that it could never be greatly altered in the course of a single generation," is the result of a history of perpetual war; a natural environment encompassing a climate conducive to short, explosive campaigns, and endless plains in turn generating endless, universal ideas of extreme kinds; the Byzantine heritage, with its notion of Moscow as the Third Rome, with its "dark cruelty" and "political servility"; the Oriental heritage of despotism, the shifting Asiatic borders, the emphasis on dignity and face and the absence of any sense of compromise; and finally, an inferiority complex on account of being developmentally two centuries behind the West.[40]

4. The Soviet Union as the resurrection of Old Muscovy: The Revolution was another chapter in the continuing dialectic between two ways of modernizing—that of following the West and that of going it alone. Tsarism, an example of the former, fell because its elite became Westernized and lost its roots. At present, there is a return to Old Muscovy and the non-Western path:

> Again we have the capital back in Moscow, and Petersburg sinking back into the swamps out of which it was erected . . . We have again an Oriental . . . holding court in the barbaric splendor of the Moscow Kremlin. Again we have the same Byzantine qualities in Russian politics, the same intolerance, the same dark cruelty, the same religious dogmatism in word and form, the same servility, the same lack of official dignity, the same all-out quality of all of official life. Finally we have the same fear and distrust of the outside world.

The difference is merely that unlike in the seventeenth century, Moscow is now a military world power.[41]

Except for the doctrinal thesis (1), these explanations are not mutually exclusive. Only the bizarrely quasi-marxist argument (2), concerning capitalism and imperialism, similar in spirit to Mao's subsequent view of Moscow, would not reappear. The others are perhaps more appropriately dealt with later. Still, a few remarks are in order. There is, first of all, no obvious relation between endless plains and endless political aspirations: denizens of the midwestern American expanse count among their number some of the most inveterately staid people anywhere.[42] Second, to argue that Westernization of the elite caused the downfall of tsarism is unwittingly to render the tsarist (and later Stalinist) attempt to suppress foreign influence rational and imperative, for solely by such a course could the elite avoid losing its indigenous roots. Third, it is strange simply to classify the Revolution as an anti-Western return to Old Muscovy: Soviet marxism was after all a profoundly Western theory of progress and production, and even the alleged "Oriental despot" in the Kremlin espoused the keenest admiration for American technology and efficiency.[43]

Of wider significance is the progression from a distinctly idealist position (1), according to which everything had been caused by the existence of a doctrine, to the historically and geographically oriented arguments (3 and 4). Though an improvement of nuance, it was not really a movement toward greater explanatory power. The doctrinal thesis, while drastically inadequate, did have the advantage of being straightforward. Its successors, by contrast, very largely assume the character of a string of factors without criteria by which they can be internally ranked. The effect is to make explanation an unending and theoretically blurry process of weighing these factors.

Ideology (in Kennan's sense) undergoes by degrees a radical devaluation from fundamental cause to a subordinate part of the Byzantine heritage, namely religious dogmatism. Its status thus varies, but reflection on its nature is held throughout to a minimum. This comparative neglect was a product not of somnolence but of the pervasive distaste for the tedious particulars of communist theory and practice that so characterized the Foreign Service, including its Russianists. The result was sheer ignorance of areas such as the Communist International and a certain lack of depth in understanding Soviet strategy and tactics, linked as the latter were to a distinct political tradition of fronts and alliances. Finally, there was also enduring confusion about Moscow's attitude toward war.

The essence of this last question was really whether the Soviet regime officially envisaged offensive war as a means by which to spread its influence and domination. Kennan's earliest account here was also one of his plainest: "War and revolution are identified, but war is not desirable at the present time: it would interfere with socialist construction in Russia and the longer it can be staved off the stronger the international proletariat will become. When war and revolution are inevitable anyway, and when every day sees an increase in the strength of the Soviet Union, it would be foolish to precipitate the crisis."[44] Apparently, then, the Soviet leadership thought war was good insofar as it gave rise to revolution but premature at the moment because the power of the USSR and its international allies was continually improving. But if this were true, it would be rational for the USSR to perpetuate the state of nonwar, thus never reaching the stage of conflated war and revolution. In a way, this was less a contradiction of Kennan's reasoning than of Soviet foreign policy. For once the notion of a proletarian Fatherland had become orthodoxy, struggles everywhere became by definition subordinate to Moscow's immediate national interests—interests that, as Kennan pointed out in this initial effort, tended to lie in the direction of absence of war. Yet his failure to explain what the Russians actually meant when they "identified" war and revolution—that is, war waged by who against whom, and for what purposes?—suggested that Moscow was actually in the business of advocating revolutionary war.

The same silence marked a more ambitious analysis made in 1935. The axiomatic essence of international relations for the Kremlin, he said, is conflict, which eventually will turn into war. Peace is thus a mere armistice, which is to be prolonged "until Russia should become independent in a military sense." A tremendous program of militarization, extending into the political, economic, and cultural sphere, has accordingly been commenced and is now creating the conditions for its own fulfillment, as extended peace would mean that "the lives and works of an entire generation will have been sacrificed in vain."[45]

The unspoken assumption is that no such sacrifice to peace is likely. While mentioning that conflict is usually depicted as an attack on the USSR, Kennan does not clarify the underlying rationale and leaves one with a sense that this stance is an arbitrarily chosen convenience. An air of measured ambiguity marks the analysis: "Truly, the universal pretensions of Moscow communism have their roots deep in the Eurasian past. And if they have been held in abeyance for a time through the exigencies of a period of intensive military industrialization, who shall say that they will not reappear with renewed vigor when the goal of this period—military independence—has been substantially attained?"[46] The feeling he conveys is that the Soviet Union is a nation restrained from jumping on its neighbors only because circumstances have not yet provided the opportunity; once current "exigencies" have been mastered, that opportunity will be deemed to have arrived.

What the Russians are said to be saying, as opposed to what Kennan thinks they are up to, is difficult to distinguish in this account. If the rhetorical device here leaves room for doubt about his opinion, uncertainty all but disappears in a subsequent effort:

> In actuality, it is . . . only the distribution of force which determines the Soviet attitude toward world affairs, and the world may as well reckon with the fact that the character of Soviet policy will vary in exact relationship to the actual force which the Soviet leaders feel they can exert in international affairs. An increase in the strength of the country will invariably lead to increased arrogance and aggressiveness . . . The epoch during which this policy has been largely defensive, designed to preserve the existence of the country throughout a crucial phase of change and reconstruction, is coming to an end. A new era is approaching in which the Kremlin will be able to take the offensive in the affairs of the world, to retract one after another concessions [*sic*] which it has made to its capitalist environment, and apply the enormous weight of its concentrated political and economic power for the achievement of positive goals. These goals are essentially imperialistic.[47]

I take this to mean that the Soviet Union is by nature aggressive and, after a period of imposed quietude, is now about to enter a period of actual offensive, the precise form of which is typically left to the reader's imagination. As the reference to "concentrated political and economic power" indicates, Kennan probably did not believe in the immediate possibility of a Soviet military attack; more likely he expected increased "arrogance and aggressiveness" *based* on military power. This, however, is not spelled out, and the argument as a whole can legitimately be read to predict almost any Russian act of aggression.

To assess the question in all its particulars would be premature. My remarks for now will be limited to two claims: first, that Kennan's depiction of the Soviet conception of war was incomplete to the point of being directly misleading; and second, even if for the moment we grant the possibility that the Russians either conceived of war and other aggressive means as a way to achieve their imperialistic goals or,

irrespective of stated position, would in fact engage in such activity
when given the proper chance, his vaticination in 1936 of an offensive
was wrong.

Kennan had correctly attributed to the Bolshevik conception of
international relations the idea of essential conflict.[48] Certainly contradiction (or conflict) was, and still largely is, something akin to an
ontological principle in Soviet thinking. That the USSR and its sur-
rounding capitalist adversaries would be locked into dialectical conflict
was thus no more subject to debate than the analogous contradiction
between labor and capital: neither can meaningfully be said to exist
without the other. The expressive *form* of such a contradiction, however, is not a given and has indeed been subject historically to several
different positions.

It is in this context that the issue of inevitable war arises. The
premise is simple: war is the organic product of capitalism in its period
of historic decline (imperialism). If war is hence intrinsic to capitalism,
it must be extrinsic to the antithesis—socialism—for which read the
USSR and associates. The central question then becomes, will these
capitalist-instigated wars be internal ones, or will they be directed
against the Soviet Union?[49] It was Kennan's silence on the conceptual
underpinnings of the Soviet thesis of inevitable conflict that made
possible the auxiliary insinuations that offensive war was somehow
part of official Russian doctrine.

One may still regard professed doctrine as immaterial to the real
nature of things, insisting that the Kremlin intended to unleash aggression of whatever kind whenever a suitable occasion arose. Kennan,
then, thought that such a moment was imminent in 1936, military
industrialization apparently having reached requisite levels. Taking his
view for an instant, I think he should have seen two strong indications
suggesting no such thing (though, admittedly, some form of push
toward the Baltic was not wholly inconceivable).

The first concerns the calculation of what he refers to as the "distribution of force." All ruling groups, unless irresponsible, perform
this task in some form or other; and no doubt their external policy
bears some (if incomplete) correlation to the result of this assessment.
At the bottom of the Stalinist computation lay, not surprisingly, the
aspect of economic strength. It was believed that the economically
dominant party normally wins any war.[50] To my knowledge there is
no sign that the Russians, despite herculean efforts at militarization,
ever entertained any delusion of economic, or for that matter military,

superiority over the West in the 1930s. An offensive posture in those circumstances would have implied a recklessness bordering on the suicidal, something to which the Stalinist regime was not subjectively inclined.[51]

An even more obvious indication was to be found in the Communist International, whose activities, indeed whose very existence, was often construed as a form of aggression. Kennan showed no great interest in this organization, for which he had little understanding in the first place; but of its importance as a barometer of Soviet intentions he was nevertheless quite aware: "If the ends can be achieved by a softening of international communist activities, this will be done. If, on the other hand, Moscow comes to the conclusion that it could to its own advantage utilize ruthlessly the apparatus of the Comintern, it will not hesitate to do so."[52] Yet not a single noteworthy analysis of the Comintern ensued. Nor, for that matter, did the Moscow embassy or the State Department generate any.[53] A brief note on the Comintern may thus be in order.

The most cursory examination would have revealed the International in a state of advanced decrepitude. Once the various Comintern parties had been subordinated to the needs of "Socialism in One Country," there was really no need for any International, merely an officially proclaimed line to be followed. Around 1934–35 this line— until then an egregiously self-destructive form of ultraleftism—was radically altered as a result of the disaster in Germany. Mirroring the Soviet policy of international alliances, communist parties sought thenceforth to create national class alliances for the defense of bourgeois democracy against fascism. Thus was born the People's (or the Popular) Front, scarcely, whatever else one might think of it, an offensive political strategy.[54]

This point escaped the State Department and its Moscow embassy, indeed most embassies. While the Comintern Congress of 1935 (the last, as it turned out) caused a vigorous American protest as a breach of the 1933 recognition agreements, the proceedings themselves received little attention. Eventually the Soviet embassy in Washington felt compelled to impress privately upon the State Department that the event actually signified real political change, but the response was merely one of bemused incomprehension.[55] Kennan's lack of interest is partially explained by the fact that he spent much of 1935 convalescing in Vienna and thinking about problems other than the Comintern. Nevertheless, a superficial acquaintance with the congress would not have been out of place. Certainly it would have given him cause to pause before predicting Soviet offensives.

Commensurately slender, one should add, was the attention to doctrine in his few examinations of state and party, though he claimed dubiously at the end of the decade to have read a fair amount of Marx and Lenin. He had, as he then described his position of a few years before, been unable to see in the party leaders anything but ordinary "hard-boiled political bosses":

> Before devout lip-service to a dogma never entirely understood, before the unquestionable desire to modernize a backward country, there naturally took precedence the instinct of self-preservation, the fear of popular revolt and of foreign intervention, the pressing urge to bolster and fortify personal power. It was obvious to us then, as it is to many more today, that the Moscow leaders had no energy to spare for the salvation of the working classes of other countries, that the Comintern was an instrument of power like the Red Army or the foreign trade monopoly, that idealism was the only luxury which the Kremlin was able to feed the masses but could not afford to partake of itself.[56]

As a personal retrospective this is less than satisfactory, it having been far from "obvious" to him in the 1930s "that the Moscow leaders had no energy to spare for the salvation of the working classes of other countries." More noteworthy, however, is the inclination to reduce idealism once again to a simple instrument of manipulation and, ipso facto, something essentially trivial that need not be examined.

This was indicative of an order of reflection devoid of any proper taxonomy in which to situate the phenomenon of Soviet communism itself. Once, it will be recalled, he had characterized the system as a gigantic form of capitalism. On another occasion he considered it a version of fascism, in turn defined as the "rule by a small irresponsible group, whose sanctions of power [rest] alone in a combination of repressive policy power on the one hand and 'bread and circuses' on the other."[57] Regardless of whether this is a good way to grasp fascism, one would have been hard pressed to find any pervasive presence of bread and circuses in the Soviet Union of the late 1930s.

The conflation of fascism and communism was based on the emphatic valorization of means over ends, on the way things are done rather than what is actually done. For Kennan, accordingly, the abominable ingredient in Bolshevism was not its aims but the proposition that those aims justify any means.[58] Taking the opposite position led Kennan to a favorable disposition toward various "civilized" dictatorships—notably Austria in the 1930s and Portugal in the 1940s—where the masses (the circus) were not much in evidence. Given this precedence of style over content, method over direction, it is possible to see how Hitler and Stalin might be consigned to the same species. Such a move, however, tells us next to nothing about who is most likely to engage in aggression, all of which brings us back to the question of anti-fascist cooperation and Munich.

Munich, and the subsequent volte-face has remained a sensitive topic for Kennan. Thus, perhaps feeling his own notion of the West betrayed, he was prepared less than a decade after the war to call Hitler's pact with Stalin and consequent war against France and Britain "a monumental betrayal of Western civilization" and to imagine that the German leaders had felt a guilt about 1939 that had been erased from their minds only through the "sufferings and sacrifices" incurred during the ensuing war against the East. Moreover, one of his first (unrealized) plans after leaving the State Department in 1950 was to write an article eliminating residual Western discomfort over this event. In 1960 Kennan still held that antifascist cooperation would have been wrong, mainly on the moral grounds that the Soviet Union of the 1930s had been "the scene of nightmarish, Orwellian orgies of modern totalitarianism."[59]

It seems clear, however, that the primary object of inquiry in assessing international power politics is not the internal level of Orwellian orgy but the potential in any conceivable adversary for external aggression.[60] Here Kennan's overly sanguine view of Nazi Germany was inversely mirrored in the conception of a Soviet Union not only hostile to Western interests but also on the verge of some undefined form of offensive. Trotsky, to cite a contemporary, captured the situation more perceptively:

> In reality, the political methods of Stalin are in no way distinguished from the methods of Hitler. But in the sphere of international politics, the difference is obvious. In a brief space of time Hitler has recovered the Saar territory, overthrown the Treaty of Versailles, placed his grasp on Austria and the Sudetenland, subjected Czechoslovakia to his domination and a number of other second-rate and third-rate powers to his influence. During the same years Stalin met only defeats and humiliations on the international arena (China, Czechoslovakia, Spain).[61]

Whence the immediate danger stemmed was thus fairly obvious, and as Kennan himself would actually agree in 1960, the prewar USSR was not a power either intent on or capable of large-scale aggression.[62]

It does not necessarily follow, of course, that antifascist collaboration with Moscow was to be recommended. One might have rejected it on other grounds, for example by taking the view that the Soviet policy was little but a propaganda decoy designed to create Western discord. The argument is not implausible. A variety of Russian actions cast doubt on the underlying commitment to collective security.[63] Yet the riposte is ultimately simple and identical to that of a more recent Kennan, when Russian proposals are similarly dismissed: one cannot know if they are serious unless they are taken seriously.[64] This the Western European powers cannot be said to have done, perhaps because it never became clear to the Chamberlains and Daladiers who the main tactical enemy in fact was. Moscow, by contrast, had argued throughout that the Western powers might be the first to suffer from any appeasement of Hitler. And so it happened.[65]

Although resurrected after the war in the conceptual guise of totalitarianism, Kennan's identification of communism with fascism never became a prominent part of his thinking. The theme of means over ends, however, was to become pivotal to his entire outlook.

The Soviet Union, then, was a historico-geographical entity with assorted features but of indeterminate generic concept. How to deal with it was for Kennan not a complicated problem, since the geopolitical and economic facts rendered conflicting or converging interests between the two nations extremely limited, and the United States was not at any rate prepared to engage in power politics.[66] The economic side of this argument suggested oddly that the two countries were similar and therefore had little to offer each other. In reality, all things being equal, there was an enormous need in the USSR for industrial goods from the United States. Nevertheless, Kennan was probably right in stressing the lack of a basis for developed relations, although in doing so he also issued a prescription for American policy that is well worth quoting in full:

> The primary quality must be patience. We must neither expect too much nor despair of getting anything at all. We must be as steady in our attitude as Russia is fickle in hers. We must take what we can get when the atmosphere is favorable, and do our best to hold on to it when the wind blows the other way. We must remain as unperturbed in the face of expansive professions of friendliness as in

the face of slights and underhand opposition. *We must make the weight of our influence felt steadily over a long period of time, in the direction which best suits our interests.*[67]

To this counsel he has, with minor alterations, always remained faithful. Fickleness, however, was something he would encounter far more often in American than in Soviet foreign policy.

The analytical traces from the 1930s do not on the whole impress. Kennan's portrait of Soviet foreign policy fails to meet the case as both a depiction of what the USSR was really up to and a demonstration of what the Russians thought they were doing. It betrays no consistent idea of how to analyze the subject matter and expresses a related reluctance to take ideology seriously. Most important, it is marked by a tendency to deny the legitimacy of the regime as one power among others in international politics. Short of transforming itself into something altogether different, there seems to be nothing the Soviet Union could have done to qualify. Such a maximalistic stance is not a realistic basis for judgment in diplomacy, which counts among its postulates that nations conduct foreign policy according to perceived interest and thus should be assessed in relation to what is possible within their constituted bounds. To reject this rule is therefore in some sense to exit from the domain of diplomatic discourse, either in effect proposing termination of relations (probably Kennan's most heartfelt view) or assuming for oneself a position other than that of a diplomat. A Catalan anarchist fighting in the Spanish Civil War, for example, might well have been entirely justified in rejecting Soviet foreign policy as a whole and in calling for the overthrow of the Stalinist regime. Diplomatic reason, however, is something altogether different.

2

War and Alliance

Bedridden with ulcers in Vienna in 1935, Kennan took it upon himself to translate the new Austrian social security law. Disporting oneself under such circumstances with an ordinance of some two hundred pages in a "formidable sort of German legal verbiage" might seem curious, even for such an exemplary specimen of the Calvinist work ethic as Kennan.[1] However, the political genesis of the law had excited his interest. By his own account a few years later, the social insurance system under the old parliamentary regime had been close to bankruptcy because the politicians had not dared to brave the displeasure of the electorate, when in 1933–34 along came an authoritarian government whose promptly appointed committee of experts was able, in the absence of external political pressure, to recast the system without further ado. The lesson was clear:

> There seemed to be little doubt that if malicious despotism had greater possibilities for evil than democracy, benevolent despotism likewise had greater possibilities for good. An intelligent, determined ruling minority, responsible in a general sense to the people at large rather than in a direct sense to groups of politicians and lobbyists or to the voters of individual districts, could function not only more efficiently but also, when it wished to, more beneficially than could the average "democratic" regime.[2]

The "benevolent" credentials of this Austrian regime of Engelbert Dollfuss and Kurt von Schuschnigg ("conservative, semi-fascist but still moderate," as Kennan was to describe it some years later), were perhaps not entirely in order.[3] The methods employed in suppressing the social-democratic movement had included incarcerating twenty thousand people and ruining the innovative and enlightened Austromarxist government of municipal Vienna. More peculiar was the expressed desire of this truly reactionary (and I use the term with all due circumspection) regime to impose a simulacrum of the old feudal estates as a replacement for parliament. Sources of support for that extraordinary idea were found in two surviving and still powerful elements of Hapsburg absolutism, the state bureaucracy and the Catholic hierarchy. In contrast to what Kennan doubtless considered the "malicious despotisms" in Germany and Italy, there was consequently no attack on religion and the clergy, no enthusiasm for mass mobilization, and no bombastic cult of the bright and modern future.[4]

A static and rigid hierarchy led by "an intelligent, determined ruling minority" and based on omnicompetent bureaucracy and strict religion: this, then, was for Kennan a compelling political model. In September 1942, as it happened, he was sent to Lisbon, where he found a leader of similar persuasion. Antonio Salazar, like his Austrian counterpart Schuschnigg, was an ascetic and devout Catholic who abhorred mass movements and liked corporatist ideas, though he never advanced the latter very far in practice. Replacing (let it be said) a clientist parliamentarism that was both corrupt and inefficient, Salazar's Estado Nuovo seemed to have as its aim absolute stasis. In this it was quite successful, for by the end of the 1960s, after four decades of Salazar's rule, Portugal remained a country of abject poverty and widespread illiteracy, nothing much apparently having changed since he was ushered into power by the very same force—the military—that was eventually to destroy his legacy. To what an extent he had been "responsible in a general sense to the people at large" is thus a matter of opinion.[5]

Kennan actually became a personal friend of this reclusive man and consistently supported his colonial empire until it finally crumbled in the 1970s.[6] Salazar, as Kennan saw it in the 1940s, understood the psychology of his people and had created a system better suited for them than that of his allegedly democratic predecessors. Convincing Washington of this, however, was difficult, since an immense war effort was at that very moment (1942–43) being launched against powers bearing more than a little resemblance to the intended Estado Nuovo, thus earning right-wing dictatorships a bad name in official political discourse. Indeed there was something forced and apologetic about Kennan's attempts in various reports to render Salazar's domestic rule palatable.[7]

It was much easier then to find justification for Portugal's foreign policy, a cautious one based on long-standing historical precedents. While tending to eternalize past determinants, Kennan's despatches lucidly delineated Lisbon's geopolitical options and likely direction. Excellent though they were, these analyses failed to command proper attention from his departmental colleagues; but by means of some exceedingly unorthodox maneuvers he managed nevertheless to resolve to mutual satisfaction the imbroglio of Washington's immediate dealings with Salazar—the projected air base on the Azores—as well as to discourage any American intentions to eliminate the Portuguese ruler.[8]

This keen diplomatic understanding of constraints and openings in foreign policy differed sharply from his earlier posture toward the Soviet Union. Political proximity no doubt played a role here. Schuschnigg and Salazar personified what Kennan deemed a reasonable and moderate way of coping with the unappealing realities of political life. Hitler and Stalin (a "gang leader") were by contrast utterly devoid of ethical restraint, products of that "sense of insecurity which makes all parvenu regimes seek a constant broadening of their police power as a compensation for their lack of sanction in public opinion and tradition." Communism and Nazism, in short, seemed to signal a descent from Western culture and tradition, a sort of spiritual departure from the West.[9]

Thus they also appeared to be beyond Kennan's immediate categorical universe. Just as he had previously formed no stable concept of Soviet society, so the sojourn in Berlin in 1939–40 failed to result in any clear conclusions with regard to the Nazi phenomenon. On occasion, he proclaimed it to be a product of the lower-middle class. Elsewhere he described it as being without a real social base, a mere mentality marked by the absence of "shame or discrimination in the selection of methods."[10] As a rule the latter perspective predominated. Thus he left the problem of social structure aside, lapsing instead into what might inelegantly be called the psychologism of compensation. Nazi aggression, he typically claimed, originated in "the jealousy, the uncertainty, the feeling of inferiority, the consequent lust to dominate Europe which is all that most Germans really have in common."[11] Given this image of ruthless abandon, it is rum that in his most ambitious study of the period, one characteristically concerned with the organization and methods of the German occupation, he found the Nazis to have been fairly restrained.[12]

Pan-Germanism was, however, in his view an insuperable barrier to any real support among the subjugated nations. In this respect the Nazi regime compared unfavorably with the mature and absorptive force of domination formerly represented by the Hapsburg empire.[13] Kennan's elective affinity with the old Austro-Hungarian empire, whose demise he has always thought a calamity of the highest order, was probably also what had made him such a detached chronicler of the annihilation of Czechoslovakia in 1938–39.[14] The Czechoslovaks, he had argued then, "suffered from the short-comings generic to social-democracy in small European countries" such as lack of "courage," "imagination," and "self-confidence." The ensuing *Anschluss* he saw as an adjustment in deplorably brutal form to the historic power shift from Vienna to Berlin, a transfer of subordination from one to the other by a people tragically devoid of a natural ruling class. But when Norway was engulfed a year later, he extolled as a great virtue the historic absence of a natural nobility, and his tone was one of anguish; for marital bonds had made Norway a second homeland.[15]

The underlying point here is that a break with Western tradition and culture was not for Kennan identical to a step in the direction from democracy to dictatorship. On the contrary, he found that issue of political regimes, so prevalent at the time, a "fancied" one about which he "could not get excited":

> I never doubted that there was something real behind this effort of our people to distinguish between certain things they liked and certain things they did not like in the art of government. But it was fairly obvious that the issue had been deliberately confused . . . by the propaganda groups with selfish purposes to pursue, and the real distinction had become obscure. Were not dictatorship and democracy only phrases? Was it not actually cruelty, stupidity, ignorance, violence and pretense which we hated? And could these not appear in any regime, no matter what it called itself?[16]

Simple division of the world into democracy and dictatorship may well have been a conceptual error (which Kennan would castigate more perceptively after the war), but the political issue itself was scarcely a "fancied one." Alienation, discomfort, and marginality would indeed be the lot of any American diplomat who chose to base his political allegiance in this epoch on a general dislike of "cruelty, stupidity, ignorance, violence and pretense," while dismissing democracy and dictatorship as mere "phrases." For the enemy-to-be was of course parading an aggressive contempt precisely for democracy, thereby allowing the other side, at the eager instigation of the United States, to assemble under that very sign. If democracy and dictatorship were rhetorical emblems, they were nonetheless rhetorical emblems with a great deal of materiality.

Given Kennan's political taxonomy, he would at any rate be less than enthusiastic about the antifascist war that was to come, especially since it involved a configuration of forces that he had rejected as wrong and unfeasible: a coalition of Western powers and the Soviet Union against Germany and Italy, nations he considered Western. Within such an alignment, Kennan's subjective, psychological concepts made only limited sense.

By way of this digression on political attitudes, we are now in a position to return to the Soviet analysis, especially as it pertained to the relations between the USSR and the West during and immediately after the Second World War. First, however, the biographical aspect should be brought up to date.

After his release from German internment in 1942, Kennan was dispatched to Lisbon. In the fall of 1943 he was reassigned to the European Allied Commission in London, a cooperative organ meant to establish future occupation zones and surrender terms. Here he suffered acutely from the lack of a precise American position on which to base negotiations with the Russians and the British, and from the less than delightful English cuisine. The result was a bad case of ulcers. He also became known in the department as something of a nuisance, demanding clear instructions and taking personal initiatives not deemed proper for a man of his secondary station. Despite official misgivings, he was appointed counselor at the Moscow embassy in mid-1944 to serve under W. Averell Harriman. The following two years were mostly unhappy. Harriman was a strong ambassador with direct access to the White House, while Kennan's duties were chiefly administrative. More important, he disagreed with the official policy of cooperation with the Soviet Union. By the summer of 1945 he had become so disenchanted that he resigned, and it required some degree of departmental persuasion (Russianists being in short supply) to change his mind. Souring Russo-American relations eventually created an audience more receptive to his views, and particularly receptive to his famous Long Telegram of February 1946. When he left Moscow in May that year it was as a man much in demand, a major new luminary in the foreign policy apparatus. He was to be political commandant at the new National War College, an influential position in Washington at the time, which would afford him excellent opportunities to lecture leading policymakers.[17]

Prospects at the end of 1941 must have seemed to Kennan nothing short of disastrous. Ever since his time in the Weimar Republic he had been acutely aware of the likely results of general warfare: the First World War had not only devastated European culture but had also brought in its wake a profoundly important revolution, the shadow of which was now looming darkly in the east. This time, with a major revolutionary participant, the outcome might very likely be even worse. It was difficult for him to see what benefits could be derived from intimate association with Moscow but not difficult at all to conjure up a wide variety of potential disasters. That the Germans and Russians would exhaust each other was perhaps the only slim foundation of hope. Kennan's, at any rate, was not an antifascist war, much less one for the purpose of creating global democracy. It was a catastrophic eruption pitting the West against itself with the added horror of Eastern involvement.[18]

The Soviet Union, as he came to see it, would be "the only expansionist power left in the world after this war." This he seemed to consider virtually self-evident, and so not in need of much explanation. The causal story most readily available here was probably that of marxist "aspirations" to spread the revolution. As we have seen, however, Kennan had relied decreasingly on the ideological model, displaced to a corresponding degree by various geographical, psychological, and above all historical factors. This explanatory trend toward, in his words, "tradition and environment" continued, fueled no doubt by the emphasis on patriotism in wartime Russia.[19] The country depicted in his major writings was thus a locus of intense nationalism, where people had turned to private concerns; where the church exerted greater spiritual attraction than the stale, ossified party; where marxism, having taken on qualities of Byzantine scholasticism, was pretty much spent as a motivating force; where the radical intelligentsia had been obliterated and cultural life atrophied; where the old autocracy had come back in new form with Stalin "settled firmly back into the throne of Ivan the Terrible and Peter the Great." In Kennan's metaphor, after the purges the "ship of state had been cut loose from the bonds of Communist dogma. Only the captain now plotted the course."[20]

Seen in this national perspective, Soviet expansionism was hence the product of "the age-old sense of insecurity of a sedentary people reared on an exposed plain in the neighborhood of fierce nomadic people," resulting in a historical dialectic of perpetual struggle and an absence of any "conception of permanent friendly relations between states." Once this dialectic of unending conflict had been established, there was no need for further inquiry into origins and causes. Similarly, one might as well dispose of the fruitless exercise of moralizing over what was historically given.[21] The Soviet Union, in brief, was looking for security and power as it always had and should be dealt with on that basis alone.

Consequently Kennan had little interest in the role of ideology in Russian policy; and in the actual doctrine he had no interest at all. Except for the somewhat anomalous Long Telegram, which I shall examine later in considerable detail, the matter hardly ever arises in his Moscow despatches. In fact a hasty search through embassy records revealed but a single serious analysis, on closer inspection actually emanating from the British embassy (and arguing, not unreasonably, that the idea that Soviet marxism had been replaced by nationalism was the equivalent of imagining that Pope Julius II had abandoned Catholicism because he happened to engage in imperialism).[22]

There one might think the ideological question exhausted: marxism was at most one instrument among others, and not a very effective one at that, for the aggrandizement of a peculiar permutation of traditional Russian autocracy. Kennan, however, was capable of saying very different and contradictory things within one and the same analysis, particularly if it was long and literary in form. On the very same occasion, for instance, that he wrote of the ship being cut loose from ideology, he also argued that the communist leaders were "as often as not victims of their own slogans, the slaves of their own propaganda," thus making propaganda "true . . . not only for those to whom it is addressed, but for those who invent it as well." Accordingly, he concluded, "the power of autosuggestion plays a tremendous part in Soviet life."[23]

If the producers of instrumental myths become enmeshed in their own creations, it would seem to follow that they will act in a fashion at least related to these propagations. If the myth is effective, if it transcends its original purpose and comes back as in a loop, if it in some sense becomes "true," then it must surely also be important. Yet there were no real investigations of the sources of Soviet "autosuggestion."

His assessment in other domains is also surprisingly cursory and internally conflictual. On the one hand, the Russian people are said to be retreating into conservative introspection and privacy; on the other, he describes them as "united under the firm and ruthless leadership, master of its own territory, and its own philosophy, beholden to no one, thirsting for prosperity, power and glory, looking into the future, as far as its weariness permits, with pride, confidence, and a new sense of national solidarity." Graphic accounts of stupendous devastation and loss of life are combined with exaggerated notions of easy reconstruction. The grave domestic consequences of acquiring Westernized provinces are emphasized, but at the same time these alien territories and peoples are simply added to the tabulation of future Soviet strength. On the whole, Kennan's USSR seems more forceful and filled with grim fortitude than was actually ever the case.[24]

Once the war was practically over, there was a shift in his analysis to the difficulties of holding Western provinces in submission and to the logistic limitations on expansionism: "Further military advances in the west could only increase the responsibilities already beyond the Russian capacity to meet. Moscow has no naval or air forces capable of challenging the sea or air lanes of the world."[25] This essentially correct estimate was, however, seldom articulated, and it was supplanted, peculiarly, by the claim that Moscow's foreign policy was based on the overall premise that the West would lack the psychological resolve to stand up to Soviet displeasure, no matter what happened. This is highly unlikely. Stalin was after all a man with a consuming interest in steel production and similar objective measures. To conduct long-term policy on the basis of what could be perceived about the subjective state of mind among foreign statesmen would have struck him as wholly idealistic.

What, then, would Moscow actually aim for? Calling it a "jealous land power," Kennan once argued that the USSR "must always seek to extend itself to the west and will never find a place, short of the Atlantic Ocean, where it can from its own standpoint safely stop."[26] He may have had the very long perspective in mind here. A more typical view was this:

> The Soviet Government since the time of Munich has never relaxed its determination to have a fairly extensive sphere of influence in certain neighboring areas of Europe and Asia, in which its power would be unchallenged. In the mind of the Kremlin this has been the *sine qua non* for Soviet post-war policy. In contemplating and discussing collaboration with other great powers, they have always gone on the assumption that this primary and minimum requirement

would be at least tacitly recognized. They have also never envisaged that collaboration with other powers would mean permanent relaxation of the controls they have set up to prevent the outside world from learning too much about Russia and the Russian people from learning too much about the outside world.[27]

Exactly how far into these adjacent areas they would try to go he was unable to say. Probably, he opined, they did not know themselves but were waiting instead for the Western side to make its bid before decisively staking their own claim.

One thing was nevertheless abundantly clear to Kennan. Whatever its final boundaries, the area in question would enjoy a less than pleasant future. "Prosperity and happiness," he wrote with peremptory accuracy, "have always been, like warm summer days, fleeting exceptions in the cruel climate of Eastern Europe."[28] The Russians wanted power, pure and simple: "It is a matter of indifference to Moscow whether a given area is 'communistic' or not. All things being equal, Moscow might prefer to see it communized, although even that is debatable. But the main thing is that it should be amenable to Moscow influence, and if possible to Moscow authority."[29] Thus he envisaged in Poland "extensive control of foreign affairs, military matters, public opinion, and economic relations with the outside world," leaving the Poles with their domestic culture to nurture. Not wont to accept much beyond the familiar in dealing with internal opposition, Moscow would certainly also implant its own system of police control. Though the result would not necessarily be Soviet-style communism, any future Polish government would have to understand the gloomy historical fact that "there is nothing in Russian thought or tradition which should cause Russia to tolerate in Poland, at a time when Germany is weak, any manifestations of independent policy which are not agreeable to the interests of the Russian Government."[30]

These were prescient words. Yet, as Kennan also pointed out, domination would not be unproblematic. The Russians enjoyed considerable advantages: ready access to the territories, modern police technology, and the unmatched strength of the communists amidst "the general bankruptcy of rival political tendencies and the widespread confusion and disorientation in the popular mind." But the difficulties were also considerable: the sheer size of the policing operation, the mark of Quisling stamped on their local representatives, the overt chauvinism of their armies, the limited political and economic value of potential land reforms, and the basic problem of reconstructing the economies of these areas without, in all probability, any assistance from the West. Furthermore, the Soviet Union now included those very western provinces that had played an important role in the downfall of tsarism; and chances were that history would repeat itself, "civil disintegration" perhaps being in the offing within a decade.[31] Russian success in controlling the sphere of influence was thus uncertain.

Outside this as yet unspecified domain in the West, Soviet aims, according to Kennan, were far more amorphous. Despite his remarks about Atlantic extension, he had argued in 1942 that Moscow had no interest in the rest of Europe as long as it remained militarily weak. Three years later he added in a similar vein that "Russia's security . . . means absence of cohesion, of balance, of harmony, in the rest of Europe."[32] Much more than that he did not say about the subject of western expansion.

Approaching from a different angle, he thought that Soviet policy generally followed the principle of maximum influence with minimum actual responsibility. Toward the underdeveloped nations, for example, this meant that Moscow would assume a posture of "flexible multiformity": "Nationalism and irredentist sentiments are encouraged among the Armenians. Tribal revolt and autonomy is incited among the Kurds. The export brand of Stalinist ideology is sold to the Jews. The doctrine of Church unity under the patronage of the Soviet State is propagated in Orthodox communities."[33] Here he found the postwar push in northern Iran wholly predictable and the (then) quiescent Russo-Turkish relations odd. Strategic considerations dictated that the Iranian area, close to the Caucasian oil fields, should be denied other great powers. Similar concerns governed the Russian approach to China, where, apart from the ever-present desire to reclaim tsarist property, the Soviet Union intended to keep all options open for its own strategic benefits. When Moscow denounced Syngman Rhee in Korea as a former Japanese collaborator (which he was), Kennan took this to be another act of sheer opportunism, obviously done for ulterior reasons.[34]

Moscow's policy, then, was one of pure expedience, unlimited manipulation, Machiavellian calculus, all in all rendering *any* act, however vile, justified if it happened to serve the ends of Soviet expansion. Should the Russians acquire atomic capabilities, Kennan doubted "that they would hesitate for a moment to apply this power against us if by doing so they thought they might materially improve their own power position in the world."[35] The effect of this kind of state-

ment on, say, a policymaker in Washington suffering from disillusion-
ment with Moscow will readily be appreciated. From that standpoint
his conjecture was frivolous. It was also dubious, for the Politburo,
whatever its ethical deficiencies, was not simply power-maximizing in
the sense that a business is profit-maximizing. Still, the image of a
completely unconscionable adversary entailed a supposition that,
though not very evident to his contemporaries, is of some importance.
As Kennan was aware, no Machiavellian calculus can be successful in
the long run without a reasonably accurate assessment of the opponent's strength, and here Moscow possessed, in his opinion, a very
keen intelligence. Like any bright practitioner of power politics, the
Kremlin knew when to retreat in the face of imposing opposition.
Unlike Hitler, Stalin was not reckless. The prescription for dealing
with the Russians, therefore, was quite simply to put up some sort of
determined resistance to their various expansionist moves.[36]

This was also the origin of Kennan's pervasive pessimism. The
Soviet Union had come into being deeply marked by the Russian
habit of regarding the outside world as inherently hostile; it was thus
a nation by definition engaged in a struggle. The problem now was
that its traditional enemies Germany and Japan (the containing surroundings so to speak) were facing precipitous decline, thereby in
effect dissolving the dialectic. That the United States would reconstitute it by rising to the task of replacing these powers he considered
entirely improbable.[37] In short, he doubted that the United States
would see its own interests and act accordingly. Thus we may turn to
his views on American policy.

When Hitler attacked the Soviet Union in June 1941 and some
American cooperation with the victim seemed likely as an extension
of the previous support for Great Britain, it was natural for Kennan
to take a restrictive view:

> It seems to me that to welcome Russia as an associate in the defense
> of democracy would invite misunderstanding of our own position
> and would lend the German war effort a gratuitous and sorely needed
> aura of morality. In following such a course I do not see how we
> could help but identify ourselves with the Russian destruction of the
> Baltic states, with the attack against Finnish independence, with the
> partitioning of Poland and Rumania . . . and with the domestic
> policy of a regime which is widely feared and detested.[38]

Material support might be given if American self-interest so demanded, but without political association.

It is a curious notion that the German attack, for that was what the "war effort" was, could ever have been invested with an "aura of morality." The question, however, is whether a sharp line could actually be drawn between material aid and political ties. Absolute political dissociation in times of intimate military collaboration was unlikely in the circumstances; for a good three years, after all, the Allied nations were to rely principally on the Red Army for the struggle against Nazi Germany. When the United States tried to stipulate at a late stage of the war that Lend-Lease aid was to be used exclusively for military pursuits in Eastern Europe, Kennan himself had a scathing response. "If we still think we can help Russia defeat Germany and at the same time not assist in the achievement of Russian political aims in Eastern Europe we are being seriously unrealistic. To the question 'how much to assist Russia' we must give one answer, not two."[39] Having classified the Soviet Union as "realism in its most stark and brutal form," Kennan was in effect groping for a comparable, if perhaps less brutal, form of realism.[40] The sort of policy he desired was one that would avoid, as he perceived it, both of the dominant and equally incorrect American positions:

> There seem to be numbers of people who are incapable of seeing any middle ground between a policy which would repudiate Russia at once and completely, even to the point of cutting off military assistance and risking, if not actually promoting, further nazi gains in the east, and a policy which, based on the theory that the Soviet Government can do no wrong, would capitulate in advance to all Soviet aspirations with respect to a peace settlement and would promise Russia as much of eastern and central Europe as the latter may wish to take when German military strength has been broken.[41]

By the summer of 1944, when he judged Germany essentially beaten, his "one answer" was to cease assistance at once, or at least to use it as a bargaining chip over Eastern Europe.[42]

Bartering might have accomplished something, but hovering over any such endeavor would have been the specter of a separate peace in the eastern theater; and complete termination of assistance would probably have been premature anyway for purely military reasons. The German offensive on the western front at the end of 1944 was very nearly successful, forcing Churchill to request Stalin's help.[43] Whatever one's view of self-interested aid, it is nevertheless clear, as Kennan emphasized, that to underwrite the military purposes of the Red Army was in some sense to underwrite Soviet political purposes.

From this it cannot be concluded that material assistance implied political identity, and here his earlier warning assumes more than a little validity. For political identity was precisely what Washington seems to have projected at the very outset with its Atlantic Charter, a kind of idealized self-image of freedom, democracy, and free trade to which the United States itself was hardly about to adhere in all the particulars. To advance this platform as the basis of the antifascist war was surely to "invite misunderstanding" on a colossal scale, especially since Moscow and London signed only with provisos, effectively excluding Eastern Europe and the empire, respectively, from its formal compass.[44]

Colossal misunderstandings can be quite useful, however, and from that viewpoint this one deserves a closer look. In relation to the British Empire, and indeed much of the world, the optimal generalities of the charter were anything but empty rhetoric, in due course finding tangible expression in a whole series of predominantly economic transformations of the world order, all of which can be said in some sense to have been in the American interest. The misunderstanding, then, may merely have lain in the assumption that these changes were necessarily in the interest of the British and the world at large; and thus it was perhaps a useful misunderstanding.[45]

Yet it was one thing to impose oneself on Britain, reduced by the war almost to a client state of the United States, and quite another to do it with the Soviet Union, whose strategic, economic, and political status was vastly different. Here, blithe references to democracy and free trade simply would not translate into real objectives—that is, objectives relevant to the situation in Central and Eastern Europe, where future conflict was likely. Dealing with the Russians in this sphere would have required language more attuned to their way of thinking. It is hard to see what else could have been done, since they controlled the demesnes at stake, and there was little inclination on the American side to use the universal language of violence. The United States failed, however, not only to put forth a bargaining position comprehensible in Soviet terms but also to put forth any real bargaining position at all. Largely postponing such matters until the end of the war was in sight, Washington limited the concrete war aims to one, unconditional surrender, while planning elaborately for the postwar world on the wholly unrealistic premise of an open Eastern Europe.[46] The American stance thus combined a maximalist state-ment of political and economic principles with a truly minimalist program of war aims, hence leaving a substantial vacuum in between and causing Kennan tremendous frustration.

To him it was self-evident that the United States and the Soviet Union had, or at least should have, different interests and hence equally different ideas as to what a reasonable world ought to look like: one would want restoration of the West, the other would not.[47] This being obvious, he devoted more reflection to what for him was a more pressing matter—the need to confront the Russians on their expansion. Without a viable approach in that respect, the question of restoration might become moot: there would be little left to restore.

Already in the summer of 1942 Kennan had accurately outlined the probable range of Russian aspirations in Eastern and Central Europe and put his finger on the fundamental issue: "How far can such expansion of Soviet political influence be reconciled with our own demands for the future peace and stability of the European conti-nent?"[48] To this there could be no official answer, given the maximalist-minimalist structure of policy. Kennan had learned that firsthand dur-ing his spell at the Allied Control Commission in 1944, and on returning to Moscow later that year he had grown impatient: "We must determine in conjunction with the British the limit of our com-mon vital interests on the Continent, i.e., the line beyond which we cannot afford to permit the Russians to exercise unchallenged power or take purely unilateral action. We must make it plain to the Russians in practical ways and in a friendly but firm manner where this line lies."[49] If this were done, he thought, a moderate level of collaboration might be possible on other matters of peace and security.

It is important to note that Kennan had not counted out what he considered reasonable relations with Moscow, the prerequisite being that the United States take it upon itself to define some limits. He was also aware that the Soviet Union was not merely demanding a sphere of influence for itself but also expected its allies to have theirs. Stalin, he told Harriman, would be prepared to let the United States do whatever it wished in, say, the Caribbean. Furthermore, as he wrote elsewhere, Moscow apparently conceived of the future United Nations as a coterie of the leading powers of each continent—that is, as a set of spheres wherein the lesser nations were to be more or less relegated to a status of appendages. Perhaps unbeknownst to him, Roosevelt had suggested a not entirely dissimilar arrangement.[50]

While recognizing that it was possible to do business with Moscow under certain conditions, Kennan was more interested in seeing the United States dictate the limits of Soviet expansionism than in any discussion of mutual demarcation. This was no doubt natural for someone who was trying to persuade his government to oppose, indeed notice, what he perceived as expansionist moves of the other side. But it was also a function of seeing expansionism on one side alone rather than understanding how Western interests too could be conceived in terms of spheres and expansionism. Whatever the reason, Kennan's despatches accorded little space to the Soviet willingness to recognize and respect the interests of the other great powers; and never did he admit the possibility that this pertained to Western Europe.[51]

Churchill, a product of different circumstances, did set out in the fall of 1944 to state the British case to Stalin, and thus the two concluded their notorious "percentage deal" by dividing measures of influence in Eastern Europe (Poland notably excepted). The United States remained uneasily on the sidelines.[52] With this American posture Kennan had no sympathy. In January 1945 he wrote darkly to his close friend and fellow Russianist Charles Bohlen:

> We have consistently refused to make clear what our interests and our wishes were, in eastern and central Europe. We have refused to name any limit for Russian expansion and Russian responsibilities, whether they are asking too little or whether it is some kind of trap. We have refused to face political issues and have forced others to face them without us. We have advanced no positive, constructive program for the continent: nothing that could encourage our friends, nothing that could appeal to people on the enemy's side of the line.[53]

Eminently valuable bargaining chips had thereby been squandered, leaving only a "bitterly modest program" of dividing Europe along the various zones of occupation. That would make possible rehabilitation in Western Europe, including the western zones of Germany and Austria, according to a plan of strict economic regulation and integration with the Atlantic community. Eastern Europe would be written off as a complete loss, for "where the Russians hold power, there our world stops; beyond that line we should not try to lift our voices unless we mean business." The United Nations, with its underlying notion of multilateral security, should be scrapped. Moscow, in any event, had other means of aggression than those covered by the projected UN charter.[54]

In consonance with this stance, formulated around the time of Yalta, where completely different American proposals held the day, Kennan spent 1945 pounding away at the theme that cooperation with the USSR was useless. He opposed sending any representative to the Allied occupation authority in Vienna. He opposed recognition of the Edvard Beneš government in Czechoslovakia. He opposed all compromise on Poland, considering such action little but window dressing to cover up for absolute Soviet control. He opposed, in particular, every attempt at running Germany together with the Russians as a unified entity.[55] This regression from a position of limited and, in his view, realistic dealings with the Soviet Union in September 1944 to his despairing advocacy of radical caesura in January 1945 was brought about not by any unexpected Russian wrongdoing but primarily by his complete loss of faith in the capacity of the United States to play the role of a competent adversary.

An assessment is now in order, for which purpose one may begin with a synopsis of Kennan's argument. A Soviet thrust westward, historically determined, is posited and said to be detrimental to the interests of a set of peaceful mercantile Atlantic powers. It is up to the latter to respond, but owing to the collapse of the traditional forces capable of doing so and the congenital naiveté of the objectively powerful United States, this response is in danger of falling signally short of what is required. Eastern Europe is already lost, and if the present muddle-headed line persists, the chances are that Western Europe will degenerate into some feeble appendage to the overpowering Soviet Union. Western civilization, sapped of its basic sources, would then face somber prospects and so, ipso facto, would the United States. Ergo, save what still can be saved—that is, areas beyond the reach of the Red Army. This means splitting Europe in half, right through Germany and Austria, and rebuilding the social order in the western part. The Russians, being hard-nosed exponents of realpolitik, will understand.[56]

This compellingly direct view invites wide-ranging comment, of which the following can be but a sample.

Not discernible in this period is Kennan's previous moralizing over Soviet foreign policy. Russia is now one of many actors in world diplomacy, disagreeable but with a recognized right to a foreign policy according to interest. This development marks a real gain in clarity. His account is nevertheless still marked by a certain unrealism (or blindness) concerning the Western side. Its operations seem a priori removed from expansionism. Consider too the guiding principle he detects in Moscow's policy, maximum influence with minimum actual responsibility. Surely such a general formula of economy—optimum effect with limited means—would be the prudent course for any great power (or competitive subject). Was it not in fact an outstanding feature of Britain's later imperial policy?[57]

The fixation on historical determinants is also problematic. Carried beyond a certain point, the historicist perspective tends paradoxically to eradicate the historical itself: the element of change disappears, and history appears (ahistorically) frozen in its tracks. The specifically *Soviet* aspect thus evaporates on the vast Russian expanses, serving to impede, among other things, serious consideration of ideology. Moreover, while criteria of periodization can be debated, I do not think it useful to swathe Stalin in the tsarist cloth of Ivan the Terrible and Peter the Great.[58] If anything, Stalin's Soviet Union more resembled absolutist Russia of the late eighteenth and nineteenth centuries than the rudimentary state of the Muscovite period. Not until this later stage did the state come to exercise extensive control by means of a vast and repressive bureaucracy and the trinitarian doctrine of Autocracy, Orthodoxy, and Nationality canonized by Nicholas I in the 1830s.[59] On a similar note, while meaningful geopolitical continuities can certainly be found, the Soviet Union is a very different social formation from tsarist Russia, subject to different internal and external determinants.[60]

However one looks at it, there can be no doubt that Stalin (and most of the Soviet commonalty) wanted to extend the western boundary of the USSR and acquire a sphere of influence in the vicinity.[61] The Soviet Union was thus at that moment expansionist in a limited and very traditional sense, though one should bear in mind that the immediate territorial claims did not go beyond the 1914 borders of tsarist Russia. To equate the desired extension with the salient of the Red Army strikes me, therefore, as extreme. While it is true that Moscow tended to reproduce in occupied areas its own system of internal control, Eastern Europe of 1945 was hardly irretrievably "lost" behind Soviet lines. In Vienna, for example, there appeared under the Russians' aegis (much to their later regret) a regime that according to American officials was the best possible.[62] The Beneš government in Prague, by any standards legitimate, was later sanctioned by free elections.[63] Until the freeze toward the end of 1947, Stalin's policy actually differed from place to place, allowing a considerable rein to Czechoslovakia and Hungary but virtually none to Poland.[64] This stemmed partly from uncertainty as to what the Western allies would do, especially in terms of horse trading.[65] The inherent tension between trying to obtain a sizable sphere of influence while maintaining reasonable relations with the West (of whose power Stalin was not in doubt) created a possible clearing for limited deals on Eastern Europe. The point is not that there was any great likelihood of sweetness and light but rather that, whatever one's doubts about the realism of American policy-making, the extension of Russian rule was not unalterably given.

In addition, the superimposition of a sharp line of rupture down the middle of the map would have eliminated with a simple stroke all those areas Kennan was later to appreciate as gray, for example Austria. That this would have been ill-advised will be understood if one recalls that the compromise of 1955, which made that nation a free and neutral one, would have been highly unlikely had the United States declined representation in Vienna as Kennan suggested. In Germany, by contrast, the policy of scission gradually became unshakable orthodoxy, a development that was to have a profound effect on Kennan's thinking and eventually lead him to a powerful critique of his own original argument.

Much more important to Kennan than the fate of Eastern Europe was the future of its Western counterpart, which he considered in bad shape and thereby eminently susceptible to communist advance and foul play. As a matter of fact, the old order here did seem to be facing a variety of potential challenges. A strong effort by indigenous resistance forces to get rid of all collaborationist elements would have caused trouble and embarrassment. Add to that the indisputable importance of communists in the resistance and their manifold increase, and there emerges an image that no observer of Kennan's viewpoint could have gazed at with equanimity—particularly not with the United States apparently devoted to antifascist liberation and close cooperation with the Soviet Union.[66]

During the crucial period between 1943 and 1947, however, when liberation gave way to restoration, the communist hierarchies clung with remarkable tenacity to their old policy of class alliance and antifascism, pleading for the rejuvenation of capitalism under the rule of the "progressive national bourgeoisie," all in the context of the analogous international alliance between the Soviet Union, the United States, and Great Britain. This did not mean that communists had given up their fundamental standpoint, for the policy was actually conceived to be in the long-term interests of socialism.[67] It did signify, though, that Moscow recognized Western Europe as an American and British sphere of influence. Conceptually speaking, this did not constitute any identity of long-term interest. Moscow (and probably London too) operated on the classical idea of parallel or partially overlapping interests, the shared factor consisting in the recognition that, however distinct and separate, their respective concerns would not clash in the foreseeable future and that no benefit therefore was to be derived from invading each other's domains.[68] Stalin was quite straightforward about this. Applying the Western model of political manipulation to the Polish situation, he told his allies: "I do not know whether a genuinely representative government is a genuinely democratic one. The Soviet Union was not consulted when those governments were formed, nor did it claim the right to interfere in those matters because it realizes how important Belgium and Greece are to the security of Great Britain. I cannot understand why in discussing Poland no attempt is made to consider the interests of the Soviet Union in terms of security as well."[69] As he had said earlier, the internal differences of the alliance could be resolved as long as one did not attempt to do so "against the interests of the unity of the three powers," a statement based, one imagines, on the assumption that contradictions within any constellation are inevitable but can be dealt with as long as the parallel interests that gave rise to it in the first place are not put into question.[70] In fact, his notion of interstate alliances seems to me a mere variation on the classic communist model of strategic fronts, which are conceived (and forcefully maintained) with absolute attention to the precise boundaries of their social rationale and political program.

Kennan himself was theoretically closer to the Soviet form of traditional realpolitik but differed from it insofar as he construed the parallelism of interest much more narrowly, indeed considered it exhausted by the summer of 1944.

That Western Europe did not in fact figure in Moscow's expansion plans, political or military, is an argument that needs some amplification for future reference. In the first place, true to his agreement with Churchill, Stalin refrained meticulously from aiding the Greek rebels, and when the British moved in bloodily to suppress them so as to restore to power a thoroughly compromised order, not a sound was heard from the Kremlin.[71] Nor were there any real protests about Western policies in Italy, from the occupation of which the Soviet

Union had effectively been excluded in what it took, not unreasonably, to be a precedent for its own occupation of Eastern Europe.[72] Anti-colonialism, potentially the most troublesome issue of all for countries such as Britain, France, and the Netherlands, was more or less buried. There was no serious move against Franco in Spain, though the Spanish Blue Division had fought with the Nazis on the eastern front. In France the French Communist party (PCF) worked diligently for national unity together with de Gaulle, launching a "Battle for Production" which almost eliminated strikes and other forms of working-class opposition and taking a firm stand against independent militias. The Italian Communist party (PCI) faced greater difficulties, having to implement demobilization of its exceedingly militant base and alternative administration in the north, only to see it replaced with a state machinery that owed much to its fascist predecessor. Yet the PCI played along. The revolutionary exceptions, Yugoslavia and Greece, were mainly products of local circumstances and independence of judgment, the latter not unconnected with the possession of equally independent armed forces.[73]

Kennan's understanding of international communism was at any rate deficient. Pondering the fact that nearly one of every four voters in France supported the communists, he had concluded that these people must be suffering from the misunderstanding that the PCF would actually be able to improve their conditions, a belief he attributed to "the dense type of intellectual smoke-screen which [had] been thrown up by the Soviet propaganda machine and which [was] based not on information about Russia but on lack of such information and on a series of clever suggestions and insinuations."[74] To believe that a full quarter of the French electorate could be induced to vote irrationally in this manner is certainly to ascribe extraordinary powers of persuasion to Soviet propaganda. In truth the PCF owed the large vote less to Soviet "smoke screens" than to its prominent role in the Resistance movement and strong position in the working class.[75]

Stalin, it can thus be said, paid his respects to what he perceived as the basic interests of his allies; but what Stalin did or did not intend with regard to Western Europe was for Kennan a minor consideration. For whatever Stalin's plans, a tottering social order and a seemingly meek and muddled American policy was obviously too delicious a dish to pass up. I have registered disagreement with this view, arguing that Moscow did in fact resist temptations to cause fundamental trouble in Western Europe.[76] The muddled American policy, however, warrants a comment.

Leaving issues of political right and wrong aside, Roosevelt's max-imalist-minimalist approach deserved Kennan's strictures. The reasons have already been given: without a policy related to the concrete situation, a position as to what was possible and at what price, there was no chance of getting anywhere with Stalin in the East. A more forthright, not to say cold-blooded, stance on Eastern Europe at the outset would not necessarily have ruptured or even soured relations with Moscow, provided dealings had been kept secret. Still, it is true that the Soviet Union was in control of the area, and the Western powers had only a limited array of sticks and carrots on hand. For example, it is hard to see what could have tempted Stalin to allow the strategically vital Poland any real autonomy, particularly after the earlier Western decision to exercise exclusive control in countries such as Greece and Italy. A Polish democracy acceptable to American public opinion was thus in effect impossible except by means of a successful war against the USSR. This the West was not prepared to attempt, and by the end of spring 1945 Poland had indeed largely receded from Western concern, replaced by the far more crucial problem of Germany.

Arguably, Roosevelt's course was still reasonable in view of its mediate station between domestic and foreign concerns: if one wanted to get along with Stalin and at the same time not run afoul of Con-gress, not to mention the six million Polish-Americans and their almost exclusively Democratic votes, then one had to maneuver pragmatically and hope that Moscow would not press matters. Moscow, unfortu-nately, did not show such good sense, whereupon began the cold war.[77]

There is some validity to this argument. Stalin's cast of mind was wholly foreign to the nature of Western politics and society, making it inconceivable to him that his own long-term interest might actually be better served by a more subtle and clever control over, say, Poland. Yet Stalin's way of thinking about these matters should have been obvious from the beginning, in which case Washington could have acted with greater negotiating acumen. The reference to domestic constraints here is not persuasive. Roosevelt was concerned about public opinion to the point of opportunism. Perhaps as a young assistant secretary of the navy, he had been too close a witness to Woodrow Wilson's postwar debacle.

It has also been argued that the United States actually did acknowl-edge the great-power interests of the Soviet Union; that what was refused was the demand for a sphere of absolute domination (as opposed to an American-style "sphere of predominance").[78] Bohlen and others (including Kennan) intermittently took this position. But what these policymakers may have thought now and then is quite a different matter from what was actually said and done in negotiations with the Russians. I have yet to find much clarity and forthrightness in that context. Nor in my view can one advance any single mode of great-power domination as, so to speak, legitimate. Latin America's subjugation, to take a relevant comparison, has been accomplished by means of economic, cultural, and institutional penetration, under-written by periodic military interventionism. The nature of the Soviet system and the history of Eastern Europe made such a model difficult to emulate. Domination of Latin America has also been relatively cheap and easy because no other great power has had enough at stake in the region to challenge the United States fundamentally. The stakes in Eastern and Central Europe have been rather higher.

It may finally be noted that Kennan's essentially correct diagnosis of Washington's way of handling Moscow provoked in him the in-correct notion that American policy would perpetually be lacking in vigor and force. Shortcomings in his special field of expertise were taken as a sign of general weakness and thus led to his miscalculating both the potential and actual international power of the United States. He was to be surprised.

We began with Kennan ill and bedridden in Vienna and we shall end with Kennan ill and bedridden in Moscow, a city of whose charm he had long since wearied. By the winter of 1946 relations between the United States and the Soviet Union had deteriorated to the point where Kennan's griping despatches suddenly appeared in a new and favorable light. The Soviet "election campaign" in February caused leading members of the hierarchy to hold forth in a flurry of speeches. Stalin himself gave a rare statement, received in Washington quite erroneously as a dramatic sign of belligerence.[79] Generally a bit at sea, the State Department decided to ask Kennan, in a humoring sort of way, for an interpretative report.[80] Kennan, in a foul mood, dictated from his sickbed a response that was to become one of the two or three most important texts of the early cold war. Now known as the Long Telegram, it was an evocative but theoretically disjointed piece of dictation, whose apparent clarity and real stylistic force would lay the foundation for both Kennan's success and his failure as an American policymaker. Widely disseminated, read, and discussed ever since, it deserves detailed scrutiny.[81]

The request for interpretation, combined with the unusual number of political statements from the Soviet side, made the Long Telegram more concerned with ideology than other postwar despatches. There was thus an initial overview of the Soviet outlook, which was said to rest on these propositions: (1) that the USSR is still encircled by hostile powers with which no permanent peaceful coexistence is possible; (2) that capitalism is racked by internal conflicts that cannot be resolved peacefully, the greatest being that between the United States and Britain; (3) that these conflicts generate wars that smarter capitalists try to direct against the Soviet Union; (4) that such efforts are ultimately futile but would, if successful in the short run, delay socialist construction and should hence be counteracted; (5) that intracapitalist conflicts are generally dangerous but also offer openings; (6) that the capitalist world contains some good elements such as communist and various progressive categories; (7) that the worst elements are those false friends of the people, the social democrats. From these seven premises followed a set of political imperatives: to advance Soviet power and decrease that of others; to encourage intracapitalist conflict; to use democratic-progressive elements abroad; and to launch a relentless attack on social democracy.

This would have been a fairly accurate description of the Soviet outlook in 1930, but important changes had occurred since. Premise 7, for instance, was now on the whole incorrect. Beginning in 1935 the worst element was no longer social democracy but fascism (recoded after the war as "reactionary circles"): hence the collaboration with the socialists in prewar France, in the wartime resistance movements, and in postwar Italy. True, insofar as certain social-democratic parties (the British and the French) were elaborating plans at this point for a Western bloc, Moscow was becoming harshly negative, for there was an old and almost violent antipathy toward anything even remotely resembling an anti-Soviet combination of states. Nevertheless, despite the overt hostility toward social democracy on this account, there was never any return to the ultraleftist attacks of 1928–1934. As regards propositions 2 through 6, they were not so much wrong as of limited immediate relevance to the Soviet position. That capitalism was a contradictory system generating war was quite clearly a thesis whose validity, had it been put into question, no right-thinking Russian would have denied. To illuminate this by demonstrating how it was mediated onto the level of concrete policy would, all things being equal, have been a good thing. Merely to state it, however, was to invite misunderstanding. In addition, none of Kennan's four imperatives actually followed from it.

Most important, however, premise 1 was only partly correct. Nothing in the basic configuration of Soviet marxism as it had developed after 1935 denied *in principle* the possibility of peaceful coexistence with leading capitalist nations, provided that some "progressive" or "antireaction" bourgeoisie was in charge. The index of progressivity depended largely on attitude toward the USSR: the friendlier the regime, the more progressive. With regard to the particulars, the spring of 1946 was admittedly a transitional period during which the question of imperialist war and the nature of the Western regimes once again appeared on the Kremlin agenda. Here, however, it is essential to understand the difference between references to states and references to various "reactionary circles." In February 1946 Moscow still classified the Western *states* as "freedom-loving," to use Stalin's authoritative term; this was in contrast to the reactionary anti-Soviet *elements* in the West, which, at least until Churchill's Iron Curtain speech in early March, were to remain largely unspecified.[82] The qualitative change in the Soviet line did not occur until the fall of 1947, with the reclassification of the states or regimes themselves. If, then, it was true in the abstract that there would be imperialist wars in the future, it was also true that coexistence and peace with bourgeois regimes was not a priori impossible . It was in fact probable for the foreseeable future, what with fascism defeated and the geopolitical situation greatly improved.

Kennan does mention, rightly, that Moscow wished to avoid war. All the more odd, therefore, that none of the four imperatives is related to that proposition. Offensively oriented, they are either partially wrong (the last) or so general as to border on the trivial. His readership may have benefited from the announcement that Moscow took a competitive view and thus wanted to increase its own power and decrease that of others, but it ought to have been clear, as he said years later, that the Soviet leaders like to do better rather than worse.[83]

He goes on to declare the Soviet premises untrue and then proceeds to inquire why, then, evidently wrongheaded ideas are propagated with such vehemence, a question that implies that one is dealing with manipulation and lies.[84] Enter the internal explanation: since the Soviet view is not based on "any objective analysis" of the external

situation, it must be the product of some "basic inner-Russian necessities," more precisely those arising out of the overall need to
preserve a system that the rulers themselves had historically always
known to be "relatively archaic in form, fragile and artificial in psychological foundation, unable to stand comparison or contact with
the political systems of Western countries." Add to that the exposed
Russian plains, and the result is insecure leaders who try to cut the
country off from the outside world and seek "security only in patient
but deadly struggle for the total destruction of rival power, never in
compacts and compromises with it." (This last assertion would appear
empirically false, for, demonstrably, there had been a whole string of
both tsarist and Bolshevik "compacts and compromises.")

Marxism, the analysis carries on, is in this respect "a perfect vehicle"
for a regime even more insecure than its predecessors. By producing
an imaginary external threat, that ideology serves to justify the military
establishment, the security state, and the isolation. Since, in consequence, "Soviet purposes must always solemnly be clothed" in dogma,
ideology becomes indispensable to the leaders as the "fig leaf of their
moral and intellectual responsibility."

So far the argument differs little in structure from that of any
orthodox Soviet account of the "true" nature of American foreign
policy: "They talk about democracy but in fact it is nothing but a fig
leaf to conceal the dictatorship of Wall Street and the imperialist
attempts to suppress democratic-progressive forces everywhere," and
so forth. He may have sensed something to that effect because the
finale of his background sketch effectively undermines what has just
been said. The Russian position, we are now told, is not "necessarily
disingenuous or insincere on the part of all those who put it forward."
There are those sufficiently parochial in outlook, "mentally dependent"
people given to "self-hypnosis," who will easily believe whatever is
"comforting and convenient." Considering, too, the "atmosphere of
Oriental secretiveness and conspiracy," the fact that the regime itself
might really be "a conspiracy within a conspiracy," and the disregard
"for objective truth," the question is whether anyone, Stalin included,
gets "accurate and unbiased information about the outside world."[85]

Hardly anything intelligible can ultimately be said of the vertiginous
maze of rationalization, "self-hypnosis," marxist dogmatism, instrumental lies, and multilayered conspiracy that the Long Telegram discovers at the heart of the Soviet outlook. The argument thus ends not
so much in self-contradiction as in a void where every statement

cancels out all others and only one certainty remains: "the steady advance of uneasy Russian nationalism" toward the complete destruction of every rival form of power.

There follows a description of official and unofficial Soviet policies. Among the former are maximum internal control and secrecy; timely moves to extend influence in neighboring areas; participation in international organs when opportune; efforts to cause disruption in the colonial world; cultivation of ties with nations potentially opposed to the West; economic and cultural autarky, with a measure of minor exchange; and military industrialization. Aside from this, Moscow's posture toward other governments would be "correct." Unofficially, however, the Russians would use fully the "far-flung apparatus" of various groups and forces at their disposal to sow every conceivable form of discord in the West. In other words, "all Soviet efforts on the unofficial international plane will be negative and destructive in character, designed to tear down sources of strength beyond the reach of Soviet control."[86] Thus the famous conclusion:

> In summary, we have here a political force committed fanatically to the belief that with the US there can be no permanent *modus vivendi*, that it is desirable and necessary that the internal harmony of our society be disrupted, our traditional way of life be destroyed, the international authority of our state be broken, if Soviet power is to be secure. This political force has complete power of disposition over the energies of one of the world's greatest people and the resources of the world's richest national territory, and is borne along by deep and powerful currents of Russian nationalism. In addition, it has an elaborate and far flung apparatus for exertion of its influence in other countries, an apparatus of amazing flexibility and versatility, managed by people whose experience and skill in underground methods are presumably without parallel in history. Finally, it is seemingly inaccessible to considerations of reality in its basic reactions.

Kennan adds some mitigating factors to bring the monster down to size. The Soviet Union, he reassures the reader, is, unlike Nazi Germany, "neither schematic nor adventuristic" and has a good understanding of the "logic of force," from which follows that if one has sufficient power and willingness to use it, one need not often do so. Seen as a whole, the West is also stronger than the Soviet Union, which faces problems with the succession of power, the new territories, and the level of popular enthusiasm for communist doctrine. Finally, since "Soviet propaganda beyond the Soviet security sphere is basically negative and destructive," it ought to be "relatively easy to combat it by any intelligent and really constructive program." (Only a month later he would, as we saw, find this "negative" propaganda remarkably effective with the French electorate.)

The question remained how the United States should proceed. Kennan listed five immediate steps: (1) Diagnose the problem as a "doctor studies an unruly and unreasonable individual." (2) The government must then enlighten the American public as to the "realities of the Russian situation." This would ultimately create "far less hysterical anti-Sovietism." Even if it were to worsen relations with Moscow, little would have been lost: "We have no investments to guard, no actual trade to lose, virtually no citizens to protect, few cultural contacts to preserve." (3) Since communism is a "malignant parasite which feeds only on diseased tissue," it is also imperative "to solve the internal problems of our own society, to improve the self-confidence, discipline, morale, and community spirit of our own people." (4) The United States must put forward "a much more positive and constructive picture of the sort of world we would like to see" and provide some "guidance." (5) In doing all the above, the United States must at all costs avoid the danger of adopting the opponent's ways, and thereby his character.

Many of these themes have already been discussed, and a detailed critique is therefore superfluous. In brief, I consider the image of Moscow's intentions and capabilities greatly overdrawn and the account of Soviet ideology, though comparatively extensive, ultimately inadequate. It was dubious to claim at this point that Soviet or Western communism espoused, in either theory or practice, any fanatic desire to "destroy" the "traditional way of life" in the West. More interesting, however, is the emergence of certain contradictions in Kennan's analysis. First, the compulsive Soviet need for security is said to express itself in two different objectives: the destruction of every rival internal and external center of power *and* the isolation of the country from the outside. The outward movement implied in the former aim would seem to counteract the latter. One might argue that this merely reflects a tension in the Soviet posture itself. If so, Kennan showed remarkably little curiosity in what ought to have been rather a central dilemma for the Kremlin, likely if nothing else to restrain any straightforward expansionism. Second, there is an unresolved contrast here between a Kremlin "seemingly inaccessible to considerations of reality in its basic reactions" and a Kremlin with a well-developed sense of power relations. We shall return to these contradictions in the context of the crucial issue of whether one can ever negotiate with fanatics.

The chief problem is otherwise that the Long Telegram is methodologically a dialectical inquiry that goes only halfway. It is dialectical insofar as it tries to develop an abstract, ideal truth, for essentially Kennan is answering the question "What is the animating principle of the Soviet species?" by thinking the most extreme form of his object (which turns out to be very odious indeed). The danger with this procedure is that the extremity may actually appear to be an immediate, or unmediated, truth. If one then also happens to be *wrong*, the effects of the error will be correspondingly that much worse. For example, if one were to emphasize to the American public that Moscow saw Washington as a rival, it would be well to elucidate the nature of that concept of rivalry so as to avoid inflamed apparitions of fanatic destruction. Here Kennan himself is not empirically clear on the Soviet position, leaving his readers understandably much less so, and the result was to cause serious confusion and exaggerated fear.

But the inquiry is undialectical in that it is free of any dialogical component. Kennan, if I may extend his metaphor, studies the pathology of his object in isolation as a doctor would scrutinize something malignant under a microscope. A series of characteristic features of the object are abstracted and then presented as its "real" nature.[87] Analytically, the delineation thus becomes hermetically *internal*: the USSR, historically produced, is ultimately seen as an object unto itself, devoid of a real Other. The result is a vision of Russian nationalism unfolding its teleological essence according to some inevitable, historical principle about which nothing really can be done. The discursive and political effects of this internal derivation will become more apparent later.

It is in the light of "ideal extremities" too that one should see the striking inconsonance between the initial, frightening image of the Soviet Union and the subsequent prescription for an American response. The latter really had more to do with the internal situation in the United States and the West (that is, having a clear analysis, informing people, keeping one's own house in order) than with any specific international counterpolicies (imparting reassuring "guidance" abroad as to how the world should look). The emphasis is heavily on the domestic scene. Given the nasty nature of the adversary, this is a peculiarly modest sort of response. The explanation can be found partly in the important but understated modifications of Kennan's absolute truth—that is, in his assessment of the "real" threat—and partly in the somewhat eccentric argument that nothing truly vital was at stake in the relations with the USSR itself. However formidable, Kennan seems to argue, this fanatical power is not only weaker but is also aware of that fact. Moreover, its immediate aims, its real as opposed to ideal aims, are actually restricted to autarky coupled with limited expansion in neighboring areas. As an international threat the Soviet Union is therefore quite manageable, provided the United States recognizes it for what it is, flexes its muscles a bit, and counteracts destructive Soviet propaganda with a constructive vision of the world. What is needed, then, is little more than an awakening to reality, followed by limited action. Once Soviet power has thus been brought properly in line with its objective base, there remains the political problem of international communism. Since this force is nothing but a "malignant parasite," it can be dealt with by ensuring that the West has no "diseased tissue" upon which it can feed. No real American interests being invested in the Soviet Union itself, the United States might then very well choose largely to ignore this unpleasant regime, devoting its energies instead to building a healthy and vigorous West.

Much more, it must be said, was obviously at stake in relations with Moscow than the limited matters Kennan listed, seemingly compiled from his daily agenda of embassy duties. Even reduced to its "objective" status, the Soviet Union was a nation of potentially immense power. It was fairly clear that the condition of world politics would to some not inconsiderable degree depend on its whereabouts.

I offer this as a symptomatic reading of the Long Telegram, the development of a series of latent structures and meanings. Kennan's contemporaries (indeed Kennan himself) probably read it in a rather different manner, and not without justification. Like many students of this seminal text since, they may have focused their attention on the "political force committed fanatically to the belief that with the US there can be no permanent *modus vivendi*," a passage singularly powerful in style and content, one against which the more moderate language and arguments pale. If so, they seized on a mistake. It was not true that the Soviet Union in 1946 considered peaceful relations with the United States impossible, even in the long run. An American intelligence report at the time assessed the Russian objectives more accurately: participation in the United Nations; good relations with the United States; a security ring around the motherland and extension of influence beyond that; general competition with other great powers. All of these goals would be pursued simultaneously and sometimes in contradiction with one another.[88] This summed up the facts fairly well but, I gather, without effect.

3

Back in the U.S. of A.

Kennan had spent the greater part of two generally disagreeable years in Moscow opposing what he took to be reigning views in Washington. It had often seemed a hopeless task, all the more frustrating because his diplomatic station was incompatible with the unequivocal criticism he felt was justified. A certain irritability, difficult to suppress, had thus found its way into some of his writings. Contrary to expectation, however, there had been a change of fortune. He had come to play a significant role in articulating the changing American posture, now apparently much closer to his ideal; he had been brought home recognized as the premier Soviet analyst in the administration.

It took him no more than a few weeks on domestic soil to realize that things were not quite as good as they seemed and that he would have to alter the tenor of his argument a good deal if he was to be properly understood. His new audience may thus have been surprised to hear him arguing impatiently that the Soviet Union could not "possibly be regarded as a power that has solved all its internal problems, is armed to the teeth and ready to plunge the world into war." In fact, he said, the USSR was now relatively weaker vis-à-vis the United States than in 1939; and as long as the latter was clear about its aims and ready to back them up, there was a good chance of modest cooperation. Unexpectedly, he also denounced the simplistic notion of "getting tough" with the Russians. "They have built a society," he pointed out with emphasis, "that cannot be held in contempt and must be dealt with as a power entitled to everybody's respect."[1]

What had happened was that he had encountered an old problem again, one he had described on the occasion of an earlier return in 1942:

> Articulated opinion in this country about Russia has been largely divided into two extreme groups: the emotionally pro-Soviet and the emotionally anti-Soviet. What we have obviously lacked . . . has been a body of opinion capable of viewing Russia dispassionately, without irrational alarm or irrational enthusiasm, with equal skepticism for Russian threats and Russian promises, and with the same cool cynicism and self-interest as which characterize the view of the Soviet leaders themselves on the outside world.[2]

To find secure ground between these twin errors, or better still to go beyond that framework altogether, was not an easy proposition at a time when the political atmosphere was hardly conducive to dispassionate analysis. Kennan in fact was not altogether clear about his own bearings; for after criticizing the "get-tough" line, he went on a speaking tour in the summer of 1946 to propose something that sounded very similar, eventually writing a report that ridiculed those who had used a less hawkish tone of voice.[3] Much of the subsequent year was spent wrestling with this dilemma, with no conclusive success.

The merits of his analyses during this period are nevertheless considerable. Most of them appeared in the form of lectures, either to the public or to various groups at the newly founded National War College. The spoken address was obviously a different medium of communication from the diplomatic despatch. He was now forced to present a broad and persuasive argument to an audience that could, and sometimes did, instantly challenge it. The sheer number of lectures also put him under constant time pressure. Not as wide in scope as the major Moscow writings, and occasionally marred by rhetorical excess, they were nonetheless at once more speculative and analytical than the typical diplomatic missive.

The period is also important because Kennan would not think consistently and deeply about the Soviet Union again until he became ambassador to Moscow in 1952. One reason was simply that, after his appointment to the new Policy Planning Staff (PPS) in April 1947, he was no longer primarily a Russianist. Henceforth his analytical object would be nothing less than the world.[4] In addition, both he and his department seemed to consider the fundamental aspects of the Soviet question settled. Departmental analyses turned, to put it uncharitably, into a series of declamatory generalities. The PPS itself produced one major paper on the subject between 1947 and 1950, and several of its regional studies touched on specific areas of Soviet policy; but the sustained process of examination and reexamination ceased.[5] While divergences of opinion, sometimes sharp, would arise as to the immediate nature and aims of Moscow's expansionism, the Soviet case as a whole appeared to have been closed, the debate instead typically turning to the adequacy of American countermeasures. As Kennan said in 1950, for the last three years everyone had understood "the Russian problem pretty much for what it" was, thus making "policy toward Russia . . . one of the least controversial of all our fields of policy."[6]

Engaged at that very moment in trying to convince his peers that the onset of war in Korea did not signify the beginning of the long-expected Russian conquest of the world, Kennan should have felt a certain unease about this retrospective. It is indeed a bit peculiar that he had not pursued the Soviet matter more systematically, especially since there had been a decisive break in his general outlook during the summer of 1948. His whole problematic had shifted then from the Soviet Union to Soviet-American relations. Where previously he had analyzed Russian means and ends and then devised an appropriate American response, a logical order of origin which assumed a chronological *sequence* of action and reaction, he now began to see a *simultaneous*, dialectically constituted relationship. That paradigmatic move was, as will be seen in the next chapter, the beginning of a full-fledged critique of cold war thinking. Yet at this initial stage it involved no change in his views on the Soviet Union as such. The regime in Moscow remained for him a repugnant one with interests antithetical to those of the United States. Hence, policy disagreements notwithstanding, he continued to share many basic assumptions with his departmental colleagues, assumptions he himself had been instrumental in articulating.[7]

In deciphering the materials of the 1946–47 period I shall therefore be making occasional references to the less extensive analyses up to 1950 insofar as they concern the Soviet Union itself. My account is ordered around an assumption that had taken on the air of a self-evident observation, namely, that the Soviet Union was a hostile, expansionist power. What remained to be discussed, then, was the origin of this posture; how it translated into concrete policy and with what likely success; and finally what could be done, from an American standpoint, by way of countermeasures.

Before facing these questions head on, I must first raise the matter of totalitarianism. This was a conceptual novelty for Kennan, never very significant but useful here in reintroducing the supremely important ethical problematic.

Totalitarianism is a highly politicized concept with an intriguing history. A term first used self-descriptively and hence favorably by Italian fascists in the 1920s, it originally designated a doctrine and a political system of an all-encompassing ("total") nature.[8] It had come to be used pejoratively before the war by some as a way of subsuming under one name the systems of Germany, Italy, and the Soviet Union. Only with the cold war though did it achieve true prominence as the negative Other of the new American definition of the world. By then, of course, Nazi Germany and fascist Italy had become historical artifacts, leaving the term available for exclusive reference to the Soviet Union. On the nontotalitarian side of the coin democracy was gradually replaced by the free world, a superior concept because as a simple negation it allowed more easily for the inclusion of otherwise unattractive regimes.[9] The dichotomy eventually found its mirror image in the Soviet two-camp theory, according to which everything could be classified as either progressive-democratic or imperialist. The two divisions actually referred to the same thing; and both made good use of the Munich analogy.[10]

It was the ethico-political aspect of the concept of totalitarianism that appealed to Kennan, who had earlier fused Hitler and Stalin on such grounds. A sporadic presence in his writings before the end of the war, the idea became a part, if not really an integrated one, of his outlook as it developed after he returned to the United States.[11] Denying that the basic conflict in world politics had anything to do with questions of collectivism, socialism, capitalism, or indeed with any aspect of economic conditions, he insisted that it revolved around ethics. On the one side were those who adhered to the adage that the ends justify the means and on the other those who thought unethical means ruin the end no matter how intrinsically worthwhile:

> We have on the one hand the familiar pattern of totalitarianism. This is the philosophy which holds that a single man or group of men, who have come into the monopolistic possession of the instruments of internal power, are qualified and entitled to decide what constitutes the interests of the peoples under their immediate control (and often peoples elsewhere as well), to draw up programs ostensibly for the promotion of what they have defined as public interests, and to

require unquestioning acceptance of these programs by the people at large and total collaboration in their realization. No independent values are recognized here, which might take precedence over the execution of these programs. No individual rights or liberties are allowed to impede it. Since it is predicated that the goal is a beneficial one, it is also assumed that all means which serve this goal are automatically permissible. The means are invariably justified by the prescribed end. Thus the selection and employment of method is governed by no ethical principles whatsoever. Expediency becomes supreme. Values which men have accepted for centuries are cheerfully tossed overboard and replaced by a simple mechanical scale of efficacy in the realization of the desired goal, against which all methods and all actions are measured. In this concept, there can be no deed too black, no duplicity too profound, no punishment too cruel, no sacrifices too great, if it is interpreted by those who hold power as serving the goal which they have indicated. Where this outlook comes to prevail, the machinery of human society loses its balance-wheel: the balance-wheel of the ethics common to the great religions of the world, and the engine of political power begins to race in a furious and uncontrolled orgy of acceleration which the protagonists of the system define as progress and in which others see only a horrifying plunge toward the failure and disaster of human society.[12]

This eloquent indictment of Stalinism, for that is in essence what it was, contains assertions that would require volumes to discuss fully. Nevertheless, some remarks of a provisional nature should be made.

First, no "balance-wheel of the ethics common to the great religions of the world" can be counterposed to the alleged doctrine that the ends justify the means. It is particularly surprising to see this argument, since the doctrine in question most often is associated, rightly or wrongly, with the Jesuits and the Spanish Inquisition, surely a forthright program of religious terror. Genocidal wars and a whole series of atrocities have been perpetrated precisely in the name of these "great religions," with the possible exception of Buddhism.

Second, the idea of justifying means in terms of ends is not as one-sided as Kennan would have us believe. It can be understood to mean that actions must be evaluated with reference to their consequences, in which case it is not incompatible with ethically induced restraint. The problem arises when ends are entirely externalized from activity, when the two are thought to be radically separate and everything is eventually reduced to an instrument. A society organized on such lines does indeed come to function according to "a simple mechanical scale of efficacy in the realization of the desired goal," Stalinism most certainly being an appalling example.

Here, however, it is well to recall Max Weber's classic account of instrumentalization (or "rationalization"), a logic of ordering the world strictly in terms of means and ends, which he saw as constitutive of bureaucracy in general and the capitalist enterprise in particular.[13] Ironies then begin to compound, for not only was capitalism for Weber related to the emergence of Calvinism, but the Calvinist Kennan was to become chief planner of American foreign policy and thus pre-eminently concerned, as he would later describe it, with relating means to "definite objects."[14]

Moreover, Kennan's own inversion, in theory, of the means-end relation retains the basic separation itself and thus comes to suffer from some of the same defects as its target of opprobrium. Carried to its logical extreme, the proposition that means alone matter—that methods are "real" and objectives "vainglorious," as he was to write in his *Memoirs*[15]—is an absurdity, since it would seem to rob activity of all meaning and rationality. Why one does what one does becomes a nonsensical and unresolvable question. To evaluate methods, one would have to take recourse to external factors and criteria, at which point infinite regression sets in and the whole project becomes self-defeating. Any simple binary division of means and ends actually threatens to eradicate value itself by making the posited end in practice a matter of realizing the extant means, thus turning everything into means.[16]

The problem can be overcome, in my view, only by refusing to regard the aim as extrinsic to the means: the good is, so to speak, embedded in the character of the practice at hand and not defined by external criteria such as, for instance, "What is good for General Motors is good for America," or "What is good for the Communist party is good for the universe."[17] Kennan made some gestures in this direction, typically when discussing the inherent value of good diplomatic form, only to deny them by endlessly repeating that the essential criterion "is not so much *what* is being done as *how* it is done."[18] This was merely a recoding of the means-ends couplet, from which he was never able to depart.

Thus the Soviet Union in this light might well be seen as a gigantic (indeed "total") attempt to let the logic of rationalization permeate every sphere of human life and society (although maximization of effect sometimes aims more at social control than production). "Reason," as Herbert Marcuse described the process, "is nothing but the rationality of the whole: the uninterrupted functioning and growth of the apparatus."[19] As Antonio Gramsci had pointed out very early on, civil society in tsarist Russia was undeveloped. The Soviet state in its Stalinist phase squeezed it even further. The sphere of subjective autonomy, which serves as the theoretical premise of Western ethics, is thus politicized in Soviet society and subordinated to an absolute, distant, and essentially abstract goal of future communism.[20] Since the 1930s, the *specific* moral values promoted for the growth of the apparatus have, however, been exceedingly conservative, a mixture of Russian nationalism and what appears suspiciously like the old Protestant command morality ("Thou shalt work hard and not commit adultery").[21] Many of these rules would indeed have found an ardent supporter in George Kennan.

One should beware too of letting any simple polarity come into play: democracy with its putatively unassailable private sphere on the one side and totalitarianism with its complete political control and lack of a private sphere on the other. Such a polarity exaggerates and distorts the meaning of the private sphere in the West. Democratic theory tends to posit such a domain (the individual) in order to construct a General Will, before which this private sphere then disappears. In reality, of course, a whole set of institutions, practices, and sanctioned rights prevent this from happening to the extent that it does in the Soviet case, where (until now) there have been no legitimately autonomous forms of organization between citizen and state.

To make the ethical axis a foundation of understanding the Soviet system is furthermore to displace or suppress its historical specificity, a reductionist operation that obscures more than it explains. Certainly, similarities can usefully be drawn between Hitler's and Stalin's regimes: consider for instance the extraordinary importance of the secret police. Whether the concept of totalitarianism is the best way to grasp these similarities is to me questionable. The derivation from exclusively—and therefore paradoxically partial—political and ethical categories has the effect of banishing from the inquiry such specifics as economic structure, in which we see a profound difference. To use Trotsky's apposite parallel, the operation is not unlike the Catholic identification of Freemasons, Marxists, and Darwinists as one and the same on the grounds that they all deny Immaculate Conception.[22] There is also a certain circularity to the argument. Raw materials for a definition are assumed to be found in Nazi Germany, fascist Italy and Stalinist Russia. A series of similarities is then extracted—charismatic leaders, atomization, mass movements, repression, and so on—whereupon totalitarianism has been codified and can be applied to the regimes in question: Q.E.D.[23]

Finally, according to Kennan a lack of ethical restraint (a "balance-wheel") in the Soviet regime leads to a situation in which "the engine of political power begins to race in a furious and uncontrolled orgy of acceleration." A society that has reduced ethics to a "mechanical scale of efficacy," however, does not necessarily lose its balance and fall into some kind of delirium. The opposite could just as well occur, and in fact probably did in the Soviet Union, with its immobility, rigidity, and control.

The purges might have indicated otherwise to Kennan, which brings us to another, related aspect of the totalitarian thesis: the idea that, in contrast to the "rule of law" in the West, these states are run arbitrarily.[24] Kennan made less of this argument than one might expect, but it did enter into his skepticism toward internationally binding agreements with Moscow and is therefore worth a comment.[25] Two points spring to mind. First, much of Stalin's terror was perfectly legal. As of 1934 the secret police were invested, in formally correct ways, with authority to imprison and sentence people; later they also earned the right to torture and shoot them. Prophylactic terror, the removal of people thought to be potential troublemakers, was likewise legal. And while the individual targets of the terror were often arbitrarily chosen, the process as a whole appears to have been quite methodically thought out and executed. Second, parallel with this development, Soviet law was professionalized and expanded enormously through codification in areas such as family law. Vast bureaucratization was also under way, bringing in its train an equally vast set of rules and regulations, none of which encouraged structural arbitrariness. This is not to say that massive illegalities, arbitrary or not, were never committed. They were. Criminal evidence, to take an obvious example, was habitually falsified. But it is to say that the opposition between arbitrariness and the rule of law is not automatically a basis on which to analyze totalitarianism. By the same token, it cannot be used, without other evidence, to characterize such a system as inherently disorderly or structurally unstable.[26]

Kennan would later add a metaphor of his own for totalitarian instability when he described the Soviet Union as a crust atop an underlying mass of uncertainties: were the crust to break, the whole structure might self-destruct. In other words, take away the thin ruling stratum and the result might well be complete collapse. First stated in the X-Article, written in the spring of 1947 and published in the summer, this idea originally applied only to the Soviet Union; but by 1948 it had become part of Kennan's larger concept of totalitarianism.[27]

What ought to be remembered here is probably the impression (and I use the word *impression* deliberately) of something essentially unrestrained, something extreme that is possibly on the verge of exploding or imploding. Where this leads in Kennan's accounts can be seen in his discussion of a statement by the Soviet jurist Evgeny Pashukanis:

> In their [totalitarian] view, all imperialists harbor designs on the happiness and independence of other people and these measures short of war are only cynical tricks, devices of people while they prepare for ugly operations. While Pashukanis didn't say so, he leaves us no choice but to conclude that in his opinion the Soviet State too would be naive if it failed to take full advantage of the rosy prospects which these measures hold out as a means of deceiving the enemy and disguising your own preparations . . . There are no rules of the game. They can do anything they think is in their interests . . . , persuasion, intimidation, deceit, corruption, penetration, subversion, horse-trading, bluffing, psychological pressure, economic pressure, seduction, blackmail, theft, fraud, rape, battle, murder, and sudden death . . . their choice is limited by only one thing, and that is their own estimate of the consequences to themselves of the adoption of a given measure . . . The fact is that no totalitarian dictator will rest unless he has satisfied his own totalitarian conscience that he has prodded you right to the limit of the danger zone of your patience.[28]

Thus, with regard to Soviet foreign policy specifically, the totalitarian theme signified little in Kennan's analyses but a reaffirmation of the old idea that Moscow would use any skulduggery to eliminate forces beyond its control. This ethical focus may not have been the best way to elucidate the essence of Soviet ways and means, but the assertion itself may have been right. Let us remember, however, what NSC 68, the guiding document of American foreign policy after 1950, proposed on Western means and ends: "The integrity of our system will not be jeopardized *by any measures, covert or overt, violent or non-violent, which serve the purpose of frustrating the Kremlin design,* nor does the necessity for conducting ourselves so as to affirm our values in actions as well as words forbid such measures, *provided only they are appropri-*

ately calculated to that end and are not excessive or misdirected as to make us enemies of the people instead of the evil men who have enslaved them."[29] It is hard to imagine a more uncompromising formulation of "mechanical efficiency" and the whole notion of ends justifying means.

Totalitarianism as a concept never became an organic part of Kennan's thinking. There were several reasons for this. There was the nominalist dislike for generic concepts, typical of traditional conservatism and bound to make him reticent about any promiscuous use of abstractions. There was the problem of internal coherence. He had argued that totalitarians recognize no "rules of the game." Yet he had also found realism an outstanding characteristic of Soviet foreign policy, and if this realism was not to become sheer contingency, it would certainly have to observe some "rules." The Long Telegram, for example, had established that Stalin was outwardly cautious, disinclined to adventurism of any kind. Only with some difficulty could this be squared with the image of overflowing totalitarian delirium.

Attached also to the concept of totalitarianism was a commonly accepted history according to which the Second World War had come about because the democracies had failed to stand up to the totalitarian, expansionist Hitler, a mistake not to be repeated with a regime of similar ilk.[30] Ergo, there must be no appeasement of Moscow. Under such circumstances it was to argue oneself into substantial trouble to say that, yes, here is a totalitarian regime corresponding in all essentials to the Nazis which ought not to be appeased while simultaneously maintaining that said regime was not adventuristic or interested in war. Never taken with Munich analogies, Kennan soon found reason to warn against "the danger" of "thinking of Russia as just a larger and improved 1948 version of Hitler's Germany," but such words of wisdom fell on unfertile ground.[31] The American outlook was becoming captive to the lesson of the 1930s and thus commensurately militarized.

There was finally the matter of political outlook. As we have seen, Kennan had opposed the earlier dichotomy of dictatorship and democracy. He was now unable to accept wholeheartedly the dichotomy of totalitarianism and the free world. Occasionally he would employ the image himself in a simple, binary way, but not without clear reservations: "We must not confuse the voluntary self-discipline and restraint of a free people with the restrictions of despotism. We might even do well to bear in mind the admonition of Alexander Hamilton

that the 'vigor of government is essential to the security of liberty'
and that 'a dangerous ambition more often lurks behind the specious
mask of zeal for the rights of the people, than under the forbidding
appearance of zeal for the firmness and efficiency of government.'"[32]
This Hamiltonian flourish, very much in character, indicated his democratic limits at the very moment when he was about to become head
policy planner for, so to speak, the leader of the free world. He was
in fact reluctant to use the division of totalitarianism and the free
world even for propaganda purposes.[33]

His predicament is perhaps best understood if it is rewritten in
classical Greek terms—which in any case might have been his immediate source of inspiration. Greek thinkers set forth a multitude of
political forms, but the central issue for them seems to have been the
contrast between the stable and orderly (traditional) on the one hand
and the arbitrary, capricious, and criminal on the other. From this
perspective Kennan's concept of totalitarianism may be grasped as a
fairly straightforward translation of the Greek notion of tyranny, implying as it did arbitrary despotism, immoderation, lack of respect for
the law, and insatiable desires on the part of the tyrant—all in all an
unstable compound teleologically destined for destruction.[34] Among
the positive counterpoints to tyranny (since this was not a dichotomy),
Kennan would have been more inclined to aristocracy than democracy,
though again, the form was less important than the question of order
and stability. Such an implicit typology would have had for him the
virtue of making a traditional regime such as Salazar's in Portugal
eligible for favorable classification.[35]

Totalitarianism, then, was a relatively barren concept Kennan attached to some old, and one or two new, ideas. In itself it yielded few
explanatory benefits.

Kennan's argument about totalitarianism was codified in a manner
that raised in passing the question of expansionism: totalitarian states
by nature squeeze maximum power benefits out of any situation by
whatever means they deem profitable. Hence they are also in some
sense expansionist.[36] This was an assertion about a state of affairs, not
an explanation of it. Insofar as he offered an explanation, it chiefly
took the form of a story about hostile ideology, which now acquired
a prominence it had not enjoyed during his Moscow period.

The origins of this shift of emphasis can be found in two American
developments. First, a critique of the new, more antagonistic posture

toward the Soviet Union was emerging from various quarters around Henry Wallace, and Kennan felt a need to combat what he took to be their idealistic views. This task, as it turned out, made the problem of ideology impossible to avoid. Second, Kennan was confronted with a lengthy memorandum, "Dialectical Materialism and Russian Objectives," written by one Edward F. Willet. Willet was a professor of business at Smith College who had somehow now become Secretary of the Navy James Forrestal's resident expert on marxism and Soviet foreign policy. The tract he had composed was a hodgepodge, concluding among other things that the Soviet Union would go to war with the United States because of the tenets of dialectical materialism. Forrestal, who had been an energetic disseminator of the Long Telegram, sent Willet's memorandum to Kennan for comment. Kennan conveyed some objections, which in turn sparked in him a desire to clarify the whole problem of ideology and foreign policy, an effort that would ultimately result in the X-Article.[37]

These events should also be seen in relation to the way in which Soviet ideology had been discussed in the United States. Here Kennan, as was his wont, tried to situate himself between two erroneous views, crudely encapsulated in the propositions that ideology meant nothing or that it meant everything. During the wartime alliance the dominant image of Russia had tended to be that of a traditional Great Power for which marxism had become an unwanted facade. As the discerning eye began to realize after the war that ideology was not in fact a mere facade, there was a general swing from the first proposition to the second.[38] The Soviet Union now signified communist conquest pure and simple. Luminously clear, ideology seemed to warrant no more scrutiny than it had during the Great Power period. Kennan was aware that this was quite the wrong way to pose the problem, and he made substantial efforts to reconceive it. Ultimately unable to transcend the given terms, he came instead to move across the entire spectrum of opinion, espousing the elastic view that ideology meant something: against the given either-or he could only respond "to some extent."

His story about hostile ideology actually varied substantially on the three major occasions when he presented it during 1946 and 1947. His first effort, an address at Yale in October 1946, was expressly devoted to an unconditional assessment of what he took to be Henry Wallace's position. Wallace, then a controversial figure, had just been fired from the cabinet by Truman because of his public support for improved ties with Moscow. Kennan's argument focused on whether or not seeking the trust of the Russian regime could be of any relevance to such an improvement. The answer was negative.

He began by classifying the Soviet leaders as "international Marxists of the sternest Leninist school," "committed by their own credo to certain preconceived opinions about the capitalist world."[39] While some people, he continued (perhaps referring to himself at other times), might think of them instead as "power-conscious realists whose pretensions to ideology are only a cynical sham," ideology is in fact "the only positive feature in a regime which has otherwise brought little but harshness, cruelty and physical misery to the human beings who have fallen within the range of its influence." Without it, the Russian leadership would be "exposed as only the last of the long series of cruel and wasteful rulers who have driven a great people from one military ordeal to another throughout the centuries in order to assure the security of their own oppressive regime."

This, on the face of it, would scarcely seem a refutation of the theory of "cynical sham," especially since he added that the leaders actually knew they would be naked without ideology (their "fig leaf" in an already familiar metaphor). He went on, however, to include a historical dimension:

> For 28 years . . . this theory [ideology, particularly the notion of outside hostility] has moulded the shape of power in the Soviet Union. Under its steady pressure, institutions have been crushed and other institutions have been fashioned. The nature of the Communist Party itself; the character and the role of the secret police; the degree of militarization; the direction of economic effort;—all these have been determined by the theory that Russia exists in an environment of instability, hostility, and ill-will. By this principle hundreds of thousands of people have come to gain their bread and butter; and hundreds of thousands of others have come to enjoy what is more important to them than either bread or butter: the sense of power for its own sake . . . These groups have come to constitute a great vested interest:—an interest vested in the basic precariousness of Russia's international position. Imagine their feelings when this recent war ended with the destruction of Russia's only real enemies, Germany and Japan, and they found themselves with the horrible possibility that Russia might be forced to live in a friendly world. In such a case they were superfluous people: excess baggage on the train of revolution, their talents no longer needed. Is it any wonder that they rose up as a body to deny that this precariousness had passed?

Is it any wonder that the whole propaganda machine of the State was applied to proving that the remaining great powers, England and America, were no less menacing to the Soviet Union and to the peace of the world than those which had been conquered . . . ? It can safely be said, therefore, that the fears and suspicions we are encountering in the Russians are not really fears and suspicions of us but relate to the character of the Soviet regime itself. It is themselves and their own backwardness that the Russians fear. This fear is obviously not going to be dispelled by any famous gestures of appeasement on our part.

He had made much the same point in less elaborate form before the war, on the grounds that Nazi Germany was evidently not a danger to the USSR. Events had proved otherwise. In its present version the claim was wrong in several ways. That, in the first place, there was a certain fear in the Soviet leadership of the United States, with its vast industrial machine intact and military power spiced by possession of the atomic bomb, is scarcely any wonder.[40] Moreover, it is difficult empirically to accept that an enormous vested interest actually went on a frantic search for fictitious enemies in 1945 merely to preserve its raison d'être. By then, assuredly, the USSR had had enough real ones. Finally, the United States and Great Britain, as regimes, were not then considered enemies on a par with Nazi Germany; such parallels did not occur authoritatively in Soviet statements, so far as I am aware, until the latter part of 1947.[41]

Again, the argument seems to reinforce rather than counter notions of "cynical sham," but the most important aspect is its causal logic: followers of marxist ideology come to power and transform society with particular reference to a part of this ideology, the depiction of the outside world as hostile; a dominant material structure based on this ideology emerges; when its real enemies are destroyed, the apparatus loses its rationale and must invent new enemies (England and America) to preserve power; the reasons for Soviet hostility are therefore internal and American efforts to appease useless.

The first, voluntarist or idealist part of this account strikingly resembles the Soviet self-conception after Stalin's revolution from above had begun in 1928, a self-conception devoid of allusion to social forces. Here too adherence to marxist principles causes transformations on a vast scale. The second, materialist argument is instead reminiscent of a standard Soviet portrayal of imperialist ideology: reactionary circles associated with monopoly capital are spreading slanderous lies about the Soviet Union and its peace policy so as to confuse progressive forces everywhere and conceal their own class rule and the preparations for aggression at home and abroad, or some such line. Leaving structure aside for the moment, what one should remember is the recurrent conclusion: American efforts to appease are useless because Soviet hostility is actually a product of purely internal factors.

A speech given in two versions in January 1947 offered Kennan some latitude for expanding these themes. The topic was "The Soviet Way of Thought and Its Effect on Foreign Policy," a familiar and confounding question to which he readily admitted having given differing answers in the past. The speech, particularly its second version, dealt with the subject matter in a wide sense and not solely in terms of marxism.[42]

His story was now brought back in time to include the "national tradition" of prerevolutionary Russia, a tradition whose importance he found "generally under-rated" in the United States. Thus he pointed to the usual set of factors: historical absence of peaceful relations with adjacent powers; a resultant view of the outside as "a hostile force with which there could be no possibility of peaceful co-existence"; a paradoxical mixture of xenophobia and "almost slavish curiosity and admiration for foreign things"; and the messianic tradition of Holy Russia combined with the ideological-geographical lack of a sense of limits.

To this familiar picture add the Bolsheviks and the revolution (whose causes he did not much ponder in this period). These original communists, "a fairly sophisticated group" in the first version of the speech, are described as products of a personal inability to cope with the difficulties of tsarism, the exception being Lenin, "whose integrity as an international socialist was complete and the sincerity of whose beliefs in socialist principles rose above petty egotism." For the others, however, "the ideal was a convenient rationalization and cover for the pursuit of impulses which had their origin in the normal workings of the good old human ego." Had Lenin lived, he said, a certain moderation might have occurred. Instead, enter Stalin and the rise of parvenus. This new ruling stratum suffered from the dual insecurity of being both a minority regime at large and upstarts within the party itself. In consequence, "they could not accept the risk of sharing power with other elements in Russia or of tolerating the free activity of people who might oppose them." The policies designed to secure the regime—collectivization and military industrialization—could only serve to perpetuate opposition, since they were implemented against the majority will. The consequences were grave:

> In time the entire nature of the regime became shaped to the end of internal security. Organs of power and administration which did not serve this purpose withered on the vine and had a tendency to become atrophied. Organs which did serve this purpose became vastly over-developed and swollen. The whole character and personality of the Soviet regime were thus gradually conditioned by the existence of this internal danger. And today the most important features of the regime are ones whose basic function is to assure the security of its internal power and the validity of its dictatorial authority.

This, for obvious reasons, could not be admitted by those concerned, and thus it had become necessary to externalize the opposition, to make it into some putatively foreign or foreign-inspired activity. Regardless of the degree of real external danger, consequently, the propaganda against the outside became constant. In sum:

> What we are dealing with here is a logical element of the Soviet system of thought: something that has been constructed in those times and conditions when it did not exist—a thesis indispensable to the structure of Soviet power . . . Thus Soviet officialdom has become one great vested interest committed to the principle of a hostile outside world . . . It will be seen, therefore, that the basic motive of Soviet power lies in the assurance of the internal security of the regime itself [which] in turn necessitates the maintenance of a fiction, namely the fiction of a hostile capitalist environment.

Kennan took this to be a confirmation of Marx's thesis, as he understood it, "that ideology is a product and not a determinant of social and political reality," which in this case meant "that the Soviet ideology of today flows with iron logic and with irresistible force from the inner necessities of Soviet power."[43]

One may note here in passing that the ideological causation of the October address has now been extended into a logic of *personal* insecurity resulting in revolutionary ideology, resulting in turn in postrevolutionary *political* insecurity, creating an objective (quasibiological) evolutionary process by which the entire state apparatus is molded according to the needs of internal security, which then in turn necessitates the ideological fiction of external enemies.

The emerging machinery, the argument continues, was marked by extraordinary discipline, predicating all personal advancement on absolute allegiance to the collective body and nothing else. The effect was

> that such party bodies can be impelled in the direction of caution and restraint in dealings with the outside world only when it can be demonstrated by individual members that any other course would be contrary to the interests of the Soviet Union . . . Thus foreign representatives who wish to see the Soviet Government take action along lines agreeable to the interests of their countries must make sure that it can be argued in the party councils that action along these lines would be in accordance with the most cynical and hardboiled interpretation of Soviet interests.

Once the Party was so persuaded, however, it had the capacity to alter radically and swiftly any obdurately held position into a new and equally obdurately held position; for while the party was always right, the concrete situation might well change. Thus "we obtain the curious mixture of outward obstinacy and inward flexibility which characterizes the Soviet approach to international affairs."

So far the argument is essentially an elaboration of the October address, but included, without actually being integrated, was a nuanced and most interesting reflection on the role of marxist ideology as such, a reflection parallel and partially antipodal to the previously outlined themes. This is prefaced by the disclaimer "that ideology is neither the real driving force nor the real program of Soviet action," which is rather a product of "the internal necessities of Soviet power" and other factors that "could not possibly have been foreseen by the classical fathers of Soviet thought." Nevertheless, ideology is important in three different ways:

> In the first place, it is in light of ideology, and in the language of ideology, that Soviet leaders become aware of what transpires in this world. They think of it, and can think of it, only in terms of Marxist philosophy. Their own education knows no other terms. And the people on whom they are dependent for their reports of the outside world have no other terms in which to describe to them what they see . . . It is clear, then, that it functions in effect as a prism through which the world is viewed.

Having as it were immersed the Russians in ideology, Kennan proceeds to pull them out by repeating his "fig leaf" thesis: "Therefore, all Soviet decisions and actions must appear to serve the doctrines of

Marx and Lenin, whether they do or not. This sets severe limitations on the freedom of expression and the outward behavior of the Soviet government. In all its words and deeds in the field of foreign affairs, it must do lip service to the interests of the working classes of the world." To the prism and the fig leaf he then adds a third and final ideological aspect: the theme of ends and means. "The central political philosophy of the Russian revolutionary movement" for a century, it had originated in "the dark and pagan recesses of the Russian soul itself" rather than in Marx. The Soviet regime, as a result, showed "an absence of scruple and restraint in method which [was] probably unparalleled in history."

Whether he means that the Russians were "worse" historically than, say, the Romans, indeed than most regimes until recent times, I do not know; his remark was of course a rhetorical one. More noteworthy is that he has removed from purview the eminently Western tradition of *raison d'état* (any means are justified in the interest of preserving the state), from Louis XI and Machiavelli onward, a tradition that might have given him cause to widen his search for origins beyond the "pagan recesses of the Russian soul."[44]

Trying to sum all of this up was not an easy matter. Ambiguities inevitably ensued, as evidenced by his conclusion that ideology "colors what the Russians see and what they do. Its function is to distort and embellish reality, both objective and subjective. Within the limits of this function, its influence is enormous . . . But it is important to remember that its bearing is on coloration of background, on form of expression and on method of execution, rather than on basic aim." This is a slippery pronouncement; but certainly something that colors reality, metaphorically speaking, is quite different from a "prism" through which *everything* is seen. An ideology that "sets severe limitations" on "expression" and "outward behavior" is not a "coloration of background."

Kennan's aim appears once again to have been to find a suitable spot between total fixation on ideology and total dismissal of it; but his was not a happy compromise, for he never makes it entirely clear whether the Russians were inside or outside ideology. He might have believed they were both—in other words that they were at once steeped in it *and* using it as a simple instrument. Yet such a claim is difficult to make without establishing, at the very least, a clear distinction between a general ideological universe and particular uses of the various statements made possible by it. Alternatively, he may actually have seen a dialectical, mutually reinforcing relationship between ideology and material institution; but this is hard to reconcile with expressions like "lip service," which imply that the stated position is not a "real" one.

Some of his difficulties stemmed from the notion of ideology as forming every aspect of Soviet marxism and the consequent endeavor to say something meaningful about this whole. Disinclined to think inside its boundaries, he tended to gaze at ideology as though it were one block of ideas alongside a potentially open-ended number of other blocks, such as tsarist, nomadic, or ethnic patterns of thought. This landed him in the morass of trying to find ways of measuring the relative influence of these various components on the Kremlin mind. Seen from a different angle, his outside position also had a propensity to result in one of only two views: either Soviet statements were propaganda, in which case ways and means had to be found whereby the truly intended could be distilled; or they were free-floating propositions subject to intellectual dissection and then to be dismissed as transparent fallacies. In short, he remained tied to the phenomenological question of sincerity: are they or are they not sincere in their ideological absurdities?

Some suggestions for escaping from this analytical predicament are offered in Appendix B. Here let us merely register that when all was said and done, Kennan considered the Russians marxists. In the January 7 speech he in fact called them "fanatics" who "seriously believe that they are faithful servants of Marx, Lenin and world revolution," and in whose ideology there is "no conscious hypocrisy or cynicism."

Yet these were marxist fanatics of a particular kind. Looking at the content of Soviet marxism in relation to traditional Russian ideology, Kennan found conspicuous similarities:

> The view that the outside world is a hostile force finds ready confirmation in the communist insistence that there is an inevitable conflict between the socialist state and its capitalist environment and that the great countries of the West are united in an evil conspiracy to overthrow the socialist state and to enslave the Russian people. The traditional xenophobia of Russian officialdom finds natural expression in the Soviet view of foreigners as a [*sic*] dangerous "spy, wrecker and diversionist." And the conception of the Russian state as an ideological entity destined eventually to spread to the utmost limits of the earth is reflected with almost baffling fidelity in the communist belief in the ultimate triumph of world revolution and in the resulting

tendency of the Kremlin to the quiet infiltration into, and domination of, outside centers of military and political power beyond the borders of Russia itself.

This confluence of old and new was a powerful brew which made all talk of changing the Soviet view much more questionable, for one was up against "some of the most basic and deep-seated traits of traditional Russian psychology."

His image, then, was one of an essentially unalterable, unresponsive enemy with whom little could be done by way of persuasion. One of the hallmarks of a fanatic is, after all, imperviousness, and in no case more obviously so than in the Soviet Union, where the whole material foundation of fanaticism was based on the principle of outside hostility. I shall return this argument in all its implications but must first deal with the issue of expansionism.

Laborious care had been taken in these first endeavors to show that everything unfurled with "iron logic" from within the Russian compound. About the outside we learn little except that real enemies had disappeared, leaving only the imagined ones, peaceful England and America. The historical dialectic of hostility as a *real* process appears to have come to an end. If we accept this, and also that the Russians had structural reasons to conjure up fictitious outside enemies, it is still not clear why they would actually bother powers thus designated. The conclusion of his January 24 speech had indeed pointed in the opposite direction: "We are dealing here with a political entity animated primarily by the desire to assure the security of its own internal power. History and environment impel it to seek such security in the pursuit of *military-industrial autarchy* and in the maintenance of a great *internal apparatus of repression.*"[45] Securing power by such means may make for a disagreeable regime but does not in itself constitute inherent expansionist tendencies. Autarky, it would appear, implies political isolationism. Here, as in the Long Telegram, there is an internal tension between inward and outward movement, which could not be eliminated by references to national tradition, party discipline, or any other areas discussed. The X-Article offered a simple, if partial, solution.

"The Sources of Soviet Conduct," the actual title of this singular piece of writing, was in some ways a truncated and inferior version of the two January speeches.[46] The prerevolutionary historical dimension had more or less vanished, and so had reflection on the *role* of ideology. This is a pity, for these changes gave the article a "revolutionary" tilt that is exacerbated by Kennan's use of language. The article as a whole, however, was not logically incompatible with its January progenitors, only differently focused.

Soviet behavior, according to the now famous opening sentence, is the result of "ideology and circumstance." Those categories correspond fairly closely to the idealist and materialist, between which Kennan had oscillated in his historical explanations. The story now begins with the maladjusted coterie of old Bolsheviks and their inability to cope with tsarism. From this psychological starting point he proceeds in his customary manner to the postrevolutionary exigencies of power, which explain the original dictatorship. After making that plausible point, Kennan slips back into an idealist mode. Referring to Stalin's personal insecurity, he sees the leaders of the *present* dictatorship in these terms: "Their particular brand of fanaticism, unmodified by any of the Anglo-Saxon tradition of compromise, was too fierce and too jealous to envisage any permanent shrinking of power. From the Russian-Asiatic world out of which they had emerged they carried with them a skepticism as to the possibilities of permanent and peaceful coexistence of rival forces. Easily persuaded of their own doctrinaire 'rightness' they insisted on the submission or destruction of all competing power" (p. 568). It is here that the relentlessly internal theme permutates by means of a reassertion of a point that had intermittently been made before (for example in the Long Telegram) but not really developed. The Kremlin, fanatical and "jealous" for historical reasons, is not only intent on eliminating "all competing" power inside the country, where, as Kennan puts it, the "process of political consolidation has never been completed" (p. 569) but *outside* as well. Competing power, wherever it is, must be destroyed. Such, then, is the imputed entelechy of Soviet communism. Just as this principle internally gives rise to its own opposition and the dialectical growth of repressive organs, so it generates its own external hostility: "It is an undeniable privilege of every man to prove himself right in the thesis that the world is his enemy; for if he reiterates it frequently enough and makes it the background of his conduct he is bound eventually to be right" (p. 569).

The historical dialectic of "real" hostility between the inside and the outside is thus resurrected, the fictive enemies Great Britain and the United States presumably having been forced to become real enemies. However, the "iron logic" still unfurls from within: everything can ultimately be traced back to the inside, whether it is argued that the hostility resulted from the predicament of power—interventions, counterrevolution, minority status, and so on—or from the personal shortcomings of the discontented Bolsheviks, who, for ideological reasons marxist and traditionally Russian, were unable to accept the existence of rival power domestically and elsewhere and thus ended up creating foes. If one agrees with the premise, the argument makes logical sense. The premise makes little historical sense though, since it entails the assumption that if the Bolsheviks had been more tolerant and benevolent in 1917–18, there would have been no foreign intervention (and perhaps no German invasion in 1941 either). Certainly the concept of outside hostility was inscribed in the Bolshevik regime from the outset and instantly confirmed when the Western powers backed the White counterrevolution. Indeed, it would have been frivolous and naive of the Bolsheviks to assume that the outside world would peer quietly at the rise of a major revolutionary power, especially one with internationalist ideas. Like its French (and to some extent American) predecessor in the eighteenth century, this was an upheaval of such magnitude that its impact was bound to be felt beyond its borders, even if the revolutionaries, on seizing power, had declared themselves fully content and then settled down to minding their own business. Hostility from outside was inherent in the very emergence of a new revolutionary regime, not merely an understandable reaction on the part of those subjected to Bolshevik incivility in international relations.

A few points need to be made in this context. The first concerns the suggestion that fluctuations in the actual threat never found reflection in Soviet assessments, since external enmity was a constant theme; it follows that those assessments were expressions of an inner structural need for external foes. The error here is not the detection of a functional need for outside evil: this existed to some degree and still does, just as it does for the Pentagon, a football team, or any other competitive subject (and perhaps for most human beings as well). As Kennan rightly stresses, once the idea had been institutionally embodied, it tended to be self-perpetuating, which is not to say that its concrete expressions were insincere or for that matter false. The error lies rather in making this the entire rationale for Soviet foreign policy and in confusing the general with the particular. The former argument is self-evident. The latter is a suggestion that a built-in, vested interest in outside hostility is one thing but the particular identification of that hostility quite another. Soviet assessments in fact varied substantially over time in both magnitude and target (as Kennan should have known), depending precisely on which powers seemed to pose the greatest danger. To a lesser extent the concomitant theory varied as well. Who it actually was out there, doing what to whom, were important questions to Moscow. For example, American recognition of Soviet hegemony over Poland must have been of significance in determining whether the United States was still a "freedom-loving" country.[47] The *specific* response to the outside did not follow inevitably from the structural proclivity to look for external enemies.

A strong air of mechanical determinism also characterizes Kennan's account of the Soviet doctrine regarding the incompatibility of socialism and capitalism. Here he takes the basic proposition that an "innate antagonism" exists between the two to mean "that there can never be on Moscow's side any sincere assumption of a community of aims between the Soviet Union and powers which are regarded as capitalism." This leads to the conclusion that Moscow "invariably" understands "the aims of the capitalist world" to be "antagonistic to the Soviet regime" (p. 572). I have argued against this conception. Let it be said only that the theoretical opposition of socialism and capitalism does not preclude a *community of aims* among states of different social systems. It was simply not empirically true that, as Kennan had said in his January 24 speech, Moscow professed to believe that "the great countries of the West are united in an evil conspiracy to overthrow the socialist state and to enslave the Russian people."

The final point is similar. Kennan establishes the vital principle of Soviet communism as the destruction of all competing power, from which thesis can be derived the inherent expansionism. Let us consider this statement for a moment. As in the Long Telegram he is advancing an argument about the "real" nature of his object in terms of an absolute, ideal truth; he is not saying anything about the immediate prospects. Nevertheless, how meaningful or useful is this ideal truth? Are we much wiser after having been told that the Russians wish to eliminate rivals? Is this not rather like asking Stalin, had we chanced upon him in some Kremlin corridor, if for Christmas he would like all present and potential competitors everywhere liquidated? Or, to use Kennan's own analogy of a later date, like asking Al Capone if he would wish to have some more money?[48]

It fails too on its own terms. This will perhaps best be understood if Kennan's statement is compared with another "absolute" truth about something inherently expansive, namely Marx's theory of capital accumulation. Marx contended, it will be recalled, that a capitalist enterprise must accumulate or perish because of a whole series of mechanisms over which it has no subjective control. Whether he was right or wrong is irrelevant. What is important is that he tried to demonstrate a logic independent of will that seemed to *compel* the capitalist to expand on pain of economic extinction. Kennan may have unearthed a similar logic with regard to domestic repression and dictatorship, making a reasonable case for why Bolshevism developed in the direction it did; but he had unearthed no "iron logic" that actually compelled the Soviet Union to expand anywhere. He had not shown, in other words, why Moscow *had*, as opposed to would have liked, to expand.[49] An apparatus devoted to the *idea* of outside hostility, and a set of similarly minded people keen on destroying other power centers: this, in itself, proves nothing about any outwardly mobile tendencies. One cannot readily transfer the revealed contingencies of establishing a monopoly of force *within* a state (to follow Weber's definition of state power) onto the dialectic of external competition. Once internal power has been grasped, what is there to say that security will necessarily be sought in destroying that which lies beyond?

Some of the confusion disappears if one makes a clear distinction between hostility and expansionism. Much of Kennan's explanation actually concerns Bolshevik or Soviet *hostility* toward the outside, not the nature of its expansionism. All territorial expansionism implies hostility, but the reverse is not true. Hostility does not in itself translate into expansionism. The fiercest hostility against the outside may well express itself in rejection and isolationism. Witness Albania. The point is somewhat similar to my earlier argument that internal repression does not automatically lead to external aggression. "Democratic" Athens, to use a transhistorical analogy, was expansionist, "totalitarian" Sparta isolationist.[50]

Two possible objections come to mind. First, the Soviet leadership arguably suffered from such inner psychological insecurities that they were forced, in the sense that kleptomaniacs or obsessive murderers feel forced to do their deeds, to eliminate real or imagined rivals. This is not wholly unlikely. It may be valid as a partial explanation for Stalin's purges, but it seems ultimately an excessively subjective basis on which to erect a general theory of Soviet expansionism.

Second, one might think that the nature of party discipline and personal advancement within the system was such as to oblige the structure as a whole always to get the maximum out of any outside power, and that this in turn would constitute expansionism. Kennan certainly offers a persuasive account of the first claim, but it is hard to limit applicability to the Soviet system alone. It would seem that any interest would expect its representatives to achieve maximum results in dealing with the outside and would agree to concessions only in terms of self-interest. It is difficult to imagine any other way in which the generic negotiator can approach his or her task, the "Anglo-Saxon tradition of compromise" notwithstanding. If this is expansionism, then every power is theoretically expansionist, in which case the argument is of little value. Perhaps the difficulty can be avoided if one assumes, as Americans (and Russians) sometimes have done, that one's own interest is nonexistent because it is universal: every advance achieved, for instance "free trade," is automatically an advance for everyone and therefore inconceivable as expansionism. As E. H. Carr pointedly reminds us, however, internationalism was a French idea in the era of French hegemony, a British idea in the imperial nineteenth century, and an American idea in this century.[51]

Having said all this, I finally doubt that expansionism can be approached derivatively, the simple reason being that it is hard to demonstrate how heterogeneous entities such as states and regimes are subject to any single sort of logic in the manner that, for instance, an army is obliged to destroy its enemy in battle. One thinks here of the American example. No nation expanded faster and farther than the United States in the nineteenth century, during which time a federation on the Atlantic seaboard conducted warfare against native Americans, Mexico, and Spain to become a vast transcontinental state, with additional territories stretching all the way to the Philippines. Not surprisingly, a good deal of self-serving explanation was attached to this process. As Theodore Roosevelt typically put the matter, "Every expansion of a great civilized power means a victory for law, order, and righteousness."[52] An orthodox Marxist would see the matter differently, no doubt in terms of capitalist profit and accumulation. But even if such factors were a driving element, it is difficult to derive any inner logic that would necessarily have pushed the system into territorial expansion. Explanation thus becomes less a matter of systemic compulsion than one of historical contingency.

These reflections may be regarded as scholastic pedantry, but their inclusion will perhaps be understood when it is remembered that the ineffable NSC 68 took as one of its basic propositions that the Russians could not tolerate the idea of freedom and thus were *compelled* to destroy the non-Soviet world.[53] Kennan himself espoused this commonplace of the cold war at times: "They are obliged to destroy the West, because they are obliged to destroy a record, and a standard of comparison. They are seized in the vise-like grip of an iron logic of history which makes the preservation of their rule in Russia dependent on the destruction of freedom in the western world."[54] Now, decades later, one is bound to observe that the Soviet regime must have managed to escape this "vise-like grip" since it is still in power without having destroyed the West. On this note we turn to the question of Soviet policy.

Kennan identified the abstract and ideal aims of Soviet expansionism variously but chiefly in four ways. They are, roughly in order of descending generality: (1) the elimination of all outside power centers in the world, (2) the relative strengthening of Soviet power and weakening of non-Soviet power; (3) "militant and persistent efforts toward the acquisition of a maximum amount of power with a minimum of responsibility"; and (4) the filling of "every nook and cranny available to it in the basin of world power."[55]

About the more specific Soviet aims and policies Kennan said re markably little in 1946–47. Even in the PPS period his analyses tended to have a comprehensive flavor, but by then he had at least begun to narrow down the scope of Soviet intentions. Reaffirming an earlier theme, he maintained that ever since the military victory at Stalingrad Moscow had concentrated on Europe:

> Being land power minded, the most immediate concern of the men in the Kremlin is to break up all other serious concentrations on the Eurasian land mass and to gain dominant influence over the governments on that territory. Their policies in other continents outside of Eurasia are basically subordinate to that aim at this time. Thus, with regard to ourselves, the main Soviet objective is to destroy at this time, I reiterate, our ability to intervene effectively in any way in the affairs of Europe or Asia. Soviet policy toward us at this time aims at the political, economic and military neutralization, isolation, and, if possible, weakening of our power.[56]

He also thought that plans were imminent for "consolidation of their power in Czechoslovakia as soon as possible, and the actual seizure of power by violent means in Greece and Italy and France."[57] The first part of his prediction proved very accurate, the second one not.

He held, more or less, to this perspective until the end of the 1940s, the one qualification being the assessment of Asia. For the truth was that, apart from Japan off the coast, the not insignificant Asian part of the "Eurasian land mass" never figured very prominently in Kennan's thinking about Soviet policy, and probably correctly so, since his Eurocentric conception of global strategy was shared by the Russians themselves. This neglect, incidentally, was both cause and effect of his intelligent analysis of the ever-worsening situation in China, a debacle that during the late 1940s seemed periodically to put the State Department under veritable political siege at home. Kennan, who had the utmost contempt for Chiang Kai-shek and the Kuomintang, argued throughout that the Chinese civil war was not a Soviet product and foresaw with great prescience (aided no doubt by his friend John Paton Davies)[58] that any future communist regime in Peking would be a potential source of trouble for Moscow.[59] Similarly, he was able later to take a cool view of Soviet intentions in the Korean conflict, stressing that the war did not herald the beginning of a planned Soviet attack but was more likely on the part of the Russians an opportunistic and hence limited use of an available civil war.[60] For him the really important Soviet objective since the Second World War had been, as he was to put it in 1949, the political conquest of Western Europe.[61]

This was therefore the main danger and pre-eminent problem at hand. His reasoning, extrapolated, was simple: the Soviet Union is expansionist, Western Europe is the natural target, and the method of attack is political. The first of these propositions has already been discussed. The second, given Russian history and geography, was obvious to him. By the autumn of 1948, nevertheless, he had a more precise explanation: Europe was one of the few areas in the world with the industrial capacity to sustain modern warfare on a grand scale, in addition to which it was also the closest of these regions to Moscow. Hence it was plainly the target for penetration.[62]

One need not accept Kennan's entire view of Soviet expansionism to recognize that it was valid insofar as the part of Europe beyond the control of the Red Army was indeed the area of primary interest and importance to Moscow, and precisely for the reasons given. The questions arise in determining what the Soviet Union actually was prepared to do here—whether, in other words, the Soviets ever made any real attempt politically to capture or "gain dominant influence" over Western Europe. I indicated disagreement earlier on this point, and I shall show later on that Kennan himself made contradictory statements on the subject.

His third point concerned the Soviet selection of ways and means. On one occasion he argued, surprisingly, that Soviet ideology did not entail the notion of an offensive war, and that, accordingly, one ought not to expect such an attack as a matter of course.[63] The sudden appearance of ideological constraints on the choice of means, an idea advanced without any sense of incoherence, was a rare exception to the ideal truth that, just as Soviet goals were theoretically unlimited, so was the array of conceivable means and methods. It was thus incumbent on Kennan to show why it was expedient for the Russians to proceed politically rather than militarily, or, as he sometimes transposed the question, by measures short of war rather than by measures of war. He approached this question in various ways, the most basic of which one might call Clausewitzian, though it was in fact only an adaptation of the Prussian's famous dictum about war and politics, and a dubious one at that.

The problematic was perhaps in some deeper sense Clausewitzian, but when Kennan initially referred to the military theorist, it was merely to sanction his own expedience thesis: "[Stalin's endorsement of Clausewitz] meant that the Kremlin thinks in terms of certain basic political purposes. Whether those purposes are to be pursued by the means of war or by the means of peace is simply a question of discretion which has got to be decided according to circumstances of the moment . . . But the basic political purpose remains a constant."[64] A hierarchy has thus been established: primacy is accorded to a constant, the "basic political purpose," to be carried out by the (subordinate) means of war or peace. War, as he would point out on a later occasion, then in support of the Clausewitzian formula, "makes no sense unless it serves a political purpose. Military action against the countries of Western Europe would therefore make no sense unless it served the political purpose which the Russians have in mind. That purpose, remember, is to acquire over the peoples of Western Europe—in this instance—a form of political domination which will be permanent and enduring."[65] No matter what allowances one makes for wide-ranging interpretation of a notoriously complex proposition, this carries things a bit too far. The dialectical notion of a contradiction involving two sides is replaced by a one-sided "purpose"; and the two principal ways in which the contradiction can manifest itself, war and peace, are imprecisely distinguished. The process is also subjectivized, as the argument moves along, into establishing what purpose the Russians "have in mind." To all of this Clausewitz (and his ardent reader Lenin) would probably have retorted that war is the violent expression of an objective political contradiction between any given parties. Indeed, what Stalin had actually said about Clausewitz was that "politics give birth to war," an assertion altogether different from Kennan's version of a single-sided "basic political purpose" to be carried out, as a matter of circumstantial convenience, by means of either war or peace.[66]

The issue at stake, however, is not Clausewitzian theory, fascinating though it is, but Kennan's analysis of Soviet policy, and in that respect his message was one of common sense: war is purposeful activity and not something the Russians will engage in for its own sake. This, everything considered, was doubtless a good thing to say. Here and elsewhere Kennan in fact listed a whole host of concrete conditions that, from a Soviet viewpoint, made it virtually imperative to avoid war. One was the internal situation. The country had always been very poor, burdened with severe agricultural problems, impeded by over-centralization, and lacking basic infrastructure such as roads; now, in addition, it had suffered staggering losses during the war in every domain, and public morale was at a low. Moreover, the system of an upper crust led by a stagnant Politburo and resting on "an amorphous mass of human beings" was not conducive to offensive war, particu-larly not at a time when the minorities who had brought about the downfall of tsarism were now back inside again and there was already trouble in Eastern Europe.[67] Overall, the Soviet Union was undoubt-edly weaker than the West. To attack under such conditions would be foolish, and the Kremlin knew it.

There were also sound military-strategic reasons for abstaining. The Red Army might be capable of marching to the Pyrenees or the English Channel or Cairo, but probably not to all three. True, the Russians were strong militarily, but that strength had been exagger-ated, and they might already be overextended. Above all, an attack on Western Europe would mean war with the United States, and this the Kremlin would not risk, especially not when the industrial heartland was vulnerable to air attack.

In addition, a successful westward campaign would mean installing communist regimes, but these would bear the traitor's stamp and breed popular resentment. Problems of occupation would ensue, and the army might never be able to leave. Finally, an attack would cause a worldwide political backlash and certainly spell the end of the United Nations.[68]

These arguments are accurate in my view and require but two brief comments. First, Kennan underestimated the domestic stability of the Soviet regime, particularly in his X-Article, with its quasimarxist talk of sprouting "seeds of decay," coupled with vivid evocations of Buddenbrooksian death, none of which, it seems fair to say, was anything but armchair speculation.[69] Second, the Soviet Union did not, in all probability, possess the capability of marching to the Atlantic, had that been the intention. The battle for Berlin alone had cost 300,000 men; the Red Army lacked necessary transportation; and, contrary to widespread belief, demobilization and decreased military production had followed the war. Ironically, the idea that the United States was capable of striking by air against Soviet industry seems to have been exaggerated as well.[70]

Kennan's "Clausewitzian" argument employed straightforward causal reasoning, in essence saying that, given the overarching aim, the disadvantages of the particular means of war far outweighed its possible advantages. He also approached the problem from a less systematic and more elusive stance, taking the style of Soviet foreign policy as the object of inquiry. The resultant analysis was preponderantly impressionistic and implicit in character.

The Russian manner of approach was for Kennan embodied in two archetypes: the sly, ruthless Asiatic nomad and the wily, resourceful chess player. At times he derived these descriptions from historical references, but for the most part they were stated as observations of fact. A composite portrait would look something like this: The Russians are characterized by their great patience and persistence. Exceptionally conscious of relations of power, they like to explore cautiously their immediate surroundings for possible openings, always making sure that there is a safe retreat. They feel no urgency about achieving their goals; they have no long-term plan but rely on their tactical flexibility and take one day at a time. This elasticity, however, is exclusively the property of the center, which determines the line to be followed rigidly by all other organs. The Russians, moreover, are superior practitioners of deception and dissimulation, spotting and exploiting weaknesses in others. We are dealing, in short, with a dangerous, cautious, and extremely tenacious enemy with a highly developed sense of power.[71]

Any number of things can be said about this characterological sketch, but it seems to me to ascribe to the Soviet leadership a tactical mobility and devilish cunning it did not possess. The X-Article, famously using the metaphor of a wind-up toy, suggests something centrally agile but locally rigid. Still, even if the apparatus as a whole follows the given line with unquestioning loyalty, the center's wind-up action is in itself not always swift. The built-in lack of local and subordinate initiative has always been a basic Soviet problem. In the period in question, Moscow showed rather a systematic lack of dash and indeed when Kennan had reason to look back in 1950, he found the Russians to have been less than clever.[72] More important for our purposes, however, is the depiction of dogged but cautious probing in neighboring areas by a power-sensitive regime. This is not a tradition or a style that lends itself easily to massive, offensive war, except as a last resort, and that, I take it, was Kennan's message. The way in which he formulated some of the Soviet aims underlines such an interpretation: that is, in terms of the *relative* increase in power, and the maximum amount of power with a minimum of responsibility. These rules did not imply war but rather a gradual, almost surreptitious process.

A final argument against the notion of a westward attack, and very much the odd man out, was the ideological one. The problem here is obvious: it could not simultaneously be argued that Soviet means were theoretically unlimited in scope and yet limited because the ideology did not envision offensive war. Perhaps this conceptual conflict explains Kennan's long-standing inability to state in no uncertain terms what the Soviet view of war really was.[73] It is instructive in this regard to peruse the immensely publicized X-Article, which deals proportionately more with ideology than his other analyses. The reader learns here that, according to Russian theory, "imperialism, the final phase of capitalism, leads directly to war and revolution"; and Soviet ideology obliges its votaries "eventually to overthrow the political forces beyond their borders" and to spend their time until the inevitable fall of capitalism preparing "for the final coup de grace." Our imaginary reader does *not* learn (as in the Long Telegram) that imperialism, in the Soviet view, leads not only to war but especially to war *against* the USSR; he or she may be forgiven for conjuring up the image of some fanatical Eastern horde busily preparing to strike out westward.

This is a deliberately partial reading of the X-Article; a detached observer at the time might well have chosen to focus instead on what was in fact its dominant theme: that of Soviet weaknesses. Still, in a climate of rising fear and loathing so to speak, it may have been easier to disregard the weaknesses of today and look ahead with trepidation to tomorrow when the hordes would be ready to attack. Loud calls, not unnaturally, would thus be heard for more and better arms to prepare against this threat, followed no doubt by exhortations to the greatest vigilance against all signs of appeasement, by which point the room for subtle political maneuvering in the international arena would have shrunk considerably.

Kennan's practicality argument left him open to the sort of reaction that this semicaricature is meant to illustrate. It mattered not at all how much he stressed the various Soviet shortcomings: the uncertainties of tomorrow would always be there to haunt him. Thus he found himself dragged into discussing whether the attack would come in five, ten, or fifteen years.[74] This clearly was a dead end from which his auxiliary remarks about style could not extricate him.

Soviet expansionism, then, had to take the practical form of measures short of war—measures that, if not peaceful, were at least employed under general conditions of peace. Kennan made this point constantly, but when it came to concrete analyses of the expected political conquest, he was less than forthcoming. Chiefly, he seems to have had in mind the activities of the various communist parties, a subject of which, as I have suggested, he had only superficial knowledge. Here I wish merely to illustrate a contradiction in his thinking.

A series of distinctive postwar conditions made the world, in Kennan's opinion, relatively receptive to communism. There were the usual radical waves which had followed in the wake of the "debauch" of modern war. There was, until the Marshall Plan partly changed matters, a power vacuum that created excellent space for communist machinations. There was a widespread tendency to favor personal and economic security over political freedom which left people wanting "direction" instead of merely abstract liberties.[75] To these specific conditions he added observations of a regional and cultural kind, arguing first that communism was attractive only where it was not in

power, and second, although he admitted a lack of intimate knowledge, that the problem appeared to him mainly a "Latin" as opposed
to a northern one:

> In the Germanic countries, in northern Europe and the Anglo-Saxon
> countries, where people are more experienced in the practices of
> representative government and where there is greater political ma-
> turity as well as a certain sobriety of social thought, the communist
> parties do not seem to have made any dangerous headway . . . The
> humble give-and-take of Anglo-Saxon democracy, with its constant
> resort to undramatic compromise and its general distaste for emo-
> tional display probably has little attraction for the Latin mind . . . I
> do not believe that the attraction of communism in these [Latin]
> countries is directly concerned with economic conditions. The exis-
> tence of great differences in the level of income, the violent contrasts
> of wealth and poverty, the occasional crass examples of the exploi-
> tation of man by man within the framework of the capitalist system:
> all these are levers seized upon by astute communists and utilized in
> their quest for power; they increase perhaps the vulnerability of Latin
> society to communist penetration; but they are not the basic reason
> for the spread of communism. This is readily apparent from the fact
> that the movement appeals predominantly to the intellectual and only
> secondarily to the working class. This being the case, I consider that
> the reasons are emotional and social rather than economic. Be that
> as it may, the stern apparition of disciplined, collective communist
> power has come to exercise a fatal fascination over many minds in
> the Latin countries, and not only there. People stand before it like
> the bird before the cobra, seized with dread foreboding, yet unable
> to detach its eye or to remove itself from the advance.[76]

I quote this passage less for the assertions made than for its style,
symptomatic of the somewhat complacent sort of impressionism into
which Kennan would at times lapse when not wholly on terra firma.
One point of substance is worth mentioning: his image of the generic
communist party as a constellation more attractive to intellectuals than
workers.[77] This social division corresponds partially to another he
made, that of an obsidian "hard core" surrounded by dallying liberals,
in turn related to his delineation (or story) of the two main forms of
communist tactics, violent seizure of power as opposed to semilegal
or legal political struggle.[78] In the initial stages there had been a tightly
knit party—the future hard core—with revolution in mind. Then

it was Stalin and his particular friends who thought they saw clearly two reasons for changing this situation. They saw, in the first place, that with these tactics the communist parties were condemned to remain, in most instances, futile minority groups, incapable of over-throwing capitalism but capable of being a constant source of embarrassment to the foreign policy of the USSR. Secondly, somewhat to their surprise, they saw that such popularity as the Soviet Union was acquiring abroad was not primarily among the working class people to whom they had originally tried to appeal but among the liberal bourgeois intellectuals for whom they had such contempt. And it occurred to them that even though they might be incapable of winning over the mass of the western proletariat to a devotion to their brand of communism, they still had the possibility, by exploiting the vague uneasiness and sentimentality of fellow-travellers, to confuse public opinion in the western countries, to embarrass the western governments and achieve dominion over them. This was the famous Trojan horse technique announced by Dimitrov in 1934. In the belly of the great silly horse of western liberalism the communists were to ride into the camp of western democracy and then destroy it from within . . . They posed as patriots; they did lip-service to the ideals of democracy; they tried to put themselves in the foreground of all popular grievances, just as though they really believed that liberal democratic society were there to stay, and should be improved rather than destroyed.[79]

As a genealogy of the Popular Front this account leaves a lot to be desired, and the "posing patriots" mentioned were ultimately to resist German force with a great deal more energy than many of the indigenous establishments. The sheer simplicity of the conspiracy depicted is what otherwise stands out, causing speculation that Kennan may have intended this account as a bedtime horror story for the edification of listeners as naive in their way as the "fellow-travellers" it maligned. A safe guess, anyway, is that he was using the atypical American Communist party as source material for his story. Otherwise it is difficult to explain how he got the idea that parties such as the French and Italian ones contained great numbers of liberals, or the belief that they attracted more intellectuals than workers.[80]

More interesting at this stage, however, is the tactical issue. The Trojan horse tactic, according to Kennan, had involved not only parliamentary activity but also deceptive front organizations designed to instigate various internal and external conflicts and so open up space for the sort of political techniques at which the communists, with their long experience of "penetrating, paralyzing, and capturing the liberal democratic state," were such experts.[81] By December 1946 he had become convinced that Moscow was about to abandon this coalition policy as ineffective; and to this position he clung, although for different reasons at different times. His original assumption, odd under the circumstances, was that the Soviet Union had come to realize that, in the absence of political success, and because it could not manage Eastern Europe economically, it needed the West and was thus having second thoughts. In May 1947, after six months of internal problems in Europe, Kennan was harboring no such sanguine hopes, if anything arguing the opposite. The Russians, he now claimed, were operating on the premise that Western Europe would not be able to survive without the resources of the *East*, thus putting them "in a position where they will be able practically to name the political price on which they will make them available." At the same time, with no apparent logical connection, he also suggested that "the communists, having failed to seize all governmental positions by parliamentary means, are about to apply their enormous influence in the labor movement to disrupt progress under existing regimes, to throw life into chaos, and eventually to effect the actual overthrow of existing authority and the establishment of workers' government."[82]

One is at a loss to understand why communists would embark on such a course if Moscow was in a position of economic blackmail and felt, as he put it, "that Europe is in reality already theirs."[83] The truth, as Kennan must have known, was that the communist parties in France and Italy (the two countries chiefly in question here) had to leave coalition governments for the dual reasons of domestic party politics and American influence, not because they were attempting to paralyze the bourgeois state.[84] Indeed, there would be no extensive disruption until after the Marshall Plan had been launched and autumn had arrived.[85] I suspect that this speech should not be taken too literally. Senators were in the audience, and Kennan was trying to make a convincing case for what was to become the Marshall Plan. His account may thus have been adjusted to achieve an appropriately dark picture.

Once Marshall Aid was under way and the political strikes against it had begun in late 1947, the argument clearly looked much more plausible. Kennan was then able to claim that revolution and civil war were in the offing. With waning postwar radicalism, Marshall

Aid, and the consequent disappearance of the political vacuum, Moscow had finally been forced to reveal itself, to go with the hard core and sacrifice wider support. Kennan also believed that the final option of ordering civil war would not in the Soviet estimation bring about war with the United States.[86] On what grounds that conjecture was based is not clear, for he offered no circumstantial evidence. In any event, even if one stretches the notion of "measures short of war" to include instigating civil war in the West, it would be hard to call this a "political conquest."

More or less simultaneously he pointed out that the Kremlin would be extremely upset with its communist allies were they ever to trigger a Soviet-American conflict.[87] Kennan did not normally envision Moscow's relationship with the international communist movement as a simple command structure of ordering; he saw it rather as a pool of shared values and impulses primordially emanating from the Soviet Union. His characterization of Tito (a future friend) as "a bird dog which has been so well trained that it has been taught to heel and no longer needs to go on the leash" was probably emblematic, though in this instance he, like virtually all his contemporaries, was soon to be proven quite wrong.[88] On specific actions Kennan thought the initiative usually came from below, Moscow retaining veto power.

None of this contradicted the broad argument, and it is now time to bring out a second trend in his thinking that did. He had predicted, as we saw, potential trouble for Moscow in a unified China under communist rule, and at infrequent moments he would extend the logic of this idea into a more widely applicable principle. In February 1947, for example, he told a university audience:

> Today I sometimes wonder whether, in the internationalist communist movement, the Kremlin has not got a bull by the horns . . . I sometimes think they have created something more powerful than themselves: a force which they do not dare let out of their hands because they fear that it might be turned against them, that they have sown their dragon's teeth and now find themselves, willy-nilly, for better or worse, the masters and the servants of the weird and terrifying warriors who have grown up in their pasture . . . [W]e must keep cool nerves and recognize that perhaps this bubble cannot be really pricked until one of these parties has come into power in a country not contiguous to the borders of the direct military power of Russia. Let us bear in mind that that is a test which has yet to be made. Every country which is today under the sway of Soviet com-

munist influence has a direct land border with other areas of communist power, and, in effect, with the Soviet Union itself. Whether a communist government could survive in other circumstances and still retain its subservience to Moscow, has not yet been determined. We saw that in 1931 Moscow showed a marked reluctance to let the German communists seize power in Germany and preferred that they should be sacrificed to Hitler rather than that this should happen. I think they knew that a communist Germany, in contemplating its relations with Communist Russia, would soon raise the question as to which should be the tail and which should be the dog. Similarly, the Kremlin has shown little disposition to see the *French* Communists take power.

There are two reasons why communist parties are more useful to the Soviet Government out of power rather than in power, when they lie outside the sphere of Soviet military action. In the first place, as opposition parties, they are dependent on outside support and therefore are easy to keep in line from the Kremlin disciplinary standpoint. Secondly, as opposition parties, they are free to criticize and badger other governments and in that way to weaken the potential of other powers. For this reason, I am not so sure that it would necessarily be a calamity for us to have such a regime come into power somewhere far from the shadow of the Red Army and the Soviet secret police. A communist regime in some such country which either failed to meet its responsibilities and discredited itself in the eyes of the people or which turned on its masters, repudiated the Kremlin's authority, and bit the hand which had reared it, might be more favorable to the interests of this country and to world peace in the long run than an unscrupulous opposition party spewing slander from the safe vantage point of irresponsibility and undermining the prestige of this country in the eyes of the world.[89]

These were astonishing words from a man who was about to become head planner of American foreign policy during the early cold war period. They were uttered well before the Tito controversy, of which Kennan had not the slightest inkling, and more than a decade before the Sino-Soviet split. The conspiratorial clairvoyance on the part of the Russians is exaggerated; it is, for instance, not likely that Stalin would have "preferred" to "sacrifice" the German communists to the Nazis because he feared their competition. Allegiance to Moscow, moreover, does not vary directly with distance. Even if freedom from immediate adjacency to the Soviet Union (or, in the Chinese case, sheer size) is conducive to independence, the matter is also one of global geopolitics. Cuba, exceedingly distant but threatened by another superpower, has thus stayed very close to Moscow's line; a similar dynamic can be seen in the alliance pattern of Vietnam and Cambodia. Nevertheless, the fact remains that Kennan had spotted future polycentric tendencies within international communism at an impressively early point.

He had also flatly contradicted himself. Either Moscow wanted the French communists to seize power or it did not: one could not claim both. If the latter was the case, there could obviously not be any intention of "political conquest." I have already stated my view on this matter: Stalin, regardless of his fears of potential rival communists, had no illusions about taking over Western Europe by means of proxies, and he had made that clear. In 1946 Kennan had actually said that Moscow knew the limits in Germany. Being cautious in the face of opposing power, as he had argued, the Russians must have calculated the risk of full war in the wake of any "political conquest" as quite unacceptable. For the Soviet leadership understood, one imagines, what Kennan himself concluded laconically in early 1948—namely, that the West would not "permanently tolerate a situation where substantially the whole Eurasian land mass would be under communist control."[90]

This is not to say that international communism, particularly in southern Europe, could have been ignored by anyone in Kennan's position. Here after all was a political force of considerable size and cohesion devoted to the perspective espoused by the Soviet Union. Irrespective of whether its present policies happened to be acceptable or even benign, such a force was an obvious strategic asset for Moscow and could not be overlooked, especially not at a time of perceived socioeconomic crisis. From this point, however, it is a far step to the idea of imminent communist takeovers. Even the political strikes against the Marshall Plan, after all, raised no calls for socialism but only against war and for national independence and democracy.[91] Kennan's strategic misreading of Soviet intentions in this respect was not without negative consequences: red specters always served in the long run to reduce the latitude for movement.

The idea of "political conquest" had a certain abstract quality. Having postulated an expansionist Soviet regime ready to use any means, Kennan had then endeavored to show the unlikeliness of the most extreme of these means: war. Despite the occasional ambiguity, his case in this respect was reasonable and informed. There remained, so to speak, the logical residue, an altogether more amorphous set of expansionist measures short of war. Of these Kennan knew far less. They lay beyond the Soviet field proper, where he was at home, and were fewer than he imagined. This brings us to the question of American countermeasures.

My initial thesis is this: To pose the question of containment in an either-or form—political containment of a political threat or military containment of a military threat—is to impose a sharp distinction that Kennan did not clearly make during the period (September 1946 to the publication of the X-Article in July 1947) when he first mentioned containment. In fact the distinction did not become explicit until 1948, when the trend toward militarization in American thought and policy was beginning to unsettle him and thus served to focus the issue.[92]

I am referring here to the conceptual aspect, not the practicalities. We know that Kennan was aware that the risk of military attack was small and saw the chief countermeasure of this initial period, the Marshall Plan, as an explicitly political move to undermine the Western communist parties. From this one ought not to conclude that containment was all about politics, since the practicalities did not represent the whole of his rather more nebulous, or complex, thinking on the subject. The two aspects should therefore be kept analytically distinct. My emphasis here will be on the period 1946–47; the wider tactical and strategic ramifications of containment as they pertain to the PPS period will be examined in Part II.

Seen as a simple proposition, containment was a self-evident idea. The Soviet Union had been identified as an inherently expansive force, and an expansive force presumably continues to expand until its energy is spent or contained. Though a physicist might disagree, I suppose the first option would have entailed total inertia on the part of all non-Soviet matter, in which starkly put form it seems an obvious absurdity. This left the notion of counterforce and the question of how, when, and where rather than if. More than that Kennan probably did not intend with the term *containment*, which was not a developed theory, strategic doctrine, or even concrete policy but a concept of active resistance as opposed to inertia, a new name for something he had essentially argued for ever since 1938.[93] Lest he should be accused of having uttered a platitude instead of something grand, bear in mind that he had fought for a long time against what seemed to him inertia, and the concept was not advertised as anything grand to begin with. Used sparingly in his texts, it did not fill the central terminological role it has subsequently been assigned by history.

(The present usage of *containment*, with all its connotations, owes its origin to Kennan's X-Article, though the word itself had been employed in a somewhat similar sense since the Middle Ages. Brooks Adams had used it half a century before Kennan; and Marx, who considered tsarist Russia the very heart of reaction, had exhorted his readers in the 1850s "to guard against excessive influence on the part of Russia, and to keep her influence confined within narrow bounds." Most curious among the purely semantic precedents is perhaps the appearance of the term in Gibbon's *Decline*, wherein Emperor Probus finds it impossible to "contain in obedience every part of his wide-extended dominion." Kennan read Gibbon religiously and referred to him no less than twice in the X-Article, one reason its authorship was so rapidly revealed, for his ardent admiration for the eighteenth-century historian of classical decay was well known.)[94]

If containment was a general goal following logically from the premise of Soviet expansionism and to that extent uncontroversial, the scope and means were all the more problematic. The imagery of the X-Article indicated a "fluid stream" to be contained by "unassailable barriers," but nothing much was said regarding the nature of these barriers, also called "unalterable counterforce."

Let us first dispose of the ethical aspect. Prima facie one might see a dilemma here. Having made rather a large point of the unlimited nature of Soviet methods, could Kennan advocate retaliation in kind? Were there, in other words, inherent moral constraints on the struggle against totalitarian chicanery? In the Long Telegram he had insisted emphatically that the West must never assume the opponent's character, but now, oddly, he seemed not to have felt this to be a pressing problem of principle. Rarely brought up, it was not as visible to him as it was to become during the "realist" debates and McCarthy inquisitions of the early 1950s.[95] That said, with some misgivings I have extrapolated four partly contradictory viewpoints from his writings:

1. The United States must do whatever is necessary to stop the Soviet Union from accomplishing its basic aims.

2. "What is important . . . is not so much *what* is done as *how* it is done." Put differently: we might have to do unpleasant things, but we shall do them in consonance with our concept of style and good manners.

3. The West, being essentially Christian, is based on certain moral traditions, rules, and values that will enable it instinctively to do right. The issue is therefore to some degree a pseudoissue.

4. A variety of means are clearly beyond the pale, such as intervention against any possible communist regime in Latin America, for such an action would "corrupt that basic decency of purpose" for which the United States stands.[96]

These positions, I reiterate, are extrapolations; Kennan might well have difficulty recognizing them as his, particularly number 2. They are stated mainly to point out the absence of any cohesive, developed view on the subject and thus warrant no comment in themselves, except perhaps that on the specific issue of interventionism (4) he took a very different view elsewhere, as we shall see.

Leaving the ethical domain, we may now situate the question of countermeasures in terms of war and peace and what, if anything, lay between. Whatever form Soviet expansionism might happen to take, the most extreme American response imaginable was war. Kennan did not believe in it. Such a course would have been unwise for reasons of basic strategy; and as the postwar order emerged, he thought that the conflict could be carried on (not resolved, for resolution was in a way impossible) within that wide gamut of means he sometimes referred to as measures short of war.[97] This does not mean that he never advocated military containment, a wider and more diffuse concept than war, and one to which he was far from opposed. Nor does it mean that under no conditions would he ever have proposed an attack on the Soviet Union. Any large-scale communist success in Western Europe, legal or not, would probably have constituted cause for war, or at least for a military action that in all likelihood would have led to it.[98] That was hypothetical, however; the immediate task was to manage below the level of open war.

A word or two is necessary here about Kennan's concept of measures short of war. The Soviet thrust, as he had conceived it, was a total one, requiring in principle an equally total response. It was time to realize that international politics had gone beyond "the adjustment of disputes": "[The problems we face] are caused by the conflict of interests between great centers of power and ideology in the world. They are problems of the measures short of war which such great centers of power and ideology use to exert pressure on one another for the attainment of their ends. And in that sense they are questions of the measures . . . for the promulgation of power as such."[99] In a more proto-Clausewitzian passage Kennan envisaged a drastic American reorientation as a consequence:

> If our measures short of war are going to be effective . . . we must select them and use them not hit or miss as the demand of any moment may seem to require, but in accordance with a pattern of grand strategy no less concrete and no less consistent than that which governs our actions in war. It is my own conviction that we must go further than that and must cease to have separate patterns of measures—one pattern for peace and one pattern for war. We must rather select them according to the purpose we are pursuing and classify them that way. We must work out a general plan of what the United States wants in this world and we must go after that with all the measures at our disposal, depending on what is indicated by the circumstances. It simply means that we have to learn to reclassify our weapons not primarily by whether they are military in nature or measures short of war, but by the purpose we are going to use them for.

Relations with friendly nations would naturally be a matter of measures short of war, while the whole register of potential means would be appropriate for nations that were not. Provided there was a "preponderance of strength," however, measures short of war would quite likely suffice for unfriendly states as well. In theory, then, any means at the disposal of the United States should be considered in the struggle to contain the Soviet Union, but in practice, assuming there was superior strength, only some of these means would have to be applied.[100]

Strength for Kennan was also a total concept, encompassing every aspect of internal and external life. He took particular pains to emphasize that it was in no way to be construed exclusively in military terms:

> It is a question of political, economic and moral strength. Above all, it is a question of our internal strength; of the health and sanity of our own society . . . [In] a diplomatic and military sense we are no stronger than the country we represent . . . Remember that the United States is not strong to the extent that its armed services are strong, or that its diplomacy is brilliant. It is strong to the extent that strength goes back of the armed services to the root of our society. For that reason none of us can afford to be indifferent to internal disharmony, dissension, intolerance and the things that break up the real moral and political structure of our society at home.[101]

There was an additional reason to pay close attention to the domestic situation, as Kennan argued lucidly in the X-Article:

> [The United States should] create among the peoples of the world generally an impression of a country which knows what it wants, which is coping successfully with the problems of internal life and with the responsibilities of a World Power, and which has the spiritual vitality capable of holding its own among the major ideological currents of the time. To the extent that such an impression can be created and maintained, the aims of Russian Communism must appear sterile and quixotic, the hopes and enthusiasm of Moscow's supporters must wane, and added strain must be imposed on the Kremlin's foreign policies. For the palsied decrepitude of the capitalist world is the keystone of Communist philosophy.[102]

This point should be seen in the context of his larger view of the Soviet-American struggle as "a sort of long-range fencing match in which the weapons are not only the development of military power but the loyalties and convictions of hundreds of millions of people and the control or influence over their forms of political organization." Invoking the authority of none other than V. M. Molotov, he continued: "In other words, it may be the strength and health of our respective systems which is decisive and which will determine the issue. This may be done—and probably will be won—without a war. And I think this is what Mr. Molotov means when he tells us that we live in a period of competition between social systems and chides us gently on being so hysterical about it."[103] True to his word, Kennan was at that very moment engaged in conceptualizing the Marshall Plan, a superb political maneuver which he correctly predicted would put the Western European communists on the defensive and wreak havoc on Moscow's international position: *touché* in the fencing match, one might say.[104] Unquestionably the Marshall Plan (whose economic importance has been greatly exaggerated) was the very heart of containment as he intended it to be implemented in this period; and to that degree his retrospective claims about the political nature of containment are quite correct. He held throughout that the United States in fact possessed the "preponderance of strength" and thus could make do with measures short of war.[105]

Yet there is more to it than that. The X-Article had emphasized "counter-force" but not defined it. On occasion Kennan would envisage "a counter-force of hope, of idealism and of practical determination which can win respect everywhere, in Russia as everywhere else,"[106] but the military aspect was more than a simple postulate. Although judiciously toned down in his presentations, it was in fact a vital part of his concept of strength and not without practical application. To eliminate the lack of "flexibility" and "coordination," he desired an "organic connection between military strength and political action."[107] Not then engaged in daily policy-making, he had few occasions to develop what this idea meant in military terms; but the imbroglio over Trieste may serve as an indication. Tito had stubbornly laid claims to the city—claims of his own, incidentally, and not of Soviet origin. Italy and the West opposed the Yugoslavs, too meekly in Kennan's opinion: "Our negotiations over the future of the port of Trieste [should] be backed up by quiet but effective augmentations of our military and air strength in that area, designed to discourage the Yugoslavs from hoping and planning for a future forceful seizure of the Trieste district."[108] Violence, as it were, *determines* in the last instance, though it may not *dominate* the actual proceedings. The trick, as Kennan said later, was to keep up "a posture of quiet strength and alertness combined with patience and dignity, a posture which will make it unmistakeably evident that this nation has the strength to back up its convictions if necessary." More graphically he went on:

[We must have] a certain minimum number and balance of ground force divisions of full fighting strength and with complete and up to date equipment, which would be in a position to be moved anywhere on short notice and to undertake the defense of the interests of this country or of the world community, if necessary . . . We must remember that the first line of American defense might be many thousand miles from American shores. We already hold a number of outlying bases which it is essential for us to staff, and it might be necessary for us on a very short notice to seize and hold other outlying island bases . . . [The] greatest value of our forces lies in their quality as a deterrent. If we do not maintain such forces, there will always be an incentive for unruly people elsewhere to seize isolated and limited objectives on the theory that we would be able to do nothing about it at the moment . . . I think there could be no more sobering and restraining influence on the mind of such people than the knowledge that this country had in being at all times a compact, mobile and hard-hitting task force which could make American power felt rapidly and effectively on limited fronts almost anywhere in the world.[109]

What was needed, as he would argue the following year, was "an armed establishment" that could "pack a mean punch in a short time on any limited theater of operations, even far from our shores."[110] Or, in more contemporary language, a rapid deployment force for the projection of American power on a global scale, the difference between then and now, of course, being that demobilization in Kennan's time made such a potential force far more important in relative terms than it is within today's military colossus. He did not, then, oppose military intervention in principle, espousing instead a more elaborate form of Theodore Roosevelt's old rule, "Speak softly and carry a big stick."[111]

Later as a policymaker Kennan occasionally went beyond generalities and proposed specific actions, whence originates in part the historiographic controversy over whether containment was intended to be military or political. He supported military intervention in Iceland if the communists were ever to seize power there; and also, under certain conditions, against the Chinese Nationalists on Formosa.[112] These, however, were hypothetical instances, and aside from suggestions along the lines of forceful demonstrations (as in the case of Trieste), the only bona fide case of proposed military action occurred in the spring of 1948 with regard to Italy. A short account of this singular incident is thus in order.

Washington had been worried about communist strength in Italy for some time and was eventually to funnel a great deal of money into other political parties.[113] After the ejection in early May 1947 of the PCI from the governing coalition, the ensuing communist opposition to Marshall Aid created the additional (I think largely unfounded) fear of insurrection. Yet by early 1948 it was the prospect of a communist election victory rather than a revolution that was felt oppressive in American quarters. According to the National Security Council the "well organized and dynamic electoral campaign" of the communists was "proving dangerously effective," part of the reason for which might have been that, in the American ambassador's estimation, "no party except the [PCI-led alliance had] become associated in the mind of the people with the basic reforms urgently required for the peasants, the workers and the humble white collar class so numerous in this country." To prevent an unfavorable election result, the United States intervened massively in the Italian campaign, while also preparing to respond to possible communist violence by setting up a command structure in Virginia for any military eventuality.[114] Stalin, meanwhile, was obliging enough to allow the Prague coup, thus considerably worsening the international climate and greatly facilitating the subsequent electoral defeat of the PCI. Another decisive ingredient in the picture was the war alert sent out in early March by the American commander of occupied Germany.[115] Kennan, on his way to Japan, became convinced that something drastic was afoot. Overly enthusiastic local communists and a Kremlin that, judging from the Prague events, was in a state of "extreme urgency," had combined to create that moment of real danger he had feared before but not believed probable. In Europe, as he cabled Washington,

> Italy is obviously key point. If Communists were to win election there our whole position in Mediterranean, and possibly in western Europe as well, would probably be undermined. I am persuaded that the Communists could not win without strong factor of intimidation on their side, and it would clearly be better that elections not take place at all than that the Communist win in these circumstances. For these reasons I question whether it would not be preferable for Italian Government to outlaw Communist Party and take strong action against it before elections. Communists would presumably reply with civil war, which would give us grounds for reoccupation of Foggia fields or any other facilities we might wish. This would admittedly result in much violence and probably a military division of Italy; but we are getting close to the deadline and I think it might well be preferable to a bloodless election victory, unopposed by ourselves, which would give the Communists the entire peninsula at one coup and send waves of panic to all surrounding areas.[116]

One historian, sympathetic to Kennan, has called this plan "incomprehensible and thoroughly contradictory," but it was neither of those things.[117] While it was certainly inconsistent with ethically founded imperatives against interventionism, nothing in his previously stated position on containment as such ruled out this sort of action. It was simply an instance of normal measures short of war no longer meeting the case, thus requiring exceptional means. It must have been fairly easy for him, in fact, to fit the Italian events to his prediction only a few months earlier of a clampdown in Czechoslovakia and attempts at seizing control in France and Italy. The first had just taken place, and the second seemed now about to happen. His cable was thus eminently comprehensible. That he had misunderstood the situation and conceived a potentially disastrous policy is beside the point.[118]

I have tried to show that there was no Great Wall between the political and the military in his thinking but rather an organic link; and "organically" is perhaps the best way to grasp the idea of containment. It is another matter that Kennan actually proved to be no swashbuckling interventionist. Generally judging that sort of thing imprudent and counterproductive, he much preferred the notion of casting ominous shadows of military potential—in order, as he wrote in early 1948, to "cramp the style" of the opponent. In this regard he professed himself an adherent (as, he alleged, were the Russians) of "one of the great truths of naval warfare": that "a force sufficiently superior to that of the enemy will probably never have to be used."[119]

Having, I trust, transcended the political-military antinomy, I can now move on to the more geopolitical dimensions of containment. The space and timing had been defined from the same vantage point of abstract, ideal truth as the concept itself: it was a question of principle, not practical policy. Just as containment was the principle of active resistance as such, so Kennan's habitually reiterated call for firm counterforce "at every juncture"—or, in the categorical terminology of the X-Article, "at a series of constantly shifting geographical and political points, corresponding to the shifts and maneuvers of Soviet policy"—may be seen as an abstraction, as a dialectical notion of the extreme.[120] In theory, Soviet expansionism had to be resisted wherever it popped up; but it did not necessarily follow that the countermove would be defined by the nature of the original move. It might well be strategically advantageous to respond in a wholly different manner and a wholly different theater.[121] In practice, of course, Kennan knew that Soviet expansionism was *not* popping up at an enormously varied number of spots, geographical or political; to the contrary, it was concentrated rather exclusively in Europe. As I have mentioned, he considered the rest of the world, except for Japan, of limited interest to Moscow, and so it was to him as well.

As with the Long Telegram, this is a symptomatic reading that does not lend itself to simple proof. Kennan himself, lacking developed awareness of the structure of his own argument, failed to state his case in a manner calculated to avoid misunderstanding or partial understanding. This failure, odd in view of his earlier experiences, earned him a well-deserved and merciless critique from no less a pontifical authority than Walter Lippmann, who subjected the X-Article to a series of interrogations in the *New York Herald Tribune* soon after it appeared.[122] Seemingly taking the "unassailable barriers" as a policy of building a global wall (not, under the circumstances, an unreasonable reading), he fired off the following salvo:

The policy . . . concedes to the Kremlin the strategical initiative as to when, where and under what local circumstances the issue is to be joined. It compels the United States to meet the Soviet pressure at these shifting geographical and political points by using satellite states, puppet governments and agents which have been subsidized and supported, though their effectiveness is meager and their reliability uncertain. By forcing us to expend our energies and our substance upon these dubious and unnatural allies on the *perimeter* of the Soviet Union, the effect of the policy is to neglect our natural allies in the Atlantic community, and to alienate them.[123]

The attack must have rankled considerably since Kennan largely agreed. In a belated response, never sent, he was particularly offended that Lippmann had identified him with the Truman Doctrine, which he had opposed, and then compared that policy unfavorably with the Marshall Plan, of which he had been a progenitor. Yet Kennan's plaintive letter falls signally short of recognizing the shortcomings of the original formulations. That these *did* have shortcomings should by then have been abundantly clear. Witness, for instance, the ensuing exchange of May 1947, when a Congressman Kunkel queried him after a speech: "You say you are not committed, but there is a global policy in which we are opposing communism every place in the world, and thereby we are putting ourselves under the control of Russia because wherever Russia stirs up a minority or acts aggressively, at that point we must go in or abandon the policy and make ourselves the laughing stock of the world. So actually you don't say when we will have to go in; you say it is up to Russia whether we have to go in." Kennan, probably wincing, replied:

I don't think we have to go in with financial support everywhere. If we have given that impression in advancing the Greek and Turkish program . . . I think we have given the wrong impression. There is a great difference in the danger of Communism in areas which are contiguous to Soviet military power and the danger of Communism in areas remote from it, as, for example, in South America. There is a difference in the danger of highly strategic areas such as Greece or Austria or Germany, where a Communist victory might have very, very serious results for us and for our allies, and a Communist victory in other places where it is not apt to have those results. China, for example: If I thought for a moment that the precedent of Greece and Turkey obliged us to try to do the same thing in China, I would throw up my hands and say we had better have a whole new approach to the affairs of the world.[124]

The discussion concerned the Truman Doctrine, but it might as well have been about the as yet unpublished X-Article. The idea of creating a policy that would in fact resemble the "capitalist encirclement" so often castigated by Moscow was alien to Kennan, who, one assumes, was familiar with Gibbon's peremptory dismissal of the concept of extended wall defenses on the perimeter: "An active enemy, who can select and vary his point of attack, must in the end discover some feeble spot, or some unguarded moment. The strength, as well as the attention, of the defenders is divided; and such are the blind effects of terror on the firmest troops that a line broken in a single place is almost instantly deserted."[125] Before the end of the decade Kennan would indeed find himself in opposition to the logic of extending military alliances around the Soviet perimeter, which was gaining ascendancy in Washington, the logic of a global wall of "unassailable barriers" for which Lippmann had taken him to task.

Seeing in containment a suggestion for concrete policy, Lippmann had no trouble demonstrating its vacuity: all the X-Article seemed to say was that if containment were successful, there might be a "gradual mellowing" or even collapse of the Soviet regime in a decade or so. Aside from the force-counterforce dialectic, it was not at all clear what Soviet-American relations would then be about. Pointing to the one-sided nature of Kennan's a priori assumption, the Soviet initiative, Lippmann went on to make the unanswerable riposte that, contrary to what Kennan seemed to think, diplomacy does not always mean transactions between "intimate" nations.[126]

This realist argument was eventually to exert a powerful influence on Kennan. Not long afterwards, at any rate, he would take a very similar position within the administration (more about this in Part II). During 1946–47, however, he pondered Soviet policy in general, not in particular. Hence he may not have seen any incompatibility between his stance and Lippmann's, considering them instead arguments on different levels. Be that as it may, while Lippmann had a dialogical notion of U.S.-Soviet relations, Kennan, in this period, did not. One obvious indication is the careless and opaque way in which Kennan expressed himself on the subject of negotiations with the Russians, leaving doubt whether he envisaged any such process at all.

We have thus arrived again at the important question, can one ever talk profitably with a fanatic?

Kennan's internal derivation of Soviet policy had, it is easy to see, the unfortunate structural effect of rendering dubious all responses to Moscow except the most primitive ones, rather like an exasperated parent who has to let an obstinate child bang its head against the wall until it discovers the consequences in the form of a disagreeable headache, all in the hope that the child will learn a lesson at some point and do otherwise. As Lippmann forcefully contended, this sort of policy had clear overtones of passivity and negativism.

The problem went beyond the structural aspect. Kennan had targeted for attack what he considered to be the view of Henry Wallace and the left-liberals, namely that it was possible to win Soviet trust by being nice and understanding. Dismissing trust as a fundamental concept in international (as opposed to human) relations, he found the idea particularly inappropriate in the Soviet case, since it involved the absurd assumption that "the guardians of the Revolution . . . [could] be swept off their feet and won over from their holiest articles of faith by an engaging smile, a few kind words, and some gestures of self-abnegation on the part of the other fellow."[127] This was a misrepresentation of Wallace's position, which took as its starting point the observation that the "tougher we get, the tougher the Russians will get," and consequently argued for some sort of realistic compromise from which better overall relations might then ensue.[128] In that sense the secretary of commerce, a much and undeservedly maligned figure, was a more straightforward realist at this stage than Kennan. More important, in the course of making his argument Kennan came close to denying the value of *all* discussion with Moscow: "As fanatics they are not amenable to reasonable argument. This is very important. You talk at them, not *to* them."[129] The impression of ultimatum or *Diktat*, conjured up by the play on "at" and "to," emerged more clearly in the X-Article: "Since there can be no appeal to common purposes, there can be no appeal to common mental approaches. For this reason, facts speak louder than words to the ears of the Kremlin; and words carry the greatest weight when they have the ring of reflecting, or being backed up by, facts of unchallengeable validity" (p. 574).

This statement is of the greatest interest, not only because of the unilateral demands it implies but also for the pivotal opposition be-

tween "words" and "facts." Kennan often made this distinction, sometimes using "circumstances" or "situations" instead of "facts" as the
opposite. In this habit he was obviously not alone, though the most
common contrariety to *words* is probably *action* or *act*. *Words*, one
might note, is not actually the simple antonym of these other concepts,
in themselves unthinkable without words and so in a way owing their
very existence to them.[130] The procedure as a whole is not without
effect. If the opposition is thought in a binary way, the verbal and the
nonverbal, the former being the negative pole, it is easy to end up, as
the chain of signification slips along, with the total exclusion of all
talk. At that point the matter becomes serious since one is led, in our
context, toward the notion of confronting the Russians with nonverbal
means, presumably some sign system lodged in the visibility of force.

This slippage is related to the dubious nature of the initial sentence
and premise. The absence of "common purposes" does not necessarily
mean, it seems to me, the absence of "common mental approaches."
It is indeed hard to imagine how any meaning at all—verbal or nonverbal, if nonverbal meaning there is—can be conveyed from one side
to the other when there are no common mental approaches. Kennan
did not hold so extreme a view, but the pronouncement was nevertheless a sign of conceptual uncertainty. This is perhaps more readily
seen in his divided stand on Soviet realism, where it is never clear
how fanatics impervious to reason could simultaneously be cautious,
pragmatic power politicians. The result is intermittent incoherence.
Once, for example, he argued that the experience of making peace
with Germany in 1918 had taught the Bolsheviks, if only by necessity,
to deal realistically with capitalist regimes; whereupon he concluded
by calling them "fanatics who [could not] afford to think realistically."[131]

Not a mere slip of the tongue, this contradiction represents two
different strains in his thinking, shaped, I suspect, by the domestic
targets he wished to attack: appeasers on the one hand and people
with a war fixation on the other. Convinced that the first perspective
entailed the naive expectation of a fundamental transformation of the
Soviet outlook, he wanted to stamp out this illusion once and for all
and in the process virtually painted himself into a corner. For of course
it was possible to persuade the Russians with words to take a different
view of certain questions, provided one gave them some advantageous
reason to do so. No basic revolution of outlook would have been
required, as indeed it would have been equally silly to imagine any

basic change of outlook on the American side, whose leadership, to reverse Kennan's argument about the Kremlin, could hardly "tamper with the foundations of [its] own power" either.[132]

Never a very astute reader of domestic politics, he may have exaggerated his anti-idealism because he exaggerated the size of the left-liberal forces. He should have known otherwise: hawkish fury and lack of measured debate increasingly marked the times. The X-Article, formally composed within the frame of neither appeasement nor war, in effect served the purpose of diminishing the sphere of rationality even further.

I have pointed to some discursive and political effects of Kennan's position, to its overly abstract quality and inverse lack of concrete policy. I have also hinted that he was not *really* against all forms of talk. Aside, that is, from the consequences of his discursive strategy, he had a "real" view, the sort of view he would have professed had he been asked directly what he thought of negotiations with Moscow. Very likely it was this:

> We are committed to a policy of seeking a more secure and hopeful international order through agreement with other peoples of this world . . . It implies a long and tremendously complicated road of negotiation in which hundreds of problems are probably going to come up for discussion and settlement at every turn. In treating these problems there can be no question of any universal "soft" policy or of a "tough" policy. Each individual problem must be judged on its own merits, against what we conceive to be the interests of our people and of world peace in general. Accordingly, our approach . . . cannot be one of any pre-conceived "softness" or "toughness," but must combine firm insistence on what we believe to be indispensable and vital . . . with a loyal and patient readiness to meet people half-way wherever we possibly can. There is no one connected with Russian affairs in our Government who would be foolish enough to think that we would have anything to gain at any time by a provocative and insolent approach to any other nation in the world. That is our answer to those who keep urging us to get "tough." We are equally clear in our understanding that in international affairs it is usually misleading, ineffective and unfair to the other fellow to rush forward with political favors for which you have not clearly stated the *quid pro quo* you expect to gain, or to make concessions which can only serve to obscure the real limits of your patience and your interests. And this is our answer to those who would have us pursue a "soft" policy composed chiefly of fatuous gestures of good will.[133]

On that note it must also be said that Kennan expressed willingness (but not often) to accept "Russian control for security purposes of a very wide band of territory between the Baltic and the Black Sea beyond the limits of the Soviet Union," though he thought, not unreasonably, that this control could be exerted without the massive dominance and de facto abolition of national independence that Moscow seemed to consider necessary. However, nothing very specific by way of policy followed from these sentiments and on the whole he dodged the issue of spheres.[134]

It was in fact the long-term goal of a qualitative change in Soviet behavior rather than any immediate horse trading that was first and foremost on his mind. Foiled by superior strength and intelligence everywhere, Moscow, like the child of my analogy, would learn at length about recurring headaches. In the vivid language of his X-Article, "No mystical, Messianic movement . . . can face frustration indefinitely without eventually adjusting itself in one way or another to the logic of that state of affairs" (p. 582). Thus in sanguine moments he imagined that ten or fifteen years of containment would result in the actual break-up of the Soviet system.[135] The "mellowed" Kremlin he rather more modestly envisioned most of the time was not as radically altered a place: "The best we could hope for is that they would be communists a little sobered in their attitude toward the outside world, a little more moderate with respect to us, and a little less hopeful of sowing dissension and getting anywhere through hard-boiled tactics."[136] Since Moscow indubitably did mellow as it were in the 1950s, one may ask to what extent this development was a product of containment. The question is vast and probably unanswerable. For one thing, containment in its implementation after 1948 accorded less and less with Kennan's ideas, and in that sense the question is misconceived. Yet one point should be made. Inscribed in the very metaphor of containment was the premise of Soviet expansionism. But what if the "fluid stream" was a mere trickle? Clearly the "unassailable barriers" would cause correspondingly less frustration, the opportunities to learn the hard lesson would be fewer, and no great "logic" would be seeping into the system as a consequence. If in fact the Soviet Union were better described as, say, an "isolationist autocracy" for which any political efflux was inessential, then containment (of whatever kind) would have served no purpose other than that of deepening Moscow's glacial isolation.[137] The post-Stalin thaw will thus be grasped as having happened despite rather than because of containment.

Kennan had set himself the task of going beyond both "the emotionally pro-Soviet and the emotionally anti-Soviet" poles of American public opinion.[138] At this he was not successful. Just as the Long Telegram had served to fuel alarmist sentiments inside the administration, so the X-Article now came to reinforce "the emotionally anti-Soviet" mood that was fast gaining ground among the generality of informed opinion. In both cases, let it be said, Kennan's intervention was nothing but a contributing factor to a process that would have occurred anyway. Yet the manner in which his analyses resonated was not wholly the product of circumstances beyond his control. To some degree it was simply a matter of language and style: the metaphorical imagery, potently evocative, lent itself to the subjective readings he so deplored when looking back. A little less eloquence and a little more stringency would not have been inadvisable. Kennan, however, was not a prominent specimen of *Homo politicus*. His concern was to state his case, not to analyze its possible effect and adjust accordingly. Style was not his only problem either. His account exhibited real antinomics, expressive not of obscure language but of incoherence. A reader could thus seize upon any of a series of themes and draw conclusions quite different from the thrust of the argument.

Yet the single most important factor in his failure to transcend the given polarity was that he shared "with the emotionally anti-Soviet" elements the fundamental assumption that the Soviet Union was inherently expansionist and willing in principle to use any means available to achieve its objectives. Once that ground had been conceded, it was exceedingly hard to regain by references to the practical predicaments of Soviet power and the present preponderance of the United States. Calling for "greater coolness, greater sophistication, greater maturity and self-confidence in our approach to this whole problem of Russia and communism" proved a futile exercise.[139] An indication of just how futile can be gleaned from a despatch composed by the American embassy in Moscow in the spring of 1950 and purporting to be a considered assessment, useful knowledge:

> Moscow is waging total war against the Free World, a ruthless and unrelenting struggle within which "Cold War" and "Shooting War" are merely tactical phrases. They are currently endeavoring to make the most of the tidal wave of social change generated by World War II with the minimum objective of capturing half of the world before the wave subsides and perhaps with the hope that they may be able to achieve sufficient gains to prepare the Free World for a final push without the latter having been able to attain postwar stabilization

> ... [They] are now in a second phase, an openly revolutionary offensive in which ... they hope to encompass certain given areas before the Free World can recover, perhaps by 1953. To accomplish these objectives Moscow is steering a course as close as possible to full scale war short of actually precipitating it.[140]

This grotesque vulgarization of Kennan's earlier arguments, substituting rhetorical violence for coolness, sophistication, maturity, and self-confidence, was at the same time also a clear projection of some consequences of those arguments. For the statement ultimately signifies a state of nonpolicy toward the Soviet Union. The vast abstractions of the cold war could not be translated any more easily into a concrete policy of interaction with Moscow than could the wartime notions of democracy in Eastern Europe.

Yet the same abstractions did allow a most concrete and massive American expansion of influence all over the non-Soviet and non-Chinese world, for which reason one might on balance consider American interests to have been well served. With this last notion Kennan had, as will be seen in Part II, little sympathy. Suffice it here to mention that when he and Charles Bohlen began after the successful Italian elections in April 1948 to contemplate some form of clarification of views with Stalin, based on what they considered a stabilized Europe, it became painfully obvious that the American side had little to offer; and their ill-conceived initiative ended in a pathetic debacle.[141] Kennan himself would espouse no realistic policy of negotiation until after the summer, when he had reassessed the German question. Four years later, on the very eve of his ambassadorship to Moscow, where, with essentially nothing to do, he was to suffer a defeat of a more personal kind, Kennan issued this poignant valediction:

> Such words as "negotiation" and "compromise" are not abstractions. Perhaps there are times when they can be shameful, but there are other times when they can be extremely necessary. By permitting the assumption to be established that there is something abstractly wicked about them we permit the entire nature of the diplomatic process ... to be obscured and removed from our field of vision ... The very word "diplomacy" has been semantically discredited in our American vocabulary.[142]

What can finally be said with regard to the two types of analysis I specified at the outset? On the dominant question concerning the "real" nature of the beast, I have criticized Kennan in his own terms for not demonstrating convincingly any logic that would compel the Soviet Union to expand and for his method of deriving everything from internal factors. His observations on Soviet practice, by contrast, I found more fruitful, especially his emphasis on the unlikelihood of a military attack on Western Europe and his intermittent references to potential tensions between Moscow and various communist parties. I disagree, however, with his contention that Stalin aimed at the political conquest of Western Europe, a contention I also think incompatible with the thesis about Soviet fears of centrifugal tendencies within the communist movement. As regards the subordinate task of putting oneself in the opponent's shoes, it must be said that Kennan did little along those lines. He made no real effort to visualize how the Russians perceived the United States and *its* goals in world politics. Nor did he manage to penetrate the veil of Soviet marxism or to relate it to concrete policies. While his analysis of the function of ideology advanced considerably, his interest in its content remained perfunctory. Perhaps the outstanding result was continued confusion about the Soviet view of war and of the West.

PART II

The American Problematic

A subtle, flexible, and cunning foreign policy conceived and executed by a high command of strategists far from the madding crowd may well be impossible (and undesirable) in a democracy unless there is actually a state of war, or at the very least some form of siege. It is most certainly difficult to achieve in the modern version of Madison's purposely decentered republic of conflicting interests, structural dispersal, and parochial outlooks.

Kennan knew this and resented it mightily.[1] Yet he was comparatively optimistic when, in the spring of 1947, he assumed responsibility for the articulation of a global American policy.[2] He found himself, as rarely before, largely in accord with the overall tenor of things. It was also satisfying to know that the new Policy Planning Staff (PPS) he was to head would function under Secretary of State George C. Marshall as a sort of general staff outside the old inhibiting divisional boundaries and clearance system of the State Department, thus allowing unusual freedom to make whatever proposals he wished directly to the man in charge.[3] Furthermore the period, unlike the Roosevelt era (and today), was one of indisputable prominence for the State Department in the making of foreign policy, an area whose importance was then at a historic peak in American politics. Kennan's appointment, to take a trivial but indicative example, occasioned a feature article in the *New York Times Magazine*.[4] It is hard to imagine an internal appointment in the State Department now earning more than minor interest, if any at all. Such attention was nonetheless a mixed blessing, marvelous as long as there was general agreement about the sort of anticommunism one ought to pursue but potentially paralyzing in times of controversy, as Senator Joseph McCarthy was later forcefully to demonstrate.

Minuscule (nine members, not including Kennan)[5] by the standards of today's bureaucracy, the PPS was immediately thrown into the Marshall Aid project and came to do much less long-term planning than might have been expected. Nor were its policy concerns truly global, for the PPS, Eurocentric by choice and inclination, came to discard a large part of the globe from its operational panoptic. In the domain of everyday policy it produced position papers (written almost exclusively by Kennan himself) of great quality. Proximity to the secretary, open-ended license of inquiry, and Kennan's personal ability all had a tonic effect on the various departmental divisions and in that sense probably also served to improve the level of policy-making.[6] By mid-1949, however, its influence was already on the wane: Dean Acheson had replaced Marshall as secretary of state; the PPS was eventually subordinated to the old clearing system again; and Kennan, no longer in agreement with the policy being pursued, drifted farther and farther toward the margin.[7]

The genesis and nature of this disagreement, or more precisely its conceptual aspects, form the first subject of examination in this section. At the center and the core of this story lie the two intertwined and partially successive issues of Germany and NATO, both essentially concerning the question of how Europe, against a backdrop of Soviet entrenchment in the East, could best be reconstructed without communism. Since the end of the Second World War, Kennan had assumed that agreement with the Russians on substantial issues was impossible, indeed unwise. His reasons varied, but on the whole he considered the American capacity to resist too feeble, the contradiction with Moscow too antagonistic, and the Russians themselves too negative for such agreements. During 1948 he changed. It gradually became evident to him that "his" containment policy would take the form of a system of militarized alliances, something for which he felt only the deepest aversion. Thus, while not acknowledging any previous error, he began to sense that developments were moving in an unsound direction. Yet he found himself fighting rear-guard action because he had conceded—in fact to some extent originally formulated—an important part of his opponents' argument: that confidence had to be shored up in Europe. It was under these circumstances that he switched position on Germany and the division of Europe. From

having been one of the earliest and most vocal advocates of partitioning as the answer to the Soviet problem, he moved toward the view
that, however unlikely, a settlement on Germany should be attempted.
Little support emerged for his new position, and by the end of 1949
he was no longer head of the PPS. This, simply put, is the trajectory
to be charted in Chapter 4.

If Europe constituted the chief field of intervention for the PPS,
nothing much was said about the Third World. The partial exception
was the issue of China, forced on the staff by outside political pressure.
The Republican party and factions of the press, particularly the powerful Luce organs, began making it a cause célèbre; the closer the
election of 1948, the more defensive the administration became.[8] Not
so the unrepentant Kennan, who instead dismissed China and the rest
of the Third World as unsuitable objects of policy. His rationale was
blunt. So far as he was concerned, these regions were of no particular
importance in the greater scheme of things and were basically unknowable anyway. His very concept of that greater scheme was defined
to a degree by this radical negativity, which is why it is retrospectively
significant. Chapter 5 is thus devoted to what Kennan thought *un-
important*, as evidenced by source materials from both before and after
1950.

I have chosen these two areas, respectively the most central and the
most marginal in Kennan's panorama, not only as case studies of the
counteractive aspect of containment but also as a way of raising the
larger question of American foreign policy as such, or what might
perhaps be called its parameters and conditions of possibility. This
was something Kennan himself began to ponder more systematically
after leaving the State Department in 1950. His reflections, "realist"
through and through, typically took the form of historical rather than
theoretical inquiry. Chapter 6 examines the resultant critique of American foreign policy and poses the question of how realistic was his
realism.

The three problematizations will be pursued separately over time,
so that, for instance, the disengagement controversy of the late 1950s,
in many ways a reenactment of the conflict over Germany and NATO
in 1948–49, is included in Chapter 4; then Chapter 5 returns to the
1940s and the genesis of the Third World problematic.

4

Reconstruction and Division

Kennan at the outset of the Second World War was a radically conservative man, bordering on the reactionary.[1] Though he was capable of expressing displeasure over existing conditions and advocating change, his emphasis was on the danger of sudden deviations from the time-honored and the normal, on historical and geographical constancy in the face of upheaval.[2] Once the war was under way, therefore, he took the American interest to lie in "the broadest and most stabile possible foundations for a reconstruction of Europe: in arrangements which would give maximum play to the *natural and permanent* creative forces of the continent and provide the least possible sources of national frustration and friction."[3]

Before the Soviet and American entries into the war, he defined this aim as more than just recreating the status quo ante pure and simple, for the prewar situation, so obviously a product of the First World War and Versailles, had not been healthy. His restoration model referred instead to an older epoch, seeking a "reestablishment of the delicate balance thrown out of adjustment by the rise of national states in Germany and Italy and the demise of the Hapsburg Empire." This presumably pre-Bismarckian order would entail "frank recognition of the value of particularism in European life."[4] Exactly what sort of order he had in mind is not clear, but it was probably not simply a proliferation of isolated sovereignties. For soon afterwards he showed interest in the transnational aspect of the Nazi occupation, and by 1942 he was advocating a kind of federation of "small peoples" based on "compulsion to cooperation."[5] Since the area at issue was chiefly

Central Europe, this model suggested a recycled version of the polyglot Austro-Hungarian empire, for which he still nourished admiration.[6] In this scheme he was not alone, for a Danubian federation was
also a favorite British project, finally torpedoed when Moscow could
not be persuaded that the whole thing was not just another *cordon
sanitaire*.[7]

The Hapsburg empire and the attachment to organicism played a
role as well in Kennan's hostility toward Roosevelt's plan for an
international peace organization, the United Nations. He opposed the
idea because it assumed a community of aims with the Soviet Union;
but he also found unpalatable the combination of nationality and
inviolable sovereignty that, as he saw it, was inscribed in the very
notion of such an organization.[8] Nationalism, after all, had ruined the
old European order in general and the Hapsburg empire in particular,
while inviolable sovereignty seemed to exemplify an artificial concept
of international relations, the superimposition of a universal principle
on a reality that was in fact a living organism constantly (but "naturally") changing over time and thus impervious to unnatural schemes
based on abstract equality among states:

> An international organization for the preservation of the peace and
> security cannot take the place of a well-conceived and realistic foreign
> policy. The more we ignore politics in our absorption with the
> erection of a legalistic system for the preservation of the status quo,
> the sooner and the more violently that system will be broken to
> pieces under the realities of international life . . . International politics
> is something organic, not something mechanical. Its essence is
> change; and the only systems for the regulation of international life
> which can be effective over long periods of time are ones sufficiently
> subtle, sufficiently pliable, to adjust themselves to constant change in
> the interests and power of the various countries involved.[9]

This was, by the way, probably not far from how Stalin saw things,
though that did not prevent him from seeing the United Nations as
one way of institutionalizing great power cooperation founded on
spheric interest.[10] Nor did Roosevelt, insofar as one can tell, consider
the project one of "freezing" a consciously "artificial" system of sovereignties, as Kennan also described it, characteristically taking presidential rhetoric too literally and failing to consider the political dynamic.[11]

By 1944 Kennan had become thoroughly alarmed by the drift of the American debate on reconstruction. It seemed to him to suffer from widely diffused illusions about future Soviet cooperation and the feasibility of a United Nations. There was too the common desire for a Carthaginian peace to contend with.[12] The cabinet consensus at the time favored a policy of treating Germany as a subjugated, not liberated, country to be demilitarized, de-Nazified, and decentralized, in short as a prime candidate for surgical change.[13] Most uncompromising here was the famous and for a while officially sanctioned Morgenthau Plan for the agrarianization of Germany.

Kennan's feelings about that country were (and have remained) ambivalent.[14] Raised in Milwaukee, perhaps the most Germanic of American cities, he had spent six months at Kassel in 1912 at the age of eight and had acquired some competence in the language. He had returned during the declining stages of the Weimar Republic for specialist training, and again in 1939 for two years as a diplomat at the American Embassy. As Kennan himself says, Germany "was a country with which I was never able to identify extensively in a personal sense. I knew its language nearly as well as my own, sometimes thought in it and wrote in it, but was never in character when speaking it . . . But intellectually and aesthetically, Germany had made a deep impression on me."[15]

My sense is that he was somewhat less out of character as a German than he believes.[16] In 1940, however, he had been most uncomplimentary, perhaps understandably at the time, about the essentials of the German national character, condensing it to "jealousy," "uncertainty," "feeling of inferiority," and a "lust to dominate Europe."[17] Germany appeared to him on the whole an immature nation. Some of these feelings lingered despite, as he states in his *Memoirs*, the more nuanced view he formed during the early war and through his close relationship with the anti-Nazi aristocrat Helmuth von Moltke.[18]

Doubtless much support could be found for the idea of rendering Germany once and for all incapable of launching any future wars. Kennan agreed with this objective but not with the policies proposed to achieve it.[19] In 1942 he had spoken of the need to have Germany "treated, cured of its disease and re-educated," but his more considered opinion was very much opposed to any fundamental tinkering with either German territory or German society at large. As a conservative he was not inclined to radical (by definition unnatural) incisions by vancours in the social order of the conquered. "The political development of great peoples," he wrote, "is conditioned and determined by their national experiences, but never by the manipulations of foreign powers in their internal affairs."[20] Thus he found the idea of dissolving the Junker class abhorrent and the castigation of this aristocratic segment as the source of Nazism and militarism quite mistaken.[21] Considering democracy not part of the "real" Germany, he was also against the idea, later consecrated at Yalta and Potsdam, of introducing (or reintroducing) that political system by dictation:

> I cannot accept the proposition that the most plausible hope for lasting political reconstruction and orderly development lies in the establishment of a democratic government in Germany. The only reasonably respectable tradition of orderly and humane government in Germany is actually that of a strong monarchical government limited by an efficient bureaucracy and a powerful upper class. Free democratic institutions require, if they are to be successful, an organically-formed tradition. Attempts to impose such institutions artificially on Germany may discredit further the whole conception of democracy, already strongly associated in the German mind with corruption and inefficiency. They may also be exploited by ambitious and unscrupulous minorities. A democratic system in Germany as we conceive it would probably be unstable and short-lived and lead quickly to a dictatorship of the left bearing many of the attributes of present national socialism.[22]

And:

> I think we should be extremely circumspect in counting on the existence in Germany of any democratically-minded people, strong enough to help us in our purposes. It may well be that we will have to find our support rather in repentant nationalists who have been persuaded by the force of events of the necessity of a less aggressive concept of Germany's destiny. In any case, I think the letter and connotation of the word "democracy" are both seriously compromised in Germany, and will scarcely be accepted by this generation as an acceptable substitute for a concise and constructive teleology of German national development.[23]

A "constructive teleology," according to this view, would particularly not involve the exclusion from public service, or the prosecution, of former Nazi officials. A tripartite de-Nazification program with Great Britain and the Soviet Union would be impractical. For one thing it would eliminate most of the capable individuals since, "like it or not, nine-tenths of what is strong, able, and respected in Germany has been poured into those very categories which we have in mind."

Moreover, the whole project was "unnecessary" to begin with: Germany was irrevocably nationalistic, and the best way to prevent future aggression was not "the artificial removal of any given class" but a "grim demonstration" to teach "the present ruling class" that such acts would lead to disaster. If said class were then to disappear, it would at least "be through the logic of history and through the organic development of German political life, not through the premature, and unavoidably inept, interference of foreign powers."[24]

It was presumably defeat itself, coupled with rehabilitation, that would teach the ruling class this lesson, not any postwar punishment. On the choice between punishment and rehabilitation Kennan's stance was unequivocal:

> [Punishment] means renouncing the aid of the strongest people in Europe in the rebuilding of European society. It means the long-term economic weakening of Central Europe in general: a weakening which will affect our friends no less than our enemies. It means, in effect, the acknowledgement on our part of the collapse of the unity and significance of western Europe in civilization . . . If we leave Germany a unified country, shorn of its eastern provinces, deprived of much of its shipping and its industry, more heavily populated by far than ever in its history, and excluded from cooperation in all the great colonial and international activities of the world at large, we will have written an unerring prescription for trouble . . . Nostalgia for the lost lands will become a new form of escapism for a people pathologically inclined to avoid reality. Economic handicaps will force them by sheer necessity to new feats of organization and invention. Their confinement on a reduced territory and their exclusion from the world at large will fan their already pathological sense of claustrophobia into new transports of introversion and fanaticism . . . We can leave Germany united, in circumstances which make it only a seething hot-bed of bitterness, revenge and social ferment; and we can then proceed, like a bad parent with a bad child, to punish the traits which we ourselves inspire. In this way we enter upon an indefinite program of military control and repression. Or we can, on the other hand, try to build a new Germany out of their physical and psychological introversion, remove the explosive quality of their national energy, and enlist—if possible—their astonishing national strength in the interest of the Continent as a whole.[25]

It was the last aspect, recruiting German strength for reconstruction, that actually constituted his major means of "rehabilitation." For he revived his federative idea by proposing to bring Germany into a

European framework based not on "the idea of long-term punishment and retribution" but "on the prospect of common prosperity and common security."[26] Given his gloomy expectations of future enmity with the Soviet Union, we must assume that Kennan conceived this reconstituted and integrated (western) European system as a counter-weight to the eastern antagonist.

The notion of steering Germany along toward a brighter European future (in itself scarcely an "organic" move) should be seen in the context of Kennan's broader critique of Washington's line on the postwar world. It must be remembered that in 1944 this line was still based on the premise of continued cooperation with the Soviet ally, in the projected United Nations as well as in the reconstitution of Europe. To this position Kennan took sharp exception. For him the Soviet Union had already taken on the role of main enemy, interested not in productive reconstruction but in the weakening and ultimate destruction of European life. With regard to the coming Allied occupation of Germany, he was thus convinced that the Russians would run their zone like "an outlying subjugated province" and that the country would therefore effectively "be partitioned." The future Allied Control Council there would "amount to little more than the present Advisory Council for Italy," an analogy indicating that he thought it would become a paper organ.[27] Nothing fruitful, in short, could be derived from attempting a common policy with Moscow on the reformation of Germany: "The idea of a Germany run jointly with the Russians is a chimera. The idea of both the Russians and ourselves withdrawing politely at a given date and a healthy, peaceful, stabile and friendly Germany arising out of the resulting vacuum is also a chimera. We have no choice but to lead our section of Germany . . . to a form of independence so prosperous, so secure, so superior, that the east cannot threaten it."[28] This "reality" should then be recognized in no uncertain terms:

> We should accept as an accomplished fact the complete partition of Germany along the line of the Russian zone of occupation, and begin at once in consultation with the British and the French to plan realistically for the future of that line. In this planning, we cannot avoid the conception of a western European federation, to include the various German entities west of the partition line. The Russians should be told of this at once. Into this federation, Schleswig-Holstein, the Hanseatic cities, Hanover, the Rheinland, Baden, Wurtemberg and Bavaria should enter as separate entities, together with any

zone of Austria which we or the British may consent to occupy. Outside of Germany, this framework would have to include Denmark, Holland, Belgium, France, Switzerland and Italy. Technical and economic coordination should be centralized in a place in this area but outside the German territories. Foreign trade and finance, in particular, should be closely controlled. Trade relations with the remainder of Europe should be conducted only through a single center, and on a straight clearing basis. In this, the rich experience of the Germans should be utilized. Since trade between the east and the west of Germany will be difficult and undependable, the west must be integrated into the Atlantic economy as independently as possible of the east. Its productive facilities must be to the maximum preserved, not destroyed, if it is not to become a permanent deficit area.[29]

A more "artificial" scheme imposed by outside foreign powers is hard to conceive, thus illustrating that when the real does not conform to what the conservative considers worthy of conservation, he or she can become quite radical.[30]

It was not only anticipated Russian intransigence and destructiveness that would make the cooperative running of Germany "a chimera" and partitioning an immediate item on the agenda. Kennan actually favored the idea in itself as a sound way to avoid the possibility that the Russians would beat the Americans to the post there if given a chance to operate freely. Having a low opinion of the German propensity for democracy, he considered the implementation of such a system a likely prelude to totalitarian derailment and a leftist dictatorship very similar to the Nazi regime. In sum, there was a real danger that Germany would fall under Russian influence, perhaps even veer in the direction of communism. "Better a dismembered Germany," he argued in the summer of 1945, "in which the west, at least, can act as a buffer to the forces of totalitarianism than a united Germany which again brings these forces to the North Sea." Similarly, he proposed the division of Austria along the lines of occupation and recommended that Italy, militarily in the hands of the West, should be restored with full possession of its colonies, leaving no say at all in the matter for the Soviet Union.[31] This, essentially, was to remain his position until mid-1948.

An evaluation of Kennan's argument necessitates a brief account of its larger context, the policies actually pursued on and in Germany during this period. The subject is vast and the historical excavation far from finished. I lay no claim to completeness or nuance. What is offered, rather, is one possible reading, simplified for the sake of polemical clarity and based mainly on secondary sources.

Agreement had been reached at Yalta to divide the country into zones of occupation in which the authority of the individual commanders was to be exceedingly wide. The State Department made a strong attempt to lessen that authority, but Roosevelt was not to be moved. The central government was thus to consist of the zone commanders congregated in Berlin as the Allied Control Council and functioning according to the principle of total unanimity.[32] Here was already a tendency toward the partition that Kennan so desired. It would have been better, from the opposing viewpoint, to follow the Austrian alternative of negative veto, whereby decisions of the coalition government stood fast *unless* the occupation powers (the United States having assumed a major role on Moscow's insistence) took the trouble to veto them. Elections were held, in which the communists received no more than 5 percent of the vote, and eventually the country was neutralized.[33]

The French were another problem. Despite being excluded from Potsdam, France had been allotted a German zone of its own. Thus equipped the French immediately began to obstruct almost everything in the Allied Control Council. One of their first acts, for instance, was to veto a nationwide bureau of statistics.[34] The British, on their part, appeared soon to have come unofficially to the same conclusion as Kennan that a divided Germany would be the preferable solution.[35] Certain German conservatives in the western sections, outstandingly Adenauer, were likewise in favor of getting rid of the Prussian, Protestant, and often social-democratic northeast. Indeed Adenauer had been a Rhineland separatist in the 1920s.[36]

Nor did the Potsdam Agreements themselves do much to serve the cause of unity. Germany was supposed to be treated as an economic but not political unit with some central economic agencies for transportation and the like (blocked, on the whole, by France); while reparations to the Soviet Union were largely to be taken out of the eastern zone itself. There was little here to encourage any functional interaction between the zones.[37] A final factor was the Potsdam decision to let the future Conference of Foreign Ministers (CFM) work out the "lesser" treaties with Bulgaria, Rumania, and so forth before the more central ones with Germany and Austria. It is clear that agreement on the latter two would have been more easily achieved immediately after the war, when relations were still reasonably cordial, rather than in the spring of 1947.[38]

The United States pursued a variety of policies on Germany during this period. The army, represented by General Lucius Clay, was in charge of the American zone and hence also of cooperating with the other zonal authorities in Berlin. Clay's basic policy instructions ordered him to do a wealth of contradictory things, and in trying to cope he came effectively to work out his own policy within the larger international framework.[39] From the French there was nothing but unapologetic obstruction, but with his Soviet counterparts Clay got along quite well, so in that respect the Control Council seems to have worked fairly satisfactorily. "It is difficult," as he wrote in the summer of 1946, "to find major instances of Soviet failure to carry out agreements reached in quadripartite government of Germany. Our difficulties in this field arise not so much from failure to carry out agreements but rather from failure to agree on interpretations."[40]

Clay understood that the Russians suspected American connivance in the French tactics since France was receiving sizable economic assistance from the United States.[41] In a way they were right. The European desk at the State Department was tacitly supporting the French by sidetracking attempts to put pressure on them, as Clay found out when he requested Washington to do so during the autumn of 1945. What primarily worried the Europeanists (not entirely without reason) was the potential effect of a more cooperative policy in Germany on the domestic scene in France, where the Communist party showed considerable strength. Moreover, the European desk was turning into a center for the Kennanesque view ("agreements are impossible or undesirable") of the Soviet Union. A leading representative, H. Freeman Matthews, had been lectured on the subject by Kennan while visiting Moscow in 1945 and had apparently been deeply impressed. Another, John Hickerson, was later to play an instrumental role in the creation of NATO, then in sharp conflict with a different Kennan. By 1946, in any event, the Europeanists had begun to equate a "realistic" policy toward the Soviet Union with the partitioning of Germany.[42]

In regard to the prosecution or liquidation of former Nazi officials, Kennan need not have been so concerned. After an initially serious American attempt in this direction, the whole thing petered out: 53,000 persons were purged, but only 1,000 remained permanently so after 1946; the judiciary was entirely restored; and when in 1949 the time came for Adenauer to form a cabinet for the Bundesrepublik, one-third of the members were former Nazis.[43]

What, then, of the Soviet policy and the Western response to it? While we are not privy to much of the internal Kremlin debate, a few points seem reasonably clear.

First, it is difficult to claim that the Soviet commander ruled his zone like an "outlying province" of his own country. In fact a case can be made that the three Western powers, certainly France, treated their areas more like completely subjugated provinces than did Moscow. A specifically German political system based on the Weimar parties (excluding the Nazis) was reconstituted in the Russian zone before any of the western zones followed suit. A broadly accepted land reform then eliminated what was left of the old Junker estates after the severance of the lands east of Oder-Neisse, but no real communization took place, and in 1946 open elections were held in the whole of Berlin.[44]

Second, it is equally difficult to make the related claim that Moscow was pursuing a policy of partitioning. If the Russians had been thinking along those lines, they could have turned the Control Council into the paper organ Kennan anticipated and then proceeded with extensive sovietization, neither of which happened. As late as the summer of 1947 Stalin actually informed his political allies in the eastern zone, to their chagrin, that they would have to accept a unified country under great power control.[45] While resisting purely economic unification, Moscow (alone among the occupation powers) pressed for central government and countrywide parties and unions, thus causing the American political representative considerable concern that the West would seem the perpetrator of continued division.[46] In addition to the facilitating of reparations, the Soviet Union probably expected good political returns from this policy.[47] The initial land reform in the eastern zone had improved the communist position there, and when the socialist and communist parties were then forceably merged into a type of popular front party, it was probably in order to have a pro-Soviet political presence in the anticipation of an all-German assembly. It is noteworthy, however, that this unity party was outpolled by the Social Democrats in the aforementioned Berlin elections of 1946, and that various election results elsewhere indicated only limited communist allegiances.[48]

There was, to be sure, considerable support in the country for socialization (even the Christian Democrats initially proposed it), but American and British authorities on the spot were cognizant of how very slim was the support for Soviet communism. The signs were in fact strong that "totalitarian" sentiment had diminished considerably, that if the dominant political mood was one of widespread apathy, the active minority was one vocally in favor of democracy.[49] The population was hence in a more receptive state of mind from a Western standpoint than Kennan, and increasingly Washington, seemed to fear. Yet the United States, after initially having had no particular policy, eventually came to counter Soviet proposals for a central government with plans for a strongly decentralized system.[50]

One might still claim that the structural—or objective—conditions were such that no German government, regardless of political inclination, could have coped, at which point space would have opened up for various "totalitarian" movements of revenge or revolution. Kennan, for example, had emphasized not only the presumably discredited democratic tradition but also the excellent organizational skills of pro-Soviet forces in destabilized situations.[51] This is a more difficult argument to discuss since it is hypothetical and we will never know how a central German government actually would have fared. In economic terms, however, it is clear that a good many of the problems consisted in the occupation itself.[52] Proper utilization and a concerted effort to reconstruct the transportation system would probably have resurrected industry in a relatively short time.[53] Agreement on a central government and immediate currency reform would similarly have created a situation most conducive to a Western commercial orientation, which, after all, was what Kennan wanted.[54] It should be said though that where an investigation of available empirical evidence would have straightened out misunderstandings about the political situation, the economic ramifications were more difficult to see at the time.

This brings us finally to the crucial subject of reparations. While the Kremlin must have been deeply concerned with the future political complexion of Germany, and certainly expressed strong interest in its demilitarization and decartelization, the first item on the Soviet agenda appears to have been the extraction of reparations. This is evident from their economic policies in the eastern zone, which was reconstructed with remarkable speed to make reparations possible.[55] The discussions about Germany at the Allied conferences indicate similar priorities, for beginning with Yalta the subject always figures prominently in the Soviet negotiating position.[56] All parties had agreed in principle that the Soviet Union was entitled to reparations in view of the frightful material damage that had been inflicted, estimated by American intelligence at almost $36 billion (1945 dollars).[57] The question was therefore straightforward: how much, from where, and when? The problem eventually proved to be fraught with controversy, only the most salient aspects of which can be dealt with here.[58]

The United States had been amenable at Yalta to substantial Soviet reparations and had consented to using the figure of $10 billion as a starting point for discussing final amounts. This sum subsequently became a bone of considerable contention. Washington gradually began to consider it an arbitrary number of little relevance to the actual proceedings, while Moscow felt, with some justification, increasingly cheated. A second problem was the cessation of reparations—plants to be shipped to Russia—from the American zone in May 1946. Since no agreement on economic unification was forthcoming, Clay simply stopped dismantling the plants, and the whole process thus came to an immediate halt.[59] On account of bad experiences in the eastern zone Moscow had by then lost much of its initial enthusiasm for this kind of reparation, subsequently focusing greater attention on what could be extracted from current industrial production, a form that had been formally agreed to at Yalta and not repudiated at Potsdam.

The United States, for a variety of mostly ill-founded reasons, was adamantly opposed to reparations from current production. It was believed, first, that such payments in themselves had been the basic problem in the collapse of the Versailles system of reparations in the 1920s, whereas the destructive aspect had actually been the amount and method of payment. It was also erroneously believed that the United States ("the taxpayer") had been left to pick up the bill; but if anyone had in fact picked up the bill, it was Wall Street speculators.[60] Third, and most important, Washington (and London) stubbornly maintained that Germany would be incapable of paying such reparations. This misconception was to some extent the result of overestimating the devastation of Germany's industrial capacity, which, in contrast to housing, had not suffered nearly as extensive a destruction as everyone (except the Russians) had thought. Urgent economic problems in the western zones, for instance the import and food deficit in the American zone, obviously also played a role by making the crisis seem more fundamental than it was. The United States, though it must have known the truth to be otherwise, attributed these problems directly to the reparations that had been made to the Soviet

Union, whereas the difficulties actually stemmed mainly from the British incapacity to get coal production in their zone properly into gear and from the general interzonal impasse. At any rate the historical lesson drawn from all this was that reparations from current production would either mean depression, political chaos, and totalitarianism or, alternatively, that the United States would once again have to "pay up," which was neither fair nor possible since Congress was already grumbling about having to cover the zonal deficits.

What seems extraordinary about these American misconceptions now is that there was a fair amount of contemporary evidence to challenge them. The Federal Reserve Board, the OSS, and John Maynard Keynes had all stated clearly on different occasions before the end of the war that Germany would be capable of paying reparations from current production. Clay himself, fully aware of the importance of the issue, suggested a cost-benefit analysis of a settlement on these grounds with Moscow, but to no avail. Indeed it was well known to the American side that a deal on economic or some other form of unification of Germany would be possible if the issue of reparations were settled. The Russians seemed willing to settle (for, say, $5 billion), and Germany would have been capable of paying: the demand was for reparations without interest over a period of twenty years, and by 1950 West Germany alone was able to pay $1 billion a year for Berlin and the NATO forces. As it turned out, the Bundesrepublik never paid any reparations to the Soviet Union. Even if the American taxpayer had ended up footing the bill, the cost would have been a bargain in comparison with the sum spent since then on keeping a quarter of a million American troops in West Germany, a sum by now probably exceeding $100 billion.[61]

Marshall, who became a leading proponent of the unbending American stance,[62] chose in the spring of 1947 to offer a sum equivalent to no more than what the Soviet Union could take out of its own zone in six months, a wholly unrealistic proposal. At the London Conference of Foreign Ministers at the end of the year he retrenched further, stating flatly that there would be no unification of Germany at the price of reparations, though Molotov at that point had agreed not to link the two issues directly, insisting only that both should be considered. Thus the CFM ceased for all practical purposes to exist; the British immediately began to maneuver in the direction of a Western alliance; plans for currency reform in western Germany were set in motion; Stalin decided to turn the eastern zone into a Soviet-

style system and then responded to the divisive currency reform in the
western zones by blockading Berlin: the cold war had begun in earnest.[63]

The argument here is simple. Seen from the limited perspective of
Germany, the United States need never have given up on the eastern
zone or knowingly pushed partition as it did.[64] Britain and the United
States controlled by far the greatest part of the resources and population in the country, and there was every reason to believe that a
unified Germany would have been not only politically oriented toward
the West but also capitalist in structure. Consequently, I think the
United States committed an enormous tactical error. Partitioning Germany might have been in the American interest in some other sense,
but before delving into that question we must return to Kennan and
the developments leading up to his "conversion."

Kennan never understood the significance of the reparations issue
when it was at stake and, as far as I know, has not recognized it since.
During the spring of 1945 he had to face it momentarily when the
reparations commission created at Yalta met in Moscow and he was
called upon to comment. He made two arguments: (1) that the Russians would advance enormous demands based on political rather than
economic criteria (the same argument he had once made about Soviet
trade), and (2) that the whole problem eventually would boil down
to horse-trading: "How much are we going to make available to the
Russians from our zones, and what price are we going to demand for
it?"[65] After suggesting that the United States and Britain should determine a price, he failed, unfortunately, to pursue this intriguing line
of thought, thus leaving the question a rhetorical one. Henceforth,
insofar as he thought about the problem at all, he seems to have
considered the Soviet claims ridiculously high, evidently put forth for
some ulterior political purpose rather than on the expectation of
reaching agreement. Indeed he took the Soviet requests at the 1947
Moscow CFM—where the original demands, scarcely outrageous in
themselves, had been moderated—as a sign of Kremlin procrastina-
tion, a tactical move to delay agreement while conditions in Europe
were deteriorating into crisis and chaos.[66]

In this assumption he was at one with his new chief, General
Marshall, whose similar reading of the Moscow experience—his initial
taste of negotiating with Molotov—was a determining factor in setting
the Marshall Plan into motion.[67] Looking back after this, as he rightly

considered it, bold political strike had been executed, Kennan offered the following typical assessment:

> Now, it is significant that the Russians showed no real disposition to come to an agreement over Germany last winter. They realized that the meeting of the Conference of Foreign Ministers was not the last that would take place; that there would be another one coming up this fall. They must have expected that in the meantime *their* negotiating power would increase and *ours* would decrease. Why did they expect this? Because, in the first place, they expected the outbreak of a severe economic crisis in this country which would deprive us of our economic negotiating power; and in the second place they thought that they controlled positions in Western Europe through which they could make it impossible for any real program of United States aid to Europe to be evolved and accepted and successfully promulgated. This being the case, they were confident that by fall fear and unrest and despair would have increased in Europe to a point where communist influence would have become dominant, where this country would have nothing more to hold on to, and where we would then be compelled either to accept a German settlement dictated by Russia or to abandon the field and permit Russia to have her way in Germany and Austria, and indeed in all Western Europe, regardless of us.[68]

There is no need to repeat earlier arguments that much of Kennan's understanding of Soviet intentions vis-à-vis Western Europe was mistaken. Noteworthy here, however, is that the Soviet analysis—mainly associated with Eugene Varga—of the capitalist world economy had not been quite what Kennan indicated. Varga's views had varied, but on the whole he had not predicted any acute capitalist crisis. Pointing iconoclastically to factors such as government intervention, he thought that capitalism would be able to stabilize in the short run. He had become a controversial figure in 1947, but the dispute was not resolved, at least publicly, to Varga's detriment until the end of the year.[69] By then Molotov and his eighty-nine assistant in Paris had understood that nothing would be forthcoming from the Marshall Plan as far as the USSR was concerned; Zhdanov had been sent off to organize the Cominform; and there were signs that Moscow had reassessed the situation and seriously begun to retrench.

Why Kennan thought Moscow's reparation claims so stupendous in size as not to be taken seriously is a good question, since he was aware of the damage done to Soviet society: "Remember that the destruction they had in their country was absolutely staggering. *It ran in the billions and billions of dollars.* I would imagine it makes the Marshall Plan figures look pretty small."[70] To this essentially correct estimate may be added that starvation had been widespread during the preceding year.[71] But instead of following his own (and Clay's) counsel and investigating what the Russians would in fact be prepared to pay politically in return for the kind of reparations they desired, Kennan instead repeated his dire prognostications:

> This amputation of Germany['s] eastern territories must surely have left a country seriously crippled and unbalanced economically, and psychologically extensively dependent in the first instance on the great land power to the east which controls or holds great food producing areas so necessary to German economy. It seems to me unlikely that such a country once unified under a single administration and left politically to itself and to the Russians would ever adjust itself to its western environment successfully enough to play a positive role in world society as we conceive it . . . I am sure Russians themselves are confident that if a rump Germany west of Oder-Neisse were to be united under a single administration, there would be no other single political force therein which could stand up against Left Wing bloc with Russian backing.[72]

It should be said that in this period he seems not to have followed German developments to any greater degree, a fact that casts considerable doubt on the basis for his often sweeping characterizations. The comparatively few pronouncements he made on Germany between mid-1945 and mid-1947 were more concerned with preventing unification under conditions deemed encouraging to the undemocratic German spirit than with any ponderings on what might constitute a possible settlement with Moscow.[73] Such a settlement was indeed excluded, for all practical purposes, by the manner in which he posed the alternatives: "We insist that either a central German authority be established along lines that will make it impossible for the Soviet Union to dominate Germany and tap its resources, or that we retain complete control over the western zones of Germany."[74] Since he had been arguing that conditions were such that the Russians would be in an excellent position to dominate Germany politically, it followed that a central government should never come about and that the country ought to be partitioned.

His policy proposals thus remained every bit as negative as they had been before the end of the war. Typically speaking of a "barrier to further advance of Communism from East to West" and of "walling [the Germans] off against eastern penetration," he not only stood firm against the Soviet suggestions for unification but, in May 1946, actually went so far as to propose unilateral American scrapping of the Potsdam Agreements. He thought that "plenty of justification" could be found for such a course of action but did not explain what it might be. Very much in the spirit of partitioning he subsequently included western Germany as a central part of his version of the Marshall Plan, stressing the importance of German coal for European recovery.[75]

In the fall of 1947, however, he began to show increasing sensitivity to the implications of the German problem, though his basic position remained the same: "The vital issue of world politics, particularly in relations between this country and Russia, is the German settlement. There are many questions and issues which will affect the future of Europe; but I can think of no single factor that will be of greater importance than the future of Germany. On Germany's future will probably depend the future of Austria, quite possibly of Czechoslovakia as well, and in general the nature of peace in Europe."[76] He also started to consider what, all things being equal, the Soviet attitude toward a properly democratic Germany would be: "It is now more unlikely than ever that the Russians would be willing to take their chances on a genuinely democratic, united Germany. Such a Germany, if it were to withstand communist penetration and domination, would like present day Czechoslovakia, exercise a highly disruptive influence on communist power in eastern Europe."[77] This signified a subtle shift from the simple supposition that the Russians would have a fairly easy task in Germany to the growing realization that they might face severe difficulties with a unified Germany that managed to survive expected problems. From this he did not as yet draw the obvious conclusion that the West ought then to explore very seriously how one might actually bring about a Germany that could exercise such a disruptive influence. The issue for Kennan remained, it seems, quite theoretical: since a democratic, unified Germany would clearly not be in the Soviet interest, pursuing a deal was useless. Consequently he voiced no opposition to Marshall's absolute refusal at the fatal London CFM in late 1947 to consider reparations from current production together with the proposal for economic unification.

By then another aspect of the problem had assumed importance in his outlook. The essential premise was plain enough. "It is unlikely," he said, "that approximately one hundred million Russians will succeed in holding down permanently, in addition to their own minorities, some ninety millions of Europeans with a higher cultural level and with long experience in resistance to foreign rule."[78] Provided, then, that the West managed to resist the attack in Western Europe on the Marshall Plan initiative, there was good reason to believe that Moscow would have to face the facts eventually and come around to serious negotiations. Extolling the Marshall Plan to a group of businessmen, Kennan described the prospects: "I predict to you confidently that within six months we will be able to do business over the table with our Russian friends, about the future of Germany, and about a number of other matters. A balance will have been restored on the Eurasian continent."[79] With all due allowances for the propagandistic occasion, Kennan had a tendency to exaggerate Moscow's future need to settle accounts because he also underestimated Moscow's capacity to keep the ninety million Eastern Europeans down.[80] As he wrote in April 1948: "The real truth is that the Russians can less afford to rest on the present line than can the free countries. They know it; and that explains the savage recklessness and the urgency with which they are now acting. We therefore do not need to draw up any programs for the defeat of Soviet power, if we can only be successful in the policies we are now pursuing. The Russians will defeat themselves."[81] This was no small mistake on his part. In point of fact it robbed his strategy of one of its basic components, the notion of a subsequent negotiated agreement on Europe favorable to American interests. If the Soviet Union could get along without having much to do with the West, there was naturally little impetus from a Soviet viewpoint to negotiate damaging agreements or indeed to negotiate at all. Molotov told Marshall as much in London: "It is impossible to talk to the Soviet government like you talk to the present Greek government."[82]

The possibility of a complete freeze Kennan was still unable to foresee. He was in effect proposing something close to what later became known as the policy of negotiating from a position of strength, the underlying implication being that present deals would mean an intolerable acknowledgment of bloated Soviet power. Hence the policy of waiting for that elusive moment, never seemingly quite reached, when preponderant strength would be achieved and the USSR would have to recognize its proper (and allotted) place in international life.

Kennan's views on Germany at this stage were well summarized in PPS 23, an important, broadly conceived policy document issued in February 1948. Its premise was that Western and Central Europe inevitably would face one of three futures: Russian domination, German domination, or a federation "into which parts of Germany" were integrated so that it could not dominate.[83] Naturally, Kennan argued, the last solution would be best, but unfortunately the Germans were in no mood to accept partitioning: he found them "sullen, bitter, unregenerate, and pathologically attached to the old chimera of German unity." The American example had made little impact, and to force partitioning in these circumstances would be to throw "the German people into the arms of the communists." The most likely political outcome would be "polarization into extreme right and extreme left," neither of which would be agreeable from the American standpoint. From all this Kennan then drew an inconclusive conclusion: "Our possibilities are therefore reduced, by process of exclusion, to a policy which, without pressing the question of partition in Germany, would attempt to bring Germany, or western Germany, into a European federation, but to do it in such a way as not to permit her to dominate that federation or jeopardize the security interests of the other western European countries." What this meant with respect to partitioning is hard to say. Perhaps his equivocation merely expressed an intention of quietly letting the process of splitting Germany into two (as opposed to several) parts run its course. Regarding other aspects of occupation policy, he repeated with some vehemence his old convictions and proposed a few new steps: integration of the German—or, as the case may be, western German—economy to maximum effect into the European economy at large; analogously ending the separation of the German people from Western Europe; termination of "psychologically unfortunate" policies such as de-Nazification and reeducation, indeed the removal of the large American establishment itself since it had been unable to exert much moral influence; and elimination, for similar reasons, of military *government* and introduction of greater responsibility for the Germans, though military *occupation* might have to become a "quasi permanent feature of the European scene."[84]

In this last prediction Kennan proved a more clairvoyant observer than he probably anticipated. Aside from its ambiguity on partitioning, PPS 23 reveals a great deal of continuity in his position on the German question. The misreading of German sentiments, more receptive and less "unregenerate" than he would allow, is once again striking.

By the time PPS 23 had been distributed in the State Department, the initial moves had already been made toward the very type of

Western federation that Kennan did not favor: NATO. This development had an important effect on his policy toward Europe and the
Soviet Union, but in order to understand the connection, we must
widen the inquiry by examining his general conception of American
strategic and tactical interests.

Containment, it will be recalled, was originally little more than a
proposition that since the Soviet Union represented interests inimical
to the United States, the latter had better do whatever was necessary
to prevent this power from further expansion. The concept did not
signify a worked-out strategy or tactics; nor, for the duration of 1947,
did Kennan and the Policy Planning Staff, as they expressly admitted,
develop any such thing.[85] They did, however, have a clear notion of
their priorities, which can be summed up in one word: Europe. The
whole Marshall project was thus initiated, on Kennan's part, because
of a pronounced concern with European and Western civilization, the
survival of which Kennan considered vital for the United States itself.
Germany, moreover, was considered extremely important on account
of its historically powerful role and its potential resources; indeed
denying the Soviet Union control over this prized area was a basic
reason for his opposing unification. Yet there was no systematic concept of the why and the wherefore of American foreign policy, and it
was only after Kennan had been subjected to some stinging criticism
that anything of the sort would emerge.

Mr. X had become a public figure and was increasingly the target of attacks for what he was presumed to have said and not to
have said. The most penetrating fusillades emanated from Walter
Lippmann, who in the fall of 1947 chided Kennan for having advocated a static strategy of encirclement. This was not an unreasonable
reading, but we know that Kennan really did not think in those terms.
Of greater interest now is that Lippmann also spotted a central weakness in Kennan's assumptions, the notion that diplomacy would necessitate some form of intimacy or proximity before it could be productive. On the contrary, Lippmann rightly retorted, diplomacy is not
about intimacy but about the ironing out of concrete problems
through bargaining. He went on to suggest mutual troop withdrawal
as the best area for negotiation: since the central Soviet asset was
armed strength in salient European positions, it seemed natural to
focus attention on how to rid the continent of that presence. An
agreement on troop withdrawals would allow a different political
situation to emerge and would have the added advantage of being

readily verifiable. It would be a tangible, unequivocal process, not subject to squabbles like the Yalta agreement on a democratic Poland. Moscow had also in principle agreed to negotiations on the matter.[86]

To this Kennan had no particular response when he belatedly took the occasion of an illness in the spring of 1948 as an opportunity to answer Lippmann's attack. He merely reiterated that a policy of shoring up what was already there would put such a strain on the USSR that in time negotiation on qualitatively new and different conditions would follow.[87]

If the columnist's critique of his negativism pointed in the direction of negotiations (and so partly coincided with the position of the left), there was also increasing dissatisfaction on the right. In September 1947 *Life* magazine published an article explicitly advertised (probably in error) by the editors as a critique of the "passive" containment policy.[88] What was actually said in this piece may be left aside, with one exception: the essence of world affairs, according to the author, was the balance of power, the pivotal components of which were a limited number of identifiable power centers around the globe; and American policy should be geared toward keeping these centers in balance. This, in a way, was only to restate a traditional precept of international politics, but in contrast to the bipolar image of the world then increasingly in vogue it represented a multipolar outlook. Kennan took this element to heart and quickly reinterpreted the Marshall Plan precisely as a move to restore the balance in Europe.[89] No doubt he had generally considered that to be the case even at the time when the plan was conceived, but the *Life* article placed his sentiment in more evident strategic form.

We are now, chronologically speaking, at the end of 1947, and events are developing in a direction very much opposed to Kennan's incipient strategic view. The London CFM has capsized; Moscow has decided, probably, that in the absence of agreements the alternative is relative isolation and then goes on by means of the Prague coup to abort the prospect of an unfavorable election in hitherto fairly pluralistic Czechoslovakia; Great Britain and the United States decide for all practical purposes to go ahead with a unified West German structure; Ernest Bevin broaches in vague terms the idea of a Western federation, and John Hickerson of the European Division, serving as temporary liaison in London with the British, becomes an instant devotee of the project.[90] The military vision gains increasing acceptance.

When Bevin brought up the subject of federation more formally to the United States in January 1948 it was primarily in the context of Western Europe and, ostensibly, the defense against Germany. However, a vital if partly veiled part of the project was to include the United States in some military capacity, a goal to which the British most likely had aspired ever since the end of the war, perhaps ever since the previous one.[91] Kennan, unaware of this aspect, was as an old federationist favorably disposed toward the initiative but had reservations about its military orientation. A Western European union led by France and Britain would certainly be the prerequisite for "restoring the balance of power in Europe without permitting Germany to become again the dominant power," but the starting point should be a "political, economic and spiritual union," not a military one. Beginning with a military object would only frighten "outlying" regions such as Scandinavia and complicate inclusion of Germany. "I am afraid," he wrote to Marshall, "there is a tendency among Bevin's subordinates to view it too much as just another 'framework' of military alliances." Instead Kennan wanted to include some basic "economic and technical and administrative arrangements" and a measure of "real federal authority."[92] This early reaction to the British overtures was to prove the beginning of his sustained opposition to the militarization of policy.

Soon afterwards, in PPS 23, Kennan returned to the problem of a Western European federation in the context of an idea he had first mentioned during the summer of 1947: a sort of intimate Atlantic union, prompted by "the logic of history," between the United States, Canada, and Britain.[93] As conceived, his scheme would not have been readily compatible with Bevin's initiative on Western Europe. Recognizing that, Kennan found himself in a bit of a quandary:

> In my opinion, the following facts are basic to a consideration of this problem. 1. Some form of political, military and economic union in Western Europe will be necessary if the free nations of Europe are to hold their own against the people of the east united under Moscow rule. 2. It is questionable whether this union could be strong enough to serve its designed purpose unless it had the participation and support of Great Britain. 3. Britain's long term problem, on the other hand, can scarcely be solved just by close association with the other Western European countries since these countries do not have, by and large, the food and raw material surpluses she needs; this problem could be far better met by close association with Canada

and the United States. 4. The only way in which a European union, embracing Britain but excluding eastern Europe, could become economically healthy would be to develop the closest sort of trading relationships either with this hemisphere or with Africa.

It will be seen from the above that we stand before something of a dilemma. If we are to take Britain into our US-Canadian orbit, according to some formula of "Union Now," this would probably solve Britain's long term economic problem and create a natural political entity of great strength. But this would tend to cut Britain off from the close political association she is seeking with continental nations more vulnerable to Russian pressure.[94]

Solutions to this dilemma were not readily available. One possibility, he suggested, was to bring Britain and the eventual European union as a whole closer economically to the United States; another might be to solve the economic problems by a common European development of colonial areas in Africa (though he had doubts, with good reason, about the feasibility of that project). But whatever the chosen route, he concluded, it was ultimately imperative to back Britain's proposal if "the main purpose" of the Marshall Plan was to be fulfilled, the main purpose here presumably being the resurrection of a Europe, or at least a Western Europe, without communism.[95]

The reference to the Marshall Plan was not accidental, for it was in the explicitly political terms of that move that Kennan wished to envision Bevin's initiative. The economic impact of the aid had been less important to him, as we recall, than the possibility of putting the Russians and their political cohorts on the defensive where this could profitably be done. It had been, in short, a specific action in a specific arena, both of them chosen with care.

It is against this background that one should consider another and somewhat contradictory aspect of PPS 23: it also included an implicit attack on the notion of alliances as such, an attack introduced as part of what was in fact Kennan's first systematic "realist" critique of American foreign policy. To be more precise, because he himself was a part of that policy-making effort, the critique concerned only one of the two underlying strands he identified in that policy: the "universalistic approach." Based on an all-encompassing "pattern of rules and procedures which would be applicable to all countries," universalism was not conducive to "solutions related to the peculiarities in the positions and attitudes of the individual peoples." It eliminated, in its simplicity, the need to understand specifics and to find "political solutions," the need, in short, to deal with the existing world as it actually was; and for that very reason it also enjoyed wide support.[96]

The "particularized approach," by contrast assumed "that the content is more important than the form" and "counterforce" rather than legal structures is the best way to deal with "the thirst for power." While not opposing "entirely the idea of alliance," it insisted that such formations be "based upon real community of interests and outlook" and not on any "abstract formalism." It followed that instead of starting with "the periphery of the entire circle" (the universalist United Nations), one ought to begin with "the center which is our own immediate neighborhood—the area of our own political and economic tradition," and proceed outward.

By this "tradition" Kennan seems to have meant, in the first place, the maritime group of English-speaking nations referred to earlier, and only secondly a greater group of what he called "the older, mellower and more advanced nations" for which "order, as opposed to power," was a value. These were the nations capable of that "combination of political greatness and wise restraint which goes only with a ripe and settled civilization," the sole possible basis for "a truly stable world order." Kennan's problem, not explored here but posed later with increasing frequency, was whether there was really anything terribly "ripe and settled" about the United States.

Kennan's particularism can be seen, as the term itself implies, as a pure negation of the projected opposite, universalism, although, given his characterization, there was something self-serving about the whole operation. Be that as it may, the polemic against proponents of a universal order of legal equality between states, "the theory of national sovereignty as it expresses itself today in international organization," certainly had implications beyond the simple denigration of the UN; for any extensive alliance system was bound to be laden with a measure of "abstract formalism."

Having made serious objections in PPS 23 to a military alliance, Kennan then let the matter rest while he journeyed to Japan. He did not return until April, only immediately to fall ill from exhaustion. For almost two months he was thus absent from the centers of power.[97] Events meanwhile moved rapidly ahead. Bevin and his European collaborators proceeded with what was to become the Brussels Treaty, officially a Western European alliance against Germany. Britain and Canada then went on to instigate secret trilateral talks with the United States about military collaboration, the enthusiastic Hickerson playing a leading role on the American side. The result was the so-called Pentagon proposals, which came to be the basis of the future NATO Treaty.[98] When Kennan reentered departmental circuits, the argument seemed to be less about whether a defensive arrangement would be a good thing than about what form it ought to take.[99]

As the emphasis in the West, especially in Europe, came increasingly to rest on defensive alliances against a putative Soviet offensive threat, Kennan focused his attention instead on what he considered a much greater threat, namely the indigenous communist parties. Writing just before the Italian elections, he outlined the problem as essentially one of European incomprehension: "The peoples of western Europe could do away with two-thirds of their own danger if they would face up to the problem of their own communists. Instead of this, they sit around and tremble before the prospect of an invasion which may never come, and which certainly would never have come if the problem of domestic communism had been dealt with promptly and incisively in the immediate post-hostilities period."[100] Whether the Europeans were as naive as this may well be doubted. Those among them who were actively pushing the United States toward a strong military commitment to a Western alliance probably suffered from few delusions about immediate Soviet attacks, using an inflated image of the latter instead as an intelligent way of achieving steady American protection for the future. This would make the American role altogether more predictable than before the war and no doubt also lessen the cost of defense.[101]

Somewhat surprised by the situation, Kennan repeated his basic stance and added that fixation on "the military aspect of world affairs" tended to be a self-fulfilling prophecy since "the more present differences are talked about and treated as a military problem the more they tend to become just that." While his argument (since then often repeated) in this instance was directed primarily against those who wished to reform the United Nations into a functional military force, he was making a point against wide alliances in general:

> There are few conceivable acts of aggression in present world conditions which would not automatically involve the vital interests of this country. Conversely, if this country were to become involved in a military effort, few of those other nations whose association would be important to the issue of the contest could afford to remain outside it. Insofar as our world problem is one involving questions of military security, the answer lies overwhelmingly with ourselves:

in our decisions, in our own actions, in our disposal over our own great strength, not in what we do with respect to other nations.[102]

At first, however, he assumed erroneously that the British and the French were primarily interested in military coordination. Thus, he concluded: "What the Western Europeans require from us is not so much a public political and military alliance (since the very presence of our troops between Western Europe and the Russians is an adequate guarantee that we will be at war if they are attacked) but rather realistic staff talks to see what can be done about their defense."[103] His logic may have been impeccable, but this was not quite what the Europeans had in mind.

Kennan began to grasp that his position was out of tune, and eventually he and Bohlen felt obliged to put their names together with Hickerson's on a paper that essentially cleared the way for a wide type of military alliance. The aims were formulated in a manner that reveals why Kennan went along: "To strengthen [the determination of the free nations of Europe], to resist aggression, to increase their confidence that they can successfully do so, and to reduce the risk of war by deterring any government from attempting further aggression through confronting it with evidence of collective determination, including that of the United States, to resist."[104] The order here is symptomatic, for what seemed essential was not the necessity of resisting any Soviet attack—highly improbable, as everyone knew—but the imperative to bolster "confidence" and "determination" in Europe. In other words, if there was a significant internal (and thus external) political threat, as Kennan maintained, and the Western European regimes insisted that a military umbrella was needed to infuse the requisite political will and confidence, then it was more or less irrelevant that the likelihood of a Soviet attack was very nearly nil: opposition to preparatory talks about an alliance, the immediate question at hand, would have to be based on some other grounds. A couple of weeks after Kennan had signed the document, he was actually encouraging such talks as a means "to keep the ball rolling and keep up the hopes of the peoples in Europe."[105]

When such talks got under way in Washington during the summer, Hickerson spearheaded the American effort while Kennan and Bohlen participated only occasionally.[106] Some of the sharpest disagreements arose not with the foreign representatives but within the American contingent itself. Kennan's role was effectively reduced to trying to delimit the geographical scope of the proposed alliance to the North Atlantic area proper. He opposed the inclusion of Italy and countries that were either close to the Soviet sphere or nonmilitarized.[107] He proposed, to no avail, "gradated" forms of membership and a more decentralized version with different "anchors."[108] Hickerson worked tirelessly and ultimately successfully for maximum extension, parrying Kennan's arguments with an intelligent mixture of practical objections and tactical retreats.[109] Contributing heavily to Hickerson's victory, however, was the fact that Kennan had conceded the original argument: if one accepted the imperative of creating political confidence, it was hard, all things being equal, to deny that confidence might indeed be generated by extending the alliance, whereas, conversely, what confidence there was might be imperiled by excluding potential candidates.

By the autumn of 1948 Kennan had come to understand the essential nature of this logic and break with it in no uncertain terms, for all things were in fact not equal. He was willing (he had little choice) to accept NATO as a kind of psychotherapy for nervous Europeans who did not "understand correctly their own position" in the face of a political threat. NATO would "contribute to the general sense of security in the area," though, as he pointed out, this therapy would also fuel the already widespread "preoccupation with military affairs" on both sides of the Atlantic and lead people "to take their eye off the real ball."[110] Yet he refused to invest the proposed alliance with any fundamental military significance, arguing along realist lines that "legalistic commitments" should not influence when and where one state chose to assist others.[111] Most important, he adamantly opposed letting the confidence thesis become a license for limitless expansion:

> The admission of any single country beyond the North Atlantic area would be taken by others as constituting a precedent, and would almost certainly lead to a series of demands from states still further afield that might be similarly threatened. Failure on our part to satisfy these further demands would then be interpreted as a lack of interest in the respective countries, and as evidence that we had "written them off" to the Russians. Beyond the Atlantic area, which is a clean-cut concept, and which embraces a real community of defense interest firmly rooted in geography and tradition, there is no logical stopping point in the development of a system of anti-Russian alliances until

that system has circled the globe and has embraced all the noncommunist countries of Europe, Asia and Africa.[112]

To this powerful argument there was, to my knowledge, no real reply; Hickerson for one dodged the issue by seemingly agreeing in reasonable terms that there ought indeed to be limits and so forth, but adding that if, on a practical level, he could only have Italy included, he would willingly exclude Greece and Turkey.[113] As we know, the North Atlantic was in due course conceptually extended to the eastern border of Turkey, and thus things proceeded apace until, under John Foster Dulles, the American pact system became the global circle Kennan had foreseen with such precision.[114]

By the end of 1948 Kennan had arrived at a much clearer idea of what the United States could and should do in the world, or perhaps more accurately what it could not and should not do. During the first half of 1948 his critique had been focused on the military overemphasis. Now, propelled by the dual pressure of the drift toward an extended anti-Soviet alliance and the formidable attacks generated by Chinese failures and domestic election campaigns, Kennan began to stress the theme of inherent limits. Central in this development was the question of Germany and its partitioning.

What position Germany, or parts of it, would have in relation to a possible Western alliance was still not resolved. The Brussels Treaty had supposedly been conceived as a defensive alliance against Germany, and the matter remained a sensitive one, particularly in France. Sentiment within the administration was unclear, though Hickerson had typically come to the conclusion early on that western Germany should eventually be included in the alliance.[115] The PPS was to have analyzed the German problem during the winter and spring of 1948, but Kennan, as we saw, was dispatched to Japan instead.[116] The complete breakdown of the Allied Control Council, the ensuing Berlin crisis, and the Western decision in June to let West German elements go ahead with a constituent assembly for state-forming purposes all rendered the need for an overview even more urgent. In August, too, the four occupying powers convened in Moscow in an attempt to resolve the precipitated crisis. At Bohlen's prompting Kennan and the PPS thus undertook during the summer the task of sorting out the ramifications of the German imbroglio.[117]

This effort resulted in a major change of outlook for Kennan, marking the end, for one thing, of his desire to partition Germany and, equally important, the beginning of a more realistic policy toward the Soviet Union. His transformation took place against the background of a series of important turns: the Berlin crisis, which indicated that the Soviet Union was not about to retreat from Germany, but revealed too beyond the shadow of a doubt how widespread pro-Western sentiment was among the German public; the trend toward a militarized concept of foreign policy in the West; the right-wing attack on the administration for its lack of success in China; and above all the Titoist challenge to Stalin's omnipotence in the East.

Having considered Tito one of Stalin's most faithful acolytes, Kennan must have been extremely surprised by this crack in the Soviet armor. At any rate he had little to say about it by way of causal analysis, but he counseled, probably correctly, a middle course between overt support and total disinterest so as not to furnish Moscow with any propaganda ammunition.[118] Yet the event must have raised some basic questions for him about the European situation and the possibility of a Soviet retreat, perhaps suggesting encouragement of non-aligned political forces as a way in which this might be approached.[119] Very shortly after the Tito split became public, Kennan began to stress that "it was necessary to look forward to changes in Europe in the long run which would permit a general unification of the whole continent."[120]

His first great memorandum on Germany from this angle, PPS 37, submitted to the State Department on August 12, 1948, was a long dissection of the advantages and disadvantages of breaking with the negative program the United States—and Kennan himself—had hitherto pursued: a program of continuing "with a divided Germany, holding the line with our own forces and our own prestige while we endeavor to strengthen western Europe." On balance he now found it desirable to put forth a more creative proposal: the United States should not "let the important decisions depend entirely on the action of others." At some future date both sides would have to withdraw; the question was therefore one "of timing." He further assumed that such a withdrawal, rather than four-power control, was the only way in which Germany could be unified. Pointing to what he perceived as the enhanced Western political status in Germany and to the novel disarray within the Eastern sphere, Kennan took the bold step of proposing a settlement based on indigenous German rule. Such a settlement *would avoid congealment of Europe along the present lines.* We can no longer retain the present line of division in Europe and yet hope to keep things flexible for an eventual retraction of Soviet power and for the gradual emergence from Soviet control, and entrance into a free European community, of the present satellite countries . . . If we carry on along present lines, Germany must divide into eastern and western governments and western Europe must move toward a tight military alliance with this country which can only complicate the eventual integration of the satellites into a European community. From such a trend, it would be hard—harder than it is now—to find "the road back" to a united and free Europe . . . It is my feeling that if the division of Europe cannot be overcome peacefully at this juncture, when the lines of cleavage have not yet hardened completely across the continent, when the Soviet Union (as I believe) is not yet ready for another war, when the anticommunist sentiment in Germany is momentarily stronger than usual, and when the Soviet satellite area is troubled with serious dissension, uncertainty and disaffection, then it is not likely that prospects for a peaceful resolution of Europe's problems will be better after a further period of waiting.

To propose a settlement was of course also to abandon the notion of a partitioned Germany. The old objections to unification remained, he admitted, reiterating that the optimal solution would have been a federated Europe "into which the several parts of Germany could be absorbed." This was unfortunately unfeasible because "of the tragic east-west differences which now divide Europe" and the incapacity on the part of the Europeans to create such a federation. The absence of agreement on Germany hence forced "by a sort of iron logic" the former Allies to give power back to the Germans.[121]

PPS 37 was not well received. Hickerson and the European Division opposed it, not surprisingly, as unsafe and unpredictable in its effects, though the main cause of rejection may well have been that it would have put into question the whole alliance project.[122] There was little unequivocal support, but intense work on the German problem, partly with outside consultants such as Hans Morgenthau, was nonetheless carried on by the PPS during the autumn, culminating in a long and specific proposal released in mid-November. Its essentials were mutual withdrawal to certain garrisoned areas, a provisional government, and free elections, all based on the assumption "that anti-communist forces [could] probably win a working majority in any reasonably free national election at this time and hold it for the foreseeable future."[123] Reactions to this ambitious paper were no less cold or hostile than they had been to PPS 37, and it was allowed to die a bureaucratic death.[124]

Once Kennan had made the decision to support a settlement, it was only natural that he should also begin seriously to consider the position of the other side. Though he assumed that the USSR would probably not agree to any equitable proposal, he also explicitly conceded that such a proposal would have to give the Russians "certain safeguards," for instance German demilitarization.[125] He understood too that the American negotiating position of cordially inviting Moscow to merge its zone with the West German system was not in fact a negotiating position but a demand for "complete capitulation." Instead he recommended that "legitimate Russian interests and requirements" should be given "reasonable" consideration.[126] The problem with this was that the Russians might well have to "insist on unreasonable advantages, because without unreasonable advantages they cannot hope to maintain any influence at all." Seeing the issue in that light, Kennan acknowledged that Germany was as important to the Soviet Union as it was to the West, and moreover that Moscow's "fear of western superiority" there had some substance.[127] Predictions of easy Soviet penetration had thus become a thing of the past.

With his newfound interest in agreement Kennan was particularly apprehensive of policies that would put the Russians in a situation where they could not "withdraw even when they have come to the conclusion that it would be to their own interest to do so."[128] "We could do this by overemphasizing and making too deep the line of division down the center of Europe: by failing to hold open the door for ultimate settlement in Germany and central Europe, or by concluding so sweeping and far-reaching a system of military alliances as to overshadow all other issues in Europe and leave no room for any gradations of influence between the Russians and ourselves."[129] By implication, then, these things were already taking place. Certainly, he warned, an extended version of NATO would be a fatal step. If every participant associated with the Marshall Plan were eligible to join NATO, the line of demarcation would become entirely militarized:

> Such a development would be particularly unfortunate, for it would create a situation in which no alteration, or obliteration, of that line could take place without having an accentuated significance. This would reduce materially the chances for Austrian and German settlements, and would make it impossible for any of the satellite countries even to contemplate anything in the nature of a gradual withdrawal

from Russian domination, since any move in that direction would take on the aspect of a provocative military move.[130]

If, in other words, the planned anti-Soviet alliance were to stretch all the way up to the Elbe, Moscow could not be expected to agree to any divestiture of responsibility in the East, whatever the costs of maintaining domination there, for the likely alternative of having the dominated country in question join this alliance was obviously even worse. Kennan's proposal for a unified Germany should thus be seen as a *strategic* move designed to create a neutral opening—"a third force which can absorb and take over the territory between the two"[131]— for Soviet-dominated nations on the verge of freeing themselves from their "unnatural" subservience. Without such an opening, only one of two things could happen: either there would be a stalemate, a total impasse; or there would be a disorderly breakdown of Soviet authority in the East, in which case a war of desperation would become a significant risk.[132] Neither prospect appealed. Despite exaggerating Eastern instability, Kennan had thus pinpointed the underlying logic of the subsequent European order with great accuracy.

Integral to his new outlook was a sharper definition of global priorities. In August 1948 he mentioned the Atlantic community, the Mediterranean, the Middle East (including Iran), Japan, and the Philippines as "vital" to American interests.[133] Soon, however, he recast this argument in terms of the five areas that possessed the military-industrial capability of launching modern warfare on a grand scale. In addition to the United States they were the British Isles, Europe, Russia, and Japan. Nothing much beyond this configuration was of more than peripheral interest to the United States, whereas, conversely, everything was at stake in keeping up a certain balance of power within it. Above all, it was absolutely necessary to prevent a unified continental bloc of Russia and "Europe" (for which read a German-dominated Central Europe).[134] The continuous disintegration of the Chinese regime, however lamentable, was thus a matter of indifference, since the area seemed unlikely to become a military-industrial power of note in the foreseeable future.[135]

Much of this argument can be recognized from before: the importance of Germany, the danger of allowing an extension of any great European land power. Strategically it was indeed largely a reformulation of the classic British approach to European politics.[136] Yet the singling out of five central areas of the world had wider implications. Kennan, we should remember, was inclined to delineate American interests within the larger framework of the West, the survival of whose civilization he always put before everything else. His horror at the prospect of internal Western warfare was of long standing; and the same basic concern for the welfare of Western ways of life had underlain his desire to avoid war with the Soviet Union. These considerations had now crystalized: war between any of these five areas, all situated in the northern temperate hemisphere and "relatively accessible to us in the psychological sense," would inevitably put the survival of the whole into question: "Since war on too vast a scale between the great existing power centers of the world can produce results catastrophic to the advance of civilization in general, as a result of technical progress, we must indeed try to see that at least *those* wars do not develop which could have these consequences."[137] The necessity of avoiding another Great War, a necessity rendered all the more graphic with expanding nuclear arsenals, has been Kennan's primary concern ever since this moment, around 1948 or 1949. Never altogether absent from his mind after the experience in Weimar Germany, it became the explicit axiom of his thinking about foreign policy. In this respect it is of particular interest that he included the only antagonistic force among the five centers, the Soviet Union, in the category of "relatively accessible" people and thus perhaps also in some diffuse way part of the civilization to be preserved.

The German issue was revived in a different form at Kennan's instigation in January 1949, but by then he had assumed the air of a dejected and alienated man.[138] Doubting that "we as a Government have ever made a firm determination of our view of the long-term future of Germany," he suggested half-heartedly a West German administration as a last-ditch alternative to the state and government then about to come into existence.[139] Dean Acheson, the new secretary of state, was actually quite open-minded on the subject, wondering "how we ever arrived at the decision" to create such a government; and Kennan was sent off to inspect the occupied country.[140] He returned a resigned policy planner. He had finally understood that, contrary to official policy, "we do not really want to see Germany unified at this time, and that there are *no* conditions on which we would really find such a solution satisfactory." Correctly and with no little bitterness he added:

> The wide area of agreement reached among ourselves here in Washington and with the British and the French in Paris has been achieved by the steady and progressive discarding of all possibilities which

might really have led to something like a unification of Germany under allied blessing, at the present time . . . [W]e spent eight weeks last fall working out what we felt would be a logical program for advance toward the unification of Germany. Piece by piece, in our deliberations here and in the concessions we have made to French and British feelings in Paris, the essentials of this program have been discarded, and the logic broken up.[141]

What had ruined his logic more than anything else was the movement toward a rigid anti-Soviet military alliance. In 1952, near the end of his ill-fated ambassadorship to Moscow, where, incidentally, he had been sent without instructions save that of avoiding the subject of Germany, Kennan issued a singularly poignant epitaph for American policy on that country.[142] Describing events around 1948, he mused over the Soviet reaction to the absence of an American proposal (like his own) to settle:

[The Russians] were probably puzzled by our failure to press for precisely this sort of solution. Had the circumstances been reversed, and had their cause, instead of ours, had the unquestioned political support of by far the larger portion of Germany, they would surely have been howling boldly and incessantly for the withdrawal of troops, the removal of the division of Germany and the immediate creation of a free German political life. That we, with what must have seemed to them our immense political advantage in Germany, failed to pursue this course and preferred to proceed instead to the rearmament and "integration" of Western Germany, must again have seemed to the Russian mind a policy going beyond what could be explained by mere timidity and caution, and presumably motivated by other and more sinister considerations.[143]

He was still not entirely sure why the United States had decided to divide Europe, or, putting it more charitably, to go along with those Western European politicians for whom this division was the happiest of all available solutions. That the West had no desire to reach agreement on any grounds other than complete Soviet capitulation had been evident to him already in 1949; but it was not until the harrowing disengagement controversy he sparked off in the late 1950s that he would understand the deeper logic behind this position.

Faced with overwhelming American sentiment to the contrary, Kennan persevered after 1950 in his criticism of extended alliances, in his opposition to the inclusion of West Germany in NATO, and in his advocacy of negotiations with Moscow on Central Europe.[144] Meanwhile, the official standpoint, staunchly proalliance and globalist, shunned the concept of containment in favor of what was purported to be a more active policy, the idea of "liberation" or "rollback" in Eastern Europe.[145] How, amidst the rhetoric, this was actually to be achieved was not altogether clear; and a quick glance at the map today reveals that it was wholly unsuccessful in achieving the stated aims. Kennan went in the opposite direction. As a true conservative, by the mid-1950s he had come to accept the Eastern European regimes as "real" and reasonably stable entities, from which observation he concluded that "liberation" in this region could come about only through a gradual development away from the Soviet Union and toward internal freedom.[146] It followed that a Western attempt should be made to facilitate such a gradual process.

The Western alliance did no such thing. Indeed, its compact negativism in the immediate post-Stalin period arguably squandered another opportunity to improve the overall European condition.[147] Kennan sensed this, as transpires from his reaction to the Eastern European events of 1956:

> If no major security considerations were involved—if there were no Atlantic Pact and United States forces were not in Europe—if the Soviet leaders did not have to fear that in releasing these eastern European peoples to a greater freedom it would merely be consigning them to inclusion in a hostile military bloc—then I think there is real question whether they would consider it desirable and expedient to insist on maintaining over eastern Europe the same hegemony that they are exercising today . . . [If we want to keep these countries in their place, we should thus continue] to manifest no serious interest in any European settlement and to cling steadfastly to our present German position. So long as we refrain from showing any interest in such a settlement, the Russians will have no choice but to continue as best they can their tragic effort to repress the national feelings of the Hungarians and the others and to keep them within their orbit.[148]

This, very roughly, was how the situation seemed to him when, during a visiting professorship at Oxford, he prepared to give the Reith Lectures on the BBC.

These lectures, in late 1957, offered Kennan a very substantial British audience, and he seized the opportunity to restate his position on a series of outstanding issues, among them German unification, the political nature of the competition with the Soviet Union, and the strategic irrationality of nuclear weapons. The particulars may in the main be passed over here, for essentially he repeated, with great force and clarity, what he had said in 1948–49. On two points, however, he expanded his earlier views. The argument had been advanced that mutual withdrawal from Germany would be disadvantageous for the West since its military forces would be farther removed than Soviet troops. Kennan contested this, emphasizing the underlying fixation on what was extremely unlikely, a Russian attack, and the concomitant failure to see the military advantages of a Soviet withdrawal as well as to take into account the unreliability of satellite armies in the East. He stated too that he had come to realize after some time in West Germany that the new generation of Germans was more interested in material welfare than in the primordial nationalism he had previously posited (on dubious grounds).[149]

What was extraordinary about the Reith Lectures was not so much their content but the public reaction. As the German historian Ernst Nolte later wrote, these lectures elevated Kennan "to the highest level of notoriety which the western world can confer in the political-intellectual field."[150] There was much sheer denunciation. Kennan was (wrongly) accused of advocating the unilateral scrapping of NATO and assorted other errors.[151] Dean Acheson, prominently featured on the front page of the *New York Times*, ridiculed him and emphasized that these views had nothing to do with the Democratic party. The *Times* itself took the widespread criticism as a hopeful sign that the United States might be "recovering from its old sickening isolation-ism."[152] The Socialist International, by contrast, voted overwhelmingly to endorse Kennan's views, and the Labour left in Britain was sup-portive.[153] Why there should have been such an uproar is, on the face of it, difficult to understand. Perhaps the moment was one when the cold war had lost some of its velocity and inherited truths seemed stale. If nothing else, the ferocious attacks by the Western establish-ment indicated a certain lack of confidence, a sense of vulnerability, a fear that Kennan's standpoint would find resonance.

What, then, was actually said against Kennan? Dean Acheson dis-missed the disengagement thesis, as it became known, with shopworn arguments such as the notion that "a thriving Western Europe would continue its irresistible pull on East Germany and Eastern Europe" and thus presumably render agreements unnecessary.[154] A more note-worthy critique was published by the prolific Harvard professor Henry Kissinger. Errors and misrepresentations notwithstanding, Kissinger made the substantial point that withdrawal and neutralization might actually turn discontent in the East into open revolution and thus be self-defeating in Kennan's own terms. Hedging his bets somewhat, Kissinger also argued for a set of positive and constructive Western proposals that would not "undermine legitimate Soviet interests"; but what he actually meant was that while there would be no Western withdrawal, the Soviet Union would be given assurances that no territory from which *it* withdrew would be used for anti-Soviet military purposes. I doubt that Moscow would have found this a constructive proposal. Kissinger's main objection, however, was a reverberation of Hickerson's view from 1948: the whole idea was risky and unpredictable and thus best avoided. The existing state of affairs was relatively stable, so why change it?[155] Both Raymond Aron and Walter Lippmann agreed, pointing out in more sympathetic language that neither of the two superpowers had any interest in giving up a perfectly satisfactory system of mutual hegemony, and that, therefore, Kennan's suggestions were fairly pointless.[156]

This last response apparently rendered Kennan speechless.[157] It had not occurred to him that the negative stand of the United States might not be based on the assumption that the division would and should disappear. He had noted the American disinclination toward negotiations and agreements that implied compromise, but he had not analyzed in depth why this was so. To put it bluntly, he had not posed the fundamental question whether the interests of the United States might not in some way best be served by leaving the Soviet sphere to its fate, perhaps using it symbolically to justify whatever the United States wanted to do elsewhere in the world. The singular enemy, hemmed in on the Eurasian landmass, arguably served exceedingly well as an open-ended justification for the enormous American expansion—political, economic, and military—that took place after the war, as a mechanism, in other words, for the United States to defend vigorously its global interests and to intervene without compunction wherever intervention was felt necessary. Moreover, the sealed line of division may have suppressed tendencies toward radical transformation in Western Europe, not only because of the American military umbrella but also by thoroughly changing the political climate. The price paid, indefinite Soviet control over Eastern Europe, must have seemed rather a bargain in this light. From the Western European vantage point, the extensive American military guarantees reduced uncertainty and afforded more resources to spend elsewhere (including on colonial wars), in addition to which the arrangement eliminated the unpleasant problem of an all too powerful Germany in the middle of Europe.

It is somewhat odd that Kennan should have failed to see this line of thinking since it approximated in some important ways what he himself had said before 1948. He too had stressed the uncertainties in letting politics have free play in Central Europe. He too had argued for the partitioning of Germany as a method of coming to terms with the recent historic dominance of this troublesome nation. He too had seen the division, the creation of a "barrier" against the East, as a way of ensuring stability and allowing breathing space for Western civilization.

Yet one must bear in mind that Kennan's perspective had been a temporary one and that he had expected, after some initial period of settling down and arranging forces, a future moment of negotiation. This notion of an interval of no diplomatic interaction was, as Lippmann had emphasized, a major mistake. Kennan had never been able to imagine in the immediate postwar period that the United States would soon play such an extraordinarily dominant and successful role. He had always had contempt for American universalism, which he identified with the United Nations and various legalistic schemes. That it would succeed in building worldwide military alliances based on crusading anticommunism he could not envisage. Nor did he quite realize the nature of the new world system that was about to emerge, the advent of American-led transnational capitalism in which power equations would assume a different meaning from those of the epoch of readily identifiable nation-states. I shall return to this point later. My conclusion here will be limited to some remarks on American interests in relation to the specific problem of Germany and disengagement.

One might respond to the disengagement thesis by acknowledging it as essentially accurate but deplorable. The very fact that American and Allied interests would be served by this policy would then be the reason for opposing it. This is a coherent position but irrelevant in Kennan's case, since he was arguing from the premise of advancing American interests. The issue, then, has to be approached by asking the largely hypothetical question, In what sense could those interests have been better served by the different course of action he was proposing? Kennan did not answer that very well because the whole thing seemed obvious to him, and he failed to see how far his thinking about those interests diverged from official ideas. This much can be said, however:

"If a settlement can be reached" on Germany and Austria, Kennan had noted, "the face of Europe will change overnight."[158] This seems probable. There is at any rate no doubt in my mind that a settlement with Moscow was possible. Prior to 1948 a reasonable offer on reparations and demilitarization might substantially have put an agreement through, although Kennan never recognized that possibility. The indications are that by early 1948 Moscow had given up, but its resignation was defensive. In fact for several years the Soviets attempted to reach agreement with the West, first in order to avoid a West German state and then, when that had become hopeless, to prevent West German rearmament and membership in NATO.[159] A program like Kennan's might well have been a realistic basis for negotiation even if, admittedly, it did come late in the day and contained nothing constructive about reparations.

A settlement, however, would have entailed a much more limited NATO or something in the nature of what Kennan preferred—that is, a kind of unilateral declaration that certain areas in Western Europe were vital to American security and not in any way to be touched or pressured. It would have required, too, unequivocal lecturing to the British and (especially) the French, underscored by a certain amount of economic blackmail. This could have been done had the will existed. A nonmilitary customs and coal federation might have been an integral part of the deal, provided it was clear that the United States was not a member.

Furthermore, the emerging, unattached, and demilitarized Germany would probably have espoused a social-democratic or centrist type of capitalist system. Given the staggering American dominance of the capitalist world economy, which was certainly obvious by 1947–48, and the inherent need for financial assistance, a transformation would have ensued in the direction of consumer culture and Western ideology. (Despite belief in the superiority of "free enterprise," Americans tend paradoxically to underestimate the intrinsic cultural and political power of the commodity.)

Such a Germany, though powerful, would scarcely have constituted a vacillating entity in the middle or a vacuum into which the USSR and the United States would inevitably have been drawn in destabilizing intrigue, as if carried along by some physical force. A strict hands-off policy in the military-political sphere would, in the situation sketched, have been in the interests of both powers, since the critical factor was not German support in itself but, negatively, the necessity of preventing the other side from obtaining it.

The effect on Eastern Europe is unclear, but assuredly a nonaligned capitalist Germany (and Austria) would have been less threatening to the Soviet Union than was now the case, and the repressive imperatives thus commensurately less pronounced. Assuming a certain diminution of world tension, the Soviet system itself might well have had a less painful evolution toward becoming less rigid and hostile.

Germany would in any case have had an easier task in penetrating the region economically. The world capitalist market would have been enlarged, bringing indirect benefits in power and economic influence to the United States. Against this, it must be admitted that a united Germany would have become an even more formidable competitor than the Bundesrepublik.

Finally, the arms race might have occurred anyway, but probably in less accentuated and ludicrous form. The budget on both sides would have been very different. The respective treasuries would not have been burdend by keeping twenty-five divisions facing one another in Germany for four decades. More important, of course, the United States (and much of the world) would perhaps not have had to live under the constant threat of immediate total extinction.

Whether the enormous expense incurred through the arms race actually served to stabilize—indeed expand—the economic system and was thus in some sense worthwhile, and whether the development of weapons of instant mass destruction has in turn served to deter a major war and thus been worthwhile as well I leave to the reader to decide. On the thirtieth anniversary of the Reith Lectures, I must nevertheless note that disengagement has once again become a term of political currency, that the division of Europe is now once again being questioned on both sides, that the "unnatural" might indeed eventually have to give way to its opposite, to some new and as yet unimaginable reality.

Kennan differed from most of his colleagues on the German question because he thought that a settlement would lessen the chance of war by making Soviet retraction in Eastern Europe easier. He feared that the politics of universal anti-Sovietism would lead an immature nation into an uncertain world leadership that might in some ultimate and primordial sense not be in its own interest. For him, at any rate, the universal was always abhorrent, destructive of the intimate and the naturally continuous.

5

Dark Continents

Kennan was a man of the North. Born and raised in Wisconsin, married to a Norwegian, he did not, metaphorically speaking, take easily to cultures and climates south of the Alps. Not even in established cases of implanted "Western civilization" was he without misgivings. That huge and heterogeneous area to which we now simply refer as the Third World was for him in the profoundest possible sense a foreign space, wholly lacking in allure and best left to its own no doubt tragic fate.

He was fortunate enough in this regard never to have had to experience a diplomatic posting farther south than the comparatively proximate Lisbon.[1] In consequence he had, on taking charge of the Policy Planning Staff, little experience and knowledge of the Third World, a state of affairs accurately reflected in—indeed an impetus to—the northern military-industrial focus of his strategic thinking.[2] His infrequently expressed but fairly straightforward views on the subject will be examined here in two parts, divided chronologically by his departure from the State Department in 1950.

"The older cultural centers of Europe," wrote Kennan in one of his first PPS studies, "are the meteorological centers in which much of the climate of international life is produced and from which it proceeds."[3] Restoring these centers, then, was axiomatically prior to everything else on the agenda, and the chief aspect of this primary task was obviously the exclusion of the Soviet Union from any material influence over the area. The agenda was otherwise rather amorphous, but, as I explained earlier, political problems arising out of the Chinese situation produced a sharper sense of what was at stake relative to the Third World. The position Kennan began to formulate in the latter part of 1948 can be summarized as hawkish in theory and dovish in practice, not necessarily a contradictory combination.

His fundamental premise was clear. The United States, he observed, enjoyed remarkable material privilege in a world where the gap between population and resources was growing ever more acute. At the same time, older patterns of life in the Third World were being shattered at an increasing pace. Resentment and turmoil would result, much of it anti-American in spirit and direction. That the United States would be subjected to hostility from "a jealous and embittered world" was therefore not in doubt: the question was how to deal with it.[4]

Here Kennan situated himself in stark contrast to what he called "a sort of rotarian idealism," by which he probably meant a liberal, muddle-headed American universalism, espousing firm belief in a legalistic world system and in the efficacy of prodigious doses of aid.[5] Against this, so to speak, imaginary adversary he advanced a whole series of arguments.

First, he said, economic aid, a typical American panacea, is ineffective. For one thing, unless it can be conducted on a "total" level, as was the case domestically during the New Deal with the Tennessee Valley Authority, little can be accomplished. In fact "the margin of starvation" being constant, ordinary aid tends to perpetuate the basic Malthusian predicament, since more food causes a commensurate increase in population, resulting in even worse conditions. Nor does aid inevitably bring any great political returns in terms of gratitude and popularity, for communist or anti-American sentiment is not just a product of bad economic conditions.[6]

Second, in a larger sense there is little reason to suppose that the United States constitutes a realistic model for political, economic, and cultural development in the Third World. Conditions in North America are unique, hardly lending themselves to global reproduction. Furthermore, contrary to a common American assumption, people are not everywhere essentially the same. Teleological expectations that "lesser developed" peoples are destined over time to become more similar to Americans are consequently likely to end in disappointment.[7]

Third, if people and nations are not everywhere the same, it is also unrealistic to conceive of the United Nations as a place where the states of the world will coalesce and act more or less like "good schoolboys on the bench and vote the right way and pursue as we do a stable world in which there will be pretty much a preservation of the status quo through juridical promises not to be violated." The future political representatives from the Third World, cynical and venal coteries aside, will probably be either Soviet-inspired regimes or exponents of "the fanatical and childish passion of native nationalism." In both cases the leadership will be distasteful and anti-Western.[8]

Finally, the United States has on the whole been incapable of producing coherent policies for distant lands and is unlikely to become much better at it forthwith. Its capabilities in these parts of the world are in fact considerably less potent than often thought, for Americans, unlike Russians, are limited by their inability to use crass propaganda, by lacking a "savage will to power," and by genuflecting toward giving rather than demanding. Above all, the United States has "not found a medium of communication, a language, with which to speak to the backward and poverty-stricken peoples of the world," a language that would seem as sensible as "phoney Marxism" does to them. Besides, a "satisfactory and fruitful and hopeful relationship between ourselves and the colored peoples in other parts of the globe" will always be difficult to achieve as long as the domestic race issue remains unresolved.[9]

A comment on these criticisms would not be amiss. Kennan was undoubtedly right in underlining the limited effects of economic aid and, as I take it, the need for concomitant structural changes if aid is actually to be given: the TVA model suggested some degree of social surgery. His skepticism about the United Nations as a political space functioning within essentially American perimeters was also well founded, for he foresaw the moment when the organization would be dominated numerically by forces, mainly from the Third World, much less willing to support the status quo. Yet in assuming a vicious Malthusian circle he was, I think, wrong: population levels in the Third World are not simple products of the amount of food available for consumption; and ethical imperatives aside, relief aid of this type can be, at least in the short run, an effective means of applying political pressure, should that be the aim.

Whether the universalist viewpoint in the naive form Kennan imputed to it ever had such dominant influence is doubtful; he had a tendency to see "idealism" where there was in fact a fair amount of raw and "realistic" power. And to the political implications of the other side of liberal universalism, the notion of free trade and unlimited economic penetration of the world, he was not very sensitive.

One should note that a deeply felt discomfort with American culture played an important, if often implicit, part in Kennan's argument. Whenever he sensed overconfidence in American materialism he could be very scathing indeed: "There will be no room, here, for the smug myopia which views American civilization as the final solution to all world problems: which recommends our institutions for universal adoption and turns away with contempt from the serious study of the institutions of peoples whose civilization may seem to us to be materially less advanced."[10] Unconvinced of the virtues of his own culture, he was obviously reluctant to see them bestowed indiscriminately on others.

Relentless pessimism is otherwise the pervasive impression. Not much, seemingly, could be done except to steel oneself for the day when the hungry masses of the world would come storming the rich fortress. This is perhaps in our present context the most significant aspect of his thinking, for his critique as a whole appeared to be an argument for doing less, or at least less of what Americans were generally inclined to do. This still left him with the original problem of what, if anything, was to be done to counter the projected increase in worldwide anti-Americanism. His recommendation, broadly speaking, was power politics: the United States should protect unhesitatingly its privileged status and the fertility of Western civilization by whatever means necessary: "Our real task in the coming period is to devise a pattern of relationships which will permit us to maintain this position of disparity without positive detriment to our national security. To do so, we will have to dispense with all sentimentality and day-dreaming; and our attention will have to be concentrated everywhere on our immediate national objectives. We need not deceive ourselves that we can afford today the luxury of altruism and world-benefaction."[11] Similarly he argued that "we must bring all our national power to bear, with clinical coldness and objectivity, to obtain conditions more favorable than those we have today to the survival of western civilization." The "aspiration to 'be liked'" is utterly futile, and all "talk about vague and . . . unreal objectives such as human rights, the raising of the living standards, and democratization" should be discarded. Policy ought to be based on "straight power concepts"

and aimed at pitting the country's numerous foes against one another.[12]

These were words of menace, apparently implying a very different
form of policy from what might have been imagined in view of
Kennan's earlier critique. Yet the actual direction of policy he distilled
amounted more or less to laissez-faire. There were two fundamental
reasons for this. In the first place the "rotarian idealism" against which
he had positioned himself had the character of an ideal type, which
thus called for an equally pure alternative, an abstract, dialectical
countertruth: "straight power concepts." Like containment, it was a
theoretical proposition not to be confused with concrete policy, in
which domain one might find it wise to assume the posture of "restraint" he had recommended in the case of China.[13]

His reasoning here was ultimately based on the realist premise,
already mentioned, that no nation in the Third World was capable of
producing military-industrial power worthy of serious consideration.
The only five regions with such capabilities belonged to the northern
temperate zone, and while peace among these important centers was
absolutely vital to the interest of all, wars "among peoples that are
rather tribes than nations" did not as a rule constitute cause for grave
concern.[14] Despite rising anti-Americanism, then, Third-World events
were not especially important.

Having settled that basic point, Kennan could look with a certain
detachment at the problem of what actually should be done in the
realm of realpolitik and "clinical coldness." The most extreme measure
was presumably military interventionism, but such a costly course of
action the Third World was scarcely worth. On the contrary, this
approach would have the counterproductive effect of mobilizing the
indigenous population around the very forces one wanted to liquidate,
in addition to which it often caused havoc with world opinion. Better,
then, to leave these nations to their own developmental logic while
maintaining no illusions about the nature of their inclinations.[15]

Kennan's second line of argument in support of restraint was quasi-
ethical in nature and thus partly contradictory to the principle of power
politics. I am referring to the warning he issued in the spring of
1947—one that, it should be said, he did not often reissue—that "an
ill-considered intervention, not clearly founded in American tradition,
would constitute a precedent which . . . might have a demoralizing
influence on our whole foreign policy and corrupt [our] basic decency

of purpose."[16] One might view this as in the best realist tradition: "decency" was an undeniable fact, and military intervention would in some sense violate this reality. Still, it can be reconciled with the notion of "clinical coldness" in pursuit of "immediate national objectives" only with the greatest difficulty.

This internal tension can be seen in a major analysis of early 1950, written after Kennan had been sent to Latin America on his one and only extensive trip to the Third World. He had returned steeped in gloom, having suffered, among other things, the ignominy of being burned in effigy in Rio de Janeiro. A lengthy report followed. Disclaiming pretensions to solid knowledge, Kennan introduced his subject with a battery of generalizations about the basic tragedy of Latin America and its Hispanic culture. Though in themselves interesting and revealing, these considerations were of minor relevance to the question of policy, which he discussed in the more direct context of possible communist or anti-American revolution.[17]

Surveying the scene from this angle, he found the chances of communist success very limited except in Guatemala. He noted too the peculiarly Latin American character of these communists (not, it seemed, as disciplined as their Soviet-style colleagues) and the fundamental fact that a single communist regime in itself would constitute no real threat to the United States. In fact, he suggested, the emergence of such a regime might be the only way to demonstrate to the gullible just how abominable was this alien system. Having said that, however, he changed his tone markedly and went on to paint a dire image of widespread anti-Americanism and an "inner core" of "fanatical, disciplined, industrious" communists "armed with organizational techniques which [were] absolutely first rate." The threat was assumed to lie mainly in "clever infiltration of key positions" rather than "conquest of mass support" (an assumption not borne out, incidentally, by the few subsequent instances of radical change in the region, which have been the result of either guerrilla war or electoral victory).[18] There being no cause for "complacency," the question then was how to produce conditions that would "impel the governments and societies of Latin American countries to resist communist pressures."

His basic criterion for acceptability in this regard was that a regime show "a recognition of communist penetration for what it is, a will to repel that penetration and to throw off communist influence, and effective action in response to that will." The nature of that "effective action" was a practical matter for the local regime to decide: "We cannot be too dogmatic about the methods by which local communists can be dealt with . . . [One must] concede that harsh governmental measures may have to proceed from regimes whose origins and methods would not stand the test of American concepts of democratic procedure; and that such regimes and methods may be preferable alternatives, and indeed the only alternatives, to further communist successes." Promoting democracy in the course of encouraging anticommunism would thus be pointless, except insofar as the United States constituted a living example. For if policy were to proceed "on the basis of a moral discrimination addressed to the internal-political personality of Latin American regimes," the outcome would be merely "a steadily increasing responsibility for the domestic affairs of those countries." Instead the United States ought to demonstrate that tolerance of domestic communism would bring "hardships and disadvantages." This, for Kennan, was the point where the "ethico-traditional" problem arose: "Our policies in recent years have greatly circumscribed our possibilities for inflicting hardships. We have forfeited—and rightly so—the right and the intention of any form of military intervention. Except in extremity, any direct pressure brought on Latin American countries in any internal issues where the detriment to the United States is not directly and immediately demonstrable, holds great dangers." Still, these regimes had to be brought to understand that the United States was "a great power" and "by and large much less in need of them" than vice versa. Thus, they ought simply to be told this:

> [We Americans have] a selfish stake in the preservation of your national independence and integrity which you should recognize as being of greater significance and importance to yourselves than any altruistic assurances of treaty undertakings which we could possibly extend to you. We expect, recognizing this, you to realize, then, that in matters of war and peace and of state security . . . your interests lie with ours, for reasons wholly practical and geographic, having nothing to do with any cultural or ideological affinity; and you should be careful not to wander too far from our side . . . We hold out to you what perhaps no great power . . . has ever held out to neighboring smaller powers: the most scrupulous respect for your sovereignty and independence, the willing renunciation of force in our relations with you . . . But you will appreciate that the payoff

for the unprecedentedly favorable and tolerant attitude is that you do not make your countries the sources or the seats of dangerous intrigue against us, and that you recognize that relationships no longer governed by the sanction of armed force must find their sanction in mutual advantage and mutual acceptability.

Beyond this postulated and quite minimal common interest in preserving "independence" by rejecting communism there was for Kennan nothing but distance and lack of intimacy between the United States and these regimes. Although he described the latter as independent, he would hardly have considered them in any meaningful sense "free": they were alien, different, Other. Anticommunism aside, the less the United States had to do with their internal workings the better.

The question remained what to do if a Latin American country suddenly felt disinclined to recognize any "mutual advantage and mutual acceptability": whither then the "scrupulous respect" for sovereignty and the "willing renunciation of force"? Kennan had two responses. On the one hand, since the United States had no great need for Latin American countries but the reverse was not equally true, the United States could generally afford to wait out a hostile regime, putting relations on ice until reason returned. If, on the other hand, a more active policy was appropriate, then "total diplomacy" had to be employed, involving a vast array of discreet and perhaps not so discreet pressures, political or economic according to the demands of the situation and enforced throughout the administration. This, clearly, would necessitate some improvement in the existing machinery: "We should apply ourselves to the elaboration of techniques for coercive measures which can impress other governments with the danger of antagonizing us through excessive toleration of anti-American activities and would yet not be susceptible to exploitation by our enemies as constituting intervention or imperialism or illicit means of pressure." What sort of measures he was actually contemplating he did not specify, although in an unused fragment of the report concerning threatened Guatemala he ruled out "any crude and tactless form of pressure." His alternative was warnings and unofficial but complete countering of all Guatemalan interests.[19]

The potential for "coercive measures which [could] impress other governments" but not be construed as "intervention" or "illicit means of pressure" was in my view entirely imaginary. Pressure, if exerted with any gusto, was bound to be "crude and tactless." As it turned out, the United States found it necessary for the purpose of combatting radical change to develop a range of "techniques for coercive measures" that was very wide indeed.[20] A great power pressuring its smaller neighbors by means of various threats—even barring military intervention—to liquidate certain indigenous forces so as to qualify as what the great power defines as properly independent: this is in any case an imperial policy. It bears a close resemblance to the orthodox Soviet doctrine of hegemony, wherein the great power defines independence for the small nation by singling out inherently foreign political tendencies that it, the great power, happens not to like; whereupon the small nation is punished precisely to the degree that it deviates from this externally established definition.[21]

Discernible here, then, is a conflicting impulse to play power politics and yet refrain from its more extreme expressions, to find therapeutic value in a possible communist regime and yet propose policies to prevent such a regime from coming to power. However, Latin America was a special case. With no other Third World region did the United States have such close historical links, such entrenched political and economic interests. An "active" policy was thus in some sense inevitable, and the indications are that Kennan thought of it that way. By proposing an active policy he nevertheless landed himself in contradiction, revealing the impossibility of playing power politics while trying to be ethical in the precise sense he had proposed.

Toward the rest of the Third World Kennan was able to assert his original thesis that only the most exceptional circumstances would warrant far-reaching policies of any kind, peaceful or otherwise. This proviso, it should be understood, applied to the United States, not the West as a whole. Included in the latter category, the cornerstone of Kennan's view of the world, were of course those "older cultural centers of Europe,"[22] which counted among their properties a fair number of colonies; and established colonialism was a very different matter.

Kennan had nothing against the phenomenon of colonialism, which he considered, as he put it later, a historical fact, in itself neither good nor bad.[23] During his PPS period he seems to have assumed that it would continue to exist for quite some time.[24] The effect of this misapprehension on the PPS was curious. Its major planning effort with regard to the Third World—the only major effort, in fact, outside the specific problem of China—was made not in assessing the potential collapse of colonialism and the worldwide repercussions of such a development, but in investigating the potential of a collective Western European project of *recolonization* in Africa. Kennan outlined the idea in PPS 23:

> The African Continent is relatively little exposed to communist pressures; and most of it is not today a subject of great power rivalries. It lies easily accessible to the maritime nations of Western Europe, and politically they control or influence most of it. Its resources are still relatively undeveloped. It could absorb great numbers of people, and a great deal of Europe's surplus technical and administrative energy. Finally, it would lend to the idea of a Western European union that tangible objective for which everyone has been rather unsuccessfully groping in recent months.[25]

Some eighteen months later, after a great deal of exploration, Kennan had to concede that the project could not be realized for lack of both capital and willingness on the part of existing colonial powers to pool possessions.[26]

It may appear astonishing in retrospect that anyone should have entertained such a scheme, this being the very moment when traditional colonialism was beginning to experience its historical demise. Bear in mind, however, that Ernest Bevin had suggested something quite similar right before the war, and in his later capacity of foreign minister he pursued a postwar policy based on arrantly imperial premises.[27] If that could pass for a socialist foreign policy, then Kennan's position was not by contemporary Western standards as absurd as it now seems.

Aside from proposing this ill-fated idea, Kennan took very limited interest in colonialism. His view was, as I have stated, practical. Certain peoples he considered inherently dependent on account of "their very level of civilization," from which observation he concluded that carte blanche condemnations of colonialism were unfair. Nor was colonialism a universal good: independence was justified in some cases, and in others continued control was simply causing too much trouble. For example in 1947 he regarded the Vietnamese unfit for self-government ("They're still open to foreign influence," he said with unconscious irony), but two years later the French engagement in Indochina seemed to him to have become a waste of time and energy: a Vietminh victory would be preferable to having Western weaknesses interminably revealed. Likewise a "Burmese mess" was better than a "British-Burmese mess." For the double purpose, however, of excluding Soviet influence and making life difficult for the Italian communists, as he imagined it would do, he favored the return of some of Italy's colonies.[28]

That he articulated a position at all on the subject was probably induced by a fear—largely unwarranted I think—that the United States in the name of some universalist theory of national sovereignty would unduly push the "older cultural centers of Europe" toward the dissolution of their colonial structures. Such a policy would have caused damage to these elementary components of a reasonable international order and must therefore be opposed. Here he was particularly critical of what he perceived, not without foundation,[29] as the American attempt to ride two horses at once: "So far our position has been the usual one, that all we want is sweetness and light. We don't want anybody to win and we hope they will compose their differences, and we want everybody to be happy. It is as though we said we hoped neither the Army nor the Navy would win the Army-Navy game. I am afraid the time is going to come pretty soon in international politics when this government is going to have to make political choices whether we like to or not."[30] The United States did eventually make choices, sometimes, as in Vietnam, supporting (and eventually succeeding) its European allies, sometimes, as in the Suez crisis, preferring to keep its distance. As it happened, Kennan disagreed with the choice in both instances. He also disapproved, more basically, of the American tendency to eclipse these, as he liked to think of them, "older, mellower, and more advanced nations of the world."[31]

Thus he abhorred the vigorous move to establish and defend a purely American kind of informal imperial system. Presentiments of such an unexpected development began to occur to him toward the end of the 1940s, for by then he was "fervently" hoping that "our great moment as a factor in world affairs" still lay in the future.[32] So far as he was concerned the United States was a society and a nation still very much in a stage of adolescence, certainly not ready for the dominant position, even within the West, that historical disaster in the form of war had thrust upon it. A break in the natural continuity of history had, so to speak, opened up the unsettling perspective of an extremely strong but naive junior member of the Western community upstaging its seniors. However necessary the active role now was, the potential for error in playing it at such a precocious stage was clearly worrisome. Simple anticolonialism, then, would be one such error.[33]

Not surprisingly, it was the future of the British Empire that chiefly aroused Kennan's concern. No other nation except Canada was closer to the United States in culture and tradition than Britain, and such proximity constituted grounds in Kennan's world view for intimacy and wide convergence of interest. Here lay the origin of his ambivalence toward British participation in a Western European federation and his hopes for a vast British-American-Canadian maritime system, separate in space and spirit from continental Europe. Allowing the empire to disintegrate into some decentered agglomeration of nationalistic Third World regimes would obviously not be conducive to the evolution of such an English-speaking system.[34] His hopes were of course never realized, and the period of imperial conflict and decline in the 1950s caused him considerable pain, particularly because of the American reluctance to support the British.

A revealing moment in this regard was sparked off by a message in January 1952 from the newly installed Iranian regime of Mohammed Mossadegh to the effect that Britain had to close most or all of its many consulates in the country. Allegedly they were causing a great deal of interference in Iran's domestic affairs. The message angered Kennan. Addressing himself to the secretary of state, he labeled it "Bolshevik in tone, spirit and content" and accused its authors of "debasement and medievalism."[35] The rest of this communication was an interesting meditation on Third World nationalism and the Western response to it.

A major cause of the persistent Western disasters in the Middle East and Asia, he averred, was "our inability to understand how profound, how irrational, and how erratic has been the reaction generally of the respective peoples to the ideas and impulses that have come to them from the West in recent decades." This reaction had essentially been "emotional and subconscious" to the point of neurosis, a product of the problem "of status, aggravated by a burning sense of inferiority and jealousy of us for our riches and for the relative security of our position." Above all, one should not think that these "fanatical local chauvinisms of the Middle East represent a force that can be made friendly or dependable from our point of view, or one to which we would have any right to engage ourselves in a moral sense." For immediate purposes they might have to be tolerated as preferable to the alternative, a "more powerful and disciplined force of Soviet Communism"; but in the last analysis both forms were "dangerous and revolting." In case one did find it convenient to promote nationalism, it ought consequently to be done "in the cold light of calculated self-interest."[36]

The West had a right of usage, the argument proceeded, to "the minimal facilities and privileges" it had acquired over time in the Middle East; to nullify this right on the spur of the moment as Iran had done was nothing less than "preposterous and indefensible," "a dangerous distortion of the concept of sovereignty." In dealing with these neurotic regimes, therefore, it would clearly be useless "to meet them by any verbal appeal to rational processes." Only action, and ensuing "experiences," would put them in "a more sober and sensible frame of mind"; only "military strength, backed by the resolution and courage to employ it," only "the cold gleam of adequate and determined force," would stop them from ejecting the West entirely. He concluded: "What I would plead is that we make up our minds at this time precisely what—in physical terms—it is essential that we and the British hold onto in the Middle Eastern area . . . and that we then take steps in whatever manner is most suitable to see that these objects, if they are in any way jeopardized by local hostility, are militarily secured with the greatest possible despatch."[37] This barrage occasioned a reply from the departmental division responsible arguing, not without cogency, that it was a mistake to think "that Middle Eastern nationalism should be treated merely as irrational, irresponsible, anti-American and anti-Western, or, as essentially different from that which transformed the Western World, for better or worse, into nation-states during the past several centuries."[38] Kennan then closed the argument by toning down his language somewhat, maintaining "that by virtue of the drastic decline in British influence . . . the fortunes of the area as a whole are already at the mercy of these unreliable and unpromising nationalist forces."[39]

Kennan's use of the term *Bolshevik*, as distinct from *Russian* or even *Soviet*, suggests that his analytical reference point was Moscow at its most radical and defiant; thus the reiteration of his old Soviet argument that words are pointless while action—in this case meaning force—is not. In between the extremes of having a friendly chat with Mossadegh to persuade him to be nicer and of using "determined force" fell, as earlier in the Soviet case, the whole realm of politics. What remained was either a nullity or pure violence.

Kennan need not have been so infuriated about this particular instance of Iranian nationalism. It made a fairly quick, if forced, exit as the United States came to play an instrumental role in bringing back to power the much more amenable shah; though today, given the dialectical result of that successful operation, there are perhaps those who look back at Mossadegh's removal with a certain regret.[40]

In less incensed moments Kennan could recognize the "great demand in wide areas of Asia for social reform" while still emphasizing that concomitant anti-Western feelings were "irrational" and arose "from ignorance or from emotional impulses."[41] The possibility of a connection between Western interests and the perpetuation of existing inequitable social conditions did not seriously occur to him. From his perspective, on the contrary, these nationalist intelligentsias were merely replacing "the relatively mild and rapidly mellowing restrictions of colonialism or of Western influence with a new and vastly more cruel form of authority, under which—as in Russia—a great fund of traditional cultural and spiritual values [would] be sacrificed and lost, to be recaptured, if ever, only by discovery in future ages."[42]

His ire was next aroused by the Suez crisis in 1956, when Nasser, it will be recalled, unilaterally seized the canal zone and thereby caused an unsuccessful British-French military intervention of which the United States disapproved. Kennan traced this American posture to "the belief that groups of people who experience a sense of political identity ought to be permitted to select the sovereignty under which they wish to reside," a belief embedded in the very origin of the United States itself and held ever since, though temporarily denied by the northern states in the 1860s. The United States, accordingly, had labored for the dissolution of the Hapsburg empire, for the elimination of foreign spheres of influence in China, and now for the dismantling "of the entire British military position in the Middle East." Kennan commented:

> I do not mean to say that in none of these recent instances was independence justified or necessary. Change is the rule of human life. There are unquestionably times when the situation calls for the emergence of a people from a dependent status to one less dependent. I merely wish to point out that the unlimited multiplication of sovereignties is not necessarily an absolute good. It can create problems as well as solve them. And it does seem to be regrettable that in the world which clearly needs less nationalism rather than more—which needs political frameworks larger, more inspiring, involving a focus of obligation more noble than those we have known in the past— the tendency should be so predominantly to the fragmentation rather than the unification of international society at large. The old empires were at least forms of political organization that bridged the primitive barriers of language and local feeling. If they had to go, as I am prepared to concede they did at least in part, then one could have

wished that they might have yielded their places everywhere not to something smaller but something greater, or at least as great.[43]

One might well agree with him that nationalism is not "an absolute good," but it can surely be a relative good in some historical situations as a means of resisting domination. For if the multilingual, "greater" systems have typically had dominant centers and exploited peripheries, it follows that the attempt on the part of the periphery—whether colonies or Soviet "satellites"—to break that relationship on nationalist or other grounds is not only understandable but perhaps also in some sense good. It may be noted in passing that, whether for reasons of "calculated self-interest" or not, Kennan's view of Tito's struggle for national independence had been quite favorable since 1948.[44]

The discourse on sovereignty and independence was, however, only the preamble to a most important analysis of what he sensed was a new kind of situation. In the late 1940s Kennan had argued that the United States and the West could afford to let unruly regimes in the Third World bark themselves out since they were not very powerful and at any rate they had nothing truly essential to offer in the larger scheme of things. While the former premise still seemed true, Kennan now began to worry about increasing dependence on the Third World for certain raw materials. The West, he noted, "is becoming increasingly fragile as it becomes increasingly highly organized economically, so that appalling consequences could be caused by any major interruption in the flow of a number of vital commodities"· "We are promoting the farming-out into an increasing number of sovereign hands of the control over facilities and resources important to the security of ourselves and our allies and to the stability of international life generally. We continue to concede in principle that the quality of sovereignty gives each government the right to make such facilities and resources available to other nations or to deny them to other nations pretty much at will."[45] His logical conclusion was to call for increasing self-sufficiency within the West.

The area of discussion being the Middle East, one must assume that the commodity he primarily had in mind was oil. Much credit for prescience is thus due here, for the West would not grasp the potency of this argument until 1973 and the first oil crisis, at which point Kennan found reason to look back on his 1956 lecture as "the most important statement he ever made about the problems that are currently confronting this country."[46] I think that was an exaggeration, but the clarity and originality of his analysis is undeniable. There was indeed a contradiction between increasing dependence on strategically important commodities and continued recognition of sovereign rights, no matter how abstract a form the latter took. By the late 1970s, in fact, the United States had closed the theoretical gap by unilaterally issuing the so-called Carter Doctrine, which declared the Persian Gulf area vital to American security and essentially eliminated all recognition of abstract rights to sovereign control by announcing the right to intervene whenever that security came under threat.[47]

In the 1960s and 1970s, with the British empire largely a memory, Kennan transferred what interest he had in Third World problems to two very different areas: Vietnam and southern Africa. The former was of course specifically a matter of American interventionism, which he opposed vocally for several reasons: the area in itself was not important enough to justify such a huge effort; a victory for Ho Chi Minh would probably result in a regime of nationalist persuasion, in a somewhat Titoist vein; and the war was merely fuelling a rivalry in anti-Americanism between the Soviet Union and China, thus preventing improvement in the infinitely more important relations with the Russians.[48] This view was, as will be recognized, very much in keeping with his broader conception of relations with the Third World: Vietnam, in a nutshell, was not worth the trouble.

To a considerable extent Kennan's position here coincided with that of the liberal left in the United States; this was certainly not so in the case of southern Africa. The problem there was at least dual, involving Portuguese colonialism in Angola and Mozambique and the white supremacist regimes in Rhodesia and South Africa. I have mentioned his attachment to Salazar in Lisbon, and his attachment to Salazar's colonial possessions was correspondingly close. Reiterating longstanding belief, he professed not to find anything wrong in the colonial relationship per se: what mattered was the specific situation, not the general phenomenon. As he asked rhetorically: "Is it names we are dealing with, or the realities behind them?"[49] With regard to the realities in this case, he suggested in his accustomed manner that dissatisfaction might be a product mainly of "the restlessness of individual intellectuals ambitious to replace the Portuguese in the seats of power" rather than of any widespread movement among the indigenous people. If he recognized any misrule on the part of the whites, he coupled this acknowledgment with the prediction that future black rule would be scarcely better and probably worse. As far as he was concerned, "the struggle between black leader and white leader in that part of the world is without moral connotations."[50]

That the attempt to retain Mozambique and Angola would eventually be so demoralizing for the Portuguese as to result in the destruction of the Salazar regime itself Kennan could not foresee. Neither, of course, did many others. Perhaps he should have been able to consider the possibility that relations between the newly independent states and Lisbon would improve considerably once the colonial structure had been razed. His own emphasis on shared tradition ought to have encouraged such notions, in which regard France was already an obvious model. The leaders of the victorious liberation movement in Angola, for example, were largely of mixed racial origin, educated in Portugal and with strong ties to Portuguese culture.

If Kennan's support for Portuguese colonialism is not surprising, his continued friendliness toward the South African apartheid system seems on the face of it peculiar and in need of exploration. Distance in culture and tradition was for Kennan an extremely significant factor in international as well as personal life, closeness being indicated by the key notion of intimacy. Leaving practical aspects aside for the moment, one can understand therefore how the *idea* of apartheid—institutionalized separateness between essentially distant peoples—would attract him. His misgivings lay more in the direction of implementation than of the idea itself: "With the exception of the Coloureds . . . there is nothing that offends me in principle in the creation of separate suburban communities for these various groups. I am sure that most of them would prefer, in any case, to live side by side with people of their own racial origin and culture. Everything depends, as I see it, on the manner in which the concept is carried into effect."[51] Here he had a fair number of criticisms:

> The viciousness of the pass laws and their enforcement; the absurdities and extremisms of petty apartheid; the multitudinous hardships inflicted on the urban Bantu by the regime's insistence on clinging to the absurd theory of the temporary nature of their residence in the urban areas; the power and disposition of the police to ignore, almost at will, the protection afforded to the individual by an otherwise excellent judicial system; the magnitude of the disparities in wages and in public expenditure on education as between Whites and non-Whites; and the hardships worked by the recent inclusion under the strictures of apartheid of the Asians and the Cape Coloureds—the latter, in particular, a people, largely Afrikaans-speaking,

who have no culture, no tongue and no remembered history other than those of the Whites who inflict these strictures upon them.

However, considering these objections reasonably clear to all, he saw no particular need to stress them, choosing instead to emphasize the difficulties on the part of the whites in "maintaining, in the face of a large black African majority, their own historical and cultural identity," an identity for which he had a great measure of admiration.[52] In 1970, after a third trip to South Africa, he said that he had been "moved and impressed by the personal qualities of the people we met, by their warmth of character, their generous hospitality, their deep religious sincerity, their keen sense of humour, and their vigor and competence in the development of this vast and interesting territory."[53] The pronouncement was in part directed toward the very people it described, and a certain flattering quality was thus to be expected. Nevertheless it expressed a real sentiment. Kennan's ideological makeup, after all, was in a most fundamental way similar to that of the Afrikaners: strong, unwavering Calvinism. The references to "their deep religious sincerity" and "their vigor and competence" were not accidental.

While he deemed it a hopeless task to talk to the various nationalist leaders in the Third World because of their allegedly irrational, stubbornly subjective perceptions of their surroundings, Kennan did not think it similarly useless to attempt to persuade the Afrikaners, not known for their lack of firmly held convictions, of the necessity for gradual abolition of some of the most offensive aspects of apartheid. "Peaceful persuasion," was in fact precisely his recipe for resolving what he considered a predicament equally tragic for both white and black.[54]

It may well be tragic for both in some sense, but if presented with a choice, the vast majority of South African blacks would, I am sure, gladly choose to exchange places with their counterparts in the tragedy, whereas the whites probably would not. It was in any case overly sanguine of Kennan to believe the apartheid system subject to change through persuasion when he must have realized how isolated was the Afrikaner position and how extraordinarily deeply rooted—a quality he had lauded—was the belief in their God-given right to what they had. American policies in the 1980s along Kennan's lines have not been outstandingly successful in encouraging the piecemeal "amelioration" he had hoped would come.[55]

His stand on Vietnam and southern Africa did share one feature:

in both instances he opposed strongly interventionist policies, and that, if anything, may be the unifying theme of his various analyses of Third World problems. This apparently paradoxical mixture of the progressive (Vietnam) and reactionary (southern Africa) may well be said to be typical for Kennan. His was certainly not a liberal world of Western reason and peoples teleologically aspiring toward it. On the contrary, beyond the sanctuaries of Western civilization was a seething mass of starvation, jealousy, and savage antagonism, everything the West supposedly was not (or should not be). To survive the coming siege, if you will, the West would have to invigorate itself, not so much by preparing strikes against the outside as by improving existing fortifications and the conditions within the walls. Peering out from impregnable positions, the West might then state its case with reserve and dignity while letting events on the outside take their unpleasant course.

6

The Importance of Being Realistic

As an organicist conservative Kennan tended to think of international relations as living matter, like any organism sometimes developing in natural balance, at other times afflicted with disease or disturbed by extraneous elements. Artificial tampering with the natural—"mechanical," "legalistic," or "universalistic" solutions to problems of foreign policy, as arrantly exemplified for him in the United Nations[1]—he found odious, almost perverse. Moreover such schemes were unrealistic, for eventually the fundamental nature of things would reassert itself, returning to haunt and punish the conjurers of total perfection. Nature (or the real) in this particular domain was *power*, embodied in a series of states with differing interests. The reality of power might, rather as with sex, be passed over in embarrassed silence, but ultimately it would demand its due.[2]

To be realistic in these circumstances was in a way to understand the inherent limits of things, the futility (indeed blasphemy) of extending radically beyond the existing, the real. At different moments Kennan thus criticized the Soviet Union and the United States alike for being unrealistic in this sense of not acknowledging given limits. His trajectory might in fact be described, a bit flippantly, as a movement from wanting to contain the gushing Soviet flood to wanting to contain the ensuing American one. Even if he did not normally think of it as expansionism—invading the privacy of others by trying to be too intimate and gregarious would perhaps be closer to his language—he was aware by the end of the 1940s that the United

States was embarking on a course of potentially open-ended commitments around the world, and this he could not but find dangerous and unnatural.[3]

The conceptual aspect of what might then be called Kennan's realist way of being toward the world of international relations is the object of inquiry here. Since the subject matter does not lend itself very easily to narration, I shall present it thematically without much regard to chronology. In order to have a starting point, let us begin with a summary of Kennan's general critique of American foreign policy.

Casting an envious eye in late 1948 on the cohesion of the Soviet Politburo, the head policy planner of the State Department described Washington's foreign policy as "the gross product of a series of isolated and haphazard actions, uncoordinated among themselves and only vaguely related to specific concepts."[4] Issued by the man in charge precisely of consistency, this was a grim verdict, expressive of a very deep dissatisfaction with nearly every aspect of policy-making. If, at some point in the early 1950s, Kennan had been asked to condense this dissatisfaction into a couple of pages, the result might have looked something like the following[5]:

After "a hundred years of unparalleled and intellectually debilitating security" Americans are inclined to an insularity of outlook.[6] Instead of taking the world as it is, they are fond of assuming that it is, or at any rate ought to be, like the United States, and that the imposition of a universal nation-state system based on Western democracy and equal legal status is everywhere the telos of history. This universalism comes to the fore in creations such as the United Nations and is also the conceptual foundation for the expanding system of alliances based on presumed identity of interest. Unwarranted belief in the "progressive" development of various Third World nationalisms and in the efficacy of foreign aid are similarly related to this syndrome. Moreover, encouraged perhaps by the way the country was successfully put together after the revolution, Americans are likely to privilege legal principle over existing power relations. This legalism implies a moralizing attitude, for the person who breaks the law is clearly in the wrong and should be punished. Opponents tend therefore to assume the character of a total, immoral enemy stripped of human qualities.

By failing to recognize difference, American foreign policy also fails to comprehend the power realities of many foreign situations. Indeed

the very element of power in international politics is denied: engaged
in power competition, the United States likes to think it is actually
doing something else. Real contradictions are thus made to disappear
behind a curtain of universal assumptions. Policy, consequently, is
often unrealistic.

As regards government, the country has a system that originated in
a simple agricultural society isolated from the power struggles of the
world. Despite vastly different conditions now both at home and
abroad, this decentralized, if not actually acephalous, structure remains
essentially intact. Particularly obstructive here is the division of power,
necessitating "laborious compromise" and rendering tactical moves
difficult to execute.[7] In addition to being dispersed, the government,
especially Congress, is marked by extraordinary ignorance of foreign
affairs; but instead of letting those chosen to conduct foreign policy
carry on with their job, the system seems built on the principle of
perpetual and destructive questioning, interruption, and meddling.
Scandalously, diplomats are even maligned as disloyal by various in-
quisitional organs. At some point this country must decide whether
it wants leaders who can deal with diplomacy professionally or who
simply mirror what are commonly conceived of as American virtues.
Political interference, furthermore, brings in its wake the tendency to
play to the crowd at home rather than to get on with the actual
problems abroad. These vagaries of the political system make long-
term objectives in foreign policy impossible to establish, leaving mere
directions. American democracy, then, is hampered in conceiving and
executing foreign policy by widespread ignorance, lack of central authority, and unprofessional diplomatic procedure. What is more, for
ethical and other reasons the United States is incapable of using, at
least flexibly, the means of military force in peacetime. To complete
the picture, the country has no developed propaganda machinery, is
inherently bad at conspiratorial manipulations abroad, and has not
been able to use economic policy effectively. Available instrumentalities
quite clearly do not measure up to the given tasks.

Recognizing this, one must avoid schemes of worldwide alliances
and interventions, choosing on the contrary to leave much of the
world alone. Wherever so needed a balance of power might be encouraged, but the primary concern should be one's own house. The
United States, in fact, is in dire need of some internal balance, characterized as it is by overly rapid development and fierce competition
everywhere. With better internal harmony and balance, direction and
purpose abroad will follow naturally.

Everything in this ersatz account is open to debate, but let it be said at once that I find much to agree with. Structural idiosyncracies of government, universalist assumptions, ethnocentrism—all these things are characteristic of American foreign policy. Kennan tended, however, to understate the American capacity to execute with force and expedition. Thus he could visualize his country as "one of those prehistoric monsters with a body as long as this room and a brain the size of a pin" peacefully mucking about in the mud until subjected to extreme provocation, and then, when finally aroused to anger, destroying everything in sight.[8] Yet the United States had historically been fairly quick to eliminate by violent means any serious obstacles to its relentless process of accumulation, expansion, and modernization on the American continent. Nor in the postwar period has this democratic nation been hesitant in the peacetime use of military force, indeed outdoing the nondemocratic Soviet Union in that department by a very considerable margin. It is true, all things being equal, that the political structure may well be unsuitable for the business of playing dirty tricks abroad. At the end of the day it must nevertheless be said that actions of this kind have probably often been successful, less perhaps because of clever conspiracy than sheer resources and power. Still, the metaphor is not without suggestive force, and the cold war can be seen as a period of permanent arousal for the dinosaur.

Be that as it may, I wish now to investigate Kennan's alternative concepts, beginning with the domain of policy execution. What he desired there was a clear command structure capable of making unequivocal policy decisions and moving the whole machinery along with them. In this sentiment he was like diplomats everywhere, who, as he said much later, in 1977, are inclined on these very grounds to be conservative: "[The diplomat] longs instinctively for a high concentration of authority behind him—for a government which knows what it is doing, which remains in office long enough to gain the confidence of other governments, which devises wise, far-seeing policies and sticks to them."[9] By then he had given up his hope, never deeply felt, that the United States would ever achieve the smart and sleek polity he idealized. In the late 1940s he could still argue for the concentration of all aspects of national power "into the hands of a single thinking authority—a sort of political high command" that would then be in a position to exercise it "with maximum economy, effectiveness and independence of action, in the promotion of the national interest."[10]

This imaginary government of authority, however, had better be *right*. With a personal history of nearly insolent opposition to his own government, Kennan knew that there were two sides to the coin, and he was thus wary of the wrong kind of omnipotence on the home front. In describing the relation between diplomat and domestic superiors he could be quite caustic:

> The personality of his own government presses itself upon [the diplomat] with a great vividness, with a sort of inexorable and commanding finality . . . its imperious authoritarianism toward its servants; its indomitable self-righteousness; its smugness and self-centeredness; its infuriating air of optimism and unconcern; its preposterous claim to infallibility; its frequent impoliteness; its stubborn and impudent silences; its insistence on the right not to answer letters; its bland assumption that because *it* has not made up its mind, reality should be expected to stand still until it does.[11]

It was particularly the interference of considerations of domestic politics that generated his bile, sometimes inspiring him to words of considerable intensity:

> [Domestic politics often appears to the diplomat as] the distillation of all that in human nature which is most extroverted, most thick-skinned, most pushing, most preoccupied with the present, least given to a sense of historical proportion, least inclined to be animated by any deeper and more subtle philosophy of human affairs, and—by the same token—least inclined to look deeply into the realities of international life, to comprehend the relativity of all national virtues, and to grasp the need for tolerance, forbearance, dignity, generosity, and integrity in the dealings between states.[12]

Such sentiments created, as we shall see, certain problems in his concept of what foreign policy was meant to express.

In addition to clarity, consistency, and streamlined authority, there was also urgent need for people of superlative quality, especially of course an elite corps of diplomats. Oddly, given his background, Kennan was always keen on promoting the generic diplomat rather than the bookish specialist. During the Second World War, for instance, he proposed a foreign service school based on the model of West Point, replete with spartan discipline, uniforms, and, interestingly enough, time off for invigorating work in agriculture and industry.[13] What sort of curriculum this institution (almost Maoist in conception) would offer he does not make clear, but judging from later statements the projected professionalism had little to do with

learning any finite body of theoretical knowledge. "International relations are not a science," he said in the early 1950s, intimating that,
apart from avoiding all utopianism, students of the subject should be
made to read classics such as the Bible, Shakespeare, Plutarch, and
Gibbon; and for good measure they might profit too from the sort of
basic values expressed in the Princeton honor system.[14] As he put it
on another occasion: "Take young men of high qualities of intellect
and character, train them to great hardness of mind and body, to
maturity and seriousness of purpose, and to a genuine understanding
of our society with all its virtues and imperfections; then see to it that
they function and become wise in the processes of government."[15]
This was an education designed to create a type and an attitude rather
than a technician.

Where foreign lands and problems were concerned, the "genuine
understanding" seemed analogously to be a matter of feeling and
intuition, a phenomenological as distinct from an analytical form of
comprehension:

> Useful thought in the political sciences is the product not just of
> rational deduction about phenomena external to ourselves but also
> of emotional and esthetic experience and of a recognition of the
> relationship of "self" to environment. This is particularly character-
> istic of area studies: for the real "foreignness" of other countries lies
> not in a series of physical phenomena but in an atmosphere, an
> outlook, a world of imagery,—all intimately involving man's estimate
> of himself as well as of his environment,—a substance, that is, which
> can be apprehended only through experience and participation, not
> through the algebra of symbols familiar and comprehensible only to
> Americans. Thus for people who think as I do, the judgment and
> instinct of a single wise and experienced man, whose knowledge of
> the world rests on the experience of personal emotional and intellec-
> tual participation in a wide cross-section of human effort, are some-
> thing we hold to be more valuable than the most elaborate synthetic
> structure of demonstrable fact and logical deduction.[16]

The problem, then, was chiefly how to develop the right sort of
perceptions and sensitivities in the diplomatic elite, not the dissemi-
nation of technological and formalized knowledge. One detects here
the traditional conservative distrust of theory but also shades of the
intuitive understanding so typical of vitalist and hermeneutic strands
of German thought around the turn of the century.[17]

For quite some time Kennan clung to the belief that many of the ills he had found in American policy-making could be eliminated if only this sapient kind of professional were allowed to run the show alone. By the 1960s he had come to conclude, more accurately, that the prescription for "cleverer people, or more profound thinkers, at the head of [U.S.] diplomacy" would accomplish little: "Such people would soon lose the wider consensus without which their ideas and calculations could have no enduring reality." He had been persuaded that the structural barriers were simply insuperable and an intelligent American foreign policy therefore impossible, on which grounds he counseled moderation and scaled-down ambition.[18]

We may now approach the more interesting problem of what, in earlier and more optimistic times, Kennan imagined this corps of sensitized professionals would actually do. To this question he had two different types of answers, which, for want of better terminology, I shall call the general and the particular. The latter concerned diplomacy as the art of judgment, the art of judging *particularities*. For now let us hold that solution in suspension. The former, by contrast, entailed a series of claims emanating from the basic assertion that such professionals were the protectors of the national interest in the balancing of power, indeed the very operators of that process.[19] Two decisive and related concepts—national interest and balance of power—had thus been introduced and were in need of explication. Kennan came to devote far more time and energy to the former, but let us first dispose of the latter.

Perhaps because he found power an objective fact and, like Burke and Gibbon, was attracted to the idea of a natural balance in everything, Kennan seems to have taken the existence of a balance of power rather for granted.[20] Its conceptual ramifications were in any case left unexplored. He first used the notion in 1938 to describe the sort of international power relations in which the United States presumably did not wish to participate. The concept then served a fairly clear role in his various Lisbon analyses of Anglo-Portuguese relations.[21] It was also implicitly present in his whole approach to countering and containing the Soviet Union.[22] Not until the fall of 1947, however, did it assume any clear categorical role in his strategic thinking. Then *Life* published an article that singled out a series of power centers around the globe and spoke (in a confused manner) about the necessity for balance among them.[23] Kennan used this theme during the following year to articulate his latent ponderings on the five military-industrial centers and the importance of avoiding an antimaritime combination of the two great land powers, Russia and Germany–Central Europe. Here balance meant something essentially negative: preventing the emergence of a single unfriendly force of hegemonic potential on the Eurasian land mass, historically a policy closely associated with Great Britain.[24]

Kennan also used this theme, relatedly, as the particularistic counterpoint to American universalism. The real world was for him diverse and dispersed; different areas had different powers of natural dominance. In these circumstances it would be unrealistic and foolish not to let existing (or previously existing, soon to be restored) states—especially Germany and Japan—play their natural balancing role against the Soviet Union. For similar reasons he thought it would be unwise to lasso various alien powers for the purpose of constructing some universal "free" alliance; much better to let, wherever possible, hostile forces balance one another out in "internecine warfare."[25]

If that logic were applied indiscriminately, however, the result might well be similar in scope, if not in kind, to the global alliance: interventions everywhere to maintain or create various balances. This was not what Kennan was proposing, though some of his formulations, if taken in isolation, could have been interpreted that way. His overarching view, as I have indicated, was that beyond a certain configuration of military-industrial centers nothing else much mattered.

The ethical aspect raised another problem. A simple method of engineering balances by pitting foe against foe obviously threatened to end up in outright cynicism, of which on numerous occasions he had accused the Soviet Union. In fact Kennan criticized American statesmen for not having understood (and tacitly supported) Japanese efforts in China before the Second World War, the Japanese having been not only the natural power of dominance there but also the main force counteracting communism. That Japan invaded and mutilated China in the process of this balancing act was thus essentially deemed irrelevant.[26] At other times he would take the view, as we have seen, that the United States ought to do only what could be anchored in its national mores and values.[27] Still, his position remained ambivalent: "I have never advocated that the U.S. behave in any way other than one which satisfied its own moral conscience, but I am extremely skeptical of the relevance and applicability of *our* moral principles to the problems and outlooks of others, and I suspect that what passes as the 'moral' approach to foreign policy in our country is often only another expression of the serious American tendency to smugness, self-righteousness, and hypocrisy."[28] In 1972, finally, he expressly argued against cynical use of the balancing act and simultaneously stressed the negative, or limited, aspect of his conception: "If a 'balance of power policy' means using American influence, wherever possible, to assure that the ability to develop military power on the grand scale is divided among several governmental entities and not concentrated entirely in any one of them, then I think that I favor it."[29] Ultimately, in other words, Kennan adhered to a version of the concept that favored the absence of dominance, an equilibrium among the forces of the state system rather than the manipulation of those forces for the purpose of hegemony.[30]

There is nothing particularly controversial about this, but it must be said that the whole idea of balance and what it does is far from unproblematic. It is questionable whether mechanical metaphors such as balance and its concomitant equilibrium are now of any direct relevance to international relations. These concepts presuppose clearly separable entities (states) of measurable weight functioning as independent forces in a universe of mutual antagonism, either increasing or decreasing in power and recognizing throughout that they are all part of the same game. This is probably not unreasonable as a description of nineteenth-century Europe but does not necessarily apply to our present world of criss-crossing, transnational interests.[31] Kennan in fact came to recognize that his kind of balance had come apart toward the end of the nineteenth century as the conjoined result of industrialization and the rise of nationalism, though he appears to have shunned the conclusion that it had become historically obsolete and thus impossible to restore.[32]

Nor, it is worth pointing out, does an equilibrium of power inevitably mean the absence of conflict, for two antagonistic forces in world politics do not inherently neutralize each other like the positive and negative poles in an electric field. On the contrary, a case can be made that equilibrium, as opposed to hegemony, conduces to conflict. The idea of balance in this regard involves the same kind of metaphorical trap as the notion that a vacuum (for example "neutral Germany" or "anarchic Iran") by physical necessity sucks in great-power activity, generating instability and conflict.[33] The notion of equilibrium assumes too a predetermined game with given rules and boundaries; if these are denied by one of the agents, the whole mechanism falters.[34] Finally, positing a system of balances and equilibriums reveals nothing about the nature of existing contradictions apart from the "vital principle" of power. Social, economic, and political aspects are external to the concept. This, plainly, limits its analytical value. The related Soviet term, "correlation of forces," perhaps works better in that regard since it is derived from a clear (if controversial) notion of contradiction.[35] That said, we may turn to the notion of national interest; unlike the balance of power a concept that Kennan made a strong effort to analyze.

When Kennan became head of the PPS, he had only the most rudimentary background in theories of international politics, and for the ensuing three years he did not delve into them.[36] Repairing, however, to Princeton after his exit from the State Department, he initiated a grandly conceived research project in collaboration with some younger scholars, the object being nothing less than a total inventory of the determinants of American foreign policy, a projection of its likely course, and "an outline, or theoretical framework, covering the place of foreign affairs in the work of government."[37] In this aim he failed, partly because of his temporary recall to government service in 1952 and partly because of the inherent difficulties of the project; but he did generate a serious attempt to theorize international relations. The organizing concept of this attempt was that of national interest.

National interest has an extended genealogy, which in simple terms can be said to have two different but partly overlapping traces. On the one hand the idea can be traced back with various mutations to sixteenth-century Italy and *ragione di stato*. Interest itself, on the other hand, was theorized in the eighteenth century on the basis of commercial models as primordial but positive covetousness, implying both an existing body and a logic governing that body. The interest, in other words, was not only material but objectively interested *in* something. James Madison made good use of this in his ingenious system of political checks and balances: vested interests in competition but structurally unable to dominate or cancel one another out. A precedence of more direct lineage can be found in Lord Bolingbroke's history of England, published in 1730. Centering his narrative on the opposition between national and particular interests, the good lord showed how various actors and actions had expressed one or the other. More recently American "realists" such as Kennan have appropriated

the concept to combat "idealist" notions of an international community of interests, for the realist a wholly fictitious phenomenon.
Against, so to speak, the unreality of the international, the realists
pitted the reality of the national.[38]

In this limited, heuristic sense, their argument was no doubt valid,
for the world, whether one likes it or not, is clearly conflictual, and
the most important actors involved in these conflicts are equally clearly
nations. The realist could also make the commonsensical case that if
nations were real and pursued policy, they were more likely to pursue
that policy in their own interest than in that of some other entity.
This would leave the internationalist with the not implausible counterargument that the nations of the world are a community with an
objective interest in recognizing itself as such, but for reasons of
delusion, or whatever, this unhappily is not done.[39] While the former
position tends to genuflect before the empirical and descriptive, the
latter entails a strong normative aspect; and to that extent, the debate
is perhaps a bit confused. In any event, as a theory of international
relations the realist "national interest" falls decidedly short, since it
ignores the systemic aspect of world politics and so too the dialectic
of internal and external imperatives.

No doubt this failure was a product of the concept's constitution
in struggle against (and to that degree shaped by) the already existing
and presumably dominant universalism.[40] For the mythical international interest was simply inverted into the "real" national interest;
the starting point of any ensuing theorization of international relations
seemed to lie in the *differentiae* of the nation itself. For instance, Hans
Morgenthau, a contemporary of Kennan's and a leading realist thinker,
formulated his version of the concept in the manner of Machiavelli by
projecting onto the nation the hunger for power that he deemed innate
to human beings. National interest thus became the animating principle of a series of national actors engaged in maximizing power. This
view earned the realists a reputation (undeserved, I think) for cynicism
as well as some accusations of bad theorizing.[41]

Kennan too approached the problem from the national viewpoint
but prior to 1950 seldom employed the concept explicitly. As in the
case of balance of power, he appears to have assumed the existence of
national interest as a matter of common sense: the world consists of
states with conflicting interests, which is only natural and proper and
not in itself a condition to worry about. Yet when he sat down during
the next several years to think about the nature of foreign policy, it

was to this concept that he looked in order to find a theoretical foundation.[42]

This is not surprising. Kennan was a reflective diplomat, and diplomats are after all functionaries of the nation-state, to whose emergence diplomacy in its modern form was tied from the outset. National interest in that sense was nothing but the (ideological) rationalization of what diplomats actually do. (It is perhaps in this light that one should understand Kennan's dislike for the "vox populi" of the American UN delegation, who were then supposed to be defenders in a global parliament of some "higher" peace interest, in which capacity they may have seemed to herald the decline of traditional diplomacy.)[43] His receptivity to the concept was probably enhanced too by his earlier Berlin studies, pursued in an atmosphere suffused with realpolitik; national interest as understood by the American realists was clearly related to this tradition of German political thought, with which they shared more than the purely nominal resemblance.[44]

Once he actually began to *think* about the matter, however, Kennan realized how difficult the foundational quest would be. Epistemological concerns aside, a systematic derivation of national interest would have necessitated a demonstration that there is a world system whose primary unit is really the nation and which operates according to some determinate kind of logic, compelling those nations to behave in certain "interested" ways. As in the case of expansionism, I question whether such a derivation can be made, since nations are heterogeneous entities and not subject to any single discernible logic. This is not to say, of course, that international politics is a sphere of pure contingency, impervious to theorization, but merely to suggest that any unveiling of the systemic aspect would have to be based on something other than the concept of national interest.[45] Kennan, in any event, avoided systematic derivation. His attention was drawn instead to the nation as an entity in isolation. More particularly, he raised two questions: How might the national interest be decided? and what, actually is it? In seeking to answer them, he came to render problematic what was supposed to be axiomatic: the nation itself.

He first tried to locate an identifiable common interest of which policy could be a function. "The people" was quickly discarded as subjectively having varying interests; and who was then to define their true interests? The task would require "someone standing out on an archimedian platform and deciding what 'interests' are."[46] Thus infinite regress sets in, since the criteria by which the "someone" has been empowered to do this need to be established, which necessitates someone else, and so on ad infinitum. The unsettling conclusion, then, seemed to be that there were as many national interests as there were people with definitions and no theoretical way of adjudicating between them, which in turn meant that the concept immediately lost a good deal of potency in the struggle against idealistic universalists: "It is entirely possible for a man animated by no sense of obligation to anything else than national interest, to come to the conclusion that this interest will be best served by the adherence of his own country to rules of international law or certain moral principles."[47] Recognizing the force of this point and lacking effective theoretical response, Kennan understood that the only answer was to demonstrate by *substantial argument* that the national interest would not in truth be served by such a course. Yet he could not quite abandon the effort to find some objective footing in the subjective muddle, an effort that predictably foundered on the psychological:

> Intent is paramount. Americans, for example, who favored pressure on the Dutch to relinquish their hold on Indonesia, might have had divergent reasons for doing so. One group might have taken this position because it calculated that American national interest would be in some way served by termination of this colonial relationship and the establishment of an independent Indonesian state. Another group might have taken this position because it opposed the colonial relationship, in general, as a matter of moral principle.[48]

For reasons Kennan had already outlined this was an unrewarding line of reasoning; and he sensed that. Basing the delineation of national interest on subjective intentionality would in any case severely limit the concept's practical usefulness, if not actually render it completely vacuous.

He then seized upon the more natural alternative of grounding the national interest in the structure of the state itself, in government:

> Here you've got something to go on. Governments have a purpose: the exercise, preservation, and sometimes expansion of power. Power is a clear, identifiable relationship. It can have "interests." And not only can it have interests, but it can and does have a natural identifier and definer of those interests, which is itself. The interests of nations, for all practical purposes of international relations, are what the respective governments perceive them to be . . . it is each government's assessment of the sum total of its desires and responsibilities.

And that is something no one else can really figure out abstractly, or assume. It must flow from the processes of government, themselves. And it is something that can change, and does change, day by day.[49]

This functionalist view ruined whatever theoretical potential the concept had and turned it into a banality: national interest is whatever any given national leadership says it is in its everyday exercise of power. Such a relativist definition was conceivably the only option but it said next to nothing about the nature of international politics. Furthermore it left little to do but empirically ascertain (which Kennan did) how the government, past and present, had determined the nation's interest—what its actual policies had been.

For someone who had spent a good deal of his time in government service arguing that his superiors failed to understand the real interest of the nation, this was not a very satisfying solution. Kennan was of course painfully aware that government is a cumbersome and contradictory affair, traversed by polymorphous interests and not always given to calculating the totality of the national interest. Once, in fact, he went so far as to claim that the PPS was the first American institution to see things consistently from the viewpoint of the whole rather than the part.[50] Under these conditions, did it make any sense to call government policy a priori an expression of national interest? To do so would have meant instant abandonment, for one thing, of the original search for objective foundations and of the belief, common among interest-based theories of politics, that at any given moment only one policy is really in accordance with the fundamental interest.[51] Disinclined to give up either, Kennan thus occasionally returned to the problem in the early 1950s, but without ever arriving at any fully acceptable solution.

What was overwhelmingly clear to him, after all, was that private and exceedingly partial interests exercised a good deal of control over Washington's policies. He liked to think of these interests as domestic (a term of opprobrium) in origin, which of course they were. In themselves, he asseverated, private groups could scarcely constitute a basis for calculating of the national interest:

> I know of no private interests in this country to which I feel we could properly ascribe any sweeping and intrinsic public value, in such a way that we would be warranted in supporting them blindly and unthinkingly in our conduct of foreign affairs. I know of no specific group of citizens whose selfish interests, as defined in their

own conscious pretensions and desiderata, we would be justified in viewing as invariably identical with those of the nation at large or in placing above "the substantial and permanent interests of our country," as this may seem from the highest level of objectivity and enlightenment the responsible policy maker is able to muster.[52]

He had read Madison but was probably also influenced by his long confrontation with Soviet ideology, when, after contemplating the revolutionary origins of most governments, he made some related, incisive remarks about their class nature:

> Every government has a dual quality. It is in one sense the spokesman for the nation at large. Yet at the same time it is always the representative of a single dominant political faction, or coalition of factions, within the given body politic, and thus the protagonist of the interests of that political element over and against the interests of other competing political elements . . . The degree of enlightenment in such a voice will be largely a matter of the outlook of the ruling group itself and of the independence it enjoys, at the given moment, to follow a courageous and constructive course in foreign policy.[53]

And, in a similar vein, these notes: "Extent to which our government is merely meeting-ground of private selfish interests means that *portions* of our foreign relations will always consist of satisfying such private interests at the expense of the whole. This simply means—wasted effort, contradictory behavior, inefficiency. As a retarding factor on our national conduct, it must be added to dispersal of power of decision with which it is closely connected."[54] If this was not the "neutral" state of the liberal imagination, Kennan nevertheless maintained that factional interest could sometimes coincide with the national interest he assumed theoretically to exist, whereupon he was back to the question of how one might decide where it lay. In part he had hit on a problem Rousseau had faced two centuries earlier in trying to formulate a theory of the General Will: particular interest, paradoxically, is both the opposite and the foundation of the general interest (will). The latter then becomes a functional myth with no other content than that of establishing its own existence for the purpose of silencing the particular.[55]

Given Kennan's strong belief in the competent civil servant as a disembodied eye removed from private interests, we may conclude that when all was said and done it was to this personage (of which he himself was the prototype) that one would have to look for an authoritative interpretation of the General Will in foreign policy. For diplomacy, he opined, "is best done not by professional politicians on the glaring stage of partisan rivalry, but by quieter men whose experience of the world has left them with a certain sense of the tragedy of things, of the unaccountability of the historical process, and of the persistent tendency of brave undertakings to have irrelevant and eccentric endings—men, consequently, with a certain detachment toward all movements governed by political passions, including those of [their] own country."[56] Whatever its merits, such a view was of little relevance to the American situation and hence fell, as he probably realized, within the category of wishful thinking.

Kennan stressed that national interest could not be an abstraction and was cognizant that the manner in which he had couched the argument made it incumbent upon him to state his case in the course of "the processes of government."[57] He did so very directly during the PPS period and afterwards, from the outside, in everything he said about American foreign policy. Most interesting here, however, are the analyses he provided in the course of making problematic the concept itself.

These took two main forms: on the one hand historical accounts or case studies in which the actual policy was contrasted with what he considered to have been the "real" American interest, and on the other delineations of the contemporary interest. The outstanding example of the first is his now classic *American Diplomacy* (1951), a short but powerful book of lectures wherein he argued, to take a typical example, that the United States as a sea power with interests essentially similar to those of Great Britain should have intervened earlier than it did in the First World War for the sake of preserving the balance of power on the Eurasian land mass; and that it should have eschewed democratic verbiage while doing so. The object of his exercise was to show that, by now a familiar thesis, historically the United States had based policy on ethnocentric notions of little applicability abroad, whereas "conduct realistically motivated is likely to be more effective than conduct unrealistically motivated."[58] The validity of these case studies can be discussed only on their own terms, a task beyond the scope of my present purposes; but on the whole they were more persuasive as demasking operations than as alternatives.

Historical accounts of a more sweeping nature were employed to introduce the contemporary issue. The story varied somewhat, but the content can be summarized as follows. Beginning with the Founding

Fathers, and continuing through the nineteenth and well into the twentieth century, government had functioned as a protector of *private rights*. Since the preponderance of American activity abroad was commercial, "this concept became closely associated with the promotion and protection of American trade and the protection of American shipping on the high seas." However, when imperatives of the present century forced the United States to enter the field of international power, "it had to be recognized that *national* interest was something more than just the sum total of selfish individual aspirations," that foreign policy was the "collective interest of the entire nation of which it, the government, had perforce to be the interpreter." Yet, he noted, the older conception of foreign policy had by no means been superseded, old and new thus coexisting uneasily.[59]

Over time too the very *computation* of national interest had become more complicated: "In earlier times, whatever increased the country's population, the extent of its domain on this continent, and the export of its commodities, was ipso facto 'good' and could readily be accepted as serving the national interest. Today none of these criteria is fully valid."[60] This brought up the interesting question of what sort of contemporary criteria might in fact be considered valid. For it was clear that there had to be some general criteria, if not rigid objectives, in order to produce policy. These would have to "take into account the domestic aspirations and undertakings of a nation, as well as external ones, and reflect some workable determination as to the relation between the two." Thus he was brought face to face with the stark and unpleasant fact that there was little to entice him in the "basic aim of American society as expressed in civil government."[61] For one thing it seemed to him dominated to a rising degree by the notion of national security, a concept much more narrow in scope than national interest and one of which he was suspicious: "Like any political absolute, the idea of service to the 'national security' is used as a stalking-horse for a thousand ulterior purposes and often assumes forms that constitute an invitation to ridicule."[62] While accepting the concept in theory as the most basic and self-evident of foreign policy aims, he was far from fond of its political ascendancy, which was taking place against a backdrop of intense cold war and loyalty investigations. It also appeared to him to be part of the tendency to immerse policy in "abstractions and idealizations" as distinct from "specific interests," strategic and territorial. "Our policy gives the impression," he reflected, "that since the war we feel caught up in an intellectual straightjacket . . . which prevents us from acting in conformance with our interests, deprives us of flexibility, and contorts us into uncompromising and negative attitudes."[63]

There was indeed something negative about national security—"the absence of something we call military attack or danger of same, or the successful repelling of it"—which he found in keeping with traditional American hostility to positive government.[64] By the mid-1950s he was beginning to see that the trend toward collective interest in foreign policy that he had detected earlier was not really emerging. Objective conditions called for far-sighted formulations, but the nation still seemed imprisoned in the prosaic desire to protect the private tradition he disliked:

> So long as we continue to expect all blessings to flow from the unimpeded development of technological change in a free enterprise,—for that length of time, our foreign policy, insofar as it does not consist of the luxurious waste involved in catering to selfish partial interests, must continue to rest on the negativism of "national security"—i.e., on the uncritical protection of our ability to lead within our own borders whatever life may be prescribed for us by the workings of a process of evolution over which we do not pretend to have any real control & do not wish to have any.[65]

The sprawling laissez-faire system was disorderly and subject to various economic imperatives, thus causing additional difficulties in the calculation of the national interest. For as Kennan realized, the absence of control over internal processes such as economic growth—in itself a disturbing handicap—rendered panoramic control over foreign policy almost impossible. No domestic force appeared capable of articulating and imposing on the body politic any aims beyond the negative one of national security.

Just as the related thesis that the U.S.-Soviet conflict would essentially condense into a matter of whose internal order was more durable, so the nature of Kennan's national interest argument drove him back to the domestic situation. This sometimes generated images of a country that ought to be going into relative seclusion to come to terms with itself and its role in the world, leaving, as it were, the external dialectic to its fate and suspending foreign policy until further notice.[66] Such a course was clearly impossible, and Kennan specifically denied that he was proposing isolationism.[67] Nevertheless, he was of the opinion that most foreign relations of the United States had no basis in structural necessity and thus could be eliminated should that seem convenient.[68] Formulated in opposition to global interventionism, his argument did therefore take on a certain isolationist tinge.

Clamoring (with increasing exasperation) for internal balance, order, and strength was itself not without problems, for when the nation decided to do precisely that by launching into an extremely ambitious campaign to eradicate all poisonous fungi (not least in the State Department), Kennan was rightly appalled and began contradictorily to complain about "a sort of cramp of introspection" that was detracting badly from the attention that ought to be given "to things outside of our own society."[69] The "cramp" in question was of course McCarthyism. The domestic line of inquiry, in short, was yielding discouraging results.

In this national focus there was a further irony, since Kennan disliked modern nationalism, considered the nation itself a passing historical phenomenon, and ultimately preferred to think in terms of Western rather than American interests.[70] "Could anything be more absurd," he asked in the mid-1950s, "than a world divided into several dozens of large secular societies, each devoted to the cultivation of its own unlimited independence?"[71] Thereby he had also distanced himself from the nineteenth-century German traditions to which he was in other respects, consciously or not, rather close. Despite organicism and the search for a deeper national purpose, there was for instance little of Ranke's faith in nation-states as "real spiritual beings" in his use of national interest.[72] At the same time it was inconsistent of Kennan to identify American interests with those of the West: Western is indisputably a supranational category, and once the supranational interest is introduced, much of the antiuniversalist claim falls flat.

By the 1970s, in a final irony, Kennan's opposition to nuclear weapons had amplified into a personal campaign for the survival of the earth, a passionate (but not utopian) defense of the most universal of interests.[73] Against the moral authority of that project, theoretical objections somehow pale.

Little of his exploration of the national interest was published, symptomatic perhaps of a lack of certitude. In the spring of 1951, as an exception, he aired some interim reflections in a law journal.[74] The result illustrated the difficulties in synthetic form and may thus serve as a convenient conclusion to this section.

He conceded at once that he had no conceptual definition of national interest, it being "too vast, too rich in meaning, too many-sided": "Concepts and ideas are sometimes like shy wild animals. You can never get near enough to touch them and make exact measurements of them, but you can round them up and gradually pen them in; you can mark out certain directions in which they are not permitted to move. In this way you can confine them from time to time and have some idea of what they are like" (p. 730). Proceeding, then, impressionistically to contain it, he claimed (1) that the American interest was grounded in "our aspirations and problems at home" (p. 730) and certainly not measurable by any abstract concepts; (2) that the United States was still growing uncontrollably and therefore should avoid indiscriminate intimacy with other nations, particularly schemes of perfecting their "liberties"; (3) that the national purpose was the sum of what the inhabitants think, as expressed in behavior and political representation; (4) that the fundamental interest in this regard was to be allowed to continue to develop "under the most favorable possible conditions, with a minimum of foreign interference, and also with a minimum of inconvenience or provocation to the interests of other nations" (p. 734); and (5) that, the world being difficult to predict, the United States ought to concentrate less on aims than on internal discipline and style of conduct. "If we can achieve these things," he concluded, "we need not be too exacting in our demands for a definition of national interest" (p. 742).

The central thesis here was simply, it seems, that not much could actually be known about either the future or the concept of national interest, in which case it was best to tend to one's own house. This was a retreat in the face of theoretical complications, but it did not stop him from using national interest, perfectly sensibly, in the original manner as a self-evident description of how nations act in international politics.[75]

Kennan's attempt to think through systematically the activity of his ideal corps of omnicompetent, clairvoyant, tactically mobile professionals within the conceptual framework of national interest and balance of power thus ended in failure, or rather with a return to the conviction he had never relinquished: that foreign policy was an unpredictable and always changing enterprise, impossible to treat theoretically except by reference to behavioral generalities such as coolness, realism, detachment, flexibility, quickness, and economy. One would just have to choose the right people and trust them to get on with it. This "maligned and neglected process" of getting on was of course the practical task of doing diplomacy.[76] Kennan had a fairly clear idea of what that meant, and thus we have reached his second, "particular" type of account, about which I shall now be making some disjointed comments.

Though not in itself subject to systematic theorization, diplomacy could certainly be *portrayed*, and quite vividly so, as "the sitting down together of two or three men in a room, without benefit of press or publicity, and the effort to find in this the real sources of tensions, the deepest ones, the ones that really count, and to ascertain the limits of patience, of political tolerance, and vital interest on both sides and the type of accommodation between them that would be least detrimental to the future stability of international society."[77]

It is not clear whether he regarded diplomacy (or diplomatic process) as synonymous with foreign policy; it sometimes seems that way, although to my knowledge he never expressly posed the question. He did, however, think that there was more to the conduct of foreign policy than the ironing out of differences at a considerable remove from the public at large, all in order to maintain international stability. That, after all, presupposed what could not always be presupposed: a common aim among the parties. As he had often pointed out, different countries had different interests, some of them strongly antagonistic to those of the United States. And in the competition for power, diplomacy was a means to an end that required specific qualities: "The pursuit of power by diplomatic means—like the pursuit of power by military means—calls for discipline, security, and the ability to move your forces swiftly and surely, taking full advantage of the concealment of our own thoughts and of the factor of surprise."[78] Diplomacy was thus not the peacetime counterpoint to military maneuvers; it was maneuvers of the same kind, only carried out under conditions of peace and employing different means of power. What is at stake, then, is the art of manipulating one's forces hither and thither—that is to say, tactics and strategy. This conceptual pair, military in heritage, is rather more operational than either balance of power or national interest, by dint of which it ought to have been closer to Kennan's immediate experience as a policy planner. All the more peculiar therefore that he did not devote any time to this couplet during his post-1950 period of reflection. Despite this silence, it is nevertheless of certain relevance in the present context.

The definition of tactics and strategy is problematic. Insofar as a conventional one exists, *tactics* (etymologically "arrangement") means ordering formations for the purpose of a specific battle, whereas *strategy* ("generalship") connotes the configuring of battles from a longer perspective. Above and beyond that, *strategy* denotes, so far as I am concerned, a calculation or manipulation of force based on spatial identity and knowledge, thus presupposing a circumscribed space defined in opposition to an exteriority of threats or targets and featuring a process of distant scanning by which foreign objects of power can be transformed into something readable and predictable. *Tactics*, meanwhile, is the calculation of action within a field controlled by the enemy; relying on time rather than space, it is not based on strict demarcation of exteriority and requires neither far-reaching projects nor a spatially totalized enemy. It is, in a sense wily intervention in temporary openings.[79] Great power tends therefore, if spatially fixed, to diminish the capacity for tactical maneuver—precisely what caused Kennan such trouble in the American case.

At the outset of his PPS service he had intended to produce a strategic concept, but more pressing matters interceded.[80] As time passed and his alienation from the trend of American foreign policy deepened, the urgency of the task seemed, naturally enough, to fade. Indeed, the abstractions of the evolving cold war crusade (for example NSC 68) drove him to oppose definitions of general aims and talk instead of some much vaguer "direction."[81] As we have seen, this left him with a negative notion of the five essential military-industrial centers, a concomitant attachment to the equilibrium of forces, and a profound pessimism concerning the possibility of planning very far into the future. It also left him little room for any concrete strategic concept. The subsequent research project at Princeton was partly an ambitious and ultimately unsuccessful attempt to remedy this lack, or at least to find an explanation for the crudity of official strategy.

Thus he did not disavow the necessity of having strategic concepts, for to do so would have been absurd. Consider, for example, this reference to "a single rounded and consistent political philosophy," a code for the sort of guiding principles necessary for the determination of strategy:

> It need hardly be pointed out that the position of the United States in the world today is of such a nature that its diplomacy, to be successful, must be based on the most subtle and literate comprehension of world realities. Furthermore, it must be animated by a single rounded and consistent political philosophy, must be refined at its inception by the processes of private and intimate discussion,

and must be executed in such a way as to permit maximum flexibility, instantaneous adaptation to changing world realities, and delicate shifts of emphasis in response to new situations. It must even operate with contradictory policies, deliberately and simultaneously, in order to permit the rapid exploitation of the shifting external scene.[82]

What comes to the fore here is nevertheless a tactical rather than a strategic orientation. His background as a diplomat posted almost constantly in enemy territory may have encouraged, or indeed generated, this proclivity. The notion of containment, to take a symptomatic expression of that period, had little strategic content and was if anything an exhortation to tactical use of muscle. In fact, the ensuing trajectory led to a nominalist emphasis on limits, contingencies, isolated instances, and local circumstances.

The tactical intelligence Kennan espoused in theory and would have liked to put into practice is reminiscent of nothing so much as the ancient Greek notion of *metis*, literally "informed prudence," but actually meaning something far more than that throughout its long Hellenic use. *Metis*, to quote its historians, implied

> a complex but very coherent body of mental attitudes and intellectual behaviour which combine flair, wisdom, forethought, subtlety of mind, deception, resourcefulness, vigilance, opportunism, various skills, and experience acquired over the years. It is applied to situations which are transient, shifting, disconcerting and ambiguous, situations which do not lend themselves to precise measurement, exact calculation or rigorous logic . . . It is an intelligence which, instead of contemplating unchanging essences, is directly involved in the difficulties of practical life with all its risks, confronted with a world of hostile forces which are disturbing because they are always changing and ambiguous.[83]

Polyvalent, shifting, and intensely mobile, *metis* could not be theoretically systematized. It comprised elements of *techne* ("skill," "craft") but was not open to the detailed, legislative description of a modern technology. In being able to diagnose the contingent, *metis* was in fact much more akin to the contemporary Greek practices of navigation and medicine. Experiential rather than abstract in character, it was the product of a personal accumulation of singular events into memory, thus allowing one to determine when *kairos*, the right moment to strike, had arrived. As with Aristotle's related *phronesis* ("practical intelligence"), *metis* stood opposed to *sophia*, or "philosophical thought." Indeed Plato denounced the stochastic knowledge of "the good eye" in the name of truth, logic, and identity, dominant notions of Western theory ever since.[84]

The mythical figures of *metis*—Zeus and the wise counselor of the *Iliad* who was capable of seeing simultaneously backwards and forwards—represent qualities that in part correspond to those of Kennan's clairvoyant diplomat. *Metis* was however also a principle of economy, the achievement of maximum effect with minimum force. In that regard it can be said to resemble artistic endeavor.[85] If one proceeds accordingly to think of our diplomatic archetype as an artist, it is useful to bring in another personification of artistic practice but one rather differently conceived, namely Kant's acrobat. For Kant an art (*Kunst*) of doing is, among other things, a question of judgment, a sort of harmonization between understanding and imagination, a mediation of theory and practice. Typically singular in application, the faculty of judgment is impossible to demonstrate on the basis of general concepts and rules, and hence it cannot, properly speaking, be taught. It is an acquired capacity to differentiate, appreciate, and discern, which is as good a way as any to summarize Kennan's conception of the art of diplomacy. But it signifies too the transformation of a preexisting equilibrium into another, which is where the metaphorical acrobat enters. Walking on a tightrope, he intervenes constantly to maintain the equilibrium of which he himself is a part. The condition must always be modified but not essentially changed, giving the appearance of a perpetuation that is in reality never finally achieved.[86] The pertinent analogies are self-evident.

Yet Kant also marks the subjectivization of taste and its relegation to the sphere of the beautiful alone, and from that angle Kennan unknowingly relied on an earlier tradition. When the notion of taste emerged in the sixteenth century, it implied a kind of hermeneutic practice of judging particularities across a spectrum of human activity much wider than that of beauty. It extended especially into the domain of ethics and manners: having taste meant being able to judge whether something was fitting within the social whole, which in turn presupposed a keen appreciation for, if not subordination to, the *sensus communis*. Kennan liked organically grown manners as determined by men of discernment within the community, and in that way he was closer to the older vision than to Kant's subjective concept.[87]

Another aspect of judgment relevant in this context is that of tact. Tact indicates a sensitivity to the uniqueness of a given situation and to the problem of how one ought to conduct oneself in it, a sensitivity that can be produced only by a developed historical and aesthetic consciousness. Again, it cannot be derived from general laws, and seems prima facie undefinable. As Hans Georg Gadamer formulates it, however, "tact helps one to preserve distance, it avoids the offensive, the intrusive, the violation of the intimate sphere of the person."[88] Essential here is an elective affinity for *distance*—the distance of the gaze if you will. Kennan's deep concern with intimacy in foreign relations, the frequent counsel to "cool impassivity," and the very exaltation of diplomatic form itself may thus be understood in terms of this notion of tact and, more basically, in relation to the way of being and knowing that I have outlined as judgment.

Traditional diplomacy, in the end, is also conducive to aestheticizing strategies on account of its intrinsic qualities. *Form* is foregrounded through a pronounced reliance on etiquette, procedures and protocol, elegance of dress, speech, and indeed writing. Kennan, of course, was much concerned, not to say obsessed, with the importance of style and form, in prose as well as in action, to the point where it became a sort of variation on *l'art pour l'art*. Picture if you will Kennan at the legation in Prague, shaving "meticulously" while awaiting the arriving German Anschluss troops, thus denying them the pleasure of thinking that they had induced "a harried appearance" in the American representative.[89] Foreign policy, simply put, should be beautifully executed: "The most brilliant undertaking can be turned into a failure if it is clumsily and tactlessly executed; there are, on the other hand, few blunders which cannot be survived, if not redeemed, when matters are conducted with grace and with feeling."[90] The belief in the primacy of method, style, and form over purpose deserves a more extensive comment since it harbors a straightforward contradiction. Originating partly in his diplomatic background, partly in his critique of Soviet ideology, the conviction that the how was more important than the what was, in its extreme version, merely a reversal of what Kennan had considered the unifying element in Hitler and Stalin. To that extent it suffered, as I pointed out earlier, from the same problem as its counterpart. What is of greater immediate interest is the relation between the valorization of form and his "realism."

Kennan's attack on universalism in general and the UN project in particular had centered on the impossibility of imposing legal forms on the underlying realities of power. The outer form, he argued, could not hide the essence of the inside content. In the specific case of the

UN, this meant that power would "seep" back into the "legalistic structure."[91] The real, to continue the Hegelian language, would not consent to disappear on account of the appearance.

This argument is irreconcilable with Kennan's exhortations about style. If he had limited himself to saying that one ought to pay more attention to how one behaves and less to the precise goals of what one does, a case might have been made that the "realist" argument was about something different: taking the world for what it is, one should *approach* it with manners. As Kennan knew, that prescription was in itself problematic, since battles in a world filled with bad manners could scarcely be fought without recourse at times to bad manners. In any case he carried the stylistic argument much further:

> Remember that none of us can really see very far ahead in this turbulent, changing, kaleidoscopic world of foreign affairs. A study of the great decisions of national policy in the past leaves the historian impressed with the difficulty of analyzing the future clearly enough to make really reliable calculations of the consequences of national action . . . For these reasons we would do well to learn to think of the conduct of foreign affairs as a problem of style even more than of purpose. Where purpose is dim and questionable, form comes into its own . . . *Our life is so strangely composed that the best way to make ourselves better seems sometimes to act as though we were better.*[92]

And again:

> The individual cannot do anything about the beast in himself; but he can help a lot, and make life more tolerable for his friends and neighbors, by trying to act as though the beast did not exist. Just so the nation may not be able to alter—at least not abruptly—the unreal or absurd or outdated purposes to which it seems to be the habit of nations to be theoretically dedicated; but it can, by its behavior in practice, do much to enhance the prospects for a more stable and peaceful and hopeful world.[93]

Behaving as though the beast did not exist: this was surely something to which the devoted supporter of the United Nations and every other universalist project might have given his or her most wholehearted assent. Fixation on style seemed paradoxically to lead Kennan into palpably "unrealistic" territory, where he could be found upholding the virtues of the normative outer shell against the interior essence.

The wider significance of this is beyond my present scope, but one may note for now that the point of convergence between Kennan and his opponents was probably not unconnected with their common Protestant ideology. His rhetoric sometimes had a strong flavor of Protestant moralism:

> You all know how odious, in individual life, is the sloppy person who neglects his own affairs and his own appearance and runs around in a cloud of loose ends and unfulfilled obligations and at the same time busies himself with schemes for the improvement of others . . . [The nation's] first obligation is to itself, to the cleanliness and orderliness and decency of its own national life. A nation which meets its problems, and meets them honestly and creditably, is not apt to be a problem to its neighbors. And, strangely enough, having figured out what it wants to do about itself, it will find that it has suddenly and mysteriously acquired criteria, which it did not have before, for knowing what to do about its relations with others.[94]

The passage may also serve as a convenient way to reintroduce the domestic argument, of which more needs to be said.

I criticized Kennan's approach of "domestic regeneration" mainly on the grounds that the external dialectic tended to get lost. In one important respect, however, it was quite innovative and indeed subversive of his own traditional view of international relations. By rendering problematic the internal social order of the actors involved, above all the Soviet Union and the United States, he had broken with the orthodox strategic notion of decisive battle. Clausewitz, chief originator of this idea, had been much concerned with the emergence of popular participation in the military sphere, having himself experienced crushing defeats at the hands of the new kind of army fielded by Napoleon in the wake of the French Revolution. Yet Clausewitz's strategic thinking was ultimately based on the assumption that the social order itself is inviolable and thus more or less a given. As a consequence the manipulation of force and power appears theoretically to focus on the destruction of the opponent's armed might, which then leads to preoccupation with the "decisive battle." It was Mao more than anyone else who first managed to transcend this paradigm, for his whole strategy was in fact built on the assumption that social resources were inherently unreliable and in the end were more crucial than weapons: hence the "invasion" of the Nationalist social space by means of a land revolution.[95] A quotation will illustrate: "The crucial process is the alteration of the established fabric of social relations through which the opponent draws the power to wage war so that a mass of people can be woven into a new fabric of social and power relations from which they cannot escape. In this the insurgent slowly builds up behind his will and capacity to wage war a firm social base and order by virtually consuming that of his opponent on which, of course, his will and capacity likewise rests."[96] Granted that this view was a product of peculiar local circumstances and not easily applicable in an international system of states, as the course of Chinese foreign policy was eventually to prove, and granted too that the global emergence of nuclear armadas has complicated the picture, what nonetheless remains valid is that the social order cannot be excluded in strategic calculation as it was in the classical models.

Kennan did not develop the argument to Mao's degree, but his conclusions were largely the same. Doubtless he was influenced by his early dealings with a major state in world politics which, as he saw it, dismissed the very legitimacy of other regimes and so refused to accept the rules of the game. After this threat of social invasion had subsided, Kennan remained convinced that the essential battleground would be domestic health, although he now assumed the main danger to come from self-caused factors. Yet to raise the problem of social order was also to question his own received notion of states defending their national interest within various balances of power since that postulated precisely what Clausewitzian theory postulated, namely the nation-state as an unproblematic given.

One other aspect of Kennan's way of being toward the world of international relations must briefly be brought up before the final issue of realism as such. It concerns the difference between land and sea power, an antinomy that underlay, among other things, his delineation of a divided political tradition in Germany: a Western, moderate orientation, as opposed to an Eastern, extremist one.[97] This subverted his defense of the Junker class; but the polarity itself placed him squarely in the bourgeois conception of sea power (for which read commerce) as inherently conducive to peaceful interaction, land power being the uncompromising, warriorlike opposite.[98] One need not dwell here on the mythological elements of this view.[99] That is, one need not dwell on the long history of war and liquidation of alien cultures and peoples that actually accompanied and fueled the emergence of this "peaceful" system of seafaring commerce.[100] More to point now is the partial truth of the myth. For it is true historically that sea power, however rapacious abroad, internally tended to produce a society without the dominant army-bureaucracy so typical of, say, Prussia and Russia.[101] Kennan had an inkling of this but never thought it through very much beyond the distressing image of (total-itarian) land power rising to threaten the maritime powers. This pes-simistic inversion of Captain Mahan's buoyant predictions certainly played a great role in his understanding of Western interests after the Second World War—the Atlantic seaboard versus the interior and so on—but he never turned it into any systematic whole.

The economic side of two categories, land and sea power, seems to have been of minor importance to Kennan, which brings us to the concluding problem of how realistic was his realism. It is clear that his thinking about international relations was characterized through-out by a strong streak of archaism: balance of power, national interest, diplomatic form, organic tradition, all of these venerated concepts might have been employed by any moderately conservative statesman of the nineteenth century. That in itself does not render them useless or wrong; quite to the contrary, historical distance may produce better perspectives than the voguishly contemporary. With mixed results, they were indeed to make a powerful guest appearance at the center of things through the figure of Henry Kissinger. Yet one must hasten to add that the nineteenth-century view in this case fails signally to cope with the weblike creation of transnational economic interests and connections. The present world is traversed by a myriad of relations that have little in common with the older type of national interest, which could be condensed in Otto von Bismarck's head and admin-istrated by his foreign ministry.

It is thus with certain justification that Kennan has been criticized for having no comprehension of, so to speak, the modern realities of economics in foreign policy.[102] The following observations must then be made. In the first place, he was fully aware of the increasing importance of economics in foreign policy. It was he, after all, who, against the express advice of Dean Acheson, added the economist (and future author of NSC 68) Paul Nitze to the Policy Planning Staff in order to remedy his own lack of expertise.[103] Furthermore he took a keen and knowledgeable interest in the economic negotiations be-tween the United States and Great Britain in 1949 and showed a clear understanding of their political implications.[104] He certainly grasped (and deplored) the diversification of foreign policy into a great number of not wholly controllable economic and strategic tracks. Most imag-inatively, in fact, he not only foresaw the future American reliance on foreign raw materials such as oil and understood its strategic implications but also made a concrete attempt to determine the exact economic scope of this development.[105] In short, he was hardly insensitive to economic power. What he did not manage to do was to think through its effects on international relations as a system. He appears resignedly to have stopped at the point where he realized that modern conditions in the United States were making a coherent American foreign policy virtually impossible. While avoiding further forays into systematic theorizing, he nevertheless clarified repeatedly the consequences of the diagnosed condition and what ought to be done about them.

These prescriptions had little chance of being adopted. Kennan knew this. He was not a realist in that sense and said as much.[106] His realism was based on the (disputable) claim that he had a better understanding of events beyond the borders of the land, as well as of the appropriate policies and the sort of machinery one would ideally need to produce them. He saw his task as presenting this reality to those whom it might concern—first the State Department and then the American public—but not to invest much time and effort in political wheeling and dealing.[107]

This position, or disposition rather, is paradoxical: to be realistic by posing the ideal against the dominant idealism-unrealism equation and thus in effect to be unrealistic. If, however, one distinguishes between the realistic and the realizable, it is not incoherent. For the argument relies not on immediate verification or falsification but on the long-term workability of a strategy or a policy, and in that sense it is relative. The point, then, is not that a course of action carried on for years under the sign of, say, legalistic universalism will necessarily cause a readily identifiable disaster. Events may well slide along reasonably well for a long period, leaving the realism of the realist critique untested and the critique nothing but a critique. A final disaster might in fact never come, or be so distant that it is hard to imagine. For decades, to take an example, Kennan attacked the unconscionable pollution of the environment and called—unrealistically—for action to deal with it; only in recent times has there been any wide acknowledgment that pollution constitutes a serious problem which should have been confronted long ago. A realistic policy for this particular problem was not *realizable* before (and is still only partially so now). Similarly, he would no doubt argue that a series of unrealistic but realizable policies of the postwar era has been cumulatively instrumental in creating the very real possibility that the world as we know it has become subject to instant destruction.

The argument is thus not without local force. Whether *realism* is the most appropriate term in the context is, however, dubious: a system that apparently functions on faulty assumptions but without, at least for the foreseeable future, debilitating consequences would thus rest on a truly "real" structural error that must be taken into account if one wants to be realistic. Semantics aside, it is perfectly legitimate to say that politicians and public are mistaken in taking foreign policy to be about X when it is in fact about Y, provided that one then proceeds to make a substantial argument why this is so.

Objections may be raised, though, against the nature of the argument. In the first place, the conception of reality and change is problematic: the unspoken assumption that reality is an immediate given—identical being as opposed to becoming—must be reconciled with the emphasis on the rapidly changing.[108] Second, the argument tends to pit the real against the word, the underlying truth against the emptiness of ideology. The point was made earlier at considerable length that ideology was the greatest riddle for Kennan with regard to the Soviet Union, and there is no need to reiterate. To state the obvious: words and ideology are not the opposite of the real or even the realistic.[109] In denouncing agreements and rhetoric designed to pander to current prejudice, Kennan might well have been right. It is deplorable when politicians knowingly mislead the public or translate crude ethnocentric concerns into irresponsible action in foreign places. Yet politics is not reducible to the simple calculation of state interest. One of its most prominent components today is precisely the complex process of human imagination and desire, which by that very fact assumes structural force. Utopian reason, the most disparaged form of unrealism, is itself cognitive and not of negligible effect in bringing about historical change.[110] Ideology, symbolism, mythology, and words are not inherently abstract: they constitute a material practice encapsulated in the foreign policy of every great power.

Kennan recognized this. Otherwise he would not have stressed constantly the political imperatives of the anti-Soviet struggle and pushed, accordingly, for the Marshall Plan as a means of making "mythological" gains against the communist parties of Western Europe. Nor would he have opposed general statements of purpose in foreign policy if he had not thought them effective in diminishing the room for maneuvering.[111] Indeed a good case can be made that he was much more in tune with the place, function, and importance of the symbolic diversity of world politics than his opponents. But attacking inflated universalism (and ideologically disliking ideologies) led him antinomically to a simple negation, where words and symbols became mere epiphenomena, surface manipulations covering up so-called underlying realities. The irony is that few idealists have shown a stronger belief than Kennan the realist in the efficacy and power of their own words.

PART III

Class and Country

Thomas Jefferson was a slaveholder, but the ideological formation from which he and his colonial cohorts launched their revolution was as pronounced an example of liberal Enlightenment as one could find anywhere in 1776. Inscribed to a degree in the very foundation of the "Empire of Reason" was every principle of the natural law associated with the rising Western bourgeoisie: popular sovereignty based in theory on autonomous and equal (white male) subjects; affirmation of the social contract; inherent and inalienable rights; universal and equal validity of the law; and underneath it all a belief in progress and rationality.[1] In opposition to these new notions there emerged the political orientation I have referred to as organicist conservatism, the preeminent political expression of which was Edmund Burke's critique of the French Revolution.[2]

Enlightenment discourse had gradually evolved a view (going back to Hobbes and Descartes) of society as the sum total of atomized subjects. For Burke and other organicist conservatives this was a mechanical concept: a state was not the quantitative outcome of any contract between monadic individuals but an entity in its own right, the qualitative result of organic growth over historical time.[3] Radical attempts by the human will to alter on putatively rational grounds this organism "in one impetuous gesture," to use Kennan's phrase, were thus unnatural and dangerous for the well-being of all.[4] Dismay over the subjection of traditional growth to rational manipulation also generated a disdain for abstract thought: abstraction was removed from the real and therefore in some sense rationalist hubris. For example, one finds this kind of intellectual anti-intellectualism in both Edmund Burke and T. S. Eliot.[5]

The Cartesian ego was not, however, a construct without historical foundation, for the advent of bourgeois society and industrial revolution certainly produced atomization (and alienation) in human relations. "Utility is the great idol of the time," as Friedrich Schiller lamented in the 1790s, adding that society, rather than "hastening upward into organic life," was "[collapsing] into its elements."[6] A century later his compatriot Ferdinand Tönnies was to describe this as the "fall" from Gemeinschaft (community) into Gesellschaft (society), a fall from the organic to the mechanical, from the natural to the artificial, from the traditional to the constructed. Soon afterward, Max Weber theorized the fall in terms of capitalist rationalization, the relentless compulsion to achieve the most efficient adequation between means and ends.[7] A new system now seemed dominant, subordinating for some external purpose such as profits or national aggrandizement all aspects of life to the logic of material production as measured in money, thus turning the qualitative into something merely quantitative.

Nowhere did the mechanical process of rationalization have more success than in the United States. Typical social sources of resistance to modernity—crafts-oriented strata and traditional classes of the land such as peasants and aristocrats—had become squeezed out very early on.[8] The workers' movement, which elsewhere in the West turned modernity to its own end by becoming a "state-bearing" power, proved in the face of American mobility and ethnic diversity incapable of cohesion as a political class, opting instead for minority status as one among many interest groups. These, then, were not social conditions conducive to a collective orientation, right or left.

Constitutively present from the outset, the discourse of individualism, market liberalism, and money-making has thus reigned supreme in the United States. "We are too materialistic," as Brooks Adams complained to Theodore Roosevelt. "We set a money value on everything." Adams, the last prominent member of that long dynasty of great American conservatives, suggested "military schools in which obedience, duty and self-sacrifice are taught on a great scale" as one possible way of counteracting this regrettable condition.[9] But the rule of the commodity was not to be dislodged. Paradigmatically excluding major opposition, it reduced Adams's opinion to little more than a feeble gesture of dissidence. "Unbelievers are to be met with in America," as Tocqueville had observed, "but there is no public organ of infidelity."[10]

The analytical Frenchman was also struck by the paradox of monotony amidst massive change, the continuous replacement of individual actors, fortunes, and opinions according to identical patterns.[11] Entrenched devotion to foundational beliefs is coupled, one might say, with a quest for acquisition and surface novelty. What in this regard passes for American conservatism has on the whole had more to do with militant advocacy of the Hobbesian jungle than with organicist notions of slowly changing hierarchy.[12] Alternatively, when not merely a reflexive fixation on the communist danger, it has taken the form of rural parochialism, a sort of stubborn, involuted traditionalism, embodying certain conservative notions about family cohesion and the like but relying in the final resort on an almost anarchic individualism.

Nor, in this unorganic mass, has there been much of a chance of taking refuge, as could some of Kennan's European counterparts, in the organic simulacrum of a supposedly classless and selfless bureaucracy. Founded on the idea of competence, duty, and loyalty, this institution in its ideal form is largely removed from the sphere of material production and inherently resistant to modernization for its own sake. Seemingly above the petty squabbles of politics, it is a place in which a conscientious conservative might promulgate the national interest in peace and relative comfort. However, the American civil service since Andrew Jackson has been none of these things. On the contrary, as Kennan was acutely aware, it has been a terrain openly contested by various individuals and groups for their own express interest, resulting in a bureaucracy that is neither stable nor particularly competent. The Foreign Service of old, preserving certain traditional models of form and rank, escaped the normal vagaries more than most, but any idea of sanctuary there must have been rudely dispelled by the immense outside pressures after 1947. Superior execution of duties—effective but also elegant—would have been reduced to a private act of symbolic defiance.

Although he toyed with the idea, the drastic alternative of exile, along the lines of Henry James and T. S. Eliot, to a more organic society such as Britain was for Kennan an impossibility. For first and foremost he was a civil servant, in moments of profound gloom clinging to the moral imperative that "loyalty is the only absolute virtue," even if from the mid-1930s on it was to be a "loyalty of principle, not of identification."[13] What remained, then, was the insurmountable dilemma around which Kennan's statements about the United States will be seen to revolve: how to combine organicist conservatism with political aspirations in a society that is constitutionally unorganic and apparently devoid of historical agencies capable of changing that basic condition. His solution, when not relative silence, was an amalgam: the kind of radicalism into which the conservative is sometimes propelled when circumstances are unpropitious,[14] defense of authority when a radical opposition actually appeared, and resistance to "commodified" life by means of art and style. Tolerated, in the fullness of time indeed venerated, within the public sphere of the establishment, his presence was nevertheless somewhat of an eccentricity. It is this very marginality that has allowed him to see things outside the common purview and to argue, rightly or wrongly, what no one in a "responsible" political position could.

7

No Exit

Kennan's background was free from connection with the world of capitalist production and money making: "I was brought up in a family of Puritan culture. My ancestors never owned capital. They worked with their hands, long and hard. They were neither self conscious about their poverty, nor bitter about the fact that it existed. Not one of them was to any important degree an employer: not one of them sold his labour. Thus, the classical social predicament, which provides the kernel of Marxist theory, was outside our experience."[1] There were times, therefore, when he considered himself "a socially disembodied spirit," and in some ways he was in fact devoid of class attachment.[2] Still, as the passage suggests, he was not far removed from the class of American freeholders. His family, of Scottish or Scottish-Irish ancestry, had remained largely uneducated farmers in the Midwest, a pattern first broken by his father, who became a lawyer. Kennan himself was the first to go to an eastern upper-class university, Princeton, into which he was never socially assimilated. Later on in Europe he was exposed to the aristocratic critique of both Soviet communism and Americanized capitalism.[3] It was here, possibly influenced by the Spenglerian Kulturkritik then much in vogue, that he became sensitive to, and alienated from, the modernity of his own country, with its mass production, mass consumption, and mass culture.[4] From then on he, like the Salazar of his Portuguese despatches, would always attempt to find some breathing space in between the "mob violence, atheism, social revolution and foreign domination" associated with communism and the "Wall Street materialism and

Hollywood immorality" of the United States—a "middle-way," as he wrote at the end of the 1930s, "between our stifling, demoralizing flow of commercialized mush and the ghastly laceration of the spirit which takes place under the name of government propaganda abroad in Moscow and Berlin."[5]

The problem, of course, was whether any historical agency existed that might viably serve to reimpose—or impose—organic totality and a slower pace of superficial change, whether there was any reasonable hope that one would ever achieve the sort of society where the paternal experience, in Kennan's typical figure, would again be intelligible to the son.[6] Prospects here were essentially dim, as deep down he always knew. An early attempt at political writing illustrates this very clearly.

Some time after his return from Moscow in 1937 Kennan began what appears to have been intended as a work on the domestic political problems of the United States. The project died in infancy; none of it ever saw the light of publication, which was no doubt a good thing since, in retrospect, the whole thing was a clear case of juvenilia.[7] The manuscript centers on the virtues of authoritarian rule by experts, a notion that, as we recall, Kennan was trying to use in contesting the practice of measuring political systems according to the binary op- position of democracy and dictatorship.

Suffering on his return from that "hypersensitiveness" he thought common to those who must represent their country abroad in as favorable a light as possible and then come back to face the real thing, he had been depressed by a profound sense of alienation: "For the dominant reaction on my part to that entire year in the United States was a growing understanding and nostalgia for America's past and an uneasiness about her future. I felt a powerful longing to identify myself more closely with everything that America had once been; and a decided reluctance to identify myself with what it seemed to be be- coming."[8] He was depressed and so was the country. Hence, even if the past of his imagination was a mere projection, he had no difficulty, as he began his political treatise, finding fault with existing conditions: "Hasty and uncontrolled industrialization has introduced ugly social and political problems which refuse to be ignored. Our agricultural population is largely indebted or dispossessed. Our great cities and industrial communities are not pleasant to contemplate. Our popula- tion as a whole no longer has its old fiber or its old ideals. Few are untouched by the problems of crime, corruption, and class and race antagonism." In particular he harbored dire premonitions about "the future of the federal government," which "was bound [sooner or later] to flounder hopelessly, to become extricated in its own failures, and to break down completely, as it had threatened to do in 1933." The country had developed into an immense industrial power while leaving its political system unaltered from the days of small-scale agriculture. In trying now to cope with the effects, Americans were unfortunately locked into the choice between the "paternalistic effort of central government" and the path of laissez-faire, both essentially within the old constitutional framework. This Kennan wished to leave behind in favor of an authoritarian system.

His argument was quite simple. It first assumed that the goals of human society are in themselves fairly uncontroversial:

> It is clear that a good proportion of our population should be better fed, better housed, better clothed and should enjoy better opportunities for play and relaxation and other enjoyment. They must be taught to be more human, and more decent in their relations to one another. Finally, if they are to be happy they should be given the feeling that they are participating individually in a common program towards the ends described above, that their efforts are not purely individualistic and selfish, that they are contributing toward the general improvement of the society in which they live.

To achieve these aims it was important not to get lost in labels and to remember that the world has always been ruled by minorities. Only in some neutral European countries, with their "advantages of compactness, homogeneity of population and exceptional political ability," did democracy actually have any real meaning. To speak of democracy in the usual sense of a "vague mixture of personal liberty and majority rule" was questionable in the American case, where "a good percentage of local and state governments are in the hands of political machines and where the main-springs of federal legislation are lobbies, patronage and local interests." What was wrong, then, was not that the country was ruled by a minority but that it was ruled by the wrong one: "professional politicians and powerfully-organized special interests," none of whom were espousing the national interest as their guiding principle. The task, once the old pseudoproblem of democracy had been eliminated, was thus to find or shape a ruling stratum dedicated to nothing but the national interest: "We feel that this country can be effectively and properly governed only by a minority selected from all sections and classes of the population, and selected on the basis of individual fitness for the exercise of authority. This fitness must be determined by character, education and inclination. It must be supplemented, once the original selection is made, by training and experience." Given the corruption of existing forces, only youth would be suitable material for recruitment; and to select them one would have to found a new political organization, apart from popular forces and established interests. Once formed, this "competent, disciplined and devoted organization of untrammelled young people, dedicated to the service of the state," would have to be trained. "They would have to make it their profession. They would have to abandon the attractions of private life, the prospect of making money and of keeping up with the Joneses. They would have to subject themselves to discipline as they would if they entered a religious order." Their nonpecuniary reward would lie "in the possession of authority and in the sense of real service to society."

The problem of how this new ruling minority-to-be was actually to come to power was not ignored but, there being no real resolution, was explicitly dismissed:

> We propose to leave this question unanswered. It does not bother us. We know of no instance in history where a highly-disciplined, energetic and determined minority has failed eventually to find means of coming into power in a state where political power was corrupt, chaotic, and diffused. Nor does this imply the necessity of the use of violence. If the degeneration of American political life continues, it more probably will eventually drop like a ripe apple into the hands of any organized minority which knows what it wants and which has the courage to accept responsibility. This danger already exists. We did not create it. We are only trying to anticipate it. There will be ruthless elements aplenty waiting to inherit the instruments of power which the old system has been unable to wield.

Having put his new group in power so to speak by default,[9] Kennan pondered the immediate aim of rooting out "boss-ridden democracy" and found that the best method for accomplishing this was to restrict suffrage: "When bewildered ignorant masses [obtain power], the invariable and unavoidable result is that they soon turn it over to the most determined and unscrupulous self-seekers. The broader and more remote the governmental unit in which they are supposed to be represented, the less understanding they have for its opposition and for their real interests." Three classes of people were therefore to be disfranchised, the first being "aliens and naturalized citizens." In Kennan's view this group of people had "proportionately more power in American politics than any other elements." Deprived of the vote, "several millions of bewildered semi-digested new arrivals would become for the first time the objects of benevolent good government rather than fodder for the rent-sharks, ward-heelers and confidence men of the big cities." Second, since the country was already "a matriarchy," one would have to disfranchise nonprofessional women: "As a whole, the American woman has conspicuously failed to live up to the responsibility which exercise of this power entails. Her club-life has become a symbol of the futility of inanity. In national politics she has placed enormous power in the hands of lobbyists, charlatans and racketeers." Next in line were the blacks, whose condition was "probably the outstanding disgrace of American public life." To remedy this, one would have to liberate them, as it were, from their present rulers: "The lack of franchise could make the negro little more defenseless than he is. It should serve, on the contrary, to develop something of that sense of responsibility for his welfare which is woefully lacking in the white population. It is a national characteristic that we are kinder to those who, like our children, are openly dependent on our kindness than to those who are nominally able to take care of themselves." After some introductory remarks about the legislature, castigated for its lack of concern with the national interest, the manuscript then peters out, leaving the exact nature of the authoritarian system unknown.

What may be said about this political fantasy? On one level it was little but a thinly disguised attempt to adapt Plato's *Republic* to American conditions: distrust of the *demos*; distaste for private wealth; a desire to make a clean slate of hopelessly corrupt conditions by forming a completely new ruling group of youthful guardians, schooled from scratch for national service in an academy of soldierlike education and then set ascetically apart.[10] Added inspiration was no doubt provided by the Dollfuss-Schuschnigg example in Austria, with its effort to reimpose hierarchical order and expert rule.[11] Yet there were also precedents closer to home. For what we have here is perhaps just a Wisconsin Progressive gone sour, derailed from his most natural political track (the New Deal) by having spent too much time in the *Untergang* atmosphere of interwar Europe. Although the emblem may appear wholly inappropriate in Kennan's case, the Progressive movement of the early twentieth century was in one respect precisely a middle-class attack on "boss-ridden democracy," by which was essentially meant the political organization of working-class immigrants in big cities.[12] Moreover, influenced by German prototypes, the scientifically "good government" of Wisconsin Progressivism was elitist to the core. As one historian summarizes:

> Ultimately what the "Wisconsin Idea" was aiming at was government by experts, the incorporation into the machinery of government of a corps of personnel trained in the most up-to-date technical knowledge and imbued with a public spirit. These experts, insulated by civil service or the appointive system from the pressures and compromises of electoral politics, were to be the guardians of the economic and social interests of the commonwealth . . . The power of the state would rest with these experts, whose mission would be the balancing and harmonizing of vested interests for the greater interest of society as a whole.[13]

It is worthwhile in this context to quote Kennan's father, Kossuth, on the comparative shortcomings of income tax laws in the world, a subject on which he was something of an authority, having written the first such statute in Wisconsin[14]: "The crudities and imperfections which are only too apparent in these laws are due in part to the fact that political considerations have influenced those who framed them. Important fiscal measures of this character should be formulated by commissions composed of men who are reasonably free from partisan bias and whose learning and abilities render them fitted for such a task."[15] This statement is not far in spirit from Kennan's own accolades to the Schuschnigg regime, whose social security reform had been handled in a most satisfactory manner by an expert commission after incompetent politicians had failed. The conceptual step from Progressive good government to benevolent authoritarianism was thus not necessarily a large one. Early on Kennan also evinced another, more attractive Progressive strain: conservationism, better known now as environmentalism. In the 1930s, at any rate, he was nourishing hopes that Wisconsin might, like "some of the small neutral countries of Europe," become "a reservoir of human decency and common-sense," a place where he could "do a small job" and know that he "was adding something real to human values."[16]

Most telling about his political musings is the complete absence of identifiable social sources for change. Hence the abstract quality of the exercise, featuring some imaginary, still uncorrupted category of young people to be trained for a position of power predestined in undefined ways to fall into their hands. Perhaps Kennan felt this structural inadequacy, for his critique of American society from then on came to focus not on potential changes in the political system but on sociocultural problems, on the darker effects of industrialism and the deleterious manifestations of mass culture. While sensing a duty to speak his mind, Kennan has made comparatively few public forays into domestic politics proper, except where his own area of expertise, foreign policy, has been at stake. Yet he has very much remained an organicist conservative.

"I am, I confess, a conservative by deepest conviction," wrote Kennan in 1953.[17] Thus he believed in the virtue of slow, gentle change, or more accurately growth, since he assumed society to be an organism.[18] A healthy social condition was one in which tradition and fixed procedure figured prominently, subject of course to normal metabolic transformation:

> Man is a creature of habit. He feels most comfortable, and conducts himself most quietly, in a garment made up of familiar and traditional action. It is not a matter of primary importance whether these actions have any real meaning for his life or whether they are essentially conventional and ritualistic. It is true, custom and habit are themselves subject to change and evolution. Changes in basic conditions of life; in climate, in geography, in the behavior of neighbors, in the nature of the tools man has to work with; all these things can come to bear on habit and custom and bring about their gradual evolution.

An essential advantage with this kind of order was its intelligibility: its character and boundaries could always be surveyed and understood. One generation's wisdom would not be obsolete for the next. So things would pass according to the seasonal model of a fairly static agricultural society, evolving with well-rooted practices and rituals according to its own inner principle of change.[19]

Freedom in these circumstances could not be conceived, it stands to reason, as anarchic license to do whatever happened to strike one's fancy (even if within legal bounds). Rather it was to be seen as "the humble acceptance of membership in, and subordination to, a natural order of things."[20] To be free was to recognize and submit to one's own given limits: "[Freedom] lies in the acceptance of that system of restraints most closely in tune with our own nature and with the order of this world, most conducive to the dignity of our relationship with others and to the self-respect and humility with which we contrive to accept ourselves."[21] And later, "Surely, one should be content with a modest station in life if one has modest capabilities . . . I would rather occupy a modest place in a good hierarchy than be a member of a grey, monotonous mass of mediocrity. There is a place for hierarchy and ceremony in life."[22] The natural order was thus decidedly not an equal one:

> All that equalizes, all that levels, all that standardizes is the enemy of freedom. A healthy social organism depends on a great complexity of inner tensions, so that the restraints of life may proceed from many and small causes, the reasonableness of which people can easily recognize. In the standardized and egalitarian society, these inner sources of regulation tend to disappear . . . To be safe in freedom, peoples must have the courage to differentiate where nature has differentiated—the courage to identify their best, to lean on it, to respect it.[23]

A differentiated and deferential social organism must, of course, have a clearly distinguishable top and bottom. Kennan took a certain pride in accusations of elitism: "God forbid that we should be without an elite. Is everything to be done by grey mediocrity? After all, our whole system is based on the selection of people for different functions in our life. When you talk about selection, you're talking about an elite."[24] There was more to this idea than the banal sociological fact that some people, or classes of people, in fact get ahead in life. As we have seen, Kennan considered minority rule not only a historical law but a good thing. The inevitable elite, in any case, would be a blessing for the whole of society, provided it was made up by the right people: "If great masses of people are to be elevated out of degradation or vulgarity it is important that some people should set an example of graciousness and good taste."[25] On the eugenic assumption that "we are creatures of heredity in even greater measure than environment," Kennan actually once went so far as to suggest that not everyone ought to be allowed to procreate. He also considered the generality inherently unfit for the sort of higher education necessary to produce an elite capable of meeting the case.[26] This, alas, was the crux of the matter, for the era of paragons seemed to have been consigned to the historical dustbin, as he himself had noted resignedly:

> The old concept of the individual, exalted from his fellows by wealth or birth and surrounded by a physical setting designed to fortify that

myth of individual superiority, now has for most of us a slight tinge of the ludicrous which means that its reality has passed for ever. In a way, it is too bad. The old principle of paternalism, that is, the principle of a recognized gentry, either of birth or education, endowed with recognized prestige and responsibility, was not only more colorful than our brand of democracy, but also produced in its day some of the best government the world has ever seen, including that of this country in the first decades of its existence. But no one can turn back the tide of history.[27]

Here he seems to deplore the loss of "a recognized gentry, either of birth or education"; elsewhere he proposed "an elite not of wealth or of birth but of mind and character."[28] How static or open the desired elite was supposed to be was left unanswered, possibly because he knew that there would never be one to his taste. The testy propositions about reproduction and education, futile iconoclasms of the radical right, may thus be grasped as expressions of a basic impotence: he saw little to do by way of practical politics.

Extensive commentary on these conservative views is unnecessary: disagreement is largely a matter of principle, and the arguments are well known. One might perhaps mention that few things are less in tune with the precepts of American democracy (essentially proto-Jacksonian, partly tempered by New Deal liberalism) than a clearly distinguishable and recognized hierarchy, or for that matter the idea of accepting "a modest station" in life. This is not to say, of course, that hierarchy does not actually exist or that most people do not in fact have to accept something "modest" or worse. More substantially, if freedom is a kind of cheerful submission to given personal limitations, it is nevertheless difficult to know whether these are natural or merely unjust products of the system to which one is asked to submit. Kennan had next to nothing to say about the constraints of the whole, about what might be done in order to ensure that everyone is actually in a position not only to recognize his or her potential but also to realize it, indeed about anything having to do with injurious discrimination in the system he himself disliked. Theodor Adorno's remark about Spengler's conservatism comes to mind:

His metaphysics is positivist in its resignation to what is so and not otherwise, in its elimination of the category of potentiality, and in its hatred of all thought that takes the possible seriously in its opposition to the actual . . . Whenever Spengler speaks of fate he means the subjugation of one group of men by another . . . This reflects the ominous "It shall not be otherwise" which is the end-product of the basic Protestant amalgamation of introspection and repression. Because mankind, tainted with original sin, is not capable of anything better in this world, the bettering of the world is made a sin.[29]

Unlike Spengler, however, Kennan was consistently inconsistent in trying precisely to better the world, in trying to redirect the historical tide if not actually turn it back. Still, his aim has typically been not to recast the internal order of social classes but to attack the ills affecting society as a whole, a point to which we shall return later.

As regards the related and more concrete problem of "actually existing democracy," Kennan's discomfort has already been demonstrated. I have claimed, in sum, that he was an advocate of so-called benevolent authoritarianism in the 1930s; that he refused any absolute categorical distinction between dictatorship and democracy; that he doubted the value of spreading Western-style democracy to other parts of the world; and that he found his own country's system outstandingly ill suited for the conduct of a coherent and intelligent foreign policy. Even during his most visible moments as chief American strategist in the late 1940s his attachment to hierarchy and order remained intact, his commitment to individualistic democracy correspondingly in doubt. To this I wish merely to add some remarks about the development of his position on democracy and the United States after 1950.

On occasion in the postwar period Kennan would express support for what he liked to think of as "the humble give and take" of "Anglo-Saxon democracy," usually in the context of contrasting it to Latin or Third World negatives.[30] He may have been referring to some idealized characteristics of the conservative British system rather than its American counterpart, having for the most part been an admirer of the former's adaptability and powers of execution. A salient point of attraction was the organic element of class compromise in the clearly hierarchical British society, not the sort of thing one normally associates with democratic theory.[31] In times of frustration and pessimism he was also wont to reaffirm the objective need for another type of American system:

> To try to combat what is taking place would require a firm strong government, capable of exerting extensive disciplinary power and of making people do things which they would not want to do and for which they cannot see the reason. In other words, the evils caused by a laissez-faire attitude toward technological advances have already

produced illnesses which can only be cured by a high degree of paternalism. Only some form of benevolent authoritarianism could manipulate living patterns in a manner adequate to restore a framework for healthy and vigorous citizenship.[32]

He continued, moreover, to deny that the authoritarian and the democratic system in practice were completely different:

> The authoritarian regime, despite its origins and sanctions, often rests on a wide area of popular acceptance and reflects popular aspirations in important degree. In democratic countries, on the other hand, such things as the operation of lobbies and political parties, and the inevitable control of nominations by small groups of people, tend to reduce the ideal representatives of government, making it difficult to view the political process as much more than a passive and negative expression of the popular will.[33]

Nor did he relinquish his unfavorable attitude toward participatory democracy, maintaining "that the permanence of a governmental system and its ability to sponsor and enforce a clear, rational, and reasonably benevolent order of law, are qualities more important, from the standpoint of the advance of civilization as we see it, than the degree of participation of the individual citizen in the governmental process."[34] This view should be understood in the context of what was perhaps the most important source of guidance in Kennan's life, Edward Gibbon: "For years, Gibbon's dictum 'Under a democratic government the citizens exercise the powers of sovereignty; and those powers will be first abused, and afterwards lost, if they are committed to an unwieldy multitude' has lain at the heart of my political philosophy."[35] Gibbon, an aristocrat of the eighteenth century with complex and ambivalent feelings about the emerging bourgeois order, partially influenced by the Enlightenment but profoundly opposed to abstract theory, an advocate of manifest social hierarchy, a historian of decline and fall whose narrative hero was usually some spiritual exile from the period in question: all these qualities must have seemed most congenial to Kennan, who was not only a close reader of Gibbon but also fond of stating his own affinity for the eighteenth century.[36]

The most reasonable way to characterize Kennan's later view of democracy may actually require reformulation into eighteenth-century terms. He had been pleased to discover, possibly through Charles Beard, that "the Fathers of the Constitution" had never had any "pure democracy" in mind.[37] What these lawgivers did have in mind is a controversial topic of debate, but it is clear that people such as John Adams thought about political systems in classical categories and favored a balanced mixture of democratic, aristocratic, and (pseudo)monarchical components, a position certainly finding some expression in the original American structure of government with its appointed senators and strong, indirectly elected president.[38] Kennan had no quarrels with this mixed concept. The best way to locate the mature Kennan on the political spectrum, past or present, might be to say that he is, impossibly, an archconservative Federalist (with the added complication of having a nigh-on Jeffersonian attachment to agrarianism).[39]

Given its archaic reference points, Kennan's political posture may seem of little contemporary relevance. Indeed in his *Memoirs* he claims deep alienation from the typical positions of the time, writing that liberals were "preoccupied with the achievement of a greater social justice *within* the existing system rather than with the adjustment of that system to meet the wider needs, environmental and otherwise, of the modern age. 'Conservative' opinion was committed to the resistance of these liberal impulses in the name of outraged patriotism and a compulsive, indiscriminate, anti-Communist fixation."[40] Yet the "egghead" campaigns of Adlai Stevenson in the 1950s were not wholly foreign to his viewpoint, were in fact close enough to impel him, out of character, to offer his services in 1956. The experience was profoundly discouraging. The ensuing defeat was annihilating, and he himself, a figure of some controversy, was kept at a distinct distance within the campaign.[41] It was in the wake of these events and the equally depressing uproar around disengagement that Kennan made his most critical remarks about the American political system, reaching a point where he was prepared to admit that his views might to a degree be considered "subversive."[42] One example will suffice: "In the doctrinal sense, we in America also have in certain respects a one-party system: for the two parties are ideologically indistinguishable: their pronouncements form one integral body of banality and platitude; whoever does not care to work within their common framework is also condemned, like the non-party person in Russia, to political passivity—to an internal emigration."[43] During the late 1950s such ideas may well have been subversive (and, whatever their exaggeration, not without truth). Doomed, then, to "political passivity" and "internal emigration," Kennan was locked into the conservative paradox, perhaps still regretting as he had in 1952 that the state, because it was dominated by nonideological parties, would "never be available for any program involving deliberate and fundamental alterations in the purpose and nature of our system."[44]

However, when the established system came under considerable attack in the 1960s, Kennan rose to its defense, in a measured sort of way, revising some old ideas of his own in the process: "Every legislative body is in many respects an evil; but it is a necessary one. It provides worse government, unquestionably, than does a benevolent despotism. But it provides better government than the non-benevolent despotism into which the benevolent one has a tendency eventually to evolve. The parliamentary institution, imperfect as it is, stands as a wholly indispensable link between the will of the people and the execution of supreme governmental authority."[45] More about the sixties later. Let it just be noted that his ambivalence on the subject did not disappear. When, in the 1970s, he proclaimed democracy "the most civilized form of government," it was thus on the understanding that the setting had to be right; and he still considered the American version unsuitable for effective government in the United States.[46] The arch-Federalist impulse has never been far from the surface: "Democracy is a loose term. Many varieties of folly and injustice contrive to masquerade under this designation . . . There are forms of plebiscitary 'democracy' that may well prove less favorable to American interests than a wise and benevolent authoritarianism."[47] His resentment, finally, of the established parties remained undiluted, intermittently becoming open contempt. They "cater," as he put it in 1976, "to what is basest in the American electorate."[48]

In consequence Kennan felt throughout that he had little to say about the daily issues of domestic politics, formulated as they were "on the assumption that the good life is something [that] can be bought," concerned in other words with acquisitiveness and money: "profits, wages, taxation or distribution of income." It was not only that his questions—"industrialism, mass culture, overpopulation, the decline of good living, vulgarization of taste"—were outside the "common framework" of the two parties; he himself was also stationed outside the very framework of the two main classes of industrial society. Opposed to "the utopian dream of progress and equality," he thus maintained virtual silence on economic issues and their class aspects, actually on the whole problem of class structure itself. Invoking Chekhov, he liked to see class conflict as a "misunderstanding" and to consign "the real root of poverty" to "human demoralization."[49]

His class marginality landed him to a degree in that "neither-norism" that Roland Barthes has ascribed to the petty bourgeoisie: an inclination to pose two equally disagreeable alternatives in order to eliminate the entire issue altogether by refusing said choices.[50] Yet if Kennan's targets included both organized labor (particularly the ethnic working class) and "the wealthy noveau-riche America, with all the sterility [and] negativism of its life," it was primarily the former class he scolded.[51] His singling out labor was, I think, less the product of any particular probusiness bias than of a sense that labor was a much more cohesive and visible interest group.

As a Russianist he was not wholly devoid of opinion about the economic organization of society; it would have been strange if he had been. Like many others he believed there was a global tendency toward "centralization of managerial and control functions in economic life." The distinction, he argued typically, was not a matter of the "substance of economic control, but of its method." That said, he was in favor of something within the wide area between "reckless and uncontrolled private speculation" and "totalitarian statism." While of the opinion that "there can be few greater catastrophes than for the state to get its claws on the myriad of minor economic activities which contribute so much to the immediate comforts and amenities of life in civilized society," he considered inevitable the coming of government "responsibility for wages and profits and employment practices of great industrial enterprises whose activities clearly affect the lives of millions of people and the whole trend of national economic life." He liked the TVA and found the idea of collective farms not unreasonable as such.[52]

In certain respects, then, he would not have been completely out of place on the bureaucratic wing of some Social Democratic party in Scandinavia. Indeed, favoring a strong government for the purpose of carrying out various needed reforms was a position that in the United States of the 1950s had certain overtones of socialism. Not particularly concerned with labeling his views, Kennan sometimes felt it necessary to distinguish himself on paternalistic grounds from socialist parties:

> If I am to be honest with myself, I must confess to being what they call "dirigiste"—a believer in a high degree of central direction of the economy. Is this socialism? Certainly not in the usual Marxist or even western European sense. These people all want central direction of the economy because they think it will improve the lot of the working class: raise their incomes, protect them from exploitation,

etc. I want it not to protect them from the employers but to protect them from themselves.[53]

Venting similar themes in 1960, he actually called himself a socialist of the *étatiste* variety; but that speech was intended for a Yugoslav audience and might have been adjusted to fit the occasion.[54] Nor was he consistently so favorably inclined toward *dirigisme*, particularly when it was connected with social welfarism, which he thought tended to lessen economic vibrancy and encourage sloth.[55] Labels aside, his focus was on management, not ownership, altogether in line with the idea of the how rather than the what. Beyond a basic belief in government of authority Kennan had no specific program in the economic domain, thus being at one with Benjamin Disraeli's seminal condensation of conservative politics: "Above all, no program!"[56]

His conservatism, then, when voiced at all, gave rise to no particularly penetrating views in the domain of American politics proper. There were two important series of domestic events, however, about which he did express himself with some vehemence: McCarthyism in the 1950s and the multifarious revolts of the 1960s. Connected in one way or another with the phenomenon of American conformism, they are best dealt with after we have had a glance at Kennan's cultural critique.

Utopian Containment

Organicist conservatism was part of a larger contradictory reaction to the coming of capitalist society which may be classed as romantic, though the term unfortunately has acquired a pejorative gloss in the United States as something naive, utopian, and unrealistic. By it I mean a basic negativity toward the kind of domination of nature brought about through the rise of commodity production, a negativity marked by a strong feeling that some elementary values of precapitalist society have been lost in the process.[1] Natural harmony of the whole is a central notion, and the object of the romantic critique is therefore typically the ills of society in toto, not the doings of, say, individual classes. Historically it has had no specific political identity. There have been romantics both right and left, ranging from reactionaries seeking to reconstitute a medieval system of estates to marxists such as Georg Lukács, Walter Benjamin, and Herbert Marcuse, indeed to Marx himself, for whom the lost and alienated essence of humanity could only be recuperated through a dialectical twist upward toward some radically new form of social being. Organicist conservatism I then take to be a right-wing form of the romantic current.

During the 1930s, Kennan's formative period, the primary expression of this kind of conservatism was a concern about the rise of mass culture and mass man, associated with the machine age and democracy.[2] Writers such as Oswald Spengler, José Ortega y Gasset, T. S. Eliot, Ezra Pound, D. H. Lawrence, and Wyndham Lewis all complained bitterly about the dilution of culture while flirting in various degrees with authoritarian right-wing movements. That political orientation probably resulted less from any deep affection for these movements (Pound's idolatry of Mussolini excepted) than from a general fear of socialism. For socialism was imagined to be the final and logical victory of mass civilization, the crushing elimination of difference and individuality in a totally administered and mechanized society.

The abhorrence of levelers and standardization had to be reconciled with the contradictory imperatives of hierarchy and totality: desire for collectivity on the one hand, subjectivity and imagination on the other. Whence followed the aestheticizing strategy common to some of these writers, whereby the modernist work of art was ingeniously conceived as at once organic and individual, thus affording partial escape from an otherwise intolerable dilemma, the complementary exit being that of exile itself—spiritual, geographic, or both. Lawrence was perhaps the plainest exhibit of these divergent impulses. As Terry Eagleton has strikingly described him, he wanted "men to be drilled soldiers but *individual* soldiers."[3] It was Lawrence who observed of the United States: "When pure mechanization or materialism sets in, the soul is automatically pivoted, and the most diverse of creatures fall into a common mechanical unison. This we see in America. It is not a homogeneous, spontaneous coherence so much as a disintegrated amorphousness which lends itself to perfect mechanical unison."[4] Similar Lawrencian themes were also propounded in British left-leaning circles, for instance by F. R. Leavis and his journal *Scrutiny*. Typically here a mechanized and degraded present of cities, motor cars, and advertising was contrasted with an idealized, largely bucolic homogeneity of the past, in this case the village of early seventeenth-century England. Leavis, who believed that culture is always transmitted by minorities, placed squarely in that tradition his own struggle against the alleged philistines at both ends of the social ladder.[5] It is against the background of this ambivalent constellation of ideas that Kennan's critique of American culture should be understood.[6]

Kennan believed in the typical romantic manner that a "mysterious enrichment" emanated from "being near to Nature and alone with her." Asserting "our affinity with growing things and the animal kingdom," he did not think humankind could "live successfully too far away from nature."[7] This attachment to rustic pursuits was expressed very early on. His only published piece of writing in the 1930s told readers of the *Canadian Geographical Journal* in sympathetic terms about peasant life on a Baltic island: "The people are condemned by the very meagreness of their economic resources to one form or another of poverty. But there is no form of poverty more dignified than that of the independent peasant-artisan, who can rely on his own handicraft for food and shelter and clothing. And it would be a pity if one of the last vestiges of this sort of society were to give way before the influences of an industrial age, and the independent peasant become the modern industrial proletarian."[8] Influenced by Lewis Mumford, among others, he began toward the end of the decade to feel "a growing conviction that . . . American society was becoming dangerously and sadly enmeshed in the tentacles of an uncontrolled urbanism." This was an idea he was never to abandon. "I would like," he wrote to a friend in 1964, "to live in an overwhelmingly agrarian country," a desire he had partially realized. On returning from Moscow after the war, he had bought a farm in Pennsylvania, where he spent a good deal of time laboring on the land.[9]

Modernity, in brief, had divided nature into country and city, and now the city was expanding as a series of artificial constructs, invading organic life and destroying the permanence of agrarian soil.[10] Some kind of balance had to be restored: "This society bears the seeds of its own horrors—unbreathable air, undrinkable water, starvation—and until people realise that we have to get back to a much simpler form of life, a much smaller population, a society in which the agrarian component is far greater again in relation to the urban component—until these appreciations become widespread and effective—I can see no answer to the troubles of our time."[11]

Symbolic of industrial civilization, the city was alien, literally and figuratively a space of darkness. Consider this highly suggestive, almost libidinal comparison made during a trip in 1950:

> And it occurred to me that for cities there is something sinister and pitiless about the dawn. The farm, secure in its humility and its submission, can take it. It can even welcome it, joyously, like the return of an old friend. But the city, still sleeping, cowers restlessly under it, particularly under the Sabbath dawn. In this chill, calm light, the city is helpless and, in a sense, naked. Its dreams are disturbed, its pretense, its ugliness, its impermanence exposed, its failure documented, its verdict written. The darkness, with its neon signs, its eroticism, and its intoxication, was protective and forgiving—tolerant of dream and delusions. The dawn is judgment: merciless and impassive.[12]

Alluring imagery aside, it is the dominance of the negative pole, the seductive city, that stands out here. About the positive side Kennan thought less fixedly. The real status of rural life in the United States he used more or less as a theoretically attractive backdrop for condemnations of urbanism. To my knowledge he rarely offered any examples of contemporary agrarian society as models. When he actually contemplated village life in the United States, the result was far from optimistic:

> What is happening in the small towns is also quite disturbing. I've seen it happen to my own village in Pennsylvania. The village used to have a political and communal life. People really lived there; their children went to school there; they went to church there; they did their shopping there; they worked there. To-day this is all changed. The village has become a row of houses along a highway, twenty-four minutes by automobile from the big industrial town of York. How many miles it is, is not important. Time has become important, not distance.[13]

Occasionally, after some longer excursus on urban troubles, he would also modify the contrasting terms so as not to fall into sheer rhapsody: "I don't want to idealise the village or the countryside. In England, as in America, the village has always been the seat of great pettiness and nastiness. But I am convinced that a society which is predominantly agrarian is, with all its faults, a sturdier and healthier society in the long run than one which is predominantly urban. Certainly emotional freshness gets lost in an urban environment."[14] More was lost in the city than merely "emotional freshness." Marked by atomization, passivity, and conformity, the new mass culture bred by this superficially enticing Other spelled ruin in every way for the social fabric:

> As this urbanization fragmentizes social groups, it centralizes the media of psychological influence (press, radio, television, movies) and makes recreation passive and vicarious rather than active and immediate. At the same time that it breaks up the groups in which the individual found scope for the development of leadership, self respect and self development, it provides for a vast fog of recreational stimuli which demand nothing in the individual, develop nothing in him and tend to atrophy his capacity for self expression.[15]

The chief weapon by which this urban conquest was conducted was of course "the run-away horse of technology," inducing in humankind "all sorts of Promethean ambitions and illusions." While new technology was "a fact of life," it ought to be subject to control and not introduced at too quick a pace. Thus he vigorously opposed the underlying "cult of production for the sake of production, the belief that economic development is an absolute good," as he defined it at the end of the 1950s, when such ideas were less common than today.[16] Yet there was little hope of receiving a sympathetic hearing. "We are prepared," he noted gloomily, "to let advancing technology do whatever it may to these living patterns, on the theory that anything else would be undemocratic and paternalistic." The United States, an "abnormally competitive" country, seemed governed solely by "the uninhibited flow of self-interest"[17]:

> Almost everywhere else, men are convinced that the answers to their problems are to be found in the acceptance of a high degree of collective responsibility and discipline. To many of them, the sight of an America in which there is visibly no higher social goal than that of self-enrichment of the individual, and where that self-enrichment takes place primarily in material goods and gadgets that are of doubtful utility in the achievement of the deeper satisfactions of life— this sight fails to inspire either confidence or enthusiasm.[18]

Sounding rather like Theodore Roosevelt and his exhortations to a "strenuous life," Kennan believed the culture of gadgetry would lead to decay[19]: "It seems to me that a great deal of the new technology that is being introduced into our lives is merely giving us bad habits and debilitating us: weakening our frames physically, thrusting us into an ever greater passivity of recreational and emotional life, demoralizing our youth, and probably weakening the biological foundation of our people."[20]

First among many pernicious products was that great symbol of American technology, the motor car. Unlike railroads, cars served to dismantle "all social relationships" and were thus an unmitigated evil.[21] Kennan, a defiant velocipedist long before the present fitness vogue, has appropriately reserved some of his most scathing words for this epitome of urban mass society. I can offer only a small sample from respectively, the 1960s and the 1930s:

> [The automobile is] unsocial, lonely, unhealthful, wasteful of both space and power, available for personal use to only limited portions (in age and state of health) of the population, exacting in its demand for our personal attention, neither safer nor faster than the railway system it replaced, and far less safe and fast than the railway system we could have had, had we ploughed into it even a fraction of the billions we have cheerfully turned over to the highway contractor and his bulldozers and the motor industry itself.[22]

The cars whirred past in monotonous profusion: dark streaks of motion, the occupation of which had no relationship to the road or to the landscape over which they passed . . . For me these hurtling gadgets, with their loads of cramped, motion-drugged humanity, had no more meaning than they had for the countless snakes and turtles who were my only companions on the road.[23]

Motorized society is not only irrational and fissiparous, but also deadeningly devoid of variation:

In these cars, for the most part were young men and girls,—in neat, symmetrical little parties of two or four. Precious little they had which was theirs alone. They had been seeing the same movies, hearing the same radio programs, reading the same magazine and newspaper articles as other young people for thousands of miles around. The cars they rode in were the same as those in which millions of other young people were riding, on those warm summer nights . . . [The roads] lay like great bands of concrete across the conquered countryside, stifling all spontaneity, all originality, all ordinary influences of nature, all local peculiarities. Even the colors became few and standardized. No more necessity to improve the color photographs of the magazine ads, with their six or seven standard colors. Life itself had been reduced to standard colors.[24]

The conformity so vividly depicted brings to mind Sartre's concept of seriality, designating a situation in which the individual is linked to others in a series rather than through a genuine group, doing alone, in isolation, exactly what everyone else is doing, a behavior ultimately modeled precisely on the assumption that everyone else is doing the same. The result is a form of individualized conformity.[25] Kennan's accounts of this "one-dimensional" society, to borrow Marcuse's famous phrase, suggest a monotony so dismally boundless as to be virtually inescapable:

[Mobility] is losing its meaning. What is the value of being able to move rapidly about when all things are the same? Even nature becomes ravaged, characterless and indifferent when it has been conquered by the automobile. I haven't the faintest interest in going anywhere in this country, because I know that, essentially, I am going nowhere. The road is precisely the same all the way from here to Los Angeles: the same billboards, the same cars, the same road-side blight, the same used-car lots and filling stations and motels and stuffy little boxes of restaurants, the same dazed, hypnotized, vacuous faces, veritably anaesthetized with staring at the flow of the endless concrete ribbon. To drive on such a road is not an experience in space, because one gets nowhere but where one came from; it is only an experience in time, but a horrible one, insofar as it constitutes a wastage of time in a way that time has almost never been wasted before; for the first time, men have devised a manner of wasting time which is both fatiguing and yet rules out even the possibility of thought and reflection.[26]

If this eerily oppressive and reified world was propelled, in a manner of speaking, by the motor car, its ideological underpinning and promotion was provided by the invidious mass media, at the center of which resided "the monstrous evil of American advertising." The result was "spectatoritis," a popular desire for mind-numbing leisure well satisfied by an industry chiefly devoted to profits[27]:

> Three of the greatest educational instruments in the country, the radio, the movies and periodical literature, were all in the hands of groups of persons whose primary purpose was to make money, whose higher responsibility to the public was negligible.[28]

> [The educational process is left to those] whose function and responsibility, in fact, are concerned with the peddling of what is, by definition, untruth, and the peddling of it in trivial, inane forms that are positively debauching in their effect on the human understanding.[29]

> With its characteristic staccato patterns, its lack of follow-through, and its endless abrupt transitions of theme, commercial entertainment has tended everywhere to weaken the faculty of concentration and to debauch the capacity for sustained and orderly thought.

Thus, he thought, Americans had reached a stage where they tended to be "creative only where commercial interest raises its capricious demands."[30] Rounding out this fiercely depressing social image were examples of decadent permissiveness such as drugs and pornography, and accounts of the ecosystemic destruction wrought by unhampered economic growth (likened to cancer).[31] Already in the 1950s he had expressed environmental concern about nuclear waste.[32]

To close the exposition, I quote some remarks made in 1954, in which Kennan allowed himself to dream of "a civilization in which there would be no dreary urban deserts, no wastes of stone and steel and dust and filth, no people living and working day in and day out in cubicles of concrete and metal, no over-population, no desolation and plundering of natural resources, no individual human life that did not stand in close association with the plants and animals to whose world we still in part belong."[33] This negative utopia, expressing an almost transcendental defiance of the present, may stand as a summary of the themes Kennan was likely to propound when speaking about American civilization. It was not a pretty picture, but then again Kennan was "a pessimist by nature," one whose pessimism was rendered so much deeper by the "ritualistic optimism" of official American culture.[34]

His overall predilections, by contrast, have little to do with the validity of his particular views, which should be assessed on their own merit. A few remarks:

Kennan's early concern with the environment is of obvious value. I also agree to a considerable extent with his diagnosis of the mass media, whose "stream of frivolities and inanities" is now likely on account of greatly improved communication technology to invade virtually every corner of the globe with its postmodern message.[35] My not insignificant proviso, however, is that mass culture is never as paralytically immobilizing as it may seem, harboring as it does a utopian element difficult to contain within the given limits of controlled consumption.[36] I think his analysis of motorized society largely correct, though in a country of enormous distances the car was for some a means of limited liberation. The urban-agrarian motif is on the whole unconvincing. Bucolic life in its traditional form was no doubt more communal and organic, but agrarian production today is irretrievably subordinated to a vast market system, and besides, the American farmer seems, despite attachment to the soil, for the most part to have been more of an isolated small businessman than a traditional villager. More important, if communal life has survived and to some extent been resurrected in this country, it is precisely in those cities with ethnic neighborhoods and compressed living patterns (though it must be added that when Kennan spoke of the "rapid disintegration and deterioration" of urban spaces, it was during a period of traumatic crisis).[37] Ultimately the agrarian myth blinded him to the potential of urban life.

The trouble with Kulturkritik otherwise, as Adorno pointed out, is that it tends to stop at a certain level: "Cultural consciousness rejects the progressive integration of all aspects of consciousness within the apparatus of material production. But because it fails to see through the apparatus, it turns towards the past, lured by the promise of immediacy."[38] Hence the danger of ending up, in Adorno's sardonic phrase, "a salaried and honored nuisance."[39]

And "a salaried and honored nuisance" was in part what Kennan became. Although uninhibited in denouncing profit-based mass media, he refrained from a sustained analysis of the economic structure that produced most of the litany of ills he continued to recite, assigning the blame instead to industrial society as a whole. There is nevertheless something to be said for this view. Even that left which used blithely to imagine environmental pollution to be the simple result of capitalist exploitation has now come to realize that massive industrialization in whatever form is always likely to generate these problems. To that degree the total critique of growth-oriented society was worthwhile and prescient. Still it exacted a price. For without anything by way of explanation beyond simple references to the Industrial Revolution, his critique assumed an abstract, plaintive character. Radical renunciation of modernity means radical political impotence.

Eventually there was to be much greater resonance for "his" issues, and for the first time he would gain an identifiable if fluid constituency beyond the realm of foreign policy. It was in fact only when foreign policy coalesced with the domestic in a movement against the most total of all environmental dangers, global war, that Kennan had his day. Central elements of his critique, fittingly condensing around the opposition to all things nuclear, would appear toward the end of the 1970s as powerful themes in what may generically be called the green movement. Thus we arrive at Kennan's harsh condemnations of the lineal ancestors of that movement, the student rebels of the 1960s, as well as to the whole question of political conformity in the United States.

American political life in the early 1950s seemed to be determined by what Kennan called, without exaggeration, "triumphant and excited and self-righteous anti-communism,"[40] spearheaded of course by the man who gave the era its name, Senator Joseph McCarthy. Obligingly the Truman administration had paved the way for the senator from (of all places) Wisconsin by needlessly scaring Congress and public alike about the Soviet specter. Just as Kennan had opposed any too fanatical form of anti-Sovietism in foreign policy, so he now came to oppose vigorously its domestic counterpart. There was material reason to do so. The emblematic target of McCarthy's inquisition was the State Department and its alleged myriad of communist sympathizers.

An index of the truly phantasmagorical character of this period is that the notion of Dean Acheson as a communist traitor could be seriously entertained in some congressional quarters. Kennan, though not himself under immediate attack, witnessed the humiliation of several long-time colleagues, among them John Paton Davies. A member of that select group of "old China hands" who had allegedly conspired to "lose" the Chinese mainland, Davies was eventually banished from the department and, despite having been cleared of wrongdoing, later found it necessary to leave the country.[41] Robert Oppenheimer, who had brought Kennan to Princeton, was similarly, if less acutely, dishonored. Kennan intervened with considerable courage on behalf of both.[42]

His record prior to McCarthy's assault was not otherwise one calculated to gain him credit with civil libertarians. In the 1930s he had grumbled about the absence of proper surveillance of communist activities; and after a speaking tour of the country in 1946 he had moved to collect the names of an academic gathering that had appeared hostile to his views on (non)cooperation with the Soviet Union. Even after 1950 he thought it right in principle (but unnecessary) to outlaw the Communist party and to bar its members from faculties of educational institutions, the reason being that communists showed no allegiance to the quest for truth.[43]

Proposals for *Berufsverbot* notwithstanding, Kennan was on the whole unequivocal in condemning the political and spiritual conformity that resulted from simple anticommunism, the "fear of the untypical, this quest for security within the walls of secular uniformity."[44] It was for him yet another example of the futile drive for the absolute, an "exercise which, like every form of perfectionism, undermines its own basic purpose" and ends in disaster: "We have seen our public life debauched, the faith of our people in great and distinguished fellow citizens systematically undermined; useful and deserving men hounded thankless out of honorable careers of public service; the most subtle sort of damage done to our intellectual life; our scholars encouraged to be cautious and unimaginative in order to escape being 'controversial,' a pall of anxiety and discouragement thrown over our entire scientific community."[45] He was indeed apprehensive that the United States in some perverse dialectical way would become increasingly like the Soviet Union: "Intolerant, secretive, suspicious, cruel, and terrified of internal dissension because we have lost our own belief in ourselves and in the power of our ideals."[46]

This is not just a question of the spectacle of a few men setting out
to achieve a cheap political success by appealing to primitive reactions, by appealing to the uncertain, suspicious little savage beast
that lies at the bottom of almost every human breast; it is more
importantly the spectacle of millions of our citizens listening eagerly
to these suggestions and then trotting off faithfully and anxiously,
like the victims of some totalitarian brainwashing, to snoop and check
up on their fellow citizens, to purge the libraries and the lecture
platforms, to protect us all from the impact of ideas.[47]

McCarthyism, he was convinced, provided a potential foundation for
a form of domestic totalitarianism, which he envisaged as "an Amer-
ican-type dictatorship retaining the electoral [and] constitutional
forms but filling them with an authoritarian content, picking arbitrarily some domestic scapegoat-enemy and treating as subversive all
those who would not join in this excoriation and persecution."[48]

As it happened, Stalin died; Kennan's compatriot from Wisconsin
went too far and eventually suffered the consequences; and the international climate improved, as did the domestic, though civil society
was still marked by strong pressure to conform. Kennan, dismayed at
this lack of color, spoke out for diversity in terms of "the glorious
disorder of nature."[49] His main concern may have been to preserve a
sphere of dissidence for himself and others of similar ilk, such as
Oppenheimer; but the fear of standardization was otherwise quite
genuine. During his two ambassadorial sojourns (1952 and 1961 to
1963), typically, he complained about the absence of vivacity and
imagination in his younger colleagues, and he was apt, in especially
frustrated moments, to stigmatize "many of the pillars of respectable
American society" for "vegetating in the smugness and selfishness and
superficiality of their particular brand of philistinism."[50]

In the end, however, there was always Lawrence's dilemma of drilled
but individual soldiers. On the one hand Kennan would criticize
American youth for its "veritable cult of personal sloppiness," for "the
decline in manners, the defiant irresponsibility, the exaggerated individualism, and the resentment of any social discipline."[51] On the other
hand he was displeased by the monochromatic quality of the typical
student of the 1950s: "We worry, in the case of our older student
generation, about what seems to us to be their exaggerated demand
for security, their lack of the spirit of adventure—even of protest—
their interest in knowledge for utilitarian purposes rather than for its
own sake."[52] It is well to bear these strictures in mind as we now turn

to the ensuing epoch, featuring as it did a student generation not notably lacking in enthusiasm for "adventure" and "protest."

The "glorious disorder" Kennan had praised in contrast to the massive uniformity of the 1950s had nothing to do with any disorderly disorder. The wholly unexpected advent of revolts among students and blacks in the 1960s represented something quite disorderly indeed, thus rubbing Kennan very much the wrong way. The times seemed to present an overwhelming spectacle of angry, uncouth people "milling about, screaming, shouting other people down, brawling with the police or with equally violent opponents, obstructing other people in their normal pursuits—and all this ostensibly in the effort to achieve one objective or another, not by the device of persuasion, not through the orderly processes of appointed authority or procedure, but through the devices of intimidation and blackmail."[53] This "spectacle" brought forth with a vengeance his penchant for "orderly processes of appointed authority or procedure." Whereas "human justice is always imperfect," he said, "the good order of society is something tangible and solid": "Humanity divides, it has been said, between those who, in their political philosophy, place the emphasis on order and those who place it on justice. I belong to the first of these categories."[54] Judging the country to be in the greatest danger since the Civil War, he responded with strong calls for a return to order, calls made in organs such as the *New York Times* and the *Wall Street Journal.* His initial critique of student militants and dropouts in the *Times* elicited such an enormous response that, with the addition of an extended response by Kennan, the original article and a selection of criticisms were immediately put out as a book (soon translated into several languages).[55] The essential point was crystalized in the title of the original address: "Rebels without a Program." For what disturbed him more than anything else was that the oppositional elements, whether shocking frontally against society or turning their backs to it, offered little by way of constructive alternatives; this "embittered pseudo-revolutionary nihilism" reminded him of incipient totalitarianism, primarily because of its historical affinities with Russian populism, revolutionary predecessor of Bolshevism. Consequent upon that realization he found "no other choice but to rally to the defense of a public authority" with which he might otherwise disagree.[56]

Kennan was not entirely hostile. In part, he acknowledged, these people were acting "out of sincerity and idealism, out of the unwillingness to accept a meaningless life and a purposeless society." In fact

he expressed a faint hope that critical elements of different genera-
tions—"experience on the one hand, strength and enthusiasm on the
other"—might coalesce in a common effort. Moreover, while defending the existing order (with emphasis on order), he was as critical as
ever of the official discourse that went with it: "The traditional vo-
cabulary of American politics—the hearty bombast, the banging of
the chauvinistic bell, the measureless national self-congratulation, the
huffy assertions of suspicion and truculence directed to the outside
world, and the ritualistic invocation of a pious anticommunism to
justify anything for which a more meaningful argument might seem
too subtle or too difficult—this language will no longer do."[57] Still,
these views were subsumed in the massive barrage against the rebellious. The vitriolic tone not only persisted but intensified between
1968 and 1971.

The substance of his quarrel cannot profitably be dealt with here.
Adequate representation would require too lengthy a treatment, and
besides, many of his themes were of long standing. Suffice it to say,
with some selectivity and great brevity, that he found the rebellion
another utopian attempt "to storm the bastions of society" by those
"determined to achieve the elimination of all evil and the realization
of the millennium within their own time"; that he accepted the idea
of "an idealistic, progressive and determined minority" but opposed
"a purely critical, irresponsible, and politically unorganized force";
that he thought the response on the part of the authorities one not
of brutality but rather of "feebleness and timidity"; that universities
were meant to be seats of higher learning, not protest, thus making
expulsion a reasonable policy; that as a more truly radical alternative
to the simple-minded desire to tear down the existing system he
offered structural reforms in areas such as transportation, advertising,
television, the environment, and political machines, in addition to
which he suggested new regional forms of government; that he pronounced himself against racial integration; that he abhorred, on the
whole, the student movement's "faulty philosophical foundations: its
lack of humour, its assumptions of human perfectibility, its exclusive
concentration on man's collective social behaviour, its total neglect of
individual ethics, its assumptions that any sort of personal beastliness
is justified if it serves a worthy public purpose."[58]

His typological image of the student rebel concentrated these anti-
pathies in particularly clear form. An extended quote is justified:

He is, as he might be expected to be in an overwhelmingly urban society, a distinctly urban creature. He is anxious, angry, humorless, suspicious of his own society, apprehensive with relation to his own future. Overexcited and unreflective, lacking confidence in anyone else, impatient and accustomed to look for immediate results, he fairly thirsts for action. Romantic and quixotic, he is on the prowl for causes. His nostrils fairly quiver for the scent of some injustice he can sally forth to remedy. Devoid of any feeling for the delineation of function and responsibility, he finds all the ills of his country, real or fancied, pressing on his conscience. He is not lacking in courage: he is prepared, in fact, to charge any number of windmills. But in doing so he is often aggressive and unintentionally destructive toward what he needs to live by, destructive sometimes toward himself . . .

The student is the victim of the sickly secularism of this society, of the appalling shallowness of the religious, philosophic and political concepts that pervade it. And in addition to all this, his estrangement from nature, his intimacy with the machine, his familiarity with the world of gadgetry, and his total lack of understanding for the slow, powerful processes of organic growth, all these imbue him with an impatience and an expectation of an immediate connection between stimulus and effect that does not fit even with the realities of his own development as a person, and even less with those of the development of a society.[59]

To this composite he counterpoised an equally idealized one of "normal, quiet, cheerful, orderly, and good-nature" people[60]:

This country still has within it great resources of strength and vitality, resources of good nature, common sense, neighborly generosity, cheerfulness and humor, practical ingenuity—qualities that have endowed our people with their identity and given our life the power and charm that it has had throughout our history. These qualities are visible today primarily in older people and not in younger ones; mainly in rural areas, not urban ones; primarily among people who work with their hands, not among intellectuals.[61]

The content of this contrasting sketch, certainly extraordinary, speaks for itself. Generally, as in this case, he explained rebelliousness by enumerating a series of "objective" conditions in society, such as secularism and mechanical preoccupations. Still, another model was at work as well, based on Russian history and exemplified in his depiction of the civil rights movement. Just as the Russian populists of the 1860s had gone to the peasants, American radicals were now going to the black communities, not only to aid in remedying internal problems but also to organize protest. The lesson, confirmed by other historical incidents, was this: "Hardship and injustice are real phenomena; but revolutionary protest against such things *is usually the product of stimulus from outsiders with a comfortable background*. By and large, that is the history of the entire Marxist-socialist movement."[62] The implication that black revolts were instigated by outsiders is false: in cases where the question was not just one of spontaneous riots, blacks, whether ghetto denizens or not, led the movement from start to finish; and beyond that every black in the United States had in some sense been negatively affected by racism, thus making the whole point of externality moot.

My concern here, however, is with explanatory models, not substantive argument. The outsiders inciting revolt while not being subject to oppression themselves are students (that is, intellectuals), and their most fundamental reason for doing so is *psychological*: they are rationalizing inner dissatisfactions by projecting them onto some available external misery.[63] The resultant "neurotic intellectual" is a figure on whom the right historically has blamed numerous disturbances against the ruling order, a figure who had made conspicuous appearances in Kennan's explanations of Bolshevism and Third World nationalism.[64] A passage, corrosively charged, from the X-Article may serve as an example:

> Frustrated, discontented, hopeless of finding self-expression—or too impatient to seek it—in the confining limits of the Tsarist political system, yet lacking wide popular support for their choice of bloody revolution as a means of social betterment these revolutionists found in Marxist theory a highly convenient rationalization for their own instinctive desires. It afforded pseudo-scientific justification for their impatience, for their categoric denial of all value in the Tsarist system, for their yearning for power and revenge and for their inclination to cut corners in the pursuit of it.[65]

"Intellectuals," as he wrote in 1949, "are generally more ambitious, more pretentious, vainer, more confused, more frustrated than workers"; and therefore more susceptible to communism which "addresses itself to the unsuccessful and the untalented ones."[66]

This theme of neurosis reappears in Kennan's analysis of the American student left of the 1960s. Relying heavily on the notion of resentment for its explanatory power, it should be read in the context of a concept first articulated by Nietzsche and indeed known as *ressentiment*. Nietzsche's theorization had more than one level, but for our purposes *ressentiment* may be said to feature the following essential logic: the multitude, or masses if you will, are inherently inert (otherwise they would not be masses as opposed to superiors); when the "natural" hierarchy of rulers and ruled is upset, it is either because the masters have been affected by the slave mentality or on account of outside agitation by various failed intellectuals who are finding demotic outlets for their personal problems. Represented in Nietzsche's writings by the ascetic priest, this structural character became in one guise or another the means by which a series of writers on the right, from Joseph Conrad to Wyndham Lewis, rendered the threatening rise of mass man and the revolt of the masses ideologically comprehensible and containable. Paradoxically, however, the act of imputing *ressentiment* to intellectuals is itself the result of *ressentiment* on the part of intellectuals: Nietzsche, Ortega, Lewis, Benda, and Kennan.[67]

This raises the larger question of positionality as such. Whence, in short, are these denunciations issued? And why the intemperate tone? Compare, for instance, Kennan's emotional response with that of Walter Lippmann, whose political proclivities and stand on Vietnam were fairly similar but who took a far more relaxed view of youthful militance. It is hard to imagine Lippmann going to the extreme of ascribing to the student leadership ("scoundrels") a sentiment of "delight" and "triumph" at the killing of their four fellow students at Kent State.[68]

Problems of order, symmetry, and authority had always loomed large throughout Kennan's bureaucratic life; Lippmann, a journalist secure in his sphere and not a little feared, was burdened by no such considerations.[69] The student movement, ultrademocratic in spirit (if not always in practice), consigned Kennan's foundational belief in the value of order and hierarchy to the rubbish heap. At the same time he probably found himself partly dislodged from his self-conceived place in the configuration of American life and politics. This, after all, was a man who had spent a good deal of the preceding era on the political margin, trying to gain a reasonable hearing for his case and not succeeding very well, and now finding himself uncomfortably in partial agreement with a crowd of people he otherwise considered largely rebarbative, agreement not only on the Vietnam war—outstanding issue of the day and one on which his vocal opposition was widely publicized—but also on the "appalling shallowness" of American culture, though here he failed to acknowledge the extent of this affinity. Subsequent renunciations, then, have resulted in part from a reflexive need to reestablish his proper place, to reinvent his own subjectivity some distance away from unwelcome company.

It is not surprising, therefore, that his argument should have been marked by a certain lingering ambivalence. He agreed with "the charge that our electoral system is not adequately representative" but insisted on "structural reform" instead of mere protest. In his dictum: "The problem is not how to make a bad system work well by abusing it; the problem is to change it in such a way that it will work well without abuse." Accordingly, he countered radical "rejection of the normal electoral process" by imploring dissenting minorities to "accept the responsibility of confronting the electorate at the polls."[70] This did not signify any populistic turn of mind, only the recognition in the face of ultrademocratic attacks that a mediating institution between people and government was necessary and desirable. Yet he also complained that the liberals of the 1950s had been tinkering with the existing system instead of making fundamental changes, having himself in that period gone so far as to say that his policies might be taken as "subversive."[71] He also claimed, as an afterthought, to be more pessimistic about the United States than the students, more "radical" in what he had to propose, a peculiar argument for someone calling for law and order. Finally, while criticizing puerility and nihilism of method, he himself had nothing better to suggest by way of accomplishing his radical policies than shopworn references to the need for a new party. The very strategic emptiness of this formula undermined his own case for opposition through "orderly processes of appointed authority or procedure."[72] The old problem of historical agency and social change was again making itself felt: a list of projects with no means in sight to carry them out.

Thus too the antinomies of conservative dissidence come to the fore. The premier virtue in Burkean (and Aristotelian) conservatism is prudence, but exhortations to moderation are difficult to reconcile with programs that necessitate vast institutional changes in the existing machinery.[73] Between abstract devotion to organic evolution and profound dissatisfaction with the actual discontinuities of modernity (not to mention the nearly schizophrenic discontinuities of postmodernity) there opens up a considerable political gap, closed only partially by declarations of faith in some sagely omnicompetent elite which can define and carry out what is supposedly in the interest of all. From this angle Kennan's position was every bit as abstract as the most revolutionary rhetoric. Of this he was partially aware: "Things desirable, essential, or even unavoidable in the long run often sound absurd, utopian, or just plain crazy, when placed in relation to the attitudes and possibilities of the present day."[74] The "desirable" and "essential" may indeed sound "utopian," even if right; but in that case one really has broken with the moderate and the prudent, unless these values are to be defined by some clairvoyant outside "the attitudes and possibilities of the present day," at which point we must posit a benevolent authoritarianism instead of a democracy.

Looking back at the 1960s now as one formed by it, silence largely having replaced the uproar, I am tempted to repeat Kennan's own wonderment at the quirks of history when he was then looking back at the 1950s: "The strivings of the 1950's and early 1960's seem far away now, as though seen through the wrong end of the binoculars: and in this perspective the actors, one's self included, look reduced in size and a bit silly, believing in things that had no substance, pursuing goals that had no future, entertaining hopes for which the justification was already being quietly destroyed."[75] But if many of the controversies of the 1960s now seem dated, one must add the intriguing footnote that when the period was over and the historical analogy of Russian revolutionary nihilism had proved unwarranted (to say the least), Kennan's dormant affinities with the then fading student movement were allowed to come into play. Encapsulated in the twin issues of nuclear weapons and nuclear energy was a certain convergence of political concerns, analogous in part to the British case of E. P. Thompson, another romantic (but left-wing) critic alienated from the youth protests of the 1960s.[76] The process was not one-way. While Kennan learned something about the place of passionate struggle for causes, the activists realized the relevance of nuclear disarmament and ecology (though there was always a current of Rousseauian naturalism in the sixties). Emphasizing the conservationist element of his conservatism, Kennan expressed the "deepest sympathy" for the peace movement, calling its "growth and gathering strength" on both sides of the Atlantic "the most striking phenomenon" of the early 1980s.[77] His defense of the more militant and youthful European side is worth quoting in full:

Nor is it useful to portray the entire European wing of this movement as the expression of some sort of vague and naively unrealistic sentiment. There is some of that, certainly; but where there is, it is largely a reaction to the negative and hopeless quality of our own Cold War policies, which seem to envisage nothing other than an indefinitely increasing political tension and nuclear danger. It is not surprising that many Europeans should see no salvation for themselves in this sterile perspective and should cast about for something that would have in it some positive element—some ray of hope.[78]

The strong presence of religious groups (indeed of the ethical concerns) in this movement, especially on the American side, played a considerable role in his favorable assessment: these are by now for the most part, in his words, "quiet, thoughtful, sensible people,"[79] not hordes of countercultural rejectionists. So we come to the question of Kennan's deep-seated Calvinism, the obvious significance of which I have hitherto ignored.

Although Kennan offered little until the 1960s in the way of explicit religious commentary, there was doubtless great symmetry of theme and structure between his beliefs and the typical Calvinist posture. If his religion did not provide him with an ideology in any precise doctrinal manner, it most assuredly governed at some deeper level his way of being toward the world.

Born into a fairly strict Presbyterian family, Kennan seems during the State Department years to have taken his religion largely as a matter of course, rarely, if ever, making any mention of it in personal terms. And if he happened to put religion in a historical perspective, he tended under the influence of Gibbon to turn it into something instrumental. Pondering, for example, the twin rise of dissension and repression in nineteenth-century Russia, he was struck by the following (in itself not very convincing) analogy: "[It] bears an uncomfortably close parallel to what happened in the first and second centuries of the Christian era, when a revolutionary religious movement among the Jews suddenly combined with the discontent of the whole great class of the under-privileged throughout the Roman world to produce a social and spiritual movement destined to change the entire course of history."[80] That the author of this alarming historical reference to a "revolutionary religious movement" was in reality an adherent of that same religion is perhaps difficult to discern. There was, however, nothing incoherent about his position. He assumed that religion was rather a structural necessity:

> I was not unconscious of the fact that . . . the great mass of people have always had to have some irrational spiritual solace in the face of their own imperfections and those of humanity in general . . . If men must be protected from the blinding glare of reality, let this work be done—as it has been done according to the tradition of Christian churches—by men who have been educated to it, who are openly dedicated to unselfishness in doing it, and whose public responsibility it is to see that it is done in such a way to preserve— and not destroy—spiritual health, peace of mind and sanity of aspiration among those whom it affects.[81]

I take this to mean that religion, in the institutional sense, serves the useful (indeed admirable) function of keeping the multitude in a reasonably healthy frame of mind and so keeps society together, a viewpoint not uncommon among eighteenth-century thinkers such as Gibbon and thus scarcely surprising to find in Kennan. Otherwise, he was apt to think ecumenically of established world religions in favorable distinction to the ethical morass of Soviet communism.[82]

Once Kennan was out of power and back in civil society again, religion became much more important in a directly personal manner. The first thing he did after leaving the State Department in 1950 was to read Calvin's *Institutes* for guidance. From then until the early 1960s, an existentially trying period, the religious component became diffused. His views on foreign policy, for example, were now sometimes swathed in Christian terminology, as when he illustrated the limits of acceptable violence by pointing to the ethically transgressive atom bombs inflicted on Japan. Custodianship, a strongly Calvinist notion, was similarly prominent in his critique of both nuclear weapons and environmental pollution. During his Yugoslav ambassadorship (1961–1963) he engaged in lay preaching, giving sermons on subjects such as Calvin and Freud, emphasizing their common understanding of the darker undercurrents in humanity. He often complained too, drawing directly from Calvinist sources, of a lack of higher public purpose in American society; and he expressed disgust with permissiveness.[83]

Justifying faith itself by reference to the limits of reason, he came to look upon his Christianity as a gift from history that was not to be questioned, and so it took its place as an integral part of his conservatism: "For it often occurs to me that whoever, being born in a Christian family, tries to set himself up in position wholly outside the faith of his fathers, is actually denying his entire cultural heritage and forfeiting for himself the strength that comes of being able to recognize one's self as a part of a continuity reaching far beyond the present generation."[84] His religion, then, came to be a fixed point of navigation, a source of moral and political authority, enabling him to cope with ruptures and humiliations. Yet its full importance does not become apparent until one goes beyond his explicit adherence and reflections to pose the question of deeper attitudinal effects. Here several features of Calvinism must be mentioned.

First and foremost is order itself. Calvin, concerned amidst radical Protestantism to restore the value of secular institutions, made order a central concept of fusion within his dual system of church and state, in theory as well as practice. Having theorized and built a strong political system, he liked to refer to disorderly elements as "inhuman monsters," an epithet not wholly dissimilar in spirit to Kennan's view of student militants.[85]

Other more or less related components that come to mind are devotion to "unceasing, penetrating and formative labour" as a kind of "intramundane asceticism," to use Ernst Troeltsch's (and indirectly Max Weber's) excellent formulations; concomitant abhorrence of sloth and luxury; repression of outward expressions of emotion; the salience of individual and communal discipline; a profound sense of tragedy and impending disaster; realist disdain for abstract speculation and utopian thought, the Kingdom of God (and therefore history) having been elevated to a hidden, unknowable realm; a consequent concentration on means over ends; much emphasis on excellence throughout while realizing that perfection is never possible because God is hidden and sin is original; firm adherence to the value of distinct internal hierarchy and allotted function; reverence for offices and elected polity (custodianship) over particular individuals; political rule based on deferential consent rather than fear, participation being limited to a passive role of ratification once the rulers have been elected; and a conception of the state as an institution of education and discipline.[86]

One can do little but note these obvious parallels and underline how profoundly Calvinist a personality Kennan is. In light of his deprecations of conformity, however, something remains to be said about the "other" impulse, about that urge toward expression and diversity which does not easily fit the austerity of Calvinist order.

Indeed, it took no more than a revisit in the early 1970s to one of the more orderly places on earth, the Soviet Union, to occasion complaints about the lack of "the pleasingly unstructured, unexpected and unintended."[87]

The aesthetic flavor of this remark was not accidental, for many of Kennan's texts can be arranged along a signifying axis from ethics to aesthetics, finding primary expression in the valorization of the how rather than the what. Beauty and form—in writing, in appearance, in policy—were for him an overdetermining factor. Beyond posture, aesthetics also became an object of study. Typically, the object of his first absorbing interest in Russian affairs had been Anton Chekhov, of whom he wrote an unpublished biography. (And an American Chekhov is perhaps what Kennan would really have liked to be, a placeless yet sympathetic observer of tragedy and detail, his essayistic despatches thus in part the result of authorial desire not quite realized.) Much later, on leaving behind the disappointing and alienating 1950s, he voiced an aspiration for "work that was more closely connected with such things as literature and the aesthetic side of life." Back on the academic path after the Yugoslavian interlude, furthermore, he told Oppenheimer that he wanted to study "the development of outlooks and tastes in the modern world," the "transition from the clear and symmetrical concepts of the 18th century culture to the strange Victorian world of the latter half of the century."[88]

Nothing seems to have come of this worthwhile idea, displaced by problems as unforeseen in 1963 as they were eventually to become acute. The aesthetic impulse itself was, however, not suppressed. With his *Memoirs*, published in 1967 and rightly praised for their literary qualities, Kennan achieved distinction as a man of letters.[89] He engaged himself energetically in the merging of the National Institute of Arts and Letters and the American Academy of Arts and Letters, over which he presided between 1965 and 1972.

Aestheticism in this respect was something more than a product of personal proclivities; for art was a refuge from the storm, a means of coping with cultural upheaval and disintegration. Witness his presidential address to the academy in 1968: "I like to think of [this ceremony] as an act of defiance in the face of the tempest of the time—as a testimonial to the fact that even though the political surface of our life be marred by bitterness, passion, and violence, the pulse of artistic creativity continues to beat firmly and confidently and to pro-

vide a deeper and better witness to our national identity and spirit
than all the conflicts and controversies in which our political confusion
has landed us."[90] Literary style was of course of particular significance
in this strategy of aesthetic defiance. Reference must be made here to
his other great model as a writer, Edward Gibbon. Lionel Gossman
writes aptly of the British historian:

> The studied politeness and civility of the language, the abstractness
> and generality of the vocabulary, are an essential part of the meaning.
> They affirm the value of urbanity, of cool and imperturbable detach-
> ment, and of deliberate, controlled, timeless elegance of form, against
> the ugly formlessness of uncontrolled passion and disorderly content;
> at the same time, they ensure that understanding will be reserved for
> an elite sufficiently educated and urbane to appreciate it and to find
> in its appreciation the confirmation of its superiority.[91]

This characterization may not apply in all respects to Kennan's use of
style, but the underlying intention of making style itself an affirmative
message of elegant constancy in a world of "ugly formlessness" is
clearly similar. Underscored professionally by the diplomatic devotion
to etiquette (and rank), aestheticism in the sense of shaping existence
according to principles of beauty can thus be understood as a gesture
of resistance, as well as a means of persevering in a reified, "bewildering" world.[92] Such an interpretation is particularly tempting if Kennan
is placed in the tradition of Eliot, Lawrence, and Pound, for whom
art served as a sanctuary for organic consciousness.[93] His fixation on
style, method, means over ends, ultimately art itself may be read, then,
as an attempt to escape the unresolvable dilemma with which I began:
how to be an organicist conservative in a place that is constitutionally
unorganic without ending up in a condition of what he rightly referred
to as "internal migration."[94]

The escape is certainly real in the sense that it is embedded in
practice. If analyzed as a problem of *ideology*, however, it can be recast
in quite different terms as part of the process of inventing a place for
the subject through the construction of some sort of narrative. The
aesthetic idea can then be seen as a symbolic act, as a mythical (but
nonetheless effective) resolution of an otherwise unacceptable closure
of ideology, in turn the product of an unresolvable social contradiction
or dilemma.[95]

This structuralist thesis demands some elaboration and modification,
for which purpose it is useful to begin with a list of recurring binary

oppositions in Kennan's discourse. A simple (and incomplete) table of positive and negative might read as follows:

elevated individual	masses
hierarchy	egalitarianism
order	justice
authority	anarchy, incoherence
diversity	conformity
differentiation	standardization
organic	mechanical
natural	artificial
slow change	rapid innovation
value	nihilism, totalitarianism
means	ends
community	atomized society
rural	urban
agricultural	industrial
manual labor	intellectual labor
"high" art	mass culture
railroads	motor cars
dirigisme	laissez-faire
realism	utopianism, perfectionism
realities	words, idealities
particularism	universalism
Western civilization	nationalism, Third World, Other
circular time	progressive time

Though useful as a conceptual inventory and summary, the table carries little explanatory power in itself. It does imply, however, something by way of a story rather than a mere display of binary thought. To achieve a chart of Kennan's ideological "map" more consistent with that narrative notion, the structuralist argument can be developed beyond the point of simple binary opposition with the introduction of a semiotic rectangle. This device permits greater complexity in analyzing master narratives and characterological systems. As in the structuralist model, the starting point is a contrariety, an antinomy of the mind resulting from the ideological closure of a real social contradiction or dilemma as represented in the given narrative. Completing the rectangle are the two simple negations (logically contradictories) of the contrarieties. The dynamism or meaning of the system is generated by the attempt to combine the various terms and thus resolve the unresolvable through allotment of functional slots to assorted

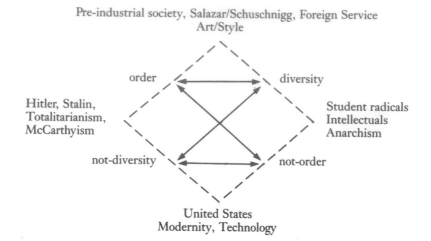

Pre-industrial society, Salazar/Schuschnigg, Foreign Service
Art/Style

order ←→ diversity

Hitler, Stalin,
Totalitarianism,
McCarthyism

Student radicals
Intellectuals
Anarchism

not-diversity ←→ not-order

United States
Modernity, Technology

characters within the narrative. The ideological closure is then over-come in the ideal synthesis of the two contrarieties.[96]

Any opposition from the list might conceivably be used, but, prima facie, the Lawrencian dilemma would offer implications of satisfactory generality. It may be reformulated as the problem of combining the positive values of order, diversity, and differentiation. For instance, Kennan's promulgation of the bureaucratic Idea contrasts with his eccentricity within, and intermittent rejection of, the actual bureaucracy. Or to put the question in terms of art: How could freedom as subordination to a natural order be reconciled with freedom as individual artistic expression (such as his own)? After all, modernist art, at least in its avant-garde form, tended to be militantly antitraditional and *transgressive*, not least in matters sexual. He was in fact aware of his difficulty in navigating between the Scylla of philistinism and the Charybdis of licentiousness.[97] I offer, then, the accompanying tentative ideological chart. Order and diversity (implying differentiation) are obviously not opposed here in a logical sense but represent rather the ideal and impossible synthesis. "Characters" listed in the combination slot of these two contrarieties—preindustrial society, Salazar, Schuschnigg, the (old) Foreign Service, art, and style—are thus the ideological (or imaginary) resolutions of the unattainable objective of finding a "real" synthesis, all of them in some symbolic manner constituting a fusion of the orderly and the diverse (and differentiated). The motley category of intellectuals occupies the next slot, combining the disorderly with the diverse (in the sense of oppositional individualism),

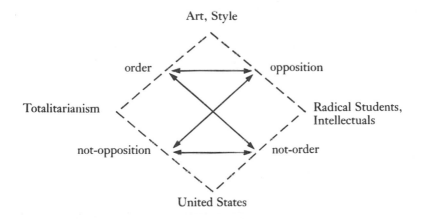

followed by the United States, unorganic, disorganized, and fluid yet standardized and conformist in its culture. The final place is taken by totalitarianism, either incipient (McCarthyism) or in full bloom (Hitler, Stalin), incorporating total order and total uniformity.

Another version may be organized around the obvious contradiction between order and opposition, in other words, the paradox of conservative radicalism. The diagram is relatively self-explanatory. The radical students constitute disorderly, nihilistic opposition; the United States symbolizes, perhaps even worse, unordered conformity; and totalitarianism the deadening alternative of order and no opposition. Art and style, then, become the only escape, the symbolic resolution that allows attachment to both order and opposition, in short, a strategy of utopian containment.

This, however, is not the end of the story. For the last decade has seen Kennan transcend these terms of ideological closure, resolving the unresolvable by assuming the defense of nothing less than the universal interest, not so much abandoning organicist conservatism as suspending judgment on American life and politics, leaving that domain to its fate and finding on the outside, at long last, a secure place for his final and prophetic stand.

Appendix A

Survey of the Soviet Analysis after 1950

Kennan's views on the Soviet Union have undergone some changes since 1950, when he became, except for two short periods, a private citizen and an outspoken critic of cold war orthodoxy. The Soviet Union has of course changed too, and thus he could claim to have been right all along. With some tenacity he has indeed defended earlier positions from this historical perspective.[1] Parallel trajectories, however, are not the whole truth. Since the entire foreign policy establishment were now hawks of one shade or another, Kennan centered his critique on them and in the process altered earlier views in a way that cannot entirely be ascribed to corresponding alterations in the Soviet Union. Previously held standpoints were not so much repudiated as allowed to lapse. One novelty, at any rate, was a better understanding of how the Soviet Union tended to see things. To get an idea of change and continuity in this post-1950 period, it will be convenient to survey briefly the main areas of examination as put forth in Part I.

Totalitarianism and the Nature of the Regime

Kennan continued to use *totalitarianism* intermittently as a designation for an almost undefinable evil, an absolute negative.[2] However, when he once tried to give it more precise meaning by reference to similarities between Nazi Germany and the Soviet Union, he had to concede defeat, in effect, by acknowledging their differences and then turning the term impressionistically into an image of something dreamlike.[3] During this period he also employed it to express contempt for McCarthyism.[4] While retaining notions of instability and crusts over something volatile, he concluded that modern technology and the destruction of primary groups in society were important factors in the emergence of totalitarianism and that technological efficiency had in fact rendered it largely impervious to resistance.[5] Yet he had expressed earlier a belief that totalitarianism was chiefly a problem pertaining to development and hence historically of passing nature; and he was convinced that change would come in the Soviet Union as everywhere else, in which supposition he proved right.[6] Noting toward the end of the 1950s a decline in "fanaticism," a greater openness, and impressive economic and technological gains, he began to think the nightmare was over.[7] The Soviet Union appeared to be moving toward the "conservative-authoritarian" state he considered to have been "the norm" in the West during the Christian era, unlike totalitarianism a political form that was not "hideous in the sight of God."[8] From then on the concept ceased to have any but historical significance for him.

Contributing to the reclassification was the notion of convergence then coming into vogue—the idea, in other words, that the two types of society were moving toward some essentially similar middle.[9] Indicatively, after the Sino-Soviet split he compared the Russian stance favorably to the Chinese on account of its *Western* filiation.[10]

The fall of Khrushchev he wrongly took as a victory for the hard-line Chinese tendency; but in seeing a certain retrogression ("neo-Stalinism") in the latter part of the 1960s he was surely correct.[11] By the 1970s, however, he had come to see Brezhnev and his oligarchic colleagues as a tired and decrepit group of bureaucrats, "perhaps the most conservative ruling group to be found anywhere in the world."[12] Looking back at that point he thought the regime remarkably similar to what it had been right after Stalin's death, despite the vast changes in Soviet society. All in all, until Mikhail Gorbachev came along, Kennan reserved his kindest words for Khrushchev. In Gorbachev, however, he has finally found a Soviet leader entirely to his liking: intelligent, imaginative, bold, realistic, and, not least, Western oriented.[13] Perhaps in contemplative moments Kennan is now wondering what might have been, what it would have been like to have had a Gorbachev rather than a Stalin to deal with.

These views are in themselves subject to dispute, but there can be no doubt that they varied over time with the regime itself.

Internal Conditions

Kennan spent a few months as ambassador to Moscow in 1952, an experience that ended abruptly in his being declared persona non grata after a singularly careless comparison, made in public, between internment in Nazi Germany and the nature of diplomatic life in the Soviet Union.

Ironically he was then on his way to an ambassadorial convocation in London to present a view far more understanding of and conciliatory to the Russian position than any other within the administration.[14] He did not return to the Soviet Union until a decade later. Removed from the primary source and occupied with domestic debates, Kennan understandably said little about internal conditions. His brief ambassadorship, unfortunately coinciding with Stalin's last phase, produced some interesting reflections (and many more, presumably, are still under classified seal). His main impression in 1952 was that the chasm between rulers and ruled had increased; the people, though physically in better shape than before, had retreated into a private sphere (an old theme of his), less an expression of "political discontent" than of a "spiritual breach."[15] Registering the sterility of cultural life, he wrote:

> The country lives today, ideologically, in a species of Wagnerian twilight, characterized by the rosy, ethereal reflections of great deeds once accomplished, breathing an atmosphere of well-deserved relaxation and smug self-congratulation over the tremendous achievements of the parting day . . . There can be no real negative characters in Soviet drama, except agents and dupes of the menacing outside world; for how could such people be produced by the influence of Soviet society alone, which has been correctly conducted for 35 years?[16]

Since then he has shown some admiration for the discipline and order of Soviet society, the inverse image of the Western promiscuity, slovenliness, and fragmentation he so detested.[17]

Soviet Foreign Policy

In this domain one can legitimately speak of a qualitative change in Kennan's outlook, chiefly the result, I think, of his having to imagine much more than before how the militarized cold war policies of the West might appear to a Russian. Although it was greatly reinforced in the latter part of the 1950s, when Soviet policy was in some ways closer to his own perspective than the American, his inclination to take a more understanding attitude toward Moscow's point of view actually originated prior to Stalin's exit.[18] Witness, for instance, a passage from his most important ambassadorial despatch of 1952, one that can still be read for its pertinence to current problems:

> Surely as one moves one's bases and military facilities toward the Soviet frontiers there comes a point where they tend to create the very thing they were designed to avoid. It is not for us to assume

that there are no limits to Soviet patience in the face of encirclements by American bases. Quite aside from political considerations, no great country, peaceful or aggressive, rational or irrational, could sit by and witness with indifference the progressive studding of its own frontiers with the military installations of a great power competitor.[19]

His fixation on Soviet expansionism as internal necessity thus waned without any attempt structurally to explain which domestic changes had brought this about. The "iron logic," at any rate, gave way to a recognition that Moscow's foreign policy was to no small degree the dialectical product of what Washington did, and vice versa. This did not mean that he saw no expansionism at all; but with the decline in "fanaticism" he tended to think of the Soviet leadership as typical great power politicians, predominantly interested in "territorial-political" questions of "who is to control whom, and where."[20] While still harboring beliefs about the ephemerality of capitalism, he said in 1956, they "are also in business. They are in the business of national power. They have inherited the governmental responsibility for a great state—one of the major traditional units in the contemporary international family—with its people, its history, its traditions, its aspirations, its prejudices, and its rivalries. Like others who are in business, they like to win friends and influence people."[21] Three years later he thought that nationalism had become more important than (marxist) ideology to the Soviet outlook on the world, an outlook modified too in another crucial respect: "In every program of imperialism there comes a point at which the obvious responsibilities and dangers of further efforts at expansion begin to outweigh the conceivable advantages."[22] In consequence, it is not surprising that he would consider the geriatric Brezhnev leadership of the 1970s cautious in its foreign policy despite its self-professed competition with the United States.[23] By then he saw Soviet "expansionism" in terms of gaining "influence" rather than extending "the formal limits" of "power and responsibility."[24]

   The effects of the great-power concept can be seen in his varying response to Soviet policies during three of the worst postwar crises in Eastern Europe: Hungary in 1956, Czechoslovakia in 1968, and Poland from 1980 on. In the first case he showed understanding if not support for the crackdown against the Nagy regime: Moscow could not be expected to ignore the signaled intention of the Hungarians to leave the Warsaw Pact. A more moderate change, not in blatant violation of the Soviet security system, might have been within the bounds of the acceptable.[25] For the same reason he was incensed by the invasion in 1968. The reform communists of the Prague Spring had taken meticulous care not to repeat Nagy's mistake. Kennan, therefore, could see no justification for the brutal Soviet action.[26] On the Polish question, finally, he voiced apprehension lest a repetition of the events of 1956 be brought about by excessive demands on the part of Solidarity.[27] His judgments, in all three instances, were based on an interpretation of what a great power with an established security system can properly be expected to tolerate, given historical peculiarities and the situation at hand.[28]

Throughout, Kennan has been sensitive to signs of dramatic swings in American public opinion on the Soviet Union. When in the 1950s he detected a belief that the change of leadership in the Kremlin also signified a basic change in the Russian propensity for offensive war, he immediately raised a word of warning: Stalin, while barbaric, had not been any more interested in war than the new leaders, and the change was therefore much less drastic in that respect than imagined.[29] The same emphasis on continuity appeared in his statements during the height of détente, the novelty of which he considered largely a ploy by the Nixon administration. Exaggerated claims, he felt, only laid the foundation for future backlashes. When détente duly collapsed, he was thus quick to criticize the notion that the Russians had ever agreed to cease competition in the Third World.[30]

War as a Soviet Means

Ambiguities on the subject of war survived, less conspicuously, into the 1950s. At one time or another he argued both that war was not a part of the Soviet ideological scheme and hence not a priori to be expected, and also that only practical considerations and caution restrained the Soviets from using any means available.[31] Still, he maintained at all times that the Soviet Union would not in fact attack Western Europe. Once the totalitarian theme became passé toward the end of the decade, his notion of unlimited Soviet means tended to fade as well.[32] The final word on war is his: "I emphatically reject the primitive thesis, drawn largely from misleading and outdated nineteenth-century examples, that the Kremlin might be inclined to resort to war as a means of resolving its internal difficulties. Nothing in Russian history or psychology supports such a thesis."[33]

Ideology

Freely confessing on several occasions his inability to deal with Soviet marxism, Kennan nevertheless found it of some importance and recognized its persuasive value in the Third World.[34] The marxist upsurge of the 1960s in the West he was, however, unable to understand. Marxism in the Soviet Union itself seemed for him to be decreasing in significance along with "fanaticism," though he never did resolve the basic question of whether it was purely a convenient instrument or something more deeply ingrained.[35] Perhaps his most interesting comment on the matter was made in 1957:

> Forty years of intellectual opportunism have wrought a strange corruption of the Communist mind, rendering it incapable of distinguishing sharply between fact and fiction in a single segment of its experience, namely in its relation to any external competitive power. Let me stress that it is only in this one sector that the Communist mind is thus affected. In other respects, it is extremely shrewd and discerning . . .
>
> They view us as one might view the inhabitants of another planet through a very powerful telescope. Everything is visible; one can see in the greatest detail the strange beings of that other world going about their daily business; and one can even discern the nature of their undertakings; but what one does not see and cannot see is the motivation that drives them in these various pursuits. This remains concealed; and thus the entire image, clear and intelligible in detail, becomes incomprehensible in its totality . . .
>
> As it is, our problem is difficult indeed; for we can never know, when we encounter their statements and reactions, whether we have to do with the substructure of sincerely held error which does indeed exist in their minds, or with the superstructure of contrived and deliberately cultivated untruth to which they are so committed.[36]

Encapsulated here are all the problems accumulated during thirty years of trying to grapple with the meaning of Soviet ideology. The first paragraph, it appears, is an attempt to provide a rationale for his old thesis that variations in the external threat had no impact on the level of Moscow's internal propaganda against it. The image, however, of a mind lost between fact and fiction in one realm while otherwise espousing great sensitivity to "realities" is hardly convincing. Much more suggestive is the parallel with a telescopic vision of a world that is in its entirety essentially different and only partly comprehensible. This inspired line of thought seems, unfortunately, to have been a flash in the pan. Did he, I wonder, consider that the vision from his side of the globe might have been impaired in equal measure by telescopic detail?

Ocularity aside, Kennan had less and less reason to take any interest in Soviet dogma, and the few times he did analyze such statements revealed a corresponding lack of insight.[37] By the 1960s he had concluded that Moscow no longer had any real belief even in the long-term prospects for a "communized world"; more recently he has said that the Russian leadership is only paying "lip-service" to the old tenets.[38]

International Communism

In light of the decreasing possibility of any communist victories in Western Europe, Kennan paid less attention to this movement. In 1952 he could still envision Moscow using the French party "to disrupt the unity and effectiveness of the Western coalition" and similarly use the East German regime to begin a civil war like that in Korea.[39] He retained the idea that foreign communists during Stalin's time had been instruments— or at least that Moscow had so conceived them—but the combination of emerging polycentrism, his related and firmly held belief that, *pari passu*, the nationalist element would always dominate over the marxist one, and the generally favorable political situation in the West served to make the problem less than urgent.[40] By the end of the 1960s he was actually calling the French and Italian communists protest parties. Farther afield, during the initial escalation in Vietnam he was already foreseeing conflicts between the Vietnamese and Chinese communists, scarcely a common idea at the time.[41]

Earlier (in 1954 and 1956) he had reiterated the familiar opinion that for reasons of potential rivalry Moscow had no desire at all to see any Western communist party come to power, that Stalin had in fact deliberately betrayed the German communists to the Nazis. What is more, according to Kennan, Moscow had always recognized the right of the other side to liquidate domestic communists, as in the German case.[42] This seems to imply some kind of recognition of spheres. Yet he could also suggest in 1967 that Stalin had been "intrigued by the possibility of extending communist power in Western Europe" and in 1960 that he had wanted to use a victory over Germany "for the purpose of expelling the British and Americans from Europe and assuring the early communization of the continent."[43] This, position, needless to say, is contradictory. The dominant theme, however, was that of a communist world marked by centrifugal or polycentric forces.

American Policy

In the early 1950s Kennan was still thinking in terms of "barriers," though much less markedly than before.[44] As time passed and his disgust with what he found a sterile, unsubtle, and dangerously militarized American policy deepened, containment assumed in his pronouncements a certain air of historical artifact. In short, he was interested in diplomacy, of which there was little of substance until after the Cuban missile crisis. His main thesis throughout was plain: if the United States was not willing to give anything up, the Soviet Union would not give anything up either; nor was it reasonable to demand that they do so.[45] No basic "intimacy of understanding" being possible, he advocated talks of a very concrete kind:

> There is only one sort of thing that can usefully be said to them and that is: what we would be prepared to do, and what we would not be prepared to do, in specific contingencies . . . [If] the tension between Russia and the Western world is to be reduced, it must be broken down into its individual components—into a number of specific problems, that is; and each of these must be treated empirically and on its merits with a view to arriving at those compromises and accommodations that would be least unsettling to world peace.[46]

In its simplistic fervor, American policy seemed to him on the contrary designed to leave little room for agreement, its primary effect actually being that of unifying the communist world.[47] The latter sentiment was not lessened by his experience when, as ambassador to Yugoslavia in the early 1960s, he found himself unexpectedly having to represent Tito before a bevy of hostile congressmen.[48] Kennan was encouraged by the improvement after 1962 in the bilateral relations with the Soviet Union but took exception to the coincident intervention in Vietnam, sheer folly in itself but also an obstacle to further improvement in U.S.-Soviet relations.[49]

The opening to Beijing thus caught him, like most others, unawares. He took a cool view of this apparent masterstroke of diplomacy. Having always supported some sort of relations with the People's Republic, he welcomed an end to the abnormal state of nonrecognition. Yet he feared a repetition of the exaggerated hopes that had followed the recognition of the USSR in 1933 and, his abhorrence for Maoist China fresh in mind, warned against taking on this decidedly non-Western power as a partner, especially versus the Soviet Union. Here his Western bias prevented him from realizing any inkling of what was about to happen. While it was for him not unlikely that the Soviet Union would develop in a more "Western" direction, the notion that China—racially, culturally, and politically alien—would open up seems to have been wholly unthinkable.[50] It will be interesting to see if the Soviet Union ever follows the Chinese example of sending thousands of graduate students to the West. Relative proximity does not necessarily make for "intimacy"; in fact often the reverse.

When détente entered a rapid decline in the mid-1970s, followed by vast rearmament and a return to cold war politics, Kennan's long-standing opposition to nuclear weapons and strategy surfaced full-blown. It had two aspects. First, he argued, these weapons are essentially unusable and cannot be related organically to any real policy objectives. Amassing ever-increasing mountains of such useless (and catastrophically dangerous) arms is therefore foolish. On the same "technical" grounds he supported improvements in conventional strength. Second, and more important, he thought that the nuclear arms race and synchronous militarization of language greatly enhanced the chances of open confrontation. No underlying contradiction between the two superpowers could possibly justify running that risk, portending as it did the destruction of civilization in toto. Everything had to be done to minimize it.[51]

To this effort Kennan has since made an outstanding contribution. With unflagging energy and profound moral conviction he has alerted the public to the danger of nuclear war and denounced the "image of the totally inhuman and totally malevolent adversary."[52]

Appendix B

On Ideology

I have heaped much criticism upon Kennan for his apparent failure to provide a satisfactory analysis of Soviet ideology and its relationship to foreign policy. Despite occasional indications in a different direction, this has been an immanent critique, concerned with internal contradictions and conceptual effects of various assumptions. It remains to demonstrate that an alternative path to Kennan's might have yielded better results. My aim is obviously not to offer a properly validated account of Soviet marxism and foreign policy but merely to suggest another way in which one might think about it, how one might escape the sincerity question. I shall make two brief points, one conceptual and the other empirical. The emphasis will be on the mediation of theory and strategic outlook, a notion often lost in Kennan's expositions.

The concept of ideology might in the first place be differentiated, or rather seen as something less than all-inclusive. The following distinctions are provisional but may be of some use.[1]

Ideology, a term coined in the 1790s by postrevolutionary thinkers in France, has meant a variety of things but is now probably commonly understood as an articulated and relatively coherent body of political positions and attitudes related to action. It is better, I think, to see as a sort of cognitive map, a representation of the individual subject's conception of the relation to his or her real conditions of existence. Being a way of coping with the real, it is thus inherently authentic. Neither composed of disembodied ideas nor synonymous with the notion of a world view, the narrative practice of mapping is material in that it is embedded in, and unthinkable without, institutions.

Theory is an activity concerned with abstract knowledge, reducible for our purposes to texts. It may be said to correspond to the most rarefied domain of what Kennan considered ideology.

Discursive formation (also master discourse or meta-language) essentially comprises the two concepts of theory and ideology. Referred to as Soviet marxism, it will be seen as a material signifying system suffused throughout a vast apparatus.

Policy is formulated within the discursive formation but constituted by the specific field on which it is an intervention, the field itself being defined by the presence of rules, adversaries, and obstacles. One may divide policy into a strategic (long-term) and tactical (short-term) aspect, the latter plainly more subject to immediate change and manipulation.

Propaganda, grasped without pejorative connotations, is simple statements, conceived, again, within Soviet marxism and designed for tactical purposes of mobilizing support for policy. Its role is wholly instrumental, which is not to say that it is necessarily made up of lies or is not believed by those who put it forth. Proposals that political subjects advance without hope, or even desire, of acceptance I see not as propaganda but as tactical policy and, like most policy, requiring propaganda for its execution. The importance of propaganda, then, resides in its instrumental quality, not in its truth value. True or not, it always has an immediate purpose.

Now, every state has some sort of self-conception that its subjects may or may not share but most often do. The Soviet Union proclaims itself marxist. It is doubtful whether that state is marxist in any sense that Marx would recognize, but the Soviet infrastructure and foreign policy are nonetheless meaningful and comprehensible within this master discourse, which subsumes and reorders other nonhegemonic discourses such as Russian traditionalism and modern scientific theories. Once that argument has been settled, causal primacy and the specific role of ideology (in Kennan's sense) becomes less important and the actual *content* commensurately more so. For it follows that Soviet marxism is, in the last analysis, both real and effective.[2]

Notions of instrumentality (as well as the metaphorical model of base and superstructure) should thus be avoided. Soviet life and propaganda certainly abound in instrumental lies and convenient covers; and there is doubtless a considerable difference between official rhetoric and what is thought and said in the inner sanctums of the Kremlin. Since time immemorial in Russia the very concept of truth (*pravda*) has partly connoted an authoritatively established truth, one whose explicit function it is to suppress any competing and potentially divisive minority views.[3] In that sense it has little in common with positivist ideas of truth. None of this, however, makes the discursive formation *as a whole* an instrument. It would be absurd to assume that a society that has gone through an immense transformation within a readily identifiable discursive formation would somehow harbor another, ultimately more "real" discourse under the surface. Such, at least, would seem the silent assumption of any theory of covers. Moreover, since what is being done can usually, coarsely put, be squared with what is being said, there appears to be no structural need for a "deeper" truth. To act and speak in the system, then, is to act and speak within the given discourse, for there is no truth outside it. Even in the unlikely case that a large number of apparatchiks happen secretly to dissent in a fundamental way, these hidden revolutionaries would, like doubting priests everywhere, be upholding the ruling logic by dint of position and function.

To accept the material reality of Soviet marxism is of course not to accept the validity of its claims. The determinants of Soviet foreign policy as far as I am concerned must in the end be sought in the objective status and structural needs of the new ruling-class system that was created in the 1930s. Such an argument is inadmissable within Soviet marxism. Yet no analysis of the real can neglect to deconstruct, if you will, the reality of self-delusion. I shall conclude, therefore, with some brief remarks about the nature of Soviet marxism and foreign policy. The distinctions I have outlined are assumed throughout but for reasons of space not extensively employed.

The organizing concept of the Soviet meta-language, particularly with regard to outside relations, is to be found not really in Marx but in Lenin and his theory of imperialism. For it was the adaptation of this theory, formulated around 1916, to the existence of a single, seemingly anomalous Soviet state that produced the framework within which *all* subsequent foreign policy has ultimately been conceived.[4] The essence of Lenin's argument was this: capitalism had reached a new stage (monopoly capitalism) signified by stagnating development of the productive forces and concomitant political inability on the part of the ruling class to keep the system afloat without resorting to extreme measures. As an organic concept of ripeness growing into overripeness, Lenin's perspective implied a downward trend but not, it is worth noting, constant depression. Rather, capitalism had come up against a *limit* (monopoly) that suggested something qualitatively new and other, namely socialism (social monopoly).[5]

One might thus have expected revolution in the advanced states of the West, but instead there arose an isolated socialist state in a backward country of the East. Marxism had made no provisions for the prolonged existence of a socialist state within a capitalist environment, indeed for the prolonged existence of a socialist state as such. According to the older vision (including Lenin's), the state, irrespective of political complexion, was innately bourgeois. Whatever the merits of this view, it is true that insofar as the world is a system of states, its members are obliged to observe a modicum of respect for the constitutive rules. A revolutionary (antisystemic) state is hence in the long run a contradiction in terms. Unless it is followed by similar transformations elsewhere, the radical state will eventually have to face the choice of conforming, perishing, or, if practically possible, withdrawing.[6] The Soviet Union tried partly to conform, partly to withdraw, and yet to lay claim to being keeper of the revolutionary faith.

The squaring of this circle could not be achieved without inflicting some violence on the received wisdom. Marxism, preeminently a theory of vertical modes of production and class structures, was turned into a partly horizontal concept, whereby the inherent contradiction between the USSR and the capitalist outside replaced the vertical between labor and capital as the governing one. By 1928, in its own eyes (and those of the communist movement), the Soviet Union had essentially become the international proletariat embodied on a state scale.[7]

The idea of a rotting monopoly capitalism unable to carry on was reinforced immensely by the depression, and for a while international communism (if not the USSR) attacked everything. Yet the same idea could profitably be employed for the entirely different type of policy that became necessary once this line of thinking had proved a disaster—in other words when, according to official thinking, "desperate monopoly capital" had proved itself capable of inflicting considerable damage in the form of fascism. Fascism had been said to originate in "the most reactionary, the most chauvinist and the most imperialist elements of finance capital," a class locus that in actual use allowed flexible application.[8] For example, the designated social base was exceedingly slim and thus made possible the recruitment of wide and diffuse categories of people (and later states) for antifascist alliances. Moreover, with regard to the actual enemy, everything depended on which forces were actually considered most hostile, the key word here being the relative *most*. This subjective property, still present in Soviet theory and foreign policy, made the exact target fairly variable according to need.

Thus emerged a complex of vertical and horizontal alliances designed to protect the newly victorious socialist fortress from any assaults and, similarly its allies from fascist liquidation. With the reactionary policies of monopolies and fascists thwarted, the question of socialism would in turn also be raised: masses of people would be mobilized in fronts based on "democratic' demands; and, eventually, influenced by the inverted images of a steadfastly progressing Soviet socialism and a capitalism no longer readily capable of meeting such democratic demands, these masses would realize where things were going. Antimonopolism and defense against reaction (if not fascism) has indeed constituted basic communist strategy ever since.[9] If, however, the premise of capitalist ripeness and decline should turn out to be wrong, the offensive aspect of the strategy falls flat. From a Western viewpoint one might then well choose to let communist parties go on defending democracy against reaction until further notice. Certainly no destruction of traditional ways of life is necessarily entailed in such a defense.

The conservative implications of this policy, defensive yet over time presumably offensive, were reinforced by the extraordinary growth of the Soviet state apparatus itself. In a reverse of original concepts, the withering away of the state was suddenly said to necessitate at this initial stage a most vigorous *expansion*.[10] The result was a vast bureaucratic machine and a fairly distinct ruling stratum with a substantial interest in maintaining internal and external stability. Foreign exceptions usually concerned cases of perceived necessity (quelling upheaval in Eastern Europe) or instances where, as Kennan had argued, the risks in disturbing the status quo were virtually nil. Add an element of inertia to the system in its mature form and the sum, as Gorbachev well knows, is an extremely conservative structure.

Since domestic contradictions were simultaneously proclaimed eradicated, Soviet society turned into an analytical nonobject. Official marxism ceased in these circumstances to be a developing theory and turned into a set of "immutable" principles guiding an essentially immutable society, thereby assuming something of the character of a state religion, replete with canon, clergy, liturgy, saints, demonology, monuments, rituals, and processions.[11] Like a religion it guarantees that its exponents are ordained and speak with authority, credibility, and seriousness. And like its religious counterparts, official Soviet language is cleansed of irony and validated by the force of the speaker's identity.[12] It permeates the apparatus that much more forcefully because literal adherence is a prerequisite for membership and advancement.[13]

By the late 1930s a set of symmetrical oppositions had thus emerged which is still very much with us. Essentially expressing one contradiction in different domains, it eliminated conceptually all possible conflict between the Soviet Union and global socialism, thus making Moscow's policy by definition one of peace and progress. These binary pairs may be codified as follows, the first being the overriding one:[14]

the Soviet Union and its allies	versus	the imperialist-fascist camp
the people	versus	monopoly capital
progress	versus	reaction
peace	versus	war

After the interlude of the Hitler-Stalin pact (concluded at sizable political cost), this matrix reached formidable legitimacy during the wartime antifascist alliance with the Western powers. The onset of cold war with these regimes brought on a period of considerable uncertainty and squabbling in the Kremlin before a firm new line could be formulated.[15] It was in fact not until Molotov had exited from the Marshall Aid negotiations in Paris and the Cominform, feeble successor to the Comintern, was about to be founded in September 1947 that Andrei Zhdanov issued an authoritative analysis. The name of the characters had changed, but the plot remained the same:

> Alarmed by the achievements of Socialism in the USSR, by the achievements of the new democracies [code word for the recent Soviet-inspired regimes in Eastern Europe], and by the post-war growth of the labor and democratic movement in all countries, the American reactionaries are disposed to take upon themselves the mission of "saviors" of the capitalist system from Communism.
>
> The frank expansionist program of the United States is therefore highly reminiscent of the reckless program . . . of the fascist aggressors, who, as we know, also made a bid for world supremacy.[16]

Amidst talk of "imperialist expansion and aggression" and the "fascization of America's political life," he went on to divide the world into an "imperialist and anti-democratic" camp and an "anti-imperialist and democratic" one, symbolized respectively of course by the United States and the Soviet Union. Harsh language notwithstanding, Zhdanov's political countermeasure was nothing more than an anti-American front that was even more diffuse and extended in scope than its purely anti-fascist predecessors, to be based on the patriotic defense of peace and "national sovereignty" (that is, opposition to the Marshall Plan). Anyone, including entire nations, could supposedly be included. Zhdanov also reiterated the principle of cooperation: "Soviet foreign policy proceeds from the fact of the co-existence for a long period of the two systems—capitalism and socialism. From this it follows that co-operation between the U.S.S.R. and countries with other systems is possible provided that the principle of reciprocity is observed and that obligations assumed are honoured."[17] The fundamental object here was still to ensure the survival of the Soviet state by a mixture of, on the one hand, adroit national and class alliances against the most powerful and threatening enemy in the opposite camp and, on the other, measures of cooperation where such were possible and not detrimental to Soviet interests. The specific policy in this case proved largely unsuccessful. Less than two years later an anti-Soviet alliance of formidable puissance had come into existence, with more of the same to follow.[18]

The thaw of the late 1950s, it is worth pointing out, was interpreted as a sign that the policy of anticommunism, to use official language, was yielding to the policy of peaceful coexistence as a result of a significant tilt in the correlation of forces toward the camp of peace and progress, leaving the other (variable) side momentarily much less capable of engaging in aggression against the Soviet Union.[19] In no way did peaceful coexistence mean that fundamental contradictions were deemed to have disappeared or that any identity of interest had suddenly emerged. A (Clausewitzian) continuation of the class struggle by other means, peaceful coexistence referred explicitly to interstate relations and involved, in the economic sphere, further demonstration of the superiority of socialism (compare Khrushchev's prediction of passing the United States in production); to the struggle on the political level to prevent imperialist war (the peace policy); and finally to uncompromising difference and opposition in the ideological domain. The aim was to allow the "progressive forces" (above all the USSR) to follow strategic policy without unduly risking nuclear annihilation.[20] These precepts are still operative, though Gorbachev's regime might well bring about significant reformulation.

Here one may stop the compressed exposition and ask whether the indicated line of inquiry has made us any wiser. The emphasis was on the mediation of policy within a discursive formation, minimally described by reference to the overdetermining concept of imperialism. One might conclude that the argument only shows the possibility of adjusting given principles to immediate national interests. The various swings in foreign policy between 1939 and 1941, to take a flagrant example, were accompanied by the utmost cynicism and dishonesty in the theoretical domain.[21] However, bending or altering apparently fundamental principles, does not in itself eliminate the semireligious nature of a society such as the Soviet Union; nor is it as effortless an operation as the period in question might suggest. If one argues that there is no contradiction between national interest and higher ideal in the Soviet Union, it is nevertheless clear that the national is inconceivable outside the master discourse, if not altogether meaningless. Instrumentalist conclusions are thus ultimately mistaken.

Yet it must be granted that the uneven but in the long term largely continuous integration of the Soviet Union into the economic and political world system has diminished the predictive value of ideologico-theoretical analysis, since policy, albeit formulated within the master discourse, is marked by its field of intervention. Moscow, to take a trivial but telling example, is a very agile currency dealer on the world market, in which it participates for the purpose of making profits. In the final analysis this policy is part and parcel of the general strategy of strengthening the Soviet state and thus officially the forces of socialism and democracy everywhere. But awareness of that is of scant use if I am a competing currency dealer with a similar desire of maximizing profits. Analogously, to a Western diplomat trying to assess Russian policy on arms control, Soviet marxism is interesting only as background; intimate knowledge of the particular terrain of arms control and Moscow's approach to it is of the essence. Layers of theories and practices situated at a considerable remove from its organizing concepts are hence steadily added to the discursive formation. Yet it remains true that one who aspires to a general understanding of Soviet foreign policy rather than technological know-how must also understand its meta-language. Kennan realized that, but the territory was too alien.

Notes

Abbreviations

Bland Files	Larry Bland, research materials
CFR	Council on Foreign Relations
DSF	U.S. Department of State Files, National Archives, Diplomatic Branch, Washington, D.C.
FO	Foreign Office, London
FRUS	U.S. Department of State, *Foreign Relations of the United States*, Washington, D.C.
FRUS: The Soviet Union	U.S. Department of State, *Foreign Relations of the United States, Diplomatic Papers: The Soviet Union, 1922–1939*, Washington, D.C., 1952
GFK	George F. Kennan
GFKP	George F. Kennan Papers, Mudd Library, Princeton University, Princeton, N.J.
HSTL	Harry S. Truman Library, Independence, Mo.
Memoirs, I	George F. Kennan, *Memoirs, 1925–1950*, Boston, 1967
Memoirs, II	George F. Kennan, *Memoirs, 1950–1963*, Boston, 1972
MPF	U.S. Department of State, Moscow Post Files, National Archives, Diplomatic Branch, Suitland, Md.
NA	National Archives, Washington, D.C.
NSC	National Security Council
PCF	French Communist party
PCI	Italian Communist party
PPS Files	Policy Planning Staff Files, National Archives, Washington, D.C.

PPSP   *The State Department Policy Planning Staff Papers*, New York, 1983
RG   Record Group
Secstate   Secretary of State

Introduction to Part I

1. An initial semantic disclaimer is in order: the use of *Russian* as synonymous with *Soviet* is a matter of convenience and should in no way be taken as support for the (ultimately chauvinistic) tendency to regard the Russian republic as the emblem of the USSR as a whole. A similar, less often noticed difficulty arises in the metonymic use of *American*.

2. The related problems of incommensurability and translation have been subject to lively debate in both Anglo-American and Continental theory, though with relatively little cross-fertilization. My position here is influenced by Michel Foucault and by Ian Hacking's essay "Styles of Scientific Reasoning," in *Post-Analytic Philosophy*, ed. J. Rajchman and C. West (New York, 1985). See also Len Doyal and Roger Harris, "The Practical Foundations of Human Understanding," *New Left Review*, 139 (May–June 1983), particularly the discussion of Willard Quine's ontological relativism.

1. The Thirties

1. This sketch is based on C. Ben Wright, "George F. Kennan, Scholar-Diplomat: 1926–1946" (Ph.D. diss., University of Wisconsin, 1972), much the best assessment of the early period; *Memoirs*, I, chaps. 1–5; GFK, personal file, DSF, 123, K 36, RG 59, Box 549, Diplomatic Branch, NA; Hugh DeSantis, *The Diplomacy of Silence* (Chicago, 1980), pp. 28–29; and Walter Isaacson and Evan Thomas, *The Wise Men: Six Friends and the World They Made* (New York, 1986), pp. 72–79, 140–150. I have reservations about the wisdom of lumping together Kennan, Bohlen, Acheson, Nitze, Lovett, and McCloy in the journalistic manner of Isaacson and Thomas. The authors, for one thing, do not make up their minds whether Kennan was a hopeless dreamer or a remarkable clairvoyant. Nor do they quite know how to square Kennan's oppositional stance with the basic idea of a group of wise men.

Incidentally, the choice of educational location for the Russian specialists was not fortuitously made; care was taken to find anti-Soviet institutions. See Frederic L. Propas, "Creating a Hard Line toward Russia: The Training of State Department Soviet Experts, 1927–1937," *Diplomatic History*, 8 (Summer 1984).

2. The account of the Foreign Service is derived from DeSantis, *Diplomacy*, pp. 13–79, 198–203; Robert Schulzinger, *The Making of the Diplomatic Mind* (Middletown, Conn., 1975), pp. 108–115; Martin Weil, *A Pretty Good Club* (New York, 1978), pp. 52–61, 93, 109, and passim. Weil, however, exaggerates Kennan's devotion to aristocratic tsarist Russia.

3. C. Ben Wright, interview with Charles Bohlen, Sept. 29, 1970, Washington, D.C.; Wright, interview with Loy Henderson, Oct. 3, 1970, Washington,

D.C. I am grateful to Larry Bland and, indirectly, C. Ben Wright, for letting me use these as well as other interviews conducted by the latter. GFK to Charles Thayer, May 22, 1935, Charles Thayer Papers, Box 3, HSTL; DSF, 123, K 36. In some form or other Kennan expressed a desire to resign in 1929, 1933, 1945, and 1950, when he did exit, two later ambassadorial stints notwithstanding.

4. DSF, 123, K 36.

5. For the Soviet side, see Adam Ulam, *Expansion and Co-Existence* (New York, 1968), pp. 113–134; E. H. Carr, *The Bolshevik Revolution, 1917–1923*, vol. 3 (London, 1953); Theodore H. von Laue, "Soviet Diplomacy: G. V. Chicherin, People's Commissar for Foreign Affairs, 1918–1930," in *Process and Power in Soviet Foreign Policy*, ed. Vernon V. Aspaturian (Boston, 1971). On the American perspective, see Joan Hoff Wilson, *Ideology and Economics* (Columbia, Mo., 1974); Thomas R. Maddux, *Years of Estrangement: American Relations with the Soviet Union, 1933–1941* (Tallahassee, 1980); Robert Browder, *The Origins of Soviet-American Diplomacy* (Princeton, 1953); Edward M. Bennet, *Recognition of Russia: An American Foreign Policy Dilemma* (Waltham, Mass., 1970), esp. chaps. 1–2. Much later Kennan said about the earliest stage of American-Soviet relations: "Persuaded of the final and absolute correctness of its own principles, each was disinclined to accept philosophically the proposition that a political system founded on the negation of those principles could endure." Unused final chapter for *The Decision to Intervene*, GFKP, Box 26.

6. Wilson, *Ideology*, pp. 121–122. Yet the Far Eastern Division within the State Department was sympathetic to recognition. See Maddux, *Years*, p. 17.

7. Take this pronouncement, for example: "An essential prerequisite to the establishment of harmonious and trustful relations with the Soviet government is the abandonment by the present rulers of Russia of their world revolutionary aims and the discontinuance of their activities designed to bring about the realization of such aims." Robert Kelley, memorandum *FRUS: The Soviet Union*, p. 7. Kelley was head of the Division of Eastern European Affairs, and it was he and Allan Dulles who had conceived the idea of specialist training. See Propas, "Creating a Hard Line." Kelley's position falls within that "impossible" category Kennan was to criticize more than half a century later: "The Western statesmen who pressed for Soviet adherence to [some parts of the Helsinki Agreements] must have been aware that some of them could not be implemented on the Soviet side, within the meanings we would normally attach to their workings, without fundamental changes in the Soviet system of power—changes we had no reason to expect would, or could, be introduced by the men then in power." "Morality and Foreign Policy," *Foreign Affairs*, 65 (Winter 1985–86), 207–208.

8. GFK to Walt Ferris, Jan. 12, 1931, as quoted in Wright, "Kennan," p. 28. A private missive, it was probably a fairly good indication of his deepest sentiments.

9. Wilson, *Ideology*, p. 125.

10. Ibid., pp. 130–131; Maddux, *Years*, pp. 14–15; Browder, *Origins*, pp. 52–62; Ulam, *Expansion*, pp. 211–214; Donald Bishop, *The Roosevelt-Litvinov Agreements* (Syracuse, N.Y., 1965). Maddux makes the most of the Japanese aspect; Bishop's is a very legalistic study concerned with the letter of the agreements and how they were carried out.

11. This account is based on Browder, *Origins*, pp. 29–30, 46–47; Maddux,

Years, p. 3; Wilson, *Ideology*, pp. 130–132; Harry Schwartz, *Russia's Soviet Economy*, 2d ed. (Englewood Cliffs, N.J., 1960), pp. 590–593.

12. "The German Export Trade to Soviet Russia," April 14, 1931, DSF, 661.6211/39; "Russian Recognition and Foreign Trade," June 1933, GFKP, Box 23. See also Wright, "Kennan," pp. 38–47. Kennan's study of earlier trade agreements is the most extensive one I have been able to find.

13. "The Gold and Foreign Currency Accounts of the Russian Government," Sept. 10, 1932, DSF, 861.51/2539; "The Foreign Trade of Russia in 1932," June 20, 1933, DSF, 661.00/175. The latter spanned 178 meticulously composed pages.

14. Memorandum, Nov. 24, 1937, *FRUS: The Soviet Union*, p. 449; Memorandum, May 11, 1938, ibid., pp. 603–604. See also GFK, *Russia and the West under Lenin and Stalin* (New York, 1960), p. 280.

15. Schwartz, *Russia's Soviet Economy*, pp. 588–592.

16. "Notes on Russian Commercial Treaty Procedure," April 5, 1933, DSF, 661.0031/30.

17. "Russian Recognition," June 1933, GFKP, Box 23. The negative model here was Weimar Germany, which he considered to have received a very raw deal in its Soviet dealings. See "The German Export Trade."

18. See George D. Holliday, *Technology Transfer to the USSR, 1928–1937 and 1966–1975: The Role of Western Technology in Soviet Economic Development* (Denver, 1977), pp. 52–55, 182–183. The actual goal of Moscow's trade was thus autarky, as Holliday rightly emphasizes, and in that sense there was obviously a political aspect to the proceedings. This only underlines, however, that the power relations may well have been quite the opposite of what Kennan thought they were. Present support for his thesis can nevertheless be found. See Jonathan Haslam, *Soviet Foreign Policy, 1930–1933* (London, 1983), p. 53. Alec Nove's argument that the unwieldy nature of the system prevents effective use of the monopoly factor seems more persuasive. A. Nove, *East-West Trade: Problems, Prospects, Issues* (Washington, D.C., 1973).

19. Memorandum, Jan. 29, 1946, MPF, Box 94, 631, "Poland," National Archives, Suitland, Md.

20. Testimony, U.S. Congress, Senate Committee on Foreign Relations, *United States Relations with Communist Countries*, Hearings, 93d Cong., 2d sess., Aug. 20, 1974. See also his somewhat ambiguous despatch, July 15, 1952, *FRUS*, 1952–1954, I, 864–865.

21. GFK, *On Dealing with the Communist World* (New York, 1964), chap. 2; Testimony, U.S. Congress, Senate Committee on Foreign Relations, *East-West Trade*, Hearings, 89th Cong., 1st sess., pt. 2, Feb. 26, 1965.

22. Karl Radek, "The Bases of Soviet Foreign Policy," *Foreign Affairs*, 12 (Jan. 1934), 206. The article had been published in Moscow a month earlier. Ridiculing the notion of continuity between tsarist and Soviet foreign policy, Radek enumerated a series of notorious targets of expansionism for the former and rightly claimed that the Bolsheviks had shown no interest in them. Murdered in the purges, Radek did not live to see Stalin refute his argument by forcefully coveting almost every single one of the areas mentioned.

23. Ulam, *Expansion*, chap. 4, remains in my view the best pro-Western survey. Jiri Hochman, *The Soviet Union and the Failure of Collective Security, 1934–*

1938 (Ithaca, N.Y., 1984), is also useful despite its distinctly one-sided emphasis on Soviet double-dealing and its weak treatment of the Comintern. For a different perspective, see Fernando Claudin, *The Communist Movement* (London, 1975), chap. 4. On Russo-German relations specifically, see Karlheinz Nicklauss, *Die Sowjetunion und Hitlers Machtergreifung* (Bonn, 1966), chaps. 8–10.

24. Radek, "Bases of Soviet Policy." See also, for example, Maxim Litvinov, *Against Aggression* (New York, 1939), p. 78: "The Soviet Union, however, does not beg to be invited into any unions, any blocs, any combinations. She will calmly let other States weigh and evaluate the advantages which can be derived for peace from close co-operation with the Soviet Union, and understand that the Soviet Union can give more than receive." On the Berlin overtures, see Hochman, *The Soviet Union*.

25. Browder, *Origins*, pp. 216–222; Bishop, *Agreements*, chap. 5 and p. 236; Ulam, *Expansion*, pp. 213–215; Maddux, *Years*, pp. 26–36, 40–43, 96–97, and chap. 7, passim. It is odd that Washington seriously thought recognition would bring about severance of the Comintern ties. Litvinov had denied this publicly in the United States at the time.

26. Memorandum, Nov. 24, 1937, *FRUS: The Soviet Union*, p. 447.

27. Bullitt [GFK] to Secstate, May 4, 1934, DSF, 761.62-305. GFK drafted the report, which was then forwarded under the ambassador's name. Hence, perhaps, the incoherence.

28. "The War Problem of the Soviet Union," March 1935, GFKP, Box 16.

29. See A. J. P. Taylor, *The Origins of the Second World War* (New York, n.d.), p. 107. Hitler's objective, as Taylor points out, was first and foremost the eradication of the Versailles system.

30. "The War Problem." This idea, which became a leading theme in Kennan's postwar analyses, will be examined more closely in that context.

31. Kennan's interpretation is an example of the psychological tendency to conclude from the conviction that one (the West in this case) is not a threat to the other, that the other obviously realizes this peaceful posture, from which it follows that the other's evident hostility is so much more reprehensible. See Robert Jervis, *Perception and Misperception in International Politics* (Princeton, 1976), pp. 354–355.

32. "The War Problem."

33. Appeasement, a bad word after the Munich debacle, had in fact designated a widely accepted British policy from the mid-nineteenth century on. See Paul Kennedy, *Strategy and Diplomacy, 1870–1945* (London, 1984), chaps. 1 and 3, for interesting remarks on the financial constraints that encouraged appeasement.

34. V. I. Lenin, *Collected Works*, vol. 31 (Moscow, 1966), p. 486. The quote is from a speech given in December 1920.

35. Quoted in Harold Nicolson, *Curzon—The Last Phase* (London, 1934), p. 37.

36. Diary note, July 28, 1950, reproduced in his statement of March 3, 1967, J. F. Dulles Oral Histories, Mudd Library, Princeton University, Princeton, N.J. See also Address, Dec. 21, 1948, GFKP, Box 17.

37. Review of *Vospominiia Sovetskogo Posla: Voina, 1939–1943*, by I. M. Maisky, *Slavic Review*, 28 (March 1969), 152n.

38. Memorandum, Riga, Aug. 19, 1932, DSF, 861.00-11496, enclosure to despatch no. 650.

39. Bullitt [GFK] to Secstate, March 19, 1936, DSF, 761.00-261.

40. Draft lecture, May 20, 1938, GFKP, Box 16.

41. Address, Bad Nauheim, 1941–42, GFKP, Box 16.

42. Four years later at Bad Nauheim (see n. 41) he realized where the geographical argument was leading but stuck to it, claiming that Iowans had unlimited "dreams," a rather more euphemistic designation. By then his geographism had reached its peak. Thinking, in somewhat Germanic fashion, that the soil determines national character, he advanced the idea that Americans in general had become like the Indians: "supple, athletic, nervously sensitive, and with relatively low powers of resistance to the natural hardships of cold, hunger and disease."

43. In Stalin's own words (1924): "American efficiency is that indomitable force which neither knows nor recognizes obstacles; which with its business-like perseverance brushes aside obstacles; which continues at a task once started until it is finished, even if it is a minor task; and without which serious constructive work is inconceivable." *Leninism* (London, 1940), p. 85. On Stalin as an Americophile, see William Taubman, *Stalin's American Policy* (New York, 1982), pp. 18–19.

44. Memorandum, Riga, Aug. 19, 1932, DSF, 861.00-11496, enclosure to despatch no. 650.

45. "The War Problem."

46. Ibid.

47. Bullitt [GFK] to Secstate, March 19, 1936, DSF, 761.00-261.

48. I have explored this in greater detail in Anders Stephanson, "On Soviet Foreign Policy," *Social Text*, 8 (Winter 1983–84).

49. See ibid. The problem is complex, and my account is necessarily brief. Relevant works are Peter Vigor, *The Soviet View of War, Peace, and Neutrality* (London, 1975), esp. pp. 54–55, 74, 80–89, 115, 127; Klaus Törnudd, *Soviet Attitudes toward Nonmilitary Regional Cooperation* (Helsinki, 1961), pp. 19, 31, 43–44, 49–52, a wider and more interesting work than the unassuming title indicates; Ulam, *Expansion*, pp. 111–207 and passim; and the pioneering study V. Kubálková and A. A. Cruickshank, *Marxism-Leninism and the Theory of International Relations* (London, 1980), esp. pp. 103–150. For primary sources, see Jane Degras, *Soviet Documents on Foreign Policy*, vol. 1 (London, 1951), pp. 33–39, 221–222, and Lenin, *Collected Works*, vols. 31 and 33.

A curious footnote was the debate in 1960 between Kennan and Russian authorities regarding Lenin's position on revolutionary war. Kennan had quoted Lenin as having said in 1918 that such a war was reasonable but not practical. The occasion for Kennan's remarks was a response, "Peaceful Coexistence: A Western View," *Foreign Affairs* (Jan. 1960), to an article by Khrushchev in the same journal. Moscow replied instantly that Lenin had been misquoted. Y. Korovin, "A Distorted View of Peaceful Coexistence," *International Affairs* (Moscow, Feb. 1960). The controversy was wrongheaded. Kennan was technically right but had quoted Lenin out of context. After all, the Soviet regime was at the moment *already* at war, and the question of whether a revolutionary war could be theoretically justified would doubtless have struck him as sheer casuistry. The Soviet answer, by the same token, is just as far off target, hiding a revolutionary past for the sake of the immediate needs of 1960. Vigor, incidentally, claims that the Soviet action against Georgia in 1921 should be seen essentially as a revolutionary war (p. 115); he may well be right. Once it had become clear in the 1920s, however, that the revolution would not spread, the option of revolutionary war faded, very quickly in practice and eventually in theory. The term appeared in the Soviet encyclopedia until 1930. War then reverted to being, as it were, the exclusive property of capitalism. One might add that the idea of spreading the blessings of liberal democracy throughout "America" by forceful means has hardly been foreign to the politicians of this country. What, for instance, was the war against Mexico, or for that matter the one against Spain, if not revolutionary wars in the name of "American" progress? Manifest Destiny was surely more than a rhetorical gesture.

50. See Vigor, *The Soviet View*, pp. 98–101, 140. He learned this from Isaac Deutscher.

51. Though Stalin's liquidation of a sizable part of the officer corps was perhaps objectively suicidal.

52. Bullitt [GFK] to Secstate, March 19, 1936, DSF, 761.00-261.

53. Betty Crump Hanson, "American Diplomatic Reporting from the Soviet Union, 1934–41," (Ph.D. diss., Columbia University, 1966), chap. 4, examines the absence of analyses of the last Comintern Congress. See also Maddux, *Years*, pp. 40–43. Maddux points to Kennan's stay in Vienna (through November) as the main reason for his silence. Yet there is no sign in his other writings that he ever took any interest in the Comintern.

54. The best work on the Comintern is Claudin, *The Communist Movement*, esp. chap. 4. See also E. H. Carr, *The Twilight of the Comintern, 1930–1935* (London, 1982), and Nicos Poulantzas, *Fascism and Dictatorship* (London, 1974), chap. 3.

55. See n. 53. A Mr. Packer from the Division of Eastern European Affairs met the Russian ambassador for lunch. The latter felt obliged to point out to Packer that "communists are instructed to preserve the existing order in this country, not to bring about its overthrow. I [Packer] said we object to any interference from abroad." Packer went on to insist that the change was merely tactical, leaving the fundamentals as before; to which the ambassador retorted that, while communists could not cease being communists, the change was really a change. Packer's subsequent account is supremely dismissive in a congenial sort of way, suggesting that for him the encounter was not to be taken seriously. Packer, memorandum, *FRUS: The Soviet Union*, pp. 260–261. This sort of posture must have been virtually incomprehensible to the Soviet side, except perhaps as dissimulation, as a maneuver to cover up actual aims. Kennan himself was later to stress Moscow's difficulties in understanding that superficial American views and attitudes often were exactly what they seemed.

56. "Fair Day, Adieu," pt. 1, 1938, p. 21, GFKP, Box 25. This unpublished memoir has two parts. The first, written in 1938, deals with his time in Moscow. The second is itself divided into two essays, covering respectively the American interlude in 1937–38 and the Prague period. The American essay may have been written in 1938 or 1939, the latter in late 1939 or 1940. These materials are very much marked by their time period and are superseded as memoirs by the more considered *Memoirs* of the 1960s and 1970s.

57. Ibid., p. 40. The point was part of an overall thesis that Stalin was turning the party into a civil service and politically relying increasingly on the masses.

58. Ibid., pp. 59–60.

59. Address, Dec. 18, 1952, GFKP, Box 17; GFK to Armstrong, Sept. 21, 1950, Hamilton Fish Armstrong Papers, Box 34, Mudd Library, Princeton University, Princeton, N.J.; *Russia and the West*, p. 294. A quote from the last: "To the moral cause of an anti-fascist coalition, the Soviet government of 1934 to 1937 could have added little but hesitant, halfway measures, and a nauseating hypocrisy" (p. 294–295). Terms like "hesitant, halfway measures" and "nauseating hypocrisy" would seem more easily employed with regard to the contemporary Franco-British policy, which Kennan does admit, retrospectively, was "vulnerable" to criticism (p. 294). More important, however, he insists that because the "purposes" of Soviet Russia were different from those of the Western democracies, there was no ground for anti-Nazi collaboration (p. 295). This is an "essentialist" (and in its ideological connotations "unrealist") position, confusing fundamental character with temporary convergence of interest in foreign policy.

His other argument was that the Soviet Union could not contribute substantially in military terms to such a coalition. Hochman, *The Soviet Union*, chap. 3, agrees, primarily citing Russian neglect of securing access routes in Eastern Europe. This is certainly arguable. But it underestimates the dynamic effects that even the *appearance* of an alliance would have had in 1938 on the Germans.

60. As Litvinov points out very straightforwardly ("realistically"), the question concerned not the internal nature of fascism but the fact that it was having determinate effects on international relations. Litvinov, *Against Aggression*, p. 63. After the war Kennan recognized that Moscow had discerned its advent accurately and had accordingly acted with chilling realism. Address, Aug. 29, 1950, GFKP, Box 18.

61. Leon Trotsky, *Writings, 1938–1939* (New York, 1974), p. 217; the quote dates from March 11, 1939.

62. This can be gleaned from the general argument of *Russia and the West*, pp. 280–296.

63. See Hochman, *The Soviet Union*, esp. chaps. 3 and 5.

64. Kennan was to propound this point during the disengagement controversy of the late 1950s. See Chapter 4.

65. On the Munich-Pact period, see Isaac Deutscher, *Stalin* (London, 1970), pp. 419–432; Ulam, *Expansion*, pp. 252–275 (on warnings to the West, see p. 221); Henry L. Roberts, "Maxim Litvinov: Soviet Diplomacy, 1930–1939," in Aspaturian, *Process* (on warning to the West, see p. 166); and Hochman, *The Soviet Union*, chap. 6 (which emphasizes Soviet duplicity). See also Litvinov's *Against Aggression*, pp. 78–79. The negative Western response to his strategic arguments for collective security brought about the end of Litvinov's prominence in Soviet policy-making. His replacement, V. M. Molotov, signaled in every way a posture much less open to Western sensibilities. See Jonathan Haslam, *The Soviet Union and the Struggle for Collective Security in Europe, 1933–39* (London, 1984).

66. "Some Fundamentals of Russian-American Relations," 1938, GFKP, Box 16.

67. Ibid.; italics added.

2. *War and Alliance*

1. "Fair Day, Adieu," pt. 1, p. 29.
2. Ibid., pp. 29–33, 31.
3. The quote is from 1960. *Russia and the West*, p. 301.
4. See F. L. Carsten, *Fascist Movements in Austria: From Schonerer to Hitler* (London, 1977), chaps. 11 and 13; Viktor Reimann, *Zu Gross für Österreich* (Vienna, 1968), pp. 1, 354–362; Manfredo Tafuri, *Vienna rossa: La politica residenziale nella Vienna sozialista, 1919–1933* (Milan, 1980); and Raimund Loew, "The Politics of Austro-Marxism," *New Left Review*, 118 (Nov.–Dec. 1979). Twelve hundred workers died and five thousand were wounded in the struggles after the Dollfuss coup in February 1934, which was followed by general imprisonments and outlawing of the Social-Democratic party (see Loew). Had he known more about it, Kennan might actually have found socialist Vienna appealing, for it had been a model city. One must add that the antidemocratic, nationalistic, and right-wing Dollfuss-Schuschnigg regime should not be confused with German Nazism: Austro-fascism, indeed, had to fight hard against Hitler's local epigones, a fight ending with the Anschluss and Schuschnigg's exile in 1938. The sort of relentless will to forget the past and create anew that one associates with fascist modernists like Filippo Marinetti was of course also foreign to Austrian reaction.
5. Like the subject matter itself, studies of Salazarist Portugal used to be an underdeveloped area. The revolution in 1974 changed this, but interest still centers, understandably enough, on the more recent period. Among the sources used in this discussion are Eric Baklanoff, "The Political Economy of Portugal's Old Regime: Growth and Change Preceding the 1974 Revolution," *World Development*, 7 (1979); and Nicos Poulantzas, *The Crisis of the Dictatorships* (London, 1976).
6. The most complete account of Kennan's period in Portugal is C. Ben Wright, "Kennan," chap. 6. See also *Memoirs*, I, chap. 6. For his personal relationship with Salazar, see GFK to Perkins, State Dept., July 24, 1951, GFKP, Box 28. For his defense of Portuguese colonialism, see GFK to Hamilton Fish Armstrong, July 25, 1970, Armstrong papers, Box 34, Mudd Library, Princeton University, Princeton, N.J. Salazar also had views similar to Kennan's on the rehabilitation of Germany as a bulwark against the Soviet Union. See Luc Crolleu, *Portugal, the U.S., and NATO* (Leuven, Belgium, 1973), pp. 39–40. Kennan mentions in *Memoirs*, I, the frantic intelligence operations in neutral Lisbon and implies that he played a role there. This may be so, though a quick look through the Office of Strategic Services (OSS) files in the NA revealed no information, and the authority on Portuguese intelligence, Douglas L. Wheeler, informs me that sources elsewhere contain little. Wheeler to the author, May 1983. It is possible that Kennan is referring to negotiations regarding Italy's removal from the war. See Joseph Barnes, oral history, Columbia Oral History Project, Columbia University, New York.
7. GFK to Mr. Ambassador, Dec. 11, 1944, GFKP, Box 23. On the apologetic tone, see GFK to Secstate, Feb. 4, 1943, DSF, 853.00-1064 (enclosure); Fish (GFK) to Secstate, April 21, 1943, DSF, 853.00-1075. That his accolades to Salazar were not always so defensive may be seen in GFK to Secstate, Oct. 5, 1943, DSF, 841.34553B-4, where he calls Salazar "a man of firmness, integrity,

and superior intelligence, with a peculiar gift for the preservation of the equilibrium of forces, and with personal predilections operating against the participation of Portugal in the war on either side. For once, due to the efforts of this same extraordinary leader, Portuguese finances have been sound and there has been no dependence on outside help in this respect." This report was composed after the Anglo-Portuguese alliance had been put into unofficial effect, just as Kennan had guessed it would be. In his elation he may have forgotten momentarily the degree to which Salazar was still a suspect character in Washington.

8. See references in n. 7 and the exchanges on the Azores in *FRUS*, 1943, II, 554–566, discussed in *Memoirs*, I, chap. 6. The departmental aspect is evident from the orders he received regarding the Azores. No one seems to have bothered to think through the effects of the American initiative on Salazar's internal and external position, and Kennan was rightly incensed about this. A month earlier he had complained pointedly that there seemed to be no American policy on Portugal for him to follow. He received a nasty response from James Clement Dunn, head of the European section, telling the chargé d'affaires in so many words to shut up. GFK to Dunn, Sept. 9, 1943; Dunn to GFK, Oct. 1, 1943, DSF, 711.53-31. See also GFK, draft letter to Shaw, n.d., GFKP, Box 23. Generally, see Wright, "Kennan," chap. 6.

9. "Fair Day, Adieu," pt. 1, p. 55; "Russia and the Post-War Settlement," unused draft, summer 1942, GFKP, Box 25 (this paper, written immediately after his release from German internment, is incomplete); "Report," quoted in *Memoirs*, I, 116. This last document is not in the GFKP. See also Letter to Mr. Ambassador, March 1944, GFKP, Box 23.

10. "Russia and the Post-War Settlement"; "The Technique of German Imperialism in Europe," April 1941, GFKP, Box 16.

11. "Report," quoted in *Memoirs*, I, 119; see also Letter to Mr. Ambassador, March 1944, GFKP, Box 23.

12. "The Technique of German Imperialism in Europe."

13. Ibid.

14. For Kennan's sentiments about the Austro-Hungarian empire, see "Report," quoted in Wright, "Kennan," p. 148; "Fair Day, Adieu," pt. 1, p. 34, and pt. 2, chap. 2; Address, Aug. 29, 1950, GFKP, Box 18; *Russia and the West*, p. 164; *Memoirs*, I, 94. There are some ironies here. The Austro-marxists crushed by the Dollfuss-Schuschnigg regime were actually very sympathetic to the multilingual political structure of the old empire so congenial to Kennan. Another irony is that Kennan's father, Kossuth, born in the 1850s, must have been named after the Hungarian nationalist who was making a much-noted visit to the United States in the wake of the failed uprisings of 1848. The eventual demise of the empire was surely long overdue and not merely the result of wrongheaded peacemaking at Versailles. As Perry Anderson writes: "The outbreak of the First World War took the trajectory of Austrian Absolutism to its conclusion: German armies fought its battles and Hungarian politicians commanded the field, the Magyar Tisza ended as effective Chancellor of the empire. Defeat razed the prison of nationalities to the ground." *Lineages of the Absolutist State* (London, 1974), p. 327.

15. "Fair Day, Adieu," pt. 2, chap. 2, pp. 33–39: "Whatever else the Czechs may be . . . they are not, at this stage of world history, a natural 'Herrenvolk.'

They are not qualified to exert authority over non-Czech neighbors: and they should, in their own interest, never have been charged with this task" (p. 36). This essay is more explicit than his collected despatches from Prague, published in *From Prague after Munich* (Princeton, 1968). On Norway, see "The Appointment of the New State Council in Norway—A Report," April 1940, GFKP, Box 23.

16. "Fair Day, Adieu," pt. 1, pp. 32–33. He considered the freedom of speech in Schuschnigg's Austria almost irresponsibly extensive in view of the precarious circumstances in which the country found itself, and certainly no less extensive than that of a typical "convention-ridden" American community (p. 31). The latter is an interesting observation.

17. Generally, see Wright, "Kennan"; *Memoirs*, I; and his personal file DSF, 123 K, 1945–1949. On his resignation, see GFK to Matthews, Aug. 21, 1945; GFK to Durbrow, Jan. 21, 1946; GFK to Hopper, April 17, 1946; all GFKP, Box 28. By the time of the third of these letters his mood had changed completely; this followed the success of the Long Telegram. It should be added that relevant materials from the period, roughly 1941–1946, originate mainly in his posting to Moscow after mid-1944 and tend therefore to project problems of the postwar era rather than of wartime.

18. See e.g. his letter to Henderson, June 24, 1941, quoted in *Memoirs*, I, 133. It is worth noting that Molotov during the interregnum (1939–1941) ridiculed the idea of an ideological, democratic war, which he likened to the old religious wars. Paolo Spriano, *Stalin and the European Communists* (London, 1985), p. 119.

19. GFK to Bohlen, Jan. 26, 1945, GFKP, Box 28. This long letter is one of his most important statements of the period.

20. "Russia—Seven Years Later," Sept. 1944, reproduced in *Memoirs*, I, 503–531 (quotation from p. 504); "Russia's International Position at the Close of the War with Germany," May 1945, reproduced in *Memoirs*, I, 532–546. Kennan's traditionalist argument shows a peculiar understanding of the early revolutionary period. Speaking of Soviet culture he states that what was valuable then was valuable insofar as it "had roots in Russian culture of the past" (p. 513). Yet the outstanding Soviet avant-garde of the 1920s, belatedly acknowledged in the West during recent years (and still largely unacknowledged in the Soviet Union itself), was remarkable precisely because of its stunningly bold modernism. It is difficult to find anything traditionally Russian about constructivist art.

21. "Russia's International Position," *Memoirs*, I, 533; "The United States and Russia," winter 1946, as reproduced in *Memoirs*, I, 560–565 (quotation from p. 560); GFK to Bohlen, Jan. 26, 1945, GFKP, Box 28.

22. Davies to Secstate, Dec. 13, 1945, MPF, Box 77, 800, "Communism," enclosure from the British embassy. John Paton Davies prefaced the memorandum by saying that Soviet ideology was important because policy always had to be put into that framework. Kennan had said something similar elsewhere, pointing to Moscow's problem in having to adapt new situations to a general line because of its presumed omniscience. Unfortunately he failed to pursue this to the point of asking what the general line actually was.

23. "Russia—Seven Years Later," *Memoirs*, I, 530. This stimulating and voluminous essay (covering twenty-eight pages in small print) sets out to analyze

the USSR in all its aspects but says virtually nothing about the content of Soviet marxism.

24. Ibid., pp. 505–509; "Lend Lease Aid to Russia," unused draft, 1945, GFKP, Box 25; *Memoirs*, I, 274–275; "Russia's International Position," in *Memoirs*, I, 533–540. Kennan argued in "Lend Lease" that only the oversized military sector would prevent Soviet recovery. The problems of reconstruction, however, would have been enormous even if the military had been completely eliminated. On the "forceful" emphasis, see also GFK to Bohlen, Jan. 26, 1945, GFKP, Box 28.

25. "Russia's International Position," *Memoirs*, I, 546.

26. GFK to Bohlen, Jan. 26, 1945, GFKP, Box 28.

27. Unused memorandum, Sept. 18, 1944, GFKP, Box 25.

28. GFK to Secstate, July 3, 1944, MPF, Box 35, 711, "Poland."

29. "Russia—Seven Years Later," *Memoirs*, I, 521.

30. GFK to Secstate, July 3, 1944, MPF, Box 35, 711, "Poland." See also *Memoirs*, I, 209.

31. "Russia's International Position," *Memoirs*, I, 535–542.

32. "Russia and the Post-War Settlement"; GFK to Bohlen, Jan. 26, 1945, GFKP, Box 28.

33. Harriman [GFK and J. P. Davies] to Secstate, Oct. 23, 1945, *FRUS*, 1945, V, 907; GFK and J. P. Davies to Harriman, April 23, 1945, *FRUS*, 1945, VII, 342. The latter is to my knowledge the first mention of the maximum–minimum formula.

34. In addition to the references given in n. 35, see, on the Korean matter specifically, GFK to Secstate, Jan. 25, 1946, *FRUS*, 1946, VIII, 619. At the same time Kennan was complaining that the Moscow embassy was not being informed of what was going on in Korea.

35. GFK to Secstate, Sept. 30, 1945, *FRUS*, 1945, V, 885. For other examples of this cynical theme, see GFK to Secstate, Aug. 2, 1945, *FRUS*, 1945, VIII, 623; GFK and WA [Ware Adams?] to Secstate, Aug. 30, 1945, MPF, Box 87, 800, " USSR," 15th interpretative report.

36. The seminal statement along these lines is "Russia's International Position." See also GFK to Bohlen, Jan. 26, 1945, GFKP, Box 28; GFK and WBS, "Embassy Comments on Policy and Information Statement on Great Britain," March 15, 1945–April 22, 1946 [*sic*, 1945?], MPF, Box 102; and the Long Telegram, in Thomas H. Etzold and John Lewis Gaddis, *Containment: Documents on American Policy and Strategy, 1945–1950* (New York, 1978), pp. 50–64.

37. "Russia's International Position"; GFK to Bohlen, Jan. 26, 1945, GFKP, Box 28; "The United States and Russia," winter 1946, GFKP, Box 23.

38. GFK to Henderson, June 24, 1941, as quoted in *Memoirs*, I, 133–134.

39. GFK to Harriman, Jan. 20, 1945, MPF, Box 77, 800.1, "Truman."

40. Draft of paper on German-Soviet relations, unused, Feb.–April 1940, GFKP, Box 25.

41. "Russia and the Post-War Settlement."

42. *Memoirs*, I, 211–212.

43. Churchill had requested assistance from Stalin in the form of an eastern offensive so as to alleviate the enormous pressure in the Ardennes. Stalin complied, though he had valid military reasons not to go ahead and could easily have let

his allies take a beating, thus easing his own path into Central Europe. Meanwhile, the British were spending military force repressing the resistance in Greece. See Claudin, *The Communist Movement*, pp. 416–419.

44. Lloyd C. Gardner, *Architects of Illusion* (Chicago, 1970), pp. 30–31; Gabriel Kolko, *The Politics of War* (London, 1968), pp. 242–243; Claudin, *The Communist Movement*, p. 397. As Claudin points out, Stalin could have complicated life considerably by asking for a clause about future colonial independence, a perfectly sensible thing to do if one wanted to maximize the antifascist forces. This he did not do.

45. The old question of the Open Door and all it implies is thereby raised. It seems clear that most American policymakers believed that the interests of the world would best be served by a transformation of the international order in the direction of economic openness or interpenetrability. They also seem to have considered commerce inherently conducive to peace, indeed necessary for democracy as such. At any rate, the United States certainly acted in accordance with such precepts (Bretton Woods, currency convertibility, free trade, and a global economy). To see matters like this is not the expression of any simple-minded economic determinism whereby American policymakers draped their actual intentions in pretty cloth; it is merely to say that economic reasoning was a justifiably integral part of how they thought about international relations. The crucial addendum is that "free" trade serves the interests of the economically strong, who, not surprisingly, are therefore to be found among its chief proponents. For a discussion of the Open Door, see Frank Ninkovitch, "Ideology, the Open Door, and Foreign Policy," *Diplomatic History*, 6 (Spring 1982).

46. Much the best treatment of the Eastern European problem in U.S. policy is Geir Lundestad, *The American Non-Policy towards Eastern Europe* (Oslo, 1978). See also Vojtech Mastny, *Russia's Road to the Cold War* (New York, 1979). Michael M. Boll, "U.S. Plans for a Postwar Pro-Western Bulgaria: A Little-Known Wartime Initiative in Eastern Europe," *Diplomatic History*, 7 (Spring 1983), demonstrates active American involvement but proves little about the region as an object of policy. A telling image of the attempt to be concrete in the abstract, as it were, can be extracted from the voluminous planning records of Harley A. Notter, RG 59, NA, Diplomatic Branch. One finds plans there for postwar TVA-style projects in Hungary and the like, all conceived on the assumption of open cooperation in the region. The extraordinary wartime planning effort, carried out under State Department auspices, was in this regard largely useless, though not for policymaking elsewhere. As far as I know, these materials still await proper historical examination.

47. GFK to Bohlen, Jan. 26, 1945, GFKP, Box 28.

48. "Russia and the Post-War Settlement."

49. Memorandum, unused, Sept. 18, 1944, GFKP, Box 25.

50. GFK to Harriman, Dec. 16, 1944, *Memoirs*, I, 222; Draft telegram, Dec. 21, 1944, GFKP, Box 23. See also *Memoirs*, I, 220. For Roosevelt's concept of the four policemen of the world, see Gardner, *Architects*, pp. 34–35.

51. See e.g. GFK to Bohlen, Jan. 26, 1945, GFKP, Box 28.

52. Claudin, *The Communist Movement*, pp. 378–379; Arthur Schlesinger, Jr., "Origins of the Cold War," *Foreign Affairs*, 46 (Oct. 1967); Mastny, *Russia's Road*, pp. 207–210. See also Churchill's own account in *The Second World War:*

Triumph and Tragedy (Boston, 1953), chap. 15. He quotes a letter (p. 233) he sent back to London on Oct. 12, 1944, wherein he denies that the agreement was a sphere-of-influence deal. Describing it as a "guide," he says that it was supposed "to express the interest and sentiment with which the British and Soviet Governments approach the problems of these countries" in order "that they might reveal their minds to each other in some way that could be comprehended." The distinctions here are somewhat blurred. Soon afterwards, however (Nov. 19, 1944), the British ambassador, Clark Kerr, was able to report that Soviet "propaganda has abandoned almost all criticism of us on the score of imperialist designs"; quoted in Graham Ross, ed., *The Foreign Office and the Kremlin: British Documents on Anglo-Soviet Relations, 1941–49* (Cambridge, 1984), p. 184. As Fraser J. Harbutt points out in *The Iron Curtain* (New York, 1986), p. 68, Churchill was moved to the agreement because of Britain's geopolitical situation between a rising USSR and a United States about to detach itself from future European affairs. This perception of the American attitude is subject to some debate. Robert Dallek, *Franklin D. Roosevelt and American Foreign Policy, 1932–1945* (New York, 1979), pp. 478–480, argues that there was ambivalence about, but acquiescence in, the agreement; and it is true that there was no clearly stated opposition (or support). Still, in his exchanges with Churchill during the summer, Roosevelt had vociferously opposed sphere-of-influence agreements. See *FRUS*, 1944, V, 117–121.

Incidentally, Schlesinger's essay contains an incorrect reading of the infamous Duclos article. Jacques Duclos, a prominent French communist, rebuked his American colleague Earl Browder in the spring of 1945 for, according to Schlesinger, supporting self-determination in Eastern Europe. In fact Duclos used Eastern Europe as an example in passing to illustrate the absence of socialism outside the USSR. The thrust of the article is directed against Browder's abandonment of antimonopolism as the basis of communist strategy and his concomitant vision of a new type of communist party. After Teheran Browder had begun to talk about admitting progressive monopolies into his front strategy and had generally become politically unpredictable. The *Daily Worker*, May 24, 1945, reproduces Duclos's article in its entirety. As for the timing, Mastny states (*Russia's Road*, p. 272), on authority of Duclos himself, that it was designed to warn the Allies against any "reversal of alliances."

53. GFK to Bohlen, Jan. 26, 1945, GFKP, Box 28.

54. Ibid.

55. GFK to Secstate, May 2, 1945, *FRUS*, 1945, III, 110; Letter to Mr. Ambassador, April 12, 1945, GFKP, Box 23; GFK to Harriman, May 14, 1945, *FRUS*, 1945, V, 295; "Comments on Treatment of Germany," Feb. 1945, GFKP, Box 23.

56. The clearest statement is GFK to Bohlen, Jan. 26, 1945, GFKP, Box 28.

57. On Britain, see Nicolson, *Curzon*, p. 49; and Kennedy, *Strategy and Diplomacy*.

58. The best example of this type of pronouncement is "Russia—Seven Years Later."

59. Anderson, *Lineages*, pp. 347–348. With regard to historical continuities, it may be remarked that the caesaro-papist structure of the Russian church had been established by Peter the Great on Lutheran models, and the antiheretical

tradition was a survival of medieval Catholic ideas, not the expression of any Byzantine totalitarianism. Simple divisions between East and West are thus problematic. See Robert E. Smith, "Russian History and the Soviet Union," *Comparative Studies in Society and History*, 4 (1961–62).

60. Dieter Geyer's introduction to his *Sowjetunion: Aussenpolitik 1917–1955* (Cologne, 1972), is a good critique of the simple continuity thesis.

61. See Roy and Zhores Medvedev, "The USSR and the Arms Race," in *Exterminism and the Cold War*, ed. E. P. Thompson (London, 1982), p. 158.

62. Dept. of State, "Briefing Book Paper on Austria" (for Potsdam), June 23, 1945, *FRUS*, 1945, I, 334–335. The government was led by the old social-democrat Karl Renner. In November 1945 elections were held. This was fatal from the Russian viewpoint, since the communist vote turned out to be very low, and the wily Renner proved capable of handling Russian pressure. That pressure grew in tandem with the worsening international situation. The American representative then assumed the role of defending the regime, originally sanctioned by the Russians. See Audrey Kurth Cronin, *Great Power Politics and the Struggle over Austria, 1945–1955* (Ithaca, 1986), pp. 23–42.

63. As Mastny points out in *Russia's Road*, Beneš was a realistic politician and far from a Soviet stooge. He was helped, of course, by the fact that the communists were quite popular in Czechoslovakia, but that in itself does not detract from the legitimacy of the regime. See also Lundestad, *American Non-Policy*, chap. 4.

64. I base this assessment on Lundestad, *American Non-Policy*, particularly the appendix; and on Claudin, *The Communist Movement*, pp. 455–465.

65. That Stalin actually thought in these terms is evident from his complaint to Truman at Potsdam that the Nationalist regime in China was unreceptive to "horse trading." *FRUS*, 1945, II, 1587. The quote is from Bohlen's minutes and hence indirect, but I doubt the original Russian term would have been very different in its connotations.

66. I say "apparently" because American policy was less idealistic here than Kennan thought. The coolness to the British counterrevolution in Greece actually covered up a good deal of support. See Lawrence S. Wittner, *American Intervention in Greece, 1943–1949* (New York, 1982).

67. Claudin, *The Communist Movement*, chap. 5. Regarding the doctrinal aspect, see also Stephanson, "On Soviet Foreign Policy."

68. As Claudin argues throughout his important work, Soviet policy under Stalin was marked by a traditional concern with spheres of influence. Recognition of mutual security zones was for Stalin, I think, the key factor in the convergence of interest, aside from the obvious need for every partner to defeat Germany. That is why he probably felt illegitimately attacked on the Polish question. Meddling with the arrangements there could, from his viewpoint, be construed only as an attack against the very basis of the alliance. Poland, after all, was his back yard. Witness here his exchange with Harry Hopkins, sent to Moscow in the spring of 1945 to sort out the Polish problem. Hopkins said that Poland had to be friendly to Moscow and democratic, although that may have been a contradiction in terms. Stalin responded that Poland had to be friendly and never again a *cordon sanitaire*, only then adding the usual shibboleths about a "democratic" Poland, by which I assume he meant, if anything, an antifascist Poland. He

concluded, with certain emphasis, that "Soviet action in Poland had been more successful than the British action in Greece and at no time had they been compelled to undertake the measures they had done in Greece." To this Hopkins had no direct reply. The point was clear: we are only doing what everyone else is doing, and if we are to be singled out for this, there will be no alliance. *FRUS*, 1945, I, 32–40. Possibly the West could have held forth Italy and France as counterexamples to Poland, but I doubt that this would have had any effect.

69. Stalin, April 1945, in Ministry of Foreign Affairs of the USSR, *Correspondence between the Chairman of the Council of Ministers of the U.S.S.R. and the Presidents of the U.S.A. and the Prime Ministers of Great Britain during the Great Patriotic War of 1941–1945*, vol. 2 (Moscow, 1957), p. 220. See also Claudin, *The Communist Movement*, p. 422. As Harriman said perceptively a month later, Stalin would not "fully understand our interest in a free Poland as a matter of principle. He is a realist in all his actions, and it is difficult for him to understand why we should want to interfere with Soviet policy in a country like Poland, which he considers so important to Russia's security, unless we have some ulterior motive. *FRUS*, 1945, I, 61.

70. *New York Times*, Nov. 7, 1944.

71. On the Greek question, see Claudin, *The Communist Movement*, pp. 372–381; and generally C. M. Woodhouse, *The Struggle for Greece, 1941–1949* (London 1976); Wittner, *American Intervention*; Procopis Papastratis, *British Policy towards Greece during the Second World War, 1941–1944* (Cambridge, 1984). Bruce Kuniholm, *The Origins of the Cold War in the Near East* (Princeton, 1980), agrees on this point but certainly not with the argument as a whole. His choice of language is very peculiar: "A source of concern not only to the Left but also to the Center was the arrest between February and July 1945 of as many as 20,000 of their supporters, many of whom were put to death" (p. 251). Decidedly. As Churchill stated to Eden: "Having paid Russia a price for freedom of action in Greece, we must not hesitate to use our troops." Quoted in Spriano, *Stalin and the European Communists*, p. 211.

72. Kennan was aware of this Italian model. Thus he thought that the projected tripartite commission in Berlin would "amount to little more than the present Advisory Council for Italy." GFK to Secstate, July 3, 1944, MPF, Box 35, 711, "Poland." The Russians were quick to bring up the subject as well. Molotov had already done so at Teheran; and at Potsdam he used Italy explicitly to defend the Soviet record in Bulgaria, Rumania, and Hungary. See James E. Miller, *The United States and Italy, 1940–1950* (Chapel Hill, 1986), p. 74; *FRUS*, 1945, II, 151, 229–230; and Kolko, *The Politics of War*, pp. 50–51. Miller, while pointing out that Stalin used Italy as a bargaining chip, puts the matter as follows: "The Soviet leader recognized Western predominance in Italy and accepted without question the right of the Western Allies to impose whatever regime they desired" (p. 74). Finally, while making the "percentage deal," Stalin had promised Churchill to encourage restraint among the Italian communists. David Carlton, *Anthony Eden* (London, 1981), p. 244.

73. Claudin, *The Communist Movement*, pp. 316–387.

74. GFK to Secstate, April 1, 1946, MPF, Box 102.

75. Stalin himself explained communist strength abroad in terms of the Resistance movement. *New York Times*, March 14, 1946. In Italy almost half of

the partisans were organized by the PCI; 42,500 died. Donald Sassoon, *The Strategy of the Italian Communist Party* (London, 1981), p. 29.

76. I disagree here with Harbutt's argument in *The Iron Curtain*. Harbutt very properly restores the tripolar nature of the alliance; that is, the role of Great Britain as the leading Western power and Soviet adversary in the European theater (before 1947) is brought to the fore. But in making this worthwhile point he comes to inflate the Anglo-Soviet conflict into a "cold war," allegedly begun in 1945 by the Russian push toward the southeast, where Britain had vital interests, and then carried over into an attack on the hitherto respected British sphere in Western Europe. That there were conflicts in the Near Eastern area is not in question; that the Russians made any significant attacks on British interests in Western Europe (aside from hypersensitive Soviet reactions to all talk of a Western bloc) I cannot see. Nor can I see that the conflicts as a whole would warrant the epithet *cold war*, a phrase that serves the conceptual function in Harbutt's account of *fusing* these events with the post-1947 period. If cold war is to be at all a meaningful term, it should be reserved for the deep freeze of the latter epoch, when the whole machinery of real diplomatic interaction virtually broke down. It is inconceivable, to take an example from the time of Harbutt's "cold war," that one would find during the later period an officially sanctioned Soviet view of British nationalization policy that would entertain the idea that "the real significance of the reform will depend on the prospects for the country's further political development in the direction of progressive democracy." M. Smith, "The Nationalization of the Bank of England and of the British Coal Industry," *New Times*, Jan. 15, 1946. In part Harbutt's problem is a product of his initial question, the ancient one of finding out exactly when the cold war began and how, which he posed without interrogating the term itself. In the later stages of his work, too, detached delineation is abandoned in favor of a simple celebration of Churchill's role in facilitating the American entry into that Anglo-Soviet "cold war" that had been discussed in the earlier stages.

77. This argument is an imaginary construct, but Schlesinger, "Origins," and Mastny, *Russia's Road*, come close to it. Mastny's work unveils Stalin's machinations in Eastern Europe at great length, which is useful but hardly a surprise; he then harshly and with justification criticizes Allied statesmen for their ineptitude in dealing with Stalin. Mastny's argument, however, seems to boil down to this: "Stalin could have taken a more enlightened view of what security meant—but only if he had not been Stalin. And the Western statesmen could have acted with fewer scruples—but then *they* would have had to be akin to Stalin. Wielding so much greater control over Russian policies than they did over theirs, the dictator may still seem to have been capable of steering away from confrontations more easily, but in the last analysis, his hands were tied by the Soviet system which had bred him and which he felt compelled to perpetuate by his execrable methods; and that system was the true cause of the Cold War" (p. 306).

After such a string of assertions, nothing more can be said except possibly to call for the elimination of the Soviet Union. Indeed, Mastny actually calls the whole process he describes "predestination." This is not very helpful. The Kremlin may well have had, as he states, an "exaggerated and quixotic notion of security," but judgments of that kind are less interesting than the question of how various notions of security might have been articulated, negotiated, and if possible reconciled.

78. The point has been made most forcefully by Eduard Mark in "Charles E. Bohlen and the Acceptable Limits of Soviet Hegemony in Eastern Europe: A Memorandum of 18 October 1945," *Diplomatic History*, 2 (Fall 1978), and "American Policy towards Eastern Europe and the Origins of the Cold War, 1941–1946," *Journal of American History*, 68 (Sept. 1981). The term "sphere of predominance" is Mark's.

79. *New York Times*, Feb. 10, 1946. On the reaction, see Walter LaFeber, *America, Russia, and the Cold War, 1945–1975*, 3d ed. (New York, 1976), p. 39. Wright, "Kennan," pp. 392–393; Gardner, *Architects*, pp. 315–316.

80. Byrnes to GFK, Feb. 13, 1946, George Elsey Papers, Box 63, HSTL. Kennan himself, in *Memoirs* I, 292, recalls that his telegram was in response to an inquiry from the Treasury Department. Although such an inquiry might have played a role, there is no doubt that the immediate origin of the famous telegram no. 511 from Moscow was Secretary of State James Byrnes's communication: the introductory paragraph of the telegram copy states explicitly that it is a reply to Byrnes. Wright remarks ("Kennan," p. 393) that it may have been Kennan's perfunctory analysis of Stalin's speech (GFK to Secstate, Feb. 12, 1946, Elsey Papers, Box 63) that caused the department to ask for a more detailed analysis.

81. C. Ben Wright, interview with Dorothy Hessman, Washington, D.C., Oct. 1, 1970, Bland Files; Wright, "Kennan," pp. 394, 411–421. Hessman took the dictation of what is often said to have been eight thousand words but was in fact shorter. Isaacson and Thomas, *Wise Men*, p. 352, seem to have counted the words of the Long Telegram pretty precisely: 5,540. I have used the text as reproduced in Etzold and Gaddis, *Containment*, pp. 50–63; all quotations are from this source.

82. Stalin used the term in his February speech. *New York Times*, Feb. 10, 1946. In view of the extraordinary misreadings of this speech—leading liberal William O. Douglas called it "the Declaration of World War III" (quoted in LaFeber, *America, Russia*, p. 39)—a comment is necessary. Stalin used orthodox language to describe the ultimate origin of the Second World War, but added the important qualification that it was "radically different" from the First World War in that it "assumed from the very beginning an anti-Fascist liberating character, having also as one of its aims the re-establishment of democratic liberties. The entry of the Soviet Union could only strengthen and did strengthen the anti-Fascist and liberating character of the Second World War. On this basis was established the anti-Fascist coalition of the Soviet Union, the United States of America, Great Britain and other freedom-loving countries." How this could have been construed as a new line (see e.g. Wright, "Kennan," p. 392) is hard to understand. The rest of the speech was mainly a defense of the regime's war record and a critique of those who had thought it internally unstable. Only in the context of rebuilding does Stalin mention anything that could be taken as a changed outlook: production levels must be raised, he says, in order to guard "against any eventuality." This single phrase, and some of his other terminology,

marks the transitional nature of the period; but it was a transition from, in Soviet eyes, active negotiation and cooperation to a state of isolationism. The future, Stalin was probably intimating, now seemed a bit murky, and one had better be prepared. Though vaguely ominous, this statement was not a declaration of another world war. The transitional aspect can be detected in other Politburo speeches as well: Zhdanov merely complains that there "are still reactionary elements who are unfriendly toward the Soviet Union" in "the freedom-loving countries," but Malenkov finds that the "weak are never respected" and talks about strengthening the Red Army. *New York Times*, Feb. 9, 1946. William O. McCagg, *Stalin Embattled* (Detroit, 1978), is an intriguing account of intraparty struggles in this period over the revival of ideology and of Stalin's relation to them; but too much is made out of slim evidence, and some of the doctrinal readings seem to me dubious.

83. "George F. Kennan's Observations on the New Soviet Leadership, August 1956," in *Ideas and Diplomacy*, ed. Norman A. Graebner (New York, 1964), pp. 823–829.

84. Thus Kennan declared that coexistence is possible; that the basic contradiction of advanced countries mainly has to do not with capitalist ownership but with urbanism and industrialism; that internal capitalist rivalries do not always result in wars and that not all wars result from capitalist conflict in the first place; that the talk of intervention against the USSR is nonsense; and that the social democrats are sincere and had improved conditions for workers in, for example, Scandinavia.

Another example of the manipulative theme is his analysis of Stalin's reaction to Churchill's Iron Curtain speech in March 1946. Churchill had spoken of the divine intention behind the American atom bomb and in favor of a "fraternal association of the English-speaking peoples" outside the United Nations for the purpose of imposing order on the world. *New York Times*, March 6, 1946. Stalin took this to be a racist call à la Hitler for an anti-Soviet offensive and an attempt to ruin cooperation between the Allies. *New York Times*, March 14, 1946. Kennan found this "the most violent reaction [he] could recall to any foreign statement" and drew the conclusion that the "Kremlin had tactical reasons of high importance and urgency for seizing upon this speech and representing it to [the] Soviet public, not for what it was [defensive], but for what [the] Kremlin wished it to appear." He speculated that the real reason for this obvious distortion of Churchill's speech was to prepare the Soviet people for aggressive operations in Iran. GFK to Secstate, March 14, 1946, *FRUS*, 1946, VI, 716. It was unthinkable to Kennan that Stalin might actually have taken Churchill's speech—by any standards a militant one—in the way he did. The search for other, more sinister motives is typical. In fact Churchill had been a leading proponent and organizer of the anti-Bolshevik intervention of 1918–19; he had been known for years as a diehard foe of the Soviet regime; the Anglo-American alliance was meant precisely as an anti-Soviet move; and the first to employ the Iron Curtain metaphor had been Goebbels. See Harbutt, *The Iron Curtain*, chap. 2 and passim. The Kremlin reaction was thus far from incomprehensible. The Fulton speech has remained vividly present in Moscow's memory: witness Gorbachev's references to it.

85. Soviet marxism in fact rests ultimately on the assumption that it is an objective, scientific truth.

86. A good argument can be made that the Russians by proxy actively supported restoration of bourgeois rule in Western Europe.

87. It is also epistemologically dubious since the procedures whereby the extraction or uncovering of knowledge takes place cannot be grounded in any independent criteria: attempts along those lines end up in infinite regress.

88. Intelligence Summary, May 2, 1946, Elsey Papers, Box 63, HSTL.

3. Back in the U.S. of A.

1. "Organization Meeting on Russia," June 12, 1946, GFKP, Box 16.

2. "Russia and the Post-War Settlement," summer 1942, GFKP, Box 25.

3. "Report to Mr. Russell on Summer 1946 Lecture Tour," Aug. 23, 1946, GFKP, Box 16.

4. On PPS and Kennan, see Wilson D. Miscamble's authoritative "George F. Kennan: The Policy Planning Staff and American Foreign Policy, 1947–1950" (Ph.D. diss., University of Notre Dame, 1980).

5. By no means did Soviet analyses completely dry up. Kennan continued to give talks now and then during the PPS period, and after 1949 he wrote articles on the subject. The initial stage of the Korean hostilities also gave rise to intensive analysis. Yet these efforts do not compare in depth to his analyses of the 1946–47 period.

6. "Background Press Conference," Washington, D.C., Aug. 22, 1950, GFKP, Box 18.

7. To question these basic assumptions would also have been to question the very arguments about the Soviet Union on which he had made his reputation, something of an existential obstacle. More prosaically, it may have seemed inopportune at times, unworthy of internal strife, to challenge overblown language, statements perhaps even to be considered useful in the greater scheme of things. When called upon to comment, he did not, for example, challenge substantially the simplifications of the important "Clifford Memorandum" of 1946, which drew on his own analyses. Actually composed by Clark Clifford's assistant George Elsey, the memorandum can speak for itself: "The language of military power is the only language which disciples of power politics understand. The United States must use that language in order that the Soviet leaders will realize that our government is determined to uphold the interests of its citizens and the rights of small nations." Reproduced in Etzold and Gaddis, *Containment*, p. 66. For Kennan's comments, see "Comments on the 'Clifford memo,'" Sept. 16, 1946, Elsey Papers, Box 63, HSTL. DeSantis, *The Diplomacy of Silence*, p. 181, suggests that Kennan's reluctance to take issue resulted from his desire, perhaps subconscious, not to jeopardize his newfound acceptance in the department. This is a credible view; yet Kennan probably did not consider his own position sufficiently removed from that of the memorandum to attack it.

8. Giovanni Gentile, Benedetto Croce's old friend and the leading philosopher of Italian fascism, spoke typically of "the total character of its doctrine, which not only pertains to the political order and development of the nation, but to its entire will, its thoughts, its feelings." Giovanni Gentile, *Grundlagen des Fascismus* (Berlin, 1936), p. 32. The book was originally written in the 1920s; the translation is my own. For an introduction to the whole problematic, see C.

J. Friedrich, M. Curtis, and B. R. Barber, *Totalitarianism in Perspective: Three Views* (New York, 1969).

9. The Truman Doctrine is symptomatic here, though the dichotomy had not yet been completely transformed, for the assistance was allegedly for "democratic Greece." This assertion should have raised eyebrows, since the Greek regime was a direct descendant of the fascist collaborators of the Second World War. For the doctrine, see Harry S. Truman, *Public Papers of the Presidents of the United States* (1947; reprint, Washington, D.C., 1963), pp. 178–179. See also NSC 68, built around the notion of a "free world" under siege, in Gaddis and Etzold, *Containment*, pp. 385–442. An interesting semantic investigation could be made of the introduction of this term.

10. See A. A. Zhdanov's speech, "The International Situation," at the founding of the Cominform, Sept. 1947, printed in U.S. Congress, House of Representatives, Committee on Foreign Affairs, 80th Cong., 2d sess., *The Strategy and Tactics of World Communism* (Washington, D.C., 1948), pp. 212–230. Zhdanov actually used the same notion of Munich and appeasement as the Western analysts, only the roles were of course reversed.

11. As far as I can determine he first used the concept, with reference to Germany, in "Comments on the Results of the Crimea Conference as Set forth in the Published Communiqué," Feb. 12, 1945, GFKP, Box 23. Six weeks later he applied it in passing to the USSR. "Report on Soviet Policy and the Policy of the Comintern Period," March 29, 1945, GFKP, Box 23.

12. Address, May 2, 1947, GFKP, Box 17. Although dismissing the economic aspect was part and parcel of the typical "totalitarian" argument (Nazi Germany and Stalinist Russia having entirely different economic systems), he made the point because, laudably, he wanted to prevent anti-Soviet sentiment from becoming a wholesale condemnation of socialism.

13. H. G. Gerth and C. W. Mills, eds., *From Max Weber: Essays in Sociology* (New York, 1946), pp. 197–215.

14. Address, Dec. 18, 1947, GFKP, Box 17. See Raymond Aron, *Clausewitz* (London, 1983), p. 93, on rationality and means and ends in the politico-military field.

15. *Memoirs*, I, 199.

16. Fredric Jameson, *The Political Unconscious* (New York, 1981), p. 250.

17. My views on ethics in this regard owe much to Alasdair MacIntyre, *After Virtue* (Notre Dame, 1981), and, through him, to Aristotle's *Ethics*, ed. J. L. Ackrill. Important too were two works by Georg Lukács, *The Young Hegel* (London, 1975), and *Tactics and Ethics: Political Writings, 1919–1929* (New York, 1975). Herbert Marcuse, *Soviet Marxism* (1958; reprint, New York, 1961), was also helpful. Finally, I learned much, as always, from conversations with Cornel West.

The criticism of Kennan should not conceal that he had put his finger on a weak spot in the marxist tradition: the ethical issue has never really been resolved, and that is true for the entire spectrum of marxism, not only its Soviet appropriation. Marx himself was a radical historicist in that he refused to base morality on universal obligation or rational necessity, since such foundations are always subject to historical change. He was not a moral relativist, however, for he did not deny the universality of moral truths in itself. Such truths, rather, could be established only through the aims and agreements of historically given societies. His followers, beginning with Engels, had difficulty with this view and began looking for epistemological ways of grounding morality in some evolutionary sense of progress. Thus the neo-Kantianism of the Second International. See Cornel West's informative "Marxism, Historicism, Ethics" (Ph.D. diss., Princeton University, 1980). The Third International, unlike the Second, largely evaded the question; and when it was not evaded, the result was very often crude utilitarianism as in Lenin. Opposing classes, it was then noted, have different moralities, and ruling-class morality naturally serves, not surprisingly, the interest of the ruling order. From functional "de-masking," the argument goes on fatally to invest with moral approval all that assists in the struggle to abolish that order; whence it is but a short step to making all action by the "true" representatives of the oppressed class inherently good. Morality has thus been lodged in an agent (the party) rather than in practice as such, and there the rot begins. The best elucidation of the problematic remains the exchange between Trotsky and John Dewey in 1938. Dewey agreed with Trotsky that moralities are historically variable and that means must be related to ends, but he rightly criticized as contradictory and illegitimate the attempt to find a foundation in the presumably suprahistorical "law of all laws," namely the class struggle. See Leon Trotsky, "Their Morals and Ours," *The New International* (June 1938), and Dewey's reply, "Means and Ends," *The New International* (Aug. 1938). Aside from Sartre, Lukács was perhaps the marxist thinker best equipped to produce an ethics, a project he planned but never accomplished during his long life. In recent years there has been a resurgence of interest among Western marxists in the area. Some have tried to construct a viable alternative to traditional dead ends by wedding Aristotle to Marx. Others deny the validity of the project to begin with. For a good introduction, see the *Canadian Journal of Philosophy, Special Supplement VII* (1980). Other pertinent works are Eugene Kamenka, *The Ethical Foundations of Marxism* (London, 1972); and Kubálková and Cruickshank, *Marxism-Leninism*. This last book makes the point about agents and deeds (pp. 196–197). Identifying agent and good is, however, not the habit of communists alone. The effort to eradicate communism and would-be communism from the world has justified a very wide range of means indeed, leading to precisely the same identification. Here I can think of no better reference than John le Carré, whose whole oeuvre explores this idea with the greatest clarity.

18. Address, Feb. 20, 1947, GFKP, Box 17.

19. Marcuse, *Soviet Marxism*, pp. 68–69. For an argument about the deviations from Weberian rationality, see F. Fehér, A. Heller, and G. Márkus, *Dictatorship over Needs* (Oxford, 1983). The authors point out that if, for some unfathomable reason, output of shoes can be maximized only at the price of less central control over the production process, those shoes will not be made. It will be interesting to see whether Mikhail Gorbachev's assault (from the center) on this logic will succeed and thus disprove the argument. The Soviet bureaucracy, by the way, is not really a meritocracy in Weber's sense. See Wladyslaw Bienkowski, *Theory and Reality* (London, 1981). Yet there has always been a Soviet infatuation, from Lenin to the present, with American Taylorism and various notions of man as a rationalized machine: thus the otherwise peculiar adoption of cybernetics, or, as Russian terminology would have it, the scientific management of society. See

Michael Waller, *Democratic Centralism: An Historical Commentary* (Manchester, 1981); and Kendall E. Bailes, "Alexei Gastev and the Soviet Controversy over Taylorism, 1918–1924," *Soviet Studies*, 29 (1977).

20. Lukács, in his essay "Tactics and Ethics" (reproduced in *Tactics and Ethics*) attacked this tendency early on (1919). The goal, he insisted, must always be immanently visible in the act lest the whole operation ends up in shortsighted "realist" maneuvers. It was this distancing of the goal that Dewey singled out as the reason for the degeneration of the formula that the ends justify the means. On Gramsci, see Perry Anderson, "The Antinomies of Antonio Gramsci," *New Left Review*, no. 100 (1976).

21. Marcuse, *Soviet Marxism*, p. 226. See also, generally, H. C. F. Mansilla, "Moraltheorien und Verhaltenssteuerung in sozialistischen System," *Osteuropa*, 34 (May 1984).

22. Trotsky, "Their Morals." This did not prevent him, by the way, from using the argument precisely in the criticized sense.

23. The popularity of the notion of totalitarianism has followed the progress of the cold war closely and has thus in recent years experienced something of a renaissance. See the classic work by Hannah Arendt, *The Origins of Totalitarianism* (1951; reprint, London, 1958), an example of the circularity argument; and Nicos Poulantzas, *State, Power, Socialism* (London, 1978). On Gramsci and Russia, see Anderson, "Antinomies." In recent use the concept appears to have served mainly as an excuse for assorted Western-backed dictatorships, categorized as authoritarian but open to democratic change, and hence by definition more benevolent than Soviet totalitarianism.

24. See Arendt, *Totalitarianism*, chap. 13. The idea is also partly present in Nicos Poulantzas, *Fascism and Dictatorship* (London, 1973), pp. 322–323.

25. See, for instance, Address, Sept. 16, 1946, GFKP, Box 16.

26. On the legality of the secret police, see John N. Hazard, *Settling Disputes in Soviet Society* (New York, 1960), p. 488; E. L. Johnson, *An Introduction to the Soviet Legal System* (London, 1969), pp. 43–54. Overall, see Robert Sharlet, "Stalinism and Soviet Legal Culture," and Moshe Lewin, "The Social Background of Stalinism," in *Stalinism*, ed. Robert C. Tucker (New York, 1977).

The paradoxes of this whole development are fascinating. Lavrenty Beria himself, ironically, was tried and executed after Stalin's death under the 1934 statute. Johnson, *Soviet Legal System*, pp. 53–54. As Poulantzas pointed out in his last work, *State, Power, Socialism*, pp. 76–77, 84–85, law is essentially an expression of the generic state monopoly on violence, and even the most murderous state is in some ways juridical. Every state engages in practices that do not fall under established legal rules and indeed consciously *breaks* those rules. State illegality is in that sense an inevitable corollary of state legality itself. I doubt that there is a secret police anywhere that does not break the law fairly constantly. Indeed, a killer operation such as the 1985 French one that blew up a Greenpeace ship, and within the jurisdiction of a presumably friendly country to boot, is bound to make one wonder whether, from a strictly juridical angle, some secret police forces of the West do not break their domestic laws just as often as the KGB. The qualitative difference between the USSR and Western democracies does not lie here but in the vastly more important role and juridical reach of the secret police in Soviet society at large.

27. GFK (under the pseudonym "Mr. X"), "The Sources of Soviet Conduct," *Foreign Affairs*, 25 (July 1947), also the X-Article; Address, Jan. 14, 1948, GFKP, Box 17.

28. Address, Sept. 16, 1946, GFKP, Box 16. As is evident from the quoted passage, Kennan is putting words into Pashukanis's mouth; he goes on to liken these imputed words to those of any Nazi jurist. Kennan had used Pashukanis (who was liquidated in 1937) as a straw man before the war as well. Bullitt (GFK) to Secstate, March 19, 1936, DSF, 761.00-261. On this occasion he misdates Pashukanis's rise to 1934; he actually became prominent in the early 1920s with his commodity theory of law, arguing that the disappearance of commodities would mean the disappearance of law. This proposition was disastrous for him in the 1930s, when the repelling Andrey Vyshinsky (an old Menshevik, later a notorious purge prosecutor, then foreign minister after Molotov) and others like him were ushering in the legal and bureaucratic Leviathan under Stalin. Although Pashukanis's essentially libertarian notion of vanishing law served in practice to simplify and politicize legal procedure, it is entirely inappropriate to compare him with Nazi jurists, even in the post-1934 period, when he had been forced to recant. See the introduction by P. Beirne and R. Sharlet, eds., in Evgeny B. Pashukanis, *Selected Writings on Marxism and Law* (London, 1980).

29. NSC 68, as cited in John Lewis Gaddis, *Strategies of Containment* (New York, 1982), p. 95; italics added. The document as a whole is a mess, and other passages can be taken to suggest a completely different viewpoint. The incoherence was a result of writing by committee and setting the aim of deliberate exaggeration. According to Paul Nitze, chief author of NSC 68, the originator of the quoted passage was none other than John Paton Davies, all of which makes his subsequent persecution at the hands of Joseph McCarthy darkly ironical in more ways than one. (I am grateful to Ronald Steel for passing this interesting piece of information along to me, Nitze having conveyed it to him in November 1987.) On NSC 68 generally, see Jerry W. Sanders, *Peddlers of Crisis: The Committee on the Present Danger and the Politics of Containment* (Boston, 1983), chap. 1; Samuel F. Wells, "Sounding the Tocsin: NSC 68 and the Soviet Threat," *International Security* (Fall 1979); and Paul Y. Hammond, "NSC 68: Prologue to Rearmament," in W. R. Schilling, P. Y. Hammond, and G. H. Snyder, *Strategy, Politics, and Defense Budgets* (New York, 1962).

30. The same history lesson, indicative of the conceptual return of totalitarianism in American political discourse, was employed in the early 1980s with respect to Nicaragua, the actual lesson drawn being that this totalitarian regime would have to be crushed to prevent a communist power move against Texas.

31. Address, Jan. 8, 1948, GFKP, Box 17. He was speaking to the Armed Services Committee on Capitol Hill.

32. Address, May 2, 1947, GFKP, Box 17.

33. He attempted, for example, to alter the wording of the Truman Doctrine. GFK to Acheson, March 6, 1947, DSF, 868.00/3-647.

34. Kennan was a self-professed admirer of *The Republic*, one of the few works he ever mentioned except for Gibbon's *Decline and Fall*. See Brooks Atkinson, "America's Global Planner," *New York Times Magazine*, July 13, 1947. My account is a gross simplification of Greek political theory but still, I hope, not without some suggestive power. Herodotus had used a simple triptych of

monarchy, aristocracy, and democracy, the degeneration of all of which he termed tyranny. Socrates then developed a typology in which tyranny was the negative of monarchy, the latter being based on consent and the upholding of the laws. This was supplanted by the opposition of aristocracy and plutocracy (rule by the few based on merit or wealth), and a fifth form, democracy. Plato seized on the difference between the law and the arbitrary in outlining three couplets, or six distinct types: (constitutional) monarchy and tyranny, aristocracy and oligarchy, constitutional democracy and democracy. Of these he ranked monarchy first. Aristotle differed from Plato in various ways but used essentially the same divisions. A striking feature throughout, however, is the contrast between the stable and orderly on the one hand and the anarchical and capricious on the other.

35. On his somewhat tentative location of Salazar, see the discussion following Address, March 7, 1947, GFKP, Box 17.

36. See Arendt, *Totalitarianism*, pp. 416–417, for a related argument. As Plato says of the despot in *The Republic*, he lives as though he is in an ordinary man's dream: "Never able to satisfy his desires, he is always in need." Kennan subsequently tried to demonstrate another underlying logic by proposing that "excess of internal authority leads inevitably to unsocial and aggressive conduct as a government among governments." Perhaps this was what he had in mind all along. "America and the Russian Future," *Foreign Affairs*, 29 (April 1951).

37. Willet's memorandum and Kennan's initial objections (GFK to Hill, Oct. 7, 1946) can be found in GFKP, Box 28. Generally, see Daniel F. Harrington, "Kennan, Bohlen, and the Riga Axioms," *Diplomatic History*, 2 (Fall 1978); George W. Sand, "Clifford and Truman: A Study in Foreign Policy and National Security" (Ph.D. diss., St. Louis University, 1973), p. 153; and Isaacson and Thomas, *The Wise Men*, pp. 381–385.

38. See Eduard M. Mark's valuable thesis, "The Interpretation of Soviet Foreign Policy in the United States, 1928–1947" (Ph.D. diss., University of Connecticut, 1978), pp. 257–258; and Adam Ulam, "Re-Reading the Cold War," in Aspaturian, *Process and Power*.

39. Address (Yale), Oct. 1, 1946, GFKP, Box 16. All quotations are from this source. He gave two addresses on this date: at Yale, and at the Naval War College in Rhode Island. His aim at Yale was to examine Wallace's position without preconceived ideas; for "the more obvious and the more familiar the postulate, the greater the danger that we may by inadvertence come to place too great a reliance upon it." Yet the analysis was far less unconditional than he imagined.

40. Marshall Shulman, *Stalin's Foreign Policy Reappraised* (New York, 1966), p. 20, summarizes it: "At the end of the war, the Soviet Union was left with a large land army and the conviction that it faced a period of extreme vulnerability. In contrast with the devastated Russian economy, American industrial power seemed towering. The United States possessed an uncertain number of atomic bombs, a large fleet of long-range aircraft, and an imposing navy." In a documentary aired on public television in New York on October 13, 1982, Kennan argued that Moscow had feared both Germany and the United States.

41. See Appendix B.

42. "The Soviet Way of Thought and Its Effect on Soviet Foreign Policy," Jan. 7, 1947, Council on Foreign Relations, Records of Groups, vol. 22, CFR

Library, New York; a second version is dated Jan. 24, 1947, GFKP, Box 16. Unless otherwise stated, all quotations are from the second version.

43. "The Soviet Way of Thought," Jan. 7, 1947.

44. From 1954. See Harold Nicolson, *The Evolution of Diplomacy* (New York, 1966), p. 47. Parenthetically, "restraint in method" did not, by any historical yardstick, characterize the Western destruction of Dresden and Hiroshima, wanton acts of terror and mass murder against civilians.

45. Italics added. "Autarchy" here probably refers to what is more often spelled autarky (that is, self-sufficiency rather than autocracy).

46. The most widely reproduced article of its kind, the X-Article is now, I think, one of those basic documents of American history. All quotations are from this source (cited in n. 27).

47. *New York Times*, Feb. 10, 1946.

48. Press conference, April 1, 1952, GFKP, Box 18.

49. Fehér et al. make such an attempt in *Dictatorship*, pp. 274–275. Not unlike Kennan, they argue that the Soviet need to conquer the outside is the result of a desire to eliminate a comparative standard and thus also eliminate the basis for any internal dissent. They also insist that the inherent aim of increasing production under complete social control means that there must be expansion. I find none of this persuasive, mostly for the same reasons I find Kennan's original arguments wanting. It is in fact odd that they should discern an expansionist logic when they also argue (p. 271) that Stalin understood quite well the advantages of autarky for his kind of despotism. The Maoist answer was more straightforward: the Soviet Union was simply a new type of capitalism and hence obviously expansionist. Western marxism, for its part, has been unable to find a satisfactory answer to the question.

50. I owe this analogy to Michael Harrington.

51. E. H. Carr, *The Twenty Years' Crisis* (London, 1940), p. 108. Similarly: "Laissez-faire in international relations, as in those between capital and labour, is the paradise of the economically strong" (p. 88).

52. Theodore Roosevelt, *The Works of Theodore Roosevelt*, vol. 13 (New York, 1926), p. 336.

53. As reproduced in Etzold and Gaddis, *Containment*, pp. 387–388. NSC 68 also espoused a kind of reversed vulgar marxist argument that the Soviet Union had to expand in order to escape from its internal contradictions: "the seeds of decay" would otherwise "begin to flower and fructify" (p. 396).

54. Address, Jan. 19, 1949, GFKP, Box 17. This view appears too in PPS 38. The Policy Planning Studies have been published in *PPSP*. The admirable feat of publishing these documents is somewhat marred by the fact that Kennan's essential addendum to PPS 4 (regarding the Marshall Plan) in 1947 is not included. PPS 4 was top secret, the explanatory note much more so (illogical as the terminology is). PPS 38 can be found in *PPSP*, II, 372–411.

55. Sources for these statements are, respectively, Address, Oct. 22, 1946, GFKP, Box 17; Address, May 9, 1947, GFKP, Box 17; "The Soviet Way of Thought," Jan. 24, 1947, GFKP, Box 17; and "The Sources of Soviet Conduct," p. 575. Most of his statements about Soviet goals involved aim number 1.

56. Address, Dec. 18, 1947, GFKP, Box 17. See also Address, Dec. 1, 1947, GFKP, Box 17.

57. Address, Dec. 18, 1947, GFKP, Box 17.

58. Davies himself minimizes this influence (interview, Asheville, N.C., April 26–27, 1981), but I think it was substantial. After firsthand experience with the Chinese communists, Davies had served with Kennan in Moscow and had been handpicked for the PPS.

59. For examples of his views on China, see Address, Feb. 20, 1947, GFKP, Box 17; and Address, June 13, GFKP, Box 17. He tended to think the communists a more capable lot than Chiang's Nationalist forces, whom he dismissed impolitely but justifiably: "We can support something; we cannot support nothing." GFK to Winnacker, Dec. 8, 1948, PPS Files, Box 13.

60. For a major statement on Korea, see GFK to Secstate, Aug. 8, 1950, *FRUS*, 1950, I, pp. 361–367. See also *Memoirs*, I, 484–500, and *Memoirs*, 26–52, on his unexpected role as a consultant during this initial stage.

61. Speech notes, Feb. 2, 1949, GFKP, Box 17; Address, June 13, 1949, GFKP, Box 17.

62. Address, Sept. 17, 1948, GFKP, Box 17. Taking Soviet goals as fairly self-evident, he tended to think of them negatively—that is, in terms of what the United States could not allow the Soviets to achieve. See e.g. Address, April 10, 1947, GFKP, Box 17, where he posits Soviet dominance over Germany as one objective definitely beyond the limit.

63. Speech notes, Feb. 2, 1949, GFKP, Box 17. Being a note, the statement is cryptic: "Soviet ideology does not envisage this type of conquest. Soviet psychology seeks maximum of power with minimum responsibility. Direct military conquest brings far too much responsibility." There is a slide here from ideology to psychology to practicalities. The other related example I have found is the one I have already quoted from the January 24, 1947, address, referring to ideological constraints on behavior. See "Soviet Way of Thought." A later, unequivocal statement is Press conference, April 1, 1952, GFKP, Box 18.

64. Address, April 10, 1947, GFKP, Box 17. Here he also uses, uniquely, a trinomial: "the measures of war or the measures of diplomacy or the measures of underhanded political penetration and intrigue."

65. Address, Dec. 1, 1947, GFKP, Box 17.

66. Kennan was referring to a peculiar reply Stalin had made to a letter from a Colonel Razin, who had taken the position that Lenin's favorable view of Clausewitz was outdated. Stalin answered that Lenin had liked the Prussian's emphasis on the "direct connection between war and politics" and on the legitimacy of retreat as "a form of struggle." Stalin was otherwise sharply critical of Clausewitz, classifying him as historically passé (premachine, in Stalin's typically rigid scheme of stages) and as one in a long row of pernicious German militarists. The Russian marshal then went on to castigate people who did not read authorities critically and to praise the virtues of counteroffensive in war (no doubt thinking fondly of his recent past). The reply, dated February 23, 1946, but published a year later, was short and not well composed. "Stalin's Reply to Professor Razin," *Political Affairs*, 26 (May 1947). It can be read in a variety of speculative ways. For one possibility, see McCagg, *Stalin Embattled*, pp. 233–235.

Clausewitz, generally speaking, has been held in high regard in Soviet military thought (but not without reservations). Lenin, as this exchange indicates, had initiated this tradition by reading Clausewitz during his intense period of Hegel studies in 1915. The Clausewitzian formula is in fact sometimes cited in Soviet works as though it originated with Lenin, whereas what is cited is of course Lenin's quote of Clausewitz. One lesson Lenin drew was indeed that "politics is the reason, and war is only the tool, not the other way around. Consequently, it remains only to subordinate the military point of view to the political." Quoted in V. D. Sokolovskiy, *Soviet Military Strategy* (London, 1975), p. 14. Despite the political theme, I think the most important aspect of Lenin's Hegelian appropriation of Clausewitz lies in the notion of a political contradiction expressing itself in several different ways (mainly peace and war) and persisting until a synthesis has been reached. An interesting introduction to the topic is Werner Hahlweg, "Lenin und Clausewitz," *Archiv für Kulturgeschichte*, 1 and 2 (1954). See also Aron, *Clausewitz* (London, 1983), where Aron claims (pp. 267–277, 302–303) that Lenin understood only one part of Clausewitz; that the latter was not really a Hegelian; and that Mao was more of a Clausewitzian than Lenin. I am not convinced of the first point. A final note: Clausewitz's dictum should not serve to conceal that, as Edward N. Luttwak argues, in *Strategy* (Cambridge, Mass., 1987), war and peace *in themselves* are subject to very different logic.

67. "The Sources of Soviet Conduct," pp. 579–580.

68. These three arguments are extracted from ibid.; Address, Dec. 1, 1947, GFKP, Box 17; Address, Feb. 10, 1947, GFKP, Box 16; and Address, Sept. 18, 1947, GFKP, Box 17.

69. "Seeds of decay" was a common term in Soviet orthodoxy, and Kennan explicitly turned it against the Soviet Union itself (as did NSC 68 later; see n. 53). The metaphor of seeds otherwise has an interesting lineage that goes back all the way to the pre-Socratic thinker Anaxagoras. Galen, in the second century A.D., used it in the sense of a growing disease, but it had probably appeared already in Lucretius in the first century B.C. See Vivian Nutton, "The Seeds of Disease: An Explanation of Contagion and Infection from the Greeks to the Renaissance," *Medical History* (Jan. 1983). Indeed, a good deal of the metaphorical apparatus used in the West to depict the Soviet danger has been concerned with disease and immunology (a fact that Andrew Ross has made clearer for me in conversation). Witness Kennan's typical references to disease, malignant parasites, and the necessity of putting the body politic in healthy order. Churchill, for whom Bolshevism was "a pestilence more destructive of life than the Black Death or the Spotted Typhus," was as always more rhetorical: "Bolshevism is not a policy; it is a disease. It is not a creed: it is a pestilence . . . It breaks out with great suddenness; it is violently contagious; it throws people into a frenzy of excitement; it spreads with extraordinary rapidity; the mortality is terrible; so that after a while, like other pestilences, the disease tends to wear itself out." From 1920. Quoted in Harbutt, *The Iron Curtain*, pp. 25, 27. The very notion of a *cordon sanitaire* thus assumes added poignancy. The disease metaphor was also common, however, in Soviet political discourse; again, in fact, it can be traced back to the Greeks. See Susan Sontag, *Illness as a Metaphor* (New York, 1978), chap. 9.

Kennan's evaluation of the political picture (admittedly not the whole realm of possible seeds of decay) was unclear. The X-Article asserts that the opposition had been crushed. Yet Kennan also argued (on unknown grounds) that two-thirds of the Russian people positively hated the Kremlin. Address, Nov. 8, 1948,

GFKP, Box 17. One can only guess at the truth of this remark, but there does seem to have been considerable popular support for the extension of the strategic borders. Roy and Zhores Medvedev, "The USSR and the Arms Race," in Thompson, *Exterminism*, p. 158. Alec Nove, *Stalinism and After* (London, 1975), p. 172, has pointed to the deep fear of disorder and anarchy among the Soviet public. Unease and anxiety over Gorbachev's present attempts to air out and animate the system is in that respect by no means limited to conservative apparatchiks. Fehér et al., *Dictatorship*, pp. 137–138, finally, make a pertinent Weberian-Habermasian point. A social order is legitimated on two conditions: first, one group considers it exemplary, and second, the rest have no alternative of equal stature. Collapse follows if neither condition is fulfilled; if only one applies, there is a legitimation crisis. Hungary in 1956 was an example of the first, while Eastern Europe generally today (except perhaps again Hungary) is an example of the second. In the Soviet Union itself, however, there are few signs of any legitimation crisis, much less of a collapse. One should be careful before assuming that there is any great mass of Soviet citizens thirsting to break down the communist dictatorship and rush into Western-style democratic freedom. Cars and refrigerators are another matter.

70. Vigor, *The Soviet View*, p. 204; R. and Z. Medvedev, "The USSR," p. 159; Wells, "Sounding the Tocsin."

71. This composite portrait is abstracted primarily from the following texts: Address, Oct. 1 (Rhode Island), GFKP, Box 16; Address, Oct. 22, 1946, GFKP, Box 16; Address, Jan. 23, 1947, GFKP, Box 16; Address, April 10, 1947, GFKP, Box 17; "The Sources of Soviet Conduct"; Lecture notes, Feb. 2, 1947, GFKP, Box 16; Address, Sept. 18, 1947, GFKP, Box 17; Address, Aug. 30, 1949, GFKP, Box 17; GFK to Kirk, Sept. 9, PPS Files, Box 23, "USSR"; Roundtable discussion, Oct. 7–9, 1949, Melby Papers, Box 4, HSTL.

72. Press conference, Aug. 22, 1950, GFKP, Box 18.

73. The best representation of the Soviet view was given in Address, May 9, 1947, GFKP, Box 17. Relating that the belief of the old Bolsheviks in foreign intervention against the Soviet Union was still official doctrine, Kennan also pointed out that Moscow did not rule out cooperation in "times and instances in which the interests of certain capitalist governments may run parallel to those of the Soviet Union." He emphasized, however, that the condition was deemed temporary, "destined to yield some day to the final showdown struggle, political or military." Yet later he states: "They do not consider the rivalry of our two systems will necessarily have to be settled some day by major war between the armed might of the Soviet Union and the armed might of our country. They conceive that this may not be necessary." Then follows the ambiguous (extemporaneous) finale: "They are pretty well persuaded that no one starts a major war these days unless he thinks he has pretty good chances of winning it. They believe that if one side or the other has a sufficient superiority of force, that side will be pretty well able to get what it wants gradually, bit by bit, without having to fight; because they don't think that the other side will dare challenge it." By dint of the posited inherent weakness of capitalism as a system, "they think there is a fair chance that they will be able to obtain such a superiority of force."

74. Address (discussion), April 10, 1947, GFKP, Box 17, is a particularly good example.

75. Speech notes, Feb. 2, 1949, GFKP, Box 17; PPS 13, Nov. 6, 1947, *PPSP*, I, 130–131; Notes for seminar at Princeton, Jan. 23, 1949, GFKP, Box 17; Address, April 10, 1947, GFKP, Box 17.

76. Address, Feb. 20, 1947, GFKP, Box 17. The problem for Kennan was how to insert the Germans into his typology since they had recently evinced less "sobriety of social thought" than one might have wished. He resolved the dilemma by stating here that, while not showing "any great understanding for democracy," they realized that communism would be a foreign type of totalitarianism. As regards the French, he thought they carried a cultural trait of strong internal criticism, which partly explained their communist proclivities. Address, Sept. 17, 1946, GFKP, Box 16.

77. See also GFK to Hooker, Oct. 17, 1949, GFKP, Box 23.

78. Address, May 6, 1947, GFKP, Box 17. For his notion of a "hard core," see also PPS 13, Nov. 6, 1947, *PPSP*, I, 136.

79. Address, Dec. 10, 1946, GFKP, Box 16.

80. It may be argued that he was speaking relatively: that is, that out of any given number of intellectuals, more would be attracted to communism than out of a corresponding number of workers. Even this is doubtful. At any rate, if the Italian case is at all indicative, the composition of mass communist parties was overwhelmingly lower class. Out of the 2.252 million members of the PCI in 1948, only 18,000 were professionals or teachers; 1.281 million were workers. Harald Hamrin, *Between Bolshevism and Revisionism: The Italian Communist Party, 1944–1947* (Stockholm, 1975), p. 232. With reference to putative liberals, it should be borne in mind that the working-class base of the French party probably resisted de-Stalinization after 1956 more than the leadership. See A. Belden Fields, "French Maoism," in Sohnya Sayres et al., *The 60s without Apology* (Minneapolis, 1984). Moreover, Palmiro Togliatti's difficulties with his militant communist base in northern Italy, seasoned by the Resistance era, are well known. In fact, while the PCI leader was firmly committed to the unity line of reconstruction as a long-term policy, the rank and file often believed, like the American officials, that this was merely a tactical maneuver. See Sassoon, *Strategy of the Italian Communist Party*, pp. 29–30.

81. Draft notes, Feb. 1948, GFKP, Box 17 (quote); Address, Oct. 22, 1946, GFKP, Box 16.

82. Address, Dec. 10, 1946, GFKP, Box 16; Address, May 6, 1947, GFKP, Box 17.

83. Address, May 6, 1947, GFKP, Box 17.

84. Because of the element of personal intrigue, the picture will probably never be complete. Italy was a clearer case than France, where conflicts within the regime, especially regarding the Renault strike, seem to have played the main role in the ejection of the PCF from the government. See James E. Miller, *The United States and Italy* (Chapel Hill, 1986), pp. 226–229, and "Taking Off the Gloves: The United States and the Italian Elections of 1948," *Diplomatic History*, 7 (Winter 1983). Paolo Spriano (a PCI historian) wrongly asserts, in *Stalin*, p. 283, that the expulsion was merely the result of domestic forces.

85. Claudin, *The Communist Movement*, pp. 466–479; Edward Mortimer, *The Rise of the French Communist Party, 1920–1947* (London, 1984), chaps. 9 and 10. Togliatti must have carried with him the memory of the turbulent Italian

period 1920–1922, the outcome of which had been fascism. He also dreaded a repetition of the contemporary Greek model: civil war and intervention. Spriano, *Stalin*, p. 225. A similar concern was at work in the 1970s, when the PCI became fixated on the necessity of entering a coalition with the Christian Democrats because of what it perceived as the prophetic disaster in Chile.

86. PPS 13, Nov. 6, 1947, *PPSP*, I, 136. See also Address, Dec. 1, 1947, GFKP, Box 17; Address, Dec. 18, 1947, GFKP, Box 17. The strikes were not entirely political: there was a lot of pent-up grassroots dissatisfaction after the period of unity.

87. Address, Jan. 8, 1948, GFKP, Box 17.

88. Address, Oct. 22, 1946, GFKP, Box 16. On the common misreading of Tito's relation with Moscow, see Michael B. Petrovish, "View from Yugoslavia," in *Witnesses to the Origins of the Cold War*, ed. T. Hammond (Seattle, 1982). Tito's militancy must have been a major factor here. Yet it is odd that Kennan, who saw through the Sino-Soviet relationship so early, did not apply the same logic to the example of Yugoslavia, also a self-made revolution based on indigenous armed force.

89. Address, Feb. 20, 1947, GFKP, Box 17.

90. Address, Sept. 17, 1946, GFKP, Box 16; Lecture draft, Feb. 17, 1948, GFKP, Box 17. My argument is set forth in Chapter 2. In December 1947, after a hot autumn of political violence in France and Italy, Stalin discouraged an Italian communist leader from further escalation in the struggle. Spriano, *Stalin*, p. 289.

91. Claudin, *The Communist Movement*, pp. 466–479. Perhaps it was unwise for the United States to rule out a priori cooperation with a communist party such as the PCI. A devious policymaker with a nose for polycentric dissension would have spotted interesting possibilities there, for relations between the PCI and Moscow had been somewhat uneasy ever since 1919. More recently (but before Gorbachev) they have been positively frosty. Yet the American posture toward the PCI, which is pro-NATO and arguably the most open political party of significance in Italy, remains stolidly the same.

92. See *Memoirs*, I, 358. Debate on the topic is extensive. Worth mentioning is the interview "X Plus 25," *Foreign Policy*, 7 (Summer 1972); Charles Gati, "What Containment Meant," ibid.; C. Ben Wright, "Mr. 'X' and Containment," *Slavic Review*, 35 (March 1976); and "George F. Kennan Replies," ibid; the interesting exchange John Lewis Gaddis, "Containment, a Reassessment," *Foreign Affairs*, 55 (July 1977); Eduard M. Mark, "The Question of Containment: A Reply to John Lewis Gaddis," *Foreign Affairs*, 56 (Jan. 1978); and John Lewis Gaddis, "Reply," ibid.; and finally the two-volume work, Terry L. Deibel and John Lewis Gaddis, eds., *Containment: Concept and Policy* (Washington, D.C., 1986).

The military-political couplet appears in Address, Oct. 1, 1946, GFKP, Box 16, but does not become an *opposition* until GFK to Secstate, Jan. 16, 1948, PPS Files, Box 27, and not firmly so until after the summer of that year.

93. See Chapter 1. I disagree, as will become evident, with Gaddis's judgment, in *Strategies*, p. 88, that Kennan's strategy "sought to achieve its objectives ultimately through psychological means—by instilling self-confidence." The *ultimate* instance in Kennan's model was not psychology but *power*.

94. On Brooks Adams, see Maurice Childs, *America's Economic Superiority*

(New York, 1947), p. 136. I have been unable to unearth Marx's German word for *confined*, but it is clearly synonymous with *contained*. His disdain for tsarism was combined with something close to adulation for Lincoln. The reference is Karl Marx, *The Secret Diplomatic History of the Eighteenth Century and The Story of the Life of Lord Palmerston* (London, 1969), p. 200. Britain's Moscow embassy, where Kennan moved in and out almost like a member, had used the term *containment* with regard to Germany in a despatch on Nov. 19, 1944. Ross, *The Foreign Office*, p. 185. On Gibbon, see Edward Gibbon, *The Decline and Fall of the Roman Empire*, vol. 1, (London, 1980), p. 324. On Kennan and Gibbon, see C. Ben Wright, interview with Dorothy Hessman, Oct. 1, 1970, Washington, D.C., Bland Files. Hessman was Kennan's long-time secretary. The references to Gibbon in the X-Article were not to the quoted passage. That he was familiar with it, however, is certain, and in *Memoirs*, I, 129–130, he actually paraphrases it with regard to the Soviet sphere of influence.

95. A strong exception (but occurring when he was on his way out) is Address, Dec. 21, 1949, GFKP, Box 17: "I am saying that the real distinction between a liberal democracy and totalitarian dictatorship lies only in the matter of method, not in the matter of aim, and that if the communists can induce us to make their methods our own, then we have lost, whether or not they have won; for that distinction of method is really all that we have to fight for."

96. Address, Sept. 16, 1946, GFKP, Box 16; Address, Feb. 20, 1947, GFKP, Box 17; Address, May 2, 1947, GFKP, Box 17 (stated more explicitly in Address, Feb. 14, 1949, GFKP, Box 17); Address, Feb. 20, 1947, GFKP, Box 17.

97. Address, Sept. 17, 1946, GFKP, Box 16. Henry Kissinger, *White House Years* (Boston, 1979), p. 61, is thus dead wrong when he asserts that containment implied the notion of a "conclusive settlement with the Soviet Union." It implied nothing of the sort. Kennan, in fact ridiculed the idea of "some broad and final political understanding with the Soviet leaders . . . after which we would all go and play golf." Address, May 31, 1948, GFKP, Box 17.

98. Address, Dec. 18, 1947, GFKP, Box 17; Address, May 31, 1948, GFKP, Box 17.

99. Address, Sept. 16, 1946, GFKP, Box 16.

100. Ibid.

101. Ibid.

102. "The Sources of Soviet Conduct," p. 581.

103. Address, May 9, 1947, GFKP, Box 17.

104. Address, May 6, 1947, GFKP, Box 17. Despite bouts of pessimism, Kennan later propagated the plan as a move of "devastating effect," as "the greatest shock to Soviet foreign policy since" the German invasion. Address, Sept. 24, 1947, GFKP, Box 17. Yet the Italian communists, for example, suffered only momentary difficulties. The PCI membership in 1950 was larger than in 1946. See Donald L. M. Blackmer, *Unity in Diversity: Italian Communism and the World* (Cambridge, Mass., 1968), pp. 14–15. On the economic aspects, see Alan S. Milward's massive study *The Reconstruction of Western Europe, 1945–1951* (London, 1984), pp. 465–466: "Marshall Aid did not save Western Europe from economic collapse. In order to defend America's own strategic interests it allowed some Western European governments to continue to pursue by means of an

extensive array of trade and payments controls the extremely ambitious, expansionist domestic policies which had provoked the 1947 payments crisis and destroyed the Bretton Woods agreements almost at birth." Milward questions particularly the received notion that there was a deep crisis in 1947, claiming on the contrary that Western European economies were reviving at a remarkable rate much before the Marshall Plan came into being.

105. See e.g. the X-Article; but he invariably pointed out that, *so far*, the United States was stronger.

106. Address, Dec. 29, 1946, GFKP, Box 16.

107. Address, Oct. 1, 1946 (Rhode Island), GFKP, Box 16 (I have wrought some violence on the word sequence); Address, March 28, 1947, GFKP, Box 17.

108. Address, Oct. 1, 1946 (Rhode Island), GFKP, Box 16.

109. Address, Jan. 23, 1947, GFKP, Box 16.

110. Address, Jan. 8, 1948, GFKP, Box 17.

111. He actually made reference to Theodore Roosevelt's formula in Address, May 9, 1947, GFKP, Box 17; and used him as a model in outlining a policy of possible intervention on Formosa. *FRUS*, 1949, IX, 358.

112. Daily Meetings of Secretary, April 28, 1949, Office of the Executive Secretariat, NA, RG 59, Box 1; *FRUS*, 1949, IX, 356–359. On the debate, see references in n. 92. C. Ben Wright, "Mr. 'X' and Containment," wrongly suggests that Kennan was in favor of military intervention in Greece. Kennan supported the concrete proposals of the Truman Doctrine (though not the overall framework) with regard to Greece but made a considerable effort to quell ideas of American troop involvement, as indeed transpires from some of the very sources Wright uses. Showing some indication of American military presence in the area was one thing; intervention in the sense of sending soldiers to shoot Greeks was another. A clear statement of Kennan's (and Bohlen's) views is in PPS 8, Sept. 18, 1947, *PPSP*, I, pp. 91–101.

When there had been talk toward the end of the war of going after Franco in Spain, Kennan had been staunchly opposed: "It is my belief that our foreign policy should be based strictly on the principle of non-interference in the internal affairs of other countries and that we should be equally strict in requiring other countries to treat us decently in international dealings. As far as I am concerned, this applies to Spain as well as to any other country." GFK to the Ambassador, Dec. 11, 1944, GFKP, Box 23. He was to show far less compunction about such interference elsewhere.

113. American involvement in Italian politics is a tangled and ongoing story marked by intrigue and murky dealings. The most comprehensive treatment of the immediate postwar period can be found in Miller, *The United States and Italy*, though the same author's article "Taking Off the Gloves" is more incisive. The background I give is the result of energetic reductionism and should thus be taken as personal opinion.

114. NSC 1/3, March 8, 1948 (released to me in sanitized form under the Freedom of Information Act); Dunn to Secstate, Feb. 7, 1948, *FRUS*, 1948, III, 828; Miller, "Taking Off the Gloves."

115. What General Lucius Clay took as a sign of a Soviet attack was in fact probably the preparatory stage of the blockade of Berlin. See *Memoirs*, I, 400–

401, for Kennan's understanding of this incident. Conspicuous by its absence here is any mention of his Italian proposal. On Clay, see also Parley W. Newman, "The Origins of the North Atlantic Treaty: A Study in Organization and Politics" (Ph.D. diss., Columbia University, 1977), p. 176.

116. GFK to Secstate, March 15, 1948, *FRUS*, 1948, III, 849. The telegram was sent from Manila. He had sketched such a scenario, for example, in PPS 13, Nov. 6, 1947, *PPSP*, I, 132.

117. Miscamble, "Kennan," p. 86n. Gaddis, *Strategies*, p. 39n. argues less strongly that this and other interventionist proposals did not express "positions consistently advocated." I think they did.

118. For his prediction, see esp. Address, Dec. 18, 1947, GFKP, Box 17. See also Address, Dec. 1, 1947, GFKP, Box 17, and PPS 13, Nov. 6, 1947, *PPSP*, I, 132. His deputy back in Washington seized upon the cable and suggested that every communist party in Europe should be similarly outlawed. Not the brightest scheme ever conceived in the department, it met the same fate as Kennan's original; squashed in infancy. George Butler, memorandum, March 16, 1948, PPS Files, Box 32.

Since the PCI lost the election, *political* interventionism (e.g. buying politicians and parties as opposed to mere attempts to influence media) was deemed to have been an enormous success. In this particular case, however, Stalin and the pope might have had more to do with the outcome. On dubious grounds the Italian case thus became a model for covert operations all over the globe. Kennan himself was instrumental in developing this capacity (which eventually assumed the character of "dirty tricks"). He managed, astonishingly, to achieve political control over the CIA bureau (Office of Political Coordination) that was to handle these operations, which would range from the political and economic to the paramilitary. No actions of the last-named kind (such as later, in Guatemala) actually took place during Kennan's period. His control was no mere formality: until 1950 he met the head of the office once a week. Kennan's assumption was that the outfit was to be used only in exceptional circumstances. Instead it expanded enormously and became permanent. By the early 1950s it was worldwide in scope and employed three thousand people. A single Central European country (unnamed) was in 1952 the target of no fewer than forty operations. See U.S. Congress, Senate, Select Committee to Study Governmental Operations with Respect to Intelligence Operations, *Final Report. Supplementary Detailed Staff Reports on Foreign and Military Intelligence, Book IV* (Washington, D.C., 1976), esp. pp. 29–36. Unfortunately Kennan's testimony before the Church Committee, on which the cited historical report is in part based, remains classified. Recently he has expressed regret over the establishment of the whole secret institution, claiming that "excessive secrecy, duplicity and clandestine skulduggery are simply not our dish" since "such operations conflict with our own traditional standards and compromise our diplomacy in other areas." "Morality and Foreign Policy," *Foreign Affairs*, 64 (Winter 1985–86), 214. I think this is too idealistic an argument, but the amateurish folly of the sinister Iran-contra affair, which happened after the article was published, certainly lends credence to his point.

119. Address, Jan. 8, 1948, GFKP, Box 17; Address, Oct. 1, 1946 (Rhode Island), GFKP, Box 16.

120. For example, see Address, Oct. 1, 1946 (Yale), GFKP, Box 16.

121. On the notion of asymmetrical response, see Gaddis, *Strategies*, chap. 3. Gaddis's whole delineation of U.S. foreign policy is based on the opposition of symmetrical and asymmetrical, as taken from Alexander George. This strategy has virtues but is in the end a bit limited.

122. The articles are collected in Walter Lippmann, *The Cold War: A Study in U.S. Foreign Policy* (New York, 1947). See also Ronald Steel, *Walter Lippmann and the American Century* (New York, 1981), pp. 443–446. Relations between Lippmann and Kennan were, despite coincidence of view, never really intimate, possibly because both had a strong sense of ego. Some of this is dealt with in Kenneth W. Thompson, *Critics and Interpreters of the Cold War* (Washington, D.C., 1978).

123. Lippmann, *The Cold War*, pp. 29–30.

124. Address, May 6, 1947, GFKP, Box 17.

125. Gibbon, *Decline*, I, 322.

126. Lippmann, *The Cold War*, esp. chap. 12.

127. Address, Oct. 1, 1946 (Yale), GFKP, Box 16.

128. *New York Times*, Sept. 14, 1946. Wallace also argued that a policy of predominance of force would be a dead end; that preventive war would only lead to occupation of Western Europe, which in turn could not be bombed. Better then to beat the communists "peacefully," as he put it, proposing trade agreements and the like. This would further an "atmosphere of mutual trust and confidence." He also expressed a desire "to allay any reasonable Russian grounds for fear, suspicions and distrust." Obviously Kennan was focusing on the last two statements. There is, however, a difference between taking trust as a fundamental category of international relations ("let's all be friends and trust one another") and taking it as a heuristic sign for an actual state of affairs: a general atmosphere of trust during negotiations is, for instance, not irrelevant to their success. Also, personal trust between leading politicians can affect the relations between their states: witness de Gaulle and Adenauer. Kennan's experience with Roosevelt's excessively personalized style probably drove him too far in the opposite direction. Wallace did not intend his stance to be one of "fatuous appeasement," as Kennan seemed to think, but a realistic exchange based on finding out exactly what the Russians deemed necessary for their security and then comparing it with what the United States could tolerate. All of which strikes me as an extremely sensible policy. It earned him no laurels. Truman, to whom he addressed his views, never bothered to make any real reply and then fired him; the *Times* dismissed them with facile reference to the Atlantic Charter. In addition to the Sept. 14 article, see also *New York Times*, Sept. 18, 1946. Kennan, as we have seen, ridiculed him as naive. Arthur M. Schlesinger, Jr., in what is generally one of the most interesting artifacts of the period, *The Vital Center* (New York, 1948), referred to the Wallace liberals as "the sentimentalists, the utopians, the wailers," in short as "Doughface progressives," in contrast to the virile and pragmatic sort of liberal (p. 159). Wallace, as far as I can judge, never got a decent hearing for his position. See also J. Samuel Walker, *Henry A. Wallace and American Foreign Policy* (Westport, Conn., 1976), chaps. 10 and 11; Norman D. Markowitz, *The Rise and Fall of the People's Century: Henry A. Wallace and American Liberalism* (New York, 1973), pp. 184–193.

Kennan's criticism of the anthropomorphic notion of trust did not prevent him from employing eminently anthropomorphic categories himself. Thus in the very speech in which he attacked Wallace he went on to speak of the "political personality" of the Soviet regime; the various archetypes he used in characterizing it were of course by definition human.

129. Address, Oct. 1, 1946 (Rhode Island), GFKP, Box 16.

130. In Wittgenstein's formulation, "Wovon man nicht sprechen kann, darüber muss man schweigen" ("Whereof one cannot speak, thereof one must be silent").

131. Address, Oct. 22, 1946, GFKP, Box 16.

132. "Comments on 'Clifford memo,'" Sept. 16, 1946, Elsey Papers, Box 63, HSTL. As Kennan used it, the epithet *fanatic* could thus have been used about his own side as well. The next day (Address, Sept. 17, 1946, GFKP, Box 16) he explained the matter further: "That doesn't mean, incidentally, that they don't understand what you are trying to say, but they don't want to admit it and they never concede that the basis of our thought would be the basis of theirs. It is a very hard thing to understand psychologically, but if you talk to any fanatic, what is in his mind is that this fellow talks from premises that are so profoundly wrong that he is trying to seduce me intellectually and my job is to try to hold out against him." The extemporaneous nature of the remarks explains in part the rambling quality, but there is also a suggestion here of some underlying obscurity of thought. Two years later he tried to get away from the difficulty by making a distinction between *assessment* (variable) and *outlook* (invariable). Address, June 13, 1949, GFKP, Box 17. This is a much more interesting avenue, but he never developed an answer to the query that inevitably follows: Where does assessment end and outlook begin?

133. Address, Dec. 29, 1946, GFKP, Box 16.

134. Address, Oct. 22, 1946, GFKP, Box 16. The issue was raised at this point (Sept.–Oct. 1946) because of Wallace's intervention. Kennan evaded the question the first time he was asked directly. Address, Sept. 17, 1946, GFKP, Box 16. Then, as the quoted passage indicates, he seemingly agreed to a sphere of some sort. In Address, Jan. 8, 1948, GFKP, Box 17, he admitted that the United States "tacitly acquiesced, as part of the whole conclusion of the war, in the Red Army advance in those countries [Eastern Europe] and in the establishment of Soviet political control in the wake of the Red Army." Six weeks later, in outlining hypothetical talks, he explicitly rejected any "sphere-of-influence agreement similar to the one concluded with the Germans in 1939." PPS 23, Feb. 24, 1948, *PPSP*, II, 119. This still leaves the possibility of some other kind of sphere agreement; what sort is not clear, and my feeling is that by then the whole question was moot as far as negotiation was concerned.

135. See the X-Article. Once he mentioned five years instead of ten as the lower limit. Address, Sept. 17, 1946, GFKP, Box 16.

136. Address, Sept. 17, 1946, GFKP, Box 16.

137. The expression is that of Sir William Hayter, former British ambassador to Moscow and former warden of New College, Oxford, as quoted in Nove, *East-West Trade*, p. 69. Joshua S. Goldstein and John R. Freeman, in their "Containment Theory and Reality: The Strategic Triangle, 1948–1978" (APSA paper, 1987), have studied quantitatively, among other things, the effects of containment

(as implemented) on relations with the USSR. They find that cooperative initiatives (as opposed to negativism) have real effects in terms of Soviet responses; while containment theory classically assumed the opposite.

138. "Russia and the Post-War Settlement."

139. Address, Feb. 20, 1947, GFKP, Box 17. Admonitions such as the following tended to be of limited effect: "In particular, I deplore the hysterical sort of anti-communism which, it seems to me, is gaining currency in our country: the failure to distinguish what is indeed progressive social doctrine from the rivalry of a foreign political machine which has appropriated and abused the slogans of socialism."

140. Joint Intelligence Committee [Moscow embassy], attached to Kirk to Secstate, April 25, 1950, *FRUS*, 1950, IV, 1165. Ambassador Kirk added: "Until they rule the world there is no real peace for them, because as world revolutionaries they must succeed or perish."

141. For documentation of the tragicomic sequence of events, see Bohlen to Lovett, April 22, 1948, Bohlen Papers, NA, Diplomatic Branch, Box 22; and *FRUS*, 1948, IV, pp. 834–871. What they wanted to convey to Stalin was, in Bohlen's words, "That any further encroachment by the Soviet Union, countries controlled by it or Communist parties dominated by it beyond the present limits of Soviet control would almost certainly be regarded by this country as an act of Soviet aggression directly inimical to the vital interests of the United States"; and "that it is definitely not true that this Government is aiming in any way, shape or form, at an imperialistic expansion of its own power or at the preparation of military aggression against the Soviet Union or any other country in eastern Europe or elsewhere." The barrenness of this proposal (which in a way relies on trust) is amazing, and one wonders what Kennan and Bohlen had thought they would accomplish. Certainly Stalin could not have taken the whole thing seriously, except perhaps as an opening shot. That is possibly the reason Moscow made the initial exchange (involving Molotov and the American ambassador Bedell Smith) public immediately, followed by an attached (positive) interpretation that the American proposal was actually addressing some comprehensive resolution of extant conflicts. Truman was instantly forced to deny that any such thing had ever been intended (*New York Times*, May 12, 1948), thus calming the British, who had been shaken by the Soviet announcement (as well they might, laboring hard as they were at the time to get NATO going). In PPS 23, 1948, *PPSP*, II, 119, Kennan argued, after excluding agreements on spheres, that once the Western European situation had stabilized and one could talk to the Russians, one should make it "worth their while" to reduce communist pressure in Europe and the Middle East, but typically he did not explain how this should be done.

142. Press conference, April 1, 1952, GFKP, Box 18. Six months later the Russians declared him persona non grata because of a bad verbal gaffe. See Appendix A, pp. 258–259.

Introduction to Part II

1. Displeasure with the lack of governmental cohesion runs through much of Kennan's critical writing, but for an early example, see "Fair Day, Adieu," pt. 2, chap. 1.

2. For his misgivings, however, see the plaintive Address, June 18, 1947, GFKP, Box 17: "Great democracies are apparently incapable of dealing with the subtleties and contradictions of power relationships."

3. Larry Bland, "Policy Planner," unpublished ms., pp. 150–155; Miscamble, "Kennan," chap. 1. Kennan's version of the origins of the PPS can be found in *Memoirs*, I, 325–329.

4. Brooks Atkinson, "America's Global Planner," *New York Times Magazine*, July 13, 1947. James Reston also supported Kennan and the PPS. *New York Times*, April 25 and May 25, 1947. In the magazine feature Kennan pinpointed the structural dilemma of the PPS: lofty distance from everyday matters would make the staff irrelevant while close attention to them would make it operational.

5. GFK to the author, Nov. 15, 1985. In the beginning the staff had only one part-time and three full-time officers, plus Kennan. See PPS 15, Nov. 13, 1947, *PPSP*, I, 140.

6. See Bland, "Policy Planner"; Miscamble, "Kennan," esp. the conclusion; Testimony, U.S. Congress, Senate Subcommittee on National Policy Machinery of the Committee on Government Operations, *Organizing for National Security, the Policy Planning Staff, and the National Security Council*, Hearings, 86th Cong., 2d sess., pt. 6, May 26, 1960.

7. His sense of failure with the PPS is graphically expressed in a diary note from Nov. 19, 1949, in *Memoirs*, I, 467. I disagree here with John Lewis Gaddis, who detects a basic parallelism between Kennan and the administration "well into 1949." *Strategies*, p. 55. The chasm was significant much earlier; and ultimately Kennan thought about foreign policy in a different manner.

8. Ross Y. Koen, *The China Lobby in American Politics* (New York, 1974), pp. 50–53, 79.

4. Reconstruction and Division

1. Just how radically conservative he was will be explored in Part III.

2. Typical statements on the theme of continuity are GFK, "Some Fundamentals of Russian–American Relations," 1938, GFKP, Box 16, and GFK to Secstate, Oct. 5, 1943, DSF, 841.34553B/4. Continuity is at once an empirical observation about history and a value, a combination resulting in a somewhat contradictory assertion that deep ruptures are largely illusory but also appalling calamities if they happen undeniably to be real, as in the case of a world war. When confronted with such events, conservatives of Kennan's type are inclined to magnify the timeless and continuous so as to be able mentally to "contain" the ruptures. During the late 1940s and after Kennan tended increasingly to stress change as a counterargument to those who wanted to lock U.S. foreign policy into a doctrinaire pattern of set goals and policies. This was not a conscious revision of the earlier stance but a product of different circumstances and targets.

3. "Russia and the Post-War Settlement;" italics added.

4. As quoted in Wright, "Kennan," p. 148. The statement was made in February 1940.

5. Memorandum for Berle, June 18, 1942, GFKP, Box 23; "Russia and the Post-War Settlement."

6. *Memoirs*, I, 94. See also *From Prague*, pp. 171, 239–240, for examples

of his attachment to the Austro-Hungarian empire and his distaste for Czech nationalism; and "Fair Day, Adieu," pt. 2, chap. 2. His most explicit statement can be found in Project notes, 1951–52, 1-E-2, Annex 4, GFKP, Box 26.

7. Törnudd, *Soviet Attitudes*, pp. 84–89; and Milton Colvin, "Principal Issues in the U.S. Occupation of Austria, 1945–48," in *U.S. Occupation in Europe after World War II*, ed. Hans A. Schmitt (Lawrence, Kans., 1978). See also the exchange between Churchill and Stalin at the Teheran conference: Stalin opposed the Danubian federation on the grounds that it would offer the Germans an excellent framework for future eastward penetration; the idea must have struck him as another scheme for a *cordon sanitaire*, as indeed did most proposals for federations. *FRUS: The Conferences at Cairo and Tehran, 1943* (Washington, D.C., 1960), pp. 602–603.

8. On the absence of common aims, see GFK to Bohlen, Jan. 26, 1945, GFKP, Box 28.

9. Diary note, *Memoirs*, I, 218–219. See also the unused "Summary of the Differences," Sept. 1951, GFKP, Box 24: "I opposed the establishment of the Organization in 1945. Once it was established, I have steadily opposed its use as an instrument in what is called the 'cold war.'" The assertion in *Memoirs*, I, 219, that he had not opposed the United Nations as such is thus odd.

10. Kennan himself recognized this in *Memoirs*, I, 220.

11. "Remarks in Lisbon," GFKP, Box 16. Roosevelt had visions of four regional policemen in the world, dominant states keeping order within their respective areas of preeminence. See Gardner, *Architects of Illusion*, pp. 35–36. Though flippant, FDR was not as simple-minded as his statements would sometimes indicate. Kennan, on his part, had difficulty understanding why agreements made beyond the political horizon of the United States would have to be translated into something recognizable.

12. See his Memorandum to Riddleberger, June 13, 1944, GFKP, Box 28. Riddleberger was head of the European Division. The memorandum is partially reproduced in *Memoirs*, I, 175–179 but referred to there as a comment from 1943 on a planning paper.

13. John H. Backer, *Priming the German Economy* (Durham, N.C., 1971), p. 10.

14. His address upon receiving an order of merit in West Germany may serve as an example, the polite tone notwithstanding. "Begegnungen mit Deutschland," *Frankfurter Allgemeine Zeitung*, June 3, 1978.

15. *Memoirs*, I, 415.

16. Harrison Salisbury, *A Journey for Our Times* (New York, 1983), p. 405, is persuasive on this point.

17. *Memoirs*, I, 118.

18. On immaturity, see for instance his comment of May 15, 1939 (*From Prague*, p. 171), later reflected in his citing Freud to the effect that Germany had been baptized late and badly. Press conference, April 1, 1952, GFKP, Box 18. Strong and good at organizing things but harboring certain pathological traits: that is perhaps the best way to summarize his characterization of Germany at the time. On the added nuance, see *Memoirs*, I, 119–123. Moltke and the anti-Nazi

Kreisau Circle he headed were Western-oriented Europeanists, one reason (aside from their courage) for Kennan's affinity. See Terence Prittie, *Germans against Hitler* (London, 1964), p. 225.

19. As late as September 1947, a time when he was mostly concerned with putting German industry to work for European recovery, he was capable of saying, "The primary objective of U.S. policy toward Germany is to prevent a recrudescence of German militarism and to see that the Germans never again menace the other peoples of Europe and the world." Address, Sept. 24, 1947, GFKP, Box 17.

20. "Russia and the Post-War Settlement"; GFK to Riddleberger, June 13, 1944, GFKP, Box 28. He had been favorably impressed with the absence of social surgery under the Nazi occupation. See "The Technique of German Imperialism in Europe," April 1941, GFKP, Box 16. The German model was important for his concept of postwar reconstruction. See for instance Memorandum for Berle, June 18, 1942, GFKP, Box 23.

Bohlen, Kennan's closest friend and a fellow Russianist, had a radically different view, taking perceived popular sentiment as the starting point: "The mood [in Europe] is definitely against the restoration of political and social forms as they existed before the war and has a decided left trend. At the present moment the only Government which is taking advantage of prevailing sentiment for progressive social development is the Soviet Government through the medium of the Communist Parties . . . The United States and British Governments are represented as favoring reaction and no opportunity is neglected to emphasize that their policies are to restore the old systems of special privilege and economic reaction. [While pressing the issue of democracy, we have not stated] that the United States stands for social and economic progress and does not intend in any way to support or favor the restoration of old forms." As a remedy Bohlen proposed, among other things, open American support for the noncommunist left in Europe. Bohlen, Memorandum, March 25, 1944, Bohlen Papers, NA, Box 4.

On the whole a keener political talent than Kennan (but less analytical), Bohlen was far better equipped to deal with bureaucratic conflicts. By the same token he was more prone to discard his positions once they seemed out of tune with the governing climate. This opportunistic (or realistic) streak made him less consistent and conceptually interesting than his more unbending friend. The best treatment of Bohlen is T. Michael Ruddy, *Cautious Diplomat: Charles E. Bohlen and the Soviet Union, 1929–1969* (Kent, Ohio, 1986). Ruddy's work does greater justice to Bohlen's virtues than Bohlen's dictated memoirs, *Witness to History* (New York, 1973).

21. "Comments on Treatment of Germany," Feb. 1945, GFKP, Box 23. He associated "continental totalitarianism" with the internal land powers; and yet he was quick to defend what must surely have been the most land-minded of all social classes, the Junkers; "Lend Lease Aid to Russia," summer 1945, GFKP, Box 25. In fact the Junker estates had partially disappeared with East Prussia and were destined to vanish completely with the cession of Silesia to Poland and the land reform in the Soviet zone.

22. "Comments," Feb. 1945, GFKP, Box 23.

23. "Comment on Paper: Germany: Occupation Period: Re-Education," May 11, 1944, GFKP, Box 23.

24. GFK to Riddleberger, June 23, 1944, GFKP, Box 28. See also GFK to Bohlen, Jan. 26, 1945, GFKP, Box 28.

25. GFK, "Letter to Mr. Ambassador," March 1944, GFKP, Box 23.

26. Ibid. Kennan was again firmly within the British tradition. Churchill had contemplated a general European federation for anti-Soviet purposes in 1942, when his Eastern ally was struggling through a desperate military situation: "I must admit that my thoughts rest primarily in Europe—the revival of the glory of Europe, the parent continent of the modern nations and of civilization. It would be a measureless disaster if Russian barbarism overlaid the culture and independence of the ancient States of Europe. Hard as it is to say now, I trust that the European family may act unitedly as one under a Council of Europe. I look forward to a United States of Europe in which the barriers between nations will be greatly minimised." Quoted in Törnudd, *Soviet Attitudes*, p. 85. The federative notion was also espoused early on by the British Labour party.

27. GFK to Secstate, July 3, 1944, MPF, Box 35, 711, "Poland." The analogy is of course interesting in itself for what it says about Western dominance in Italy.

28. "Lend Lease Aid to Russia."

29. GFK to Bohlen, Jan. 26, 1945, GFKP, Box 28.

30. One is reminded of Edmund Burke's recommendation that the French adopt an English type of constitution instead of pursuing revolution, obviously a most unorganic proposal from the organicist par excellence.

31. "Lend Lease Aid to Russia." See also GFK to Bohlen, Jan. 26, 1945, GFKP, Box 28.

32. John H. Backer, *The Decision to Divide Germany* (Durham, N.C., 1978), pp. 27, 38–39; Manuel Gottlieb, *The German Peace Settlement and the Berlin Crisis* (New York, 1960), p. 96.

33. Colvin, "Principal Issues"; Backer, *The Decision*, p. 155; W. W. Rostow, *The Division of Europe after World War II: 1946* (Aldershot, 1982), p. 55. The central point is that in Austria there was a government but in Germany there was none.

34. John H. Backer, *Winds of History: The German Years of Lucius DuBignon Clay* (New York, 1983), pp. 88–89; Backer, *The Decision*, p. 137; Lucius D. Clay *Decision in Germany* (Garden City, N.Y., 1950), pp. 39–40; Rostow, *Division*, p. 25; Martin McCauley, *The GDR since 1945* (London, 1983), p. 19; Jean Edward Smith, "The View from USFET: General Clay's and Washington's Interpretation of Soviet Intentions in Germany, 1945–1948," in Schmitt, *U.S. Occupation*; John Gimbel, *The Origins of the Marshall Plan* (Stanford, 1976), pp. 38-41; Edward N. Peterson, *The American Occupation of Germany: Retreat to Victory* (Detroit, 1977), p. 67. No one, to my knowledge, disputes that the French obstructed the Allied Control Council; Robert Murphy, the chief State Department official in Germany, spoke of a "French sabotage of the Potsdam decision." April 4, 1946, *FRUS*, 1946, V, 536.

35. Murphy thought the British had come to this view after Potsdam. See Rostow, *Division*, pp. 42–44. The question is if they ever quite abandoned the

notion of dismemberment to which they had adhered after the inception of the Anglo–Soviet alliance. See Ross, *The Foreign Office*, pp. 82, 137. My own sense, and it is only an impression based on conversations (off the record) with a few British officials who had been concerned with German problems, is that they were always strongly predisposed to see the virtues of a divided Germany and indeed still do. How deeply embedded this British inclination was can be gauged by the fact that the German policies during 1946–47 generated remarkably little dissension from the left and from the rank and file of the ruling Labour party, which in any case conducted a foreign policy almost wholly in accordance with time-honored imperial axioms. See Kenneth O. Morgan, *Labour in Power, 1945–1951* (Oxford, 1984), pp. 262, 276.

Noteworthy here, too, is Clay's negative response to the Long Telegram, which he dismissed as expressive of the British position. Clay did not like Kennan's "anti-Soviet prejudices," as he told him to his face in 1945. See Backer, *Winds of History*, p. 91; the quote is Kennan's recollection and thus not a direct one. See also Gimbel, *Origins*, p. 133. The Soviet wartime position was much more vacillating on the issue of dismemberment: at Teheran the Big Three had agreed on dismemberment in some form, but after March 1945 Moscow had clearly abandoned that position. See *FRUS, Conferences at Cairo and Tehran, 1943*, pp. 600–601; Ross, *The Foreign Office*, p. 55.

36. Adenauer seemingly never relinquished his separatist inclination. See Kees van der Pijl, *The Making of the Atlantic Ruling Class* (London, 1984), p. 71. See also Richard J. Barnet, *The Alliance* (New York, 1983), chap. 1, which offers a good sketch of Adenauer; and David Calleo, "Early American Views of NATO: Then and Now," in *The Troubled Alliance*, ed. Lawrence Freedman (London, 1983). Adenauer was instrumental in preventing the potential success of East German attempts, mainly by the socialists within the Soviet-engineered Unity party, to reunify the country. See McCauley, *The GDR*, pp. 62–63, which rightly stresses the inestimable importance of Adenauer in keeping Germany divided. A British official who played a considerable part in the British policy on Germany has stated that Adenauer, whom he knew well, liked to say that Germany had been run too long by schnapps (Prussians) and beer (Bavarians); the time had now come for "civilized" white wine. Sir Frank Roberts, address, Oxford, Nov. 1984.

37. The Potsdam protocol on Germany can be found in *FRUS, Conference of Berlin*, 1945, II, 1481–1490. See also Gottlieb, *The German Peace Settlement*, pp. 37–42; Rostow, *Division*, pp. 18–19.

38. Patricia Dawson Ward, *The Threat of Peace* (Kent, Ohio, 1979), pp. 177–178, makes this point well.

39. The authoritative text here is Backer's sympathetic *Winds of History*, but see also Gardner, *Architects*, chap. 9, where Clay's antiradicalism is properly illuminated; Barnet, *The Alliance*, chap. 1; Timothy P. Ireland, *Creating the Entangling Alliance* (Westport, Conn., 1981), pp. 17–18; and Gimbel, *Origins*, p. 68. On JCS/1067, see Backer, *Priming*, pp. 21–30. Clay's own memoirs, *Decision in Germany* (New York, 1950), are unreliable insofar as his conflict with the State Department is nowhere mentioned. JCS/1067 was issued in May 1945.

40. Quoted in Smith, "The View from USFET," in Schmitt, *U.S. Occupation*, p. 71. See also Backer, *Winds of History*, p. 92, where Clay is quoted as

saying, "The U.S.S.R. has blocked no more than one or two papers in the Control Council, whereas France has vetoed all legislative moves toward creating a central administrative machinery."

41. Clay, *Decision*, pp. 39–40; Peterson, *The American Occupation*, p. 67.

42. Gimbel, *Origins*, chap. 4, is the outstanding account, written from a pro-army, though I think largely accurate, viewpoint. A quote from the conclusion (p. 274) is useful: "Faced with the the post-Potsdam impasse in Germany caused by France's actions, and appalled at the high cost of the occupation in appropriated dollars, the Army and Clay maneuvered for two years to try to bring France around. But the State Department refused either to apply sanctions against France or to admit publicly that France was indeed the major problem in Germany. Instead, State Department functionaries expressed suspicions about Russian intentions and long range objectives, and they did so despite the Army's protests, despite the terms of the Army's evidence that the Russians were cooperating in Berlin to fulfill the terms of the Potsdam Agreement. Eventually, the State Department devised tests of Russian intentions, and finally its officials asserted openly that Russia had violated the Potsdam Agreement and other things. Meanwhile, the Russians went their own way in their zone." See also Backer, *Winds of History*, pp. 92–93. Rostow's short but biting *Division* is also a good, if partial, analysis of the intransigence of the European Division. Rostow himself was working at the State Department at the time, but as an old OSS hand he was essentially an outsider. In the spring of 1946 he was one of the main authors of a proposal for an all-European settlement, a proposal opposed mightily by the European Division. On Matthews's "conversion," see *Memoirs*, I, 288. See also Gimbel, *Origins*, pp. 131–133, on Matthews's promotion of Kennan's Long Telegram and the basic views he extracted from it. By the summer of 1947 Matthews had become ambassador to Sweden, where he launched a most energetic campaign of pressure and persuasion to coax that country away from its traditional neutrality, which he considered not only untenable but also immoral. See Geir Lundestad's excellent book *The Cold War and Scandinavia* (New York, 1980), pp. 201–202. John Kenneth Galbraith, like Rostow then an outsider economist in the department, has left an uncharitable but probably perceptive assessment of Matthews as "a banner member of the old club and a man of substantially inaccessible mind, or, to be fair, one into whose mind few found the effort at penetration rewarding." Galbraith characterizes the European Division as "rigidly monastic." *A Life in Our Times* (Boston, 1981), pp. 247, 246.

43. William D. Graf, "Anticommunism in the Federal Republic of Germany," in *Socialist Register* (London, 1984).

44. This account, obviously subject to some dispute, is based mainly on McCauley, *The GDR*, pp. 11–42. He points out that the returning communist leaders quickly dissolved the independent radical committees in the eastern zone (p. 11). See also Henry Krisch, *German Politics under Soviet Occupation* (New York, 1974), chap. 3. The French even refused to permit trade unions in their zone any contact with trade unions in other zones. Backer, *Winds of History*, p. 93.

45. Erich W. Gniffke, *Jahre mit Ulbricht* (Cologne, 1966), pp. 249–251.

Gniffke, then a socialist member of the unity party in the eastern zone, learned of this firsthand from Wilhelm Pieck, who had been part of that party contingent. See also McCagg, *Stalin Embattled*, p. 290.

46. Robert Murphy sent worried cables from Berlin alerting Washington to the dangers of letting the Russians and the communists appear the sole champions of German unity. See for example Murphy to Secstate, Feb. 24, 1946, *FRUS*, 1946, V, 505–507. For the Soviet view, see V. M. Molotov, *Problems of Foreign Policy* (Moscow, 1949), pp. 65–68, where his speech at the Paris Conference of Foreign Ministers (CFM) June 10, 1946, is reproduced. In his words (p. 65): "I proceed from the consideration that, in the interest of world economy and tranquility in Europe, it would be incorrect to adopt the line of annihilating Germany as a state, or of agrarianizing her, with the destruction of her main industrial centres. Such a line would undermine the economy of Europe, dislocate world economy [*sic*] and lead to a chronic political crisis in Germany, which would spell a threat to peace and tranquility." He went on to point out that the USSR had advocated an all-German administration for a year by then. For the most part, however, Moscow opposed steps to unify the country on the economic level alone—that is, without commensurate political unification, which was the American position. The issue did not become sharply defined until Germany came up as the main item on the CFM agenda in the spring of 1947. Molotov, after having proposed a central government, then argued that the Germans themselves ought to decide the extent to which they wished to be centralized; Bevin replied that Germans always wanted centralization and that one could not trust them to "act intelligently in this question." Stalin later told Marshall that the issue of unification should not be left to the German right. See *FRUS*, 1947, II, 314, 342. See also Krisch, *German Politics*, pp. 24–25.

47. This was essentially how Kennan perceived matters: "At the moment, the Russians are exploiting the French opposition to central agencies in order to let the Communists pose safely as the champions of German unity, with a view to gaining strength outside the Russian zone. At the same time, they are profiting from the occasion to complete political preparations within their own zone and to prepare that zone as a springboard for a Communist political offensive elsewhere in the Reich." GFK to Offie, May 10, 1946, *FRUS*, 1946, V, 555.

48. The Berlin election of 1946 showed that the Soviet-dominated party was easily defeated by the Socialists. McCauley, *The GDR*, p. 30, on land reform gains, see p. 27. Molotov acknowledged this reality at the Moscow CFM in March 1947 by pointing to the election results from the British zone: the Socialists and the Christian Democrats got 11 million votes each, the Communists 2 million (and less proportional representation). *Problems*, p. 355. Milovan Djilas, in his *Conversations with Stalin* (New York, 1962), pp. 153–154, relates that in the spring of 1946 Moscow believed (or at any rate said so to some Bulgarians and Yugoslavs) that Germany would be Soviet-dominated; he goes on to express amazement—as he did at the time—that anyone would have entertained such hopes. I agree. Whatever their hopes, by the autumn of 1946 there could have been no doubt that, politically, things would be very difficult.

49. Prior to the Berlin elections, for instance (Aug. 20, 1946), Clay sent a

soothing telegram to the War Department asserting that the United States had "created a reasonably healthy atmosphere in our zone in which there is little evidence of Communist gains." Quoted in Smith, "The View from USFET," in Schmitt, *U.S. Occupation*, p. 71. Nor was Clay's statement mere guesswork: OMGUS, the occupation authority, carried out continuous opinion polls which indicated a population largely detached from politics but receptive to Western messages and apparently quite clear on the Nazi disaster. There was a growing polarization in popular identification with either the Soviet Union or the United States which increasingly favored the latter. See A. Merrit and R. Merrit, eds., *Public Opinion in Occupied Germany* (Urbana, Ill., 1970), pp. 50–58. The authors point out (p. 57) that a unique opportunity for a broad change of popular attitudes was at hand in the American zone, but the emerging cold war turned the original democratization campaign into a propagandistic anti-Soviet one. Admist general passivity, however, there was a surviving active democratic tradition in Germany. See Peter H. Merkl, *The Origin of the West German Republic* (New York, 1963), pp. 20–21. The British estimated in October 1947 that anticommunist forces would win substantially in any national German elections. Beam, memorandum of conversation, *FRUS*, 1947, II, 692.

50. Peterson, *The American Occupation*, p. 65; Clay, *Decision*, p. 151. As Clay points out, the United States considered Soviet proposals for a strong central government tantamount to laying the foundation for "single-party domination." See also the discussions at the Moscow CFM, *FRUS*, 1947, II, 314–319, 335.

51. For example GFK to Secstate, March 6, 1946, *FRUS*, 1946, V, 516.

52. Backer, *The Decision*, pp. 90, 109–110.

53. Gottlieb, *The German Peace Settlement*, pp. 149–150; Gardner, *Architects*, pp. 237, 244. According to Gottlieb (p. 79) the facilities and the manpower existed for revived coal production but not the capacity to put them together. At the Moscow CFM Molotov chided Bevin for this. Molotov, *Problems*, p. 388.

54. Backer, *The Decision*, p. 177.

55. The eastern zone had achieved 98 percent of the 1936 level of coal production by 1946. Gottlieb, *The German Peace Settlement*, p. 80.

56. The subject of reparations was discussed at Yalta, but the actual agreement was hammered out at Potsdam; since Germany was not on the CFM agenda until Moscow in March 1947, it arose only intermittently in the interval, for instance during the Paris CFM in the summer of 1946. For the Yalta discussions, see Backer, *The Decision*, p. 66. It is interesting that in Austria, Moscow seems mainly to have been interested in the German assets. See Colvin, "The Principal Issues," in Schmitt, *U.S. Occupation*.

57. Backer, *The Decision*, p. 71.

58. The ensuing account is, unless otherwise stated, based on Gottlieb, *The German Peace Settlement*, and Backer's three works, *The Decision*, *Priming*, and *Winds of History*, particularly the first. Gottlieb's book, published in 1960, is the pioneering work, while *The Decision* gives the best contemporary overview and a most solid dissection of the whole reparations problem from the 1920s onward. See esp. chaps. 4 and 5, where, respectively, the mythological notion that the American taxpayer had ended up paying German reparations after the First World War and the twin idea that Soviet claims were exorbitant are subjected to a withering critique. Backer was a high-level American economist working in Ger-

many at the time; he is not, I hasten to add, an exponent of so-called revisionist historiography, though his argument lends itself in part to that sort of view. For a short statement of the latter kind, see Gardner, *Architects*, chap. 9, though it relies largely on the seminal work of Gottlieb (also a participant on the American side in Germany). Finally, Gimbel, *Origins*, chaps. 4–7, offers a useful treatment of the problem as well.

As for primary source materials, it is perhaps most instructive to read the proceedings of the Moscow and London CFMs of 1947 and accounts of the auxiliary Western discussions (*FRUS*, 1947, II, 197, 214, 256, 264–265, 273–274, 290, 298, 301, 303–304, 309, and 335 [Moscow], and 754–819 [London]), supplemented by Molotov's speeches (*Problems*, passim). Stalin told Marshall in Moscow (*FRUS*, 1947, II, 342) that "for economic unity there must be a government which could adopt a budget, legislation and a tax system." And, one might add, pay reparations. The meeting otherwise reveals a fairly large measure of agreement as to the general outline of Germany's future political system. See for instance *FRUS*, 1947, II, 277–278.

It is interesting, incidentally, to compare the difference in reporting between the London *Times* and the *New York Times* during the London CFM: while the former was fairly cool and neutral, the latter was shrill and partisan, almost to the point of becoming an inverted mirror image of the *Daily Worker*. See particularly the parallel accounts (Dec. 9, 1947) of a speech by Molotov. When the CFM collapsed, the *New York Times* announced, "The breakdown did not come over Germany and Austria, but over the world struggle between democracy and totalitarianism and the Russian fight against Secretary Marshall's European Recovery Program," p. 1. Subsequently it editorialized (Dec. 16, 1947) that the CFM should be abolished altogether.

59. Gimbel has made an intriguing case that Clay's move to stop plant deliveries was actually designed to get the procrastinating State Department to act against the French and is thus not to be understood as an anti-Soviet gesture. The validity of this argument is difficult to evaluate. See John Gimbel, "Cold War Historians and the Occupation of Germany," in Schmitt, *U.S. Occupation*.

60. In the period 1924–1930 American investors purchased $1.239 billion worth of German bonds. Van der Pijl, *Atlantic Ruling Class*, p. 66.

61. Backer estimated the cumulative cost when he was writing (the book was published in 1978) at $66 billion, *The Decision*, p. 170. Given inflation, the amount ought now to have reached at least $100 billion. OSS and Federal Reserve economists had estimated that Germany could pay between $2.5 and $3.5 billion annually. Ibid., p. 174.

62. A reassessment of Marshall's political role is in order. Smith, for example ("The View from USFET," in Schmitt, *U.S. Occupation*) provocatively contrasts Jimmy Byrnes the pragmatic dealer with Marshall the cold warrior, a figure on whom more work is clearly needed.

63. For the Soviet turn in January 1948, see Djilas, *Conversations*, p. 153, and McCagg, *Stalin*, pp. 291–292. That there was indeed a major shift then is underlined by the subsequent Prague coup in February.

64. Gottlieb's characterization of the American position is poignant: "In how many ways and with what enticing persuasions was this program [a divided Europe] rationalized and defended. In a winged phrase: 'we must begin with

what we have in the West.' It was easy to feel that the Soviets were merely 'stalling' for time or were deliberately procrastinating in order to obstruct Western European economic recovery. How easy to argue that the West had 'bought' unity— or the eastern zone of Germany—at Potsdam and should not be 'blackmailed' into buying the same horse 'twice' in a 'deal.'" Gottlieb, *The German Peace Settlement*, p. 162. The effects on the satellites, he adds, were thus forgotten.

65. GFK to Harriman, May 14, 1945, *FRUS*, 1945, III, 1212. The Russians, represented by Ivan Maisky, made their concern over reparations quite clear to him. Ibid, pp. 1213–1215.

66. Address, May 6, 1947, GFKP, Box 17.

67. George C. Marshall, Oral History, Oct. 30, 1952, HSTL.

68. Address, Sept. 24, 1947, GFKP, Box 17.

69. Varga was attacked at a series of seminars in May 1947, the proceedings of which were published in Moscow seven months later and in Washington in early 1948 as *Soviet Views on the Post-War World Economy: An Official Critique of Eugene Varga's "Changes in the Economy of Capitalism Resulting from the Second World War"* (Washington, D.C., 1948). Until May 1947, then, Varga's widely publicized views must have been acceptable to the Soviet leadership. On Varga, see also Jerry F. Hough, "The 'X-Article' and Contemporary Sources of Soviet Conduct," in Deibel and Gaddis, *Containment*.

70. GFK, Address, Sept. 18, 1947, GFKP, Box 17; italics added.

71. McCagg, *Stalin Embattled*, p. 96.

72. GFK to Secstate, March 6, 1946, *FRUS*, 1946, V, 519. This telegram is also notable because it contradictorily cast doubt on the Russian desire to create central agencies in Germany while arguing (pp. 516–517) that Moscow did indeed desire such agencies as "a possibly indispensable device for entering at an appropriate moment the other three zones and facilitating there accomplishment of Soviet political program."

73. Apart from the preceding despatch I know of only one other major analysis: GFK to Offie, May 10, 1946, *FRUS*, 1946, V, 555. By the time he was beginning to think about the Marshall Plan in May 1947, the western part of Germany figured prominently as the engine of reconstruction (coal for Europe), but no specific analysis of Germany was involved in that proposal.

74. Address, April 10, 1947, GFKP, Box 17.

75. GFK to Secstate, March 6, 1946, *FRUS*, 1946, V, 519; Memorandum, May 16, *FRUS*, 1947, III, 221.

76. Address, Sept. 24, 1947, GFKP, Box 17.

77. PPS 13, Nov. 6, 1947, *PPSP*, I, 133.

78. Ibid., p. 132.

79. Address, Feb. 17, 1948, GFKP, Box 17. See also his unmailed letter to Lippmann, April 6, 1948, GFKP, Box 17: "Molotov sat adamant at the Moscow council-table, because he saw no reason to pay us a price for things which he thought were bound to drop into his lap, like ripe fruits, through the natural course of events."

80. That the Soviet Union would find it not only convenient but also necessary at some future date to change its fundamental line and negotiate, and that the United States ought therefore not to do anything for the present: this seems to have been an ingrained notion in Kennan. It resurfaced during his

sojourn as ambassador to the USSR in 1952, long after he had shifted his general position toward serious negotiations. See Harrison Salisbury, *Moscow Journal* (Chicago, 1961), p. 271, and *Journey for Our Times*, pp. 411–417, where Salisbury argues (p. 416) that Kennan was actually right about this at the time when he was declared persona non grata.

81. GFK to Lippmann, April 6, 1948, GFKP, Box 17.

82. Quoted in Gottlieb, *The German Peace Settlement*, p. 181.

83. PPS 23, Feb. 20, 1948, *PPSP*, II, 110.

84. All quotations ibid., pp. 110–114.

85. PPS 15, Nov. 13, 1947, *PPSP*, I, 141.

86. Lippmann, *The Cold War*, esp. pp. 33–44, 60–62. The weakness of Lippmann's own analysis was the absence of any clear notion of the concrete Soviet aims.

87. GFK to Lippmann, April 6, 1948, GFKP, Box 17. Retrospectively Kennan tends to backdate his views on this point. In 1959, for instance, he claimed that since 1944 he had "rigorously opposed, over the course of years, everything that seemed to me to make it more difficult for the Russians to withdraw from the standpoint of prestige and everything that tended to deprive us of bargaining flexibility for a final settlement." This is an accurate account of his stance after the summer of 1948 but not really before. GFK to Whelan, July 3, 1959, GFKP, Box 31.

88. C. Dewitt Poole, "Balance of Power," *Life*, Sept. 22, 1947.

89. Notes on Poole, Oct. 13, 1947, Bland Files.

90. On Hickerson, see Newman, *The Origins of NATO*, pp. 137–138; and Miscamble, "Kennan," p. 78. For Bevin's original proposal, see *FRUS*, 1947, II, 815.

91. Bevin's memorandum to the Americans was still couched in terms of uniting "the ethical and spiritual forces inherent in this Western civilisation" and other cloudy notions. *FRUS*, 1948, III, 5; for his public rendition in Parliament, see the *Times* (London), Jan. 23, 1948. The strategic vision behind it was quite clear: to bring the United States into a network of European defense. See David Calleo's perceptive essay "Early American Views," in Freedman, *The Troubled Alliance*, and Geir Lundestad, "Empire by Invitation? The US and Western Europe, 1945–1952," *SHAFR Newsletter*, 15 (Sept. 1984). See also Nicholas Henderson, *The Birth of NATO* (London, 1982), pp. 3–6. Henderson's book, an apologia written by one of the British negotiators, is nonetheless interesting in the image it gives of Hickerson's role. Hickerson thought Bevin's goal magnificent but wanted more specifically a pact modeled on the Rio Treaty which would include the United States. Jan. 19, 1948, *FRUS*, 1948, III, 7.

92. "Memorandum for Marshall," Jan. 20, 1948, *FRUS*, 1948, III, 7–8.

93. Secret memorandum attached to PPS 4, July 23, 1947, Bland Files.

94. PPS 23, Feb. 24, 1948, *PPSP*, II, 104.

95. Ibid., pp. 104–106.

96. These and the following quotes are from PPS 23, *PPSP*, II, 124–126. It is noteworthy that Kennan, in arguing against abstract legalities, reversed the form-content opposition: content suddenly becomes more important than form.

97. A good account of this period can be found in Miscamble, "Kennan," chap. 3. See also *Memoirs*, I, chap. 17, and Henderson, *Birth of NATO*, p. 15.

98. Henderson, *Birth of NATO*; Ireland, *Creating the Entangling Alliance*, p. 95.

99. George Butler, Kennan's stand-in at PPS during his absence, composed a completely pro-NATO memorandum, PPS 27, *PPSP*, II, 161–170; Kennan, upon returning, was unsettled to see how little he had been able to bring his views across to his staff. GFK to Louis Halle, April 20, 1966, GFKP, Box 31. See also Miscamble, "Kennan," p. 88.

100. GFK to Lippmann (unmailed), April 6, 1948, GFKP, Box 17.

101. Calleo, "Early American Views," in Freedman, *The Troubled Alliance*.

102. Memorandum (unused), April 29, 1948, GFKP, Box 23.

103. GFK to Lovett, April 29, 1948, *FRUS*, 1948, III, 109.

104. Ibid., p. 117.

105. GFK to Secretary and Under-Secretary, April 29, 1948, ibid., p. 129.

106. The content of these top-secret talks must have been fairly well known to the Russians, continuously supplied with information as they probably were by Donald McLean, first secretary at the British embassy. McLean was not a direct participant, but the embassy was headquarters for the British delegation, and he was partly involved in the preliminary negotiations. Henderson, who *was* a participant, worked at the embassy. Yet McLean's possible role is nowhere mentioned in the introduction or postscript to Henderson's book, which has the self-congratulatory air of a successful schoolboy conspirator.

107. Generally, see Miscamble, "Kennan," pp. 98–101; Henderson, *Birth of NATO*; *Memoirs*, I, 406–414. Minutes of the "exploratory" talks can be found in *FRUS*, 1948, III, beginning on p. 148. On his concept of narrow membership, see GFK to Lovett, Aug. 31, 1948, *FRUS*, 1948, III, 225.

108. Fourth meeting, July 8, 1948, *FRUS*, 1948, III, 168; GFK to Lovett, Aug. 31, 1948, ibid., p. 225; Thirteenth meeting, Sept. 2, 1948, ibid., p. 226.

109. For a typical Hickerson intervention, see Thirteenth meeting, ibid. See also his draft memorandum, Aug. 31, 1948, PPS Files, Box 27.

110. PPS 43, Nov. 24, 1948, *PPSP*, II, 492, 491; Address, Nov. 8, 1948, GFKP, Box 17.

111. Draft memorandum, n.d., PPS Files, Box 27.

112. PPS 43, Nov. 24, 1948, *PPSP*, II, 493–494.

113. Hickerson, Memorandum, Nov. 27, 1948, PPS Files, Box 27.

114. Dulles himself, though enthusiastic about alliances, added only four new countries to the pact system; the central commitments had already been made during the Truman years. See Gaddis, *Strategies*, p. 152.

115. Newman, *The Origins of NATO*, p. 153.

116. There is no space to delve into Kennan's important contribution to the Japanese question, for Japan was the one Asian area in which he took an ardent interest. His logic in approaching the problem was largely similar to that in the case of Germany: Japan was the "natural" counterweight to the Soviet Union in the East and should be allowed to grow back into that role as painlessly as possible. Thus he intervened to preserve traditional ways and means, for example the industrial Zaibatsu system. Japan was not to be made into an American protectorate, but the United States had to make absolutely sure that there would be no internal communist takeovers. Considering the nature of Kennan's opposition, it is ironic that some of the unorganic reforms imposed on the Japanese,

such as the creation of a substantial class of small farmers, have served eminently conservative purposes. The farmers, disproportionately well represented in parliamentary elections, make up a good part of the voting power that has sustained the right-wing party in power ever since the war. See Howard Schonberger, "U.S. Policy in Post-War Japan: The Retreat from Liberalism," *Science and Society*, 46 (Spring 1982). For Kennan's views, see GFK to Secstate, March 14, 1948, *FRUS*, 1948, I, 531–532.

117. Miscamble, "Kennan," pp. 114–121.

118. PPS 35, June 30, 1948, *PPSP*, II, 317–321. As late as October 1948 he was still maintaining a simplistic view of the conflict, erroneously depicting Tito as a compliant servant of Moscow unfortunate enough to have his own machine and thus incur Soviet displeasure. Address, Oct. 14, 1948, GFKP, Box 17.

119. His major statement in this period on retraction of Soviet power (PPS 38, Aug. 18, 1948, *PPSP*, II, esp. 378–381, 385–387) demonstrates only a vague notion along these lines. Symptomatically, Tito's break is in part traced, entirely improbably, to the impact of the Marshall Plan, a purely *American* initiative. In the end, however, Yugoslav defiance must have suggested a trend toward the return to some "natural" state of European independence.

120. Minutes of the exploratory talks, July 9, 1948, *FRUS*, 1948, III, 177. The quote is thus indirect.

121. PPS 37, Aug. 12, 1948, *PPSP*, II, 323–333.

122. Miscamble, "Kennan," p. 119.

123. PPS 37/1, Nov. 15, 1948, *PPSP*, II, 335–371; Miscamble, "Kennan," pp. 120–132; *Memoirs*, I, 422–426.

124. Even Bohlen, generally at one with Kennan, expressed doubts. See Miscamble, "Kennan," pp. 130–131.

125. GFK, Memorandum, Sept. 17, 1948, PPS Files, Box 15; the quotation is from GFK, Memorandum for the Secretary, Oct. 18, 1948, PPS Files, Box 15. He emphasized too the sharp contradictions within the Department.

126. PPS 37/1, *PPSP*, II, 337–338. This reasonableness did not include any desire to compromise with the Russians on the issue of reparations, the importance of which for Moscow he still did not appreciate.

127. PPS 42, Nov. 2, 1948, *PPSP*, II, 481. He now thought the chief Soviet objective in Germany a negative one: the prevention of a West German state. I think he was right.

128. PPS 37/1, *PPSP*, II, 337.

129. Address, Nov. 8, 1948, GFKP, Box 17. The opposite error, he argued, would be appeasement.

130. PPS 43, Nov. 24, 1948, *PPSP*, II, 494–495.

131. Ibid., p. 495.

132. This latter view is pronounced in the X-Article.

133. Address, Aug. 20, 1948, GFKP, Box 17.

134. The first time he mentions the five world centers is, as far as I know, Address, Sept. 17, 1948. GFKP, Box 17. The idea had been present implicitly for a good while though. In early 1948, for example, he spoke of Japan and the Far East from the viewpoint of war-making potential. Sullivan, Diary note, Jan. 14, 1948, Bland Files. Moreover in Address, April 10, 1947, GFKP, Box 17, he

had already intimated that the Soviet threat would be particularly dangerous if combined with German technology.

135. See PPS 39, Sept. 7, 1948, *PPSP*, II, 412–433. With the deterioration of the Nationalist position and the upcoming American elections the Chinese issue was heating up. Kennan, partly influenced by John Paton Davies, had nothing but dislike for Chiang and considered the Chinese civil war a morass of deadly proportions. The need to oppose a Marshall Plan for China and other active measures probably did as much as anything to help him articulate a clear view of what was globally important and what was not. For an incisive comment on the issue of Chinese support, see GFK to Winacker, Dec. 8, 1948, PPS Files, Box 13.

136. See e.g. his remarks at the Council on Foreign Relations, Dec. 4, 1946, CFR, Records of Groups, vol. 20, 14th meeting, CFR Library, New York. See also Kennan's remarks, PPS Minutes, May 27, 1949, PPS Files, Box 27. From the American Revolution to the Second World War, Britain never faced two or more great powers alone in war. See Kennedy, *Strategy and Diplomacy*, p. 213.

137. PPS Minutes, June 5, 1949, PPS Files, Box 27.

138. GFK to Lovett, Jan. 11, 1949, PPS Files, Box 15.

139. Memorandum, March 8, 1949, *FRUS*, 1949, III, 96–102.

140. Murphy, Memorandum of conversation, March 9, 1949, ibid., p. 102. Materials pertaining to Kennan's German trip can be found in GFKP, Box 23.

141. GFK to Secretary, May 20, 1949, ibid., pp. 888–889.

142. *Memoirs*, II, 109.

143. "NATO and Russia," in *Memoirs*, II, 340.

144. The despatch cited in n. 143 may stand as the paradigmatic statement. See also Draft statement, Sept. 23, 1952, GFKP, Box 26; and "Notes for Essays," spring 1952, p. 195, GFKP, Box 26, File 1-E-2, where he states, "A coalition is a clumsy military entity, and the more coalition, the more clumsiness." Lippmann was one of the few established luminaries to make a similar argument. See e.g. GFK to Lippmann, Jan. 13, 1953, and Lippmann to GFK, Jan. 17, 1953, Lippmann Papers, Box 81, Yale University Library, New Haven, Conn.

145. A central role in the emergence of rollback ideology was played by James Burnham's *Containment or Liberation?* (New York, 1953), which chastised Kennan's concept as de facto appeasement. As we have seen, however, containment had already been criticized for its supposedly passive implications in the fall of 1947 in *Life* (September 22). On Dulles's liberation policy, see Gaddis, *Strategies*, pp. 155–156.

146. "The Future of Soviet Communism," *The New Leader*, June 18, 1956.

147. On the American reluctance to negotiate seriously, see Gaddis, *Strategies*, pp. 192–193. Although it is true that a more nuanced image of the Eisenhower administration was needed, Gaddis's argument is far more favorable than is warranted.

148. Address, Jan. 3, 1957, GFKP, Box 19.

149. The Reith Lectures, published as *Russia, the Atom, and the West* (New York, 1958), pp. 43–49.

150. Ernst Nolte, *Marxism, Fascism, Cold War* (Assen, Netherlands, 1982), p. 267. On the general reaction, see *Memoirs*, II, 234–237, 250–257.

151. *Memoirs*, II, 251.

152. *New York Times*, Jan. 11. See also March 30, 1958: "There are no longer any frontiers." The *Times* was giving voice to the sort of universalism that would send Kennan into a deep gloom. Acheson found one effective line of attack: Kennan had advocated a kind of localized people's defense and then imprudently offered his personal assurances that it would work. The choice of phrase was not a happy one, and it became a target for a good deal of derision.

153. *New York Times*, June 15, 1958. Dennis Healy, teaching at Harvard at the time, found almost no support there for disengagement. The exception, peculiarly enough, was Zbigniew Brzezinski. Healy traces this to Brzezinski's Polish roots: without disengagement, no chance of escaping Soviet domination. Healy to the author in conversation, Los Angeles, May 1988.

154. Dean Acheson, "The Illusion of Disengagement," *Foreign Affairs*, 36 (April 1958).

155. Henry Kissinger, "Missiles and the Western Alliance," ibid, p. 398. He wrongly imputed (on the grounds of some murky formulations Kennan had made) to the disengagement thesis the purpose that it was partly designed to persuade "the Soviet Union about the sincerity of Western intentions" (p. 394). This was precisely the kind of procedure against which Kennan had argued for decades. Moreover, Kissinger brought forth Korea as an example of disengagement and its consequences (i.e. war), an analogy completely off the mark. For Korea was a liberated country wracked by civil war and Germany a defeated one without a civil war in sight; that is, unlike in Korea, there were not two separate armed forces ready to go at each other. Withdrawal from Germany was thus not comparable to withdrawal from Korea.

156. GFK, *Memoirs*, II, 252–255. For Lippmann's views, see *New York Herald Tribune*, April 6, April 9, and Aug. 25, 1959. As he pointed out in the last, although no one would admit it openly, "the partition of Germany is regarded on both sides as not intolerable and, on the whole, preferable to reunification under any conditions that are theoretically possible." Aron had said the same thing even in the early 1950s, when it was probably not true for the Soviet side. See Raymond Aron, "The Quest for a Philosophy of Foreign Affairs," in *Contemporary Theory of International Relations*, ed. Stanley Hoffman (Englewood Cliffs N.J., 1960).

157. He wrote later, in *Memoirs*, II, 253–254: "I have often thought that we might all have been spared a lot of trouble if someone in authority had come to me before these lectures were given and had said [this]." The whole affair caused him great existential anguish. He has since defended his position. See e.g. Address, April 29, 1965, GFKP, Box 21, where he also asserted, interestingly, that the West had had no constructive policy in Eastern Europe since 1914.

158. Oral comments to Secy re Baruch letter, n.d. [Dec. 1948?], Bland Files.

159. McCauley, *The GDR*, pp. 59–66, 73–74.

5. Dark Continents

1. In *Memoirs*, I, 181, he is apologetic about his lack of Third World experience: "I recognize this to have been a regrettable limitation on both experience and intellectual horizon. The negative impressions produced by occasional brief encounters with places farther south in Africa and the Middle East . . . were

largely, I am sure, the result of these blind spots. As such they were no doubt shallow and misleading. But they, too, affected . . . future thoughts and outlooks on international affairs."

2. See Bland, "Policy Planner," p. 178. Only 10 percent of the total staff effort was spent on Latin America, Africa, or Asia during Kennan's term at PPS, and half of that on China.

3. PPS 4, July 23, 1947, *PPSP*, I, 67.

4. PPS 23, Feb. 24, 1948, *PPSP*, II, 121–123; the quotation is from Address, Dec. 21, 1948, GFKP, Box 17; Address, Feb. 16, 1949, CFR, "Records of Meetings," CFR Library, New York.

5. Address, Dec. 18, 1947, GFKP, Box 17. The origin of Kennan's negative view of foreign aid was a trip to Novosibirsk in July 1945. See *Memoirs*, I, 275. He concluded after the trip that an outsider cannot help an objectively needy people since the assistance ends up helping the regime instead. Yet his attack on foreign aid as a means of winning influence began in earnest only in the 1950s. When writing the *Memoirs*, he found no copy of his long account of the trip, but one is available in his personal file, 1945–1949, DSF 123, NA. Another copy is in the Foreign Office archives at the Public Record Office in London (July 28, 1947, FO 371/47932). It was read and commented upon, all in accordance with that FO procedure which makes its documents so much easier to follow than those of the State Department; the economic desk of the FO noting perceptively that it was the product of a "lettered traveller."

6. "Oral Report to Secretary," Feb. 17, 1950, *FRUS*, 1950, I, 160; Sullivan, diary entry, Jan. 14, 1948, Bland Files (indirect quote); Address, Dec. 18, 1947, GFKP, Box 17. This last theme became more pronounced in the 1950s. See for example Address, Nov. 8, 1951, GFKP, Box 18.

7. PPS 23, Feb. 24, 1948, *PPSP*, II, 121–123; "Report on Latin America," March 29, 1950, *FRUS*, 1950, II, 598–624.

8. Roundtable discussion, October 7–9, 1949, Melby Papers (quote), Box 4, HSTL; Address, Sept. 19, 1949, GFKP, Box 17; GFK to Acheson, Nov. 14, 1949, GFKP, Box 23.

9. Diary entry, Baghdad, June 23–25, 1944, *Memoirs*, I, 184–185; Sullivan, diary entry, Jan. 14, 1948, Bland Files; Address, Dec. 21, 1949, GFKP, Box 17; Address, Oct. 14, 1949, GFKP, Box 17.

10. Address, Jan. 19, 1949, GFKP, Box 17.

11. PPS 23, Feb. 24, 1948, *PPSP*, II, 121.

12. Address, Dec. 21, 1948, GFKP, Box 17; PPS 23, Feb. 24, 1948, *PPSP*, II, 122.

13. PPS 23, Feb. 24, 1948, *PPSP*, II, 122.

14. Introduction to meeting, June 5, 6, 1949, PPS Files, Box 27.

15. This viewpoint marks, above all, his position on China, where the issue of intervention was certainly on the agenda before the completion of the revolution in the fall of 1949. For a typical "nonmeddling" comment, see PPS minutes, Oct. 11, 1949, *FRUS*, 1949, I, 399. See also, despite its contradictions, "Report on Latin America," *FRUS*, 1950, II, 598–624.

16. Address, Feb. 20, 1947, GFKP, Box 16.

17. "Report on Latin America," pp. 598–624. Unless otherwise noted, all quotations are from this source. See also *Memoirs*, I, 474–484, and Roger R.

Trask, "George F. Kennan's Report on Latin America (1950)," *Diplomatic History*, 2 (Summer 1978), on the background and character of this report. Kennan's comments about Latin American culture were exceedingly negative, though not without a (misplaced) tragic sense of sympathy. In retrospect the northern puritan was ambivalent: "I am not sure that I do not prefer [the human ego] in its Latin American manifestations: spontaneous, uninhibited and full-throated, rather than in those carefully marked and poisonously perverted forms it assumes among the Europeans and the Anglo-Americans." *Memoirs*, I, 483.

18. There have been three cases of sustained radical change in Latin America: Cuba in 1959, Chile in 1970, and Nicaragua in 1979. The first and third were guerrilla victories. The one electoral case, Chile, was a failure and ended in a right-wing coup. The point, at any rate, is negative: "clever infiltration" was not the main "danger."

19. Fragment, spring 1950, GFKP, Box 24. It is paginated 42 and was probably part of a draft of the Latin American report.

20. U.S. postwar interventionism in the Third World, direct or by proxy, is a matter of common knowledge, but for a graphic illustration, see John L. S. Girling, *America and the Third World* (London, 1980), pp. 140–141, table 3. Guatemala itself was of course to be subject to a very "crude and tactless" example of this in 1954. See Stephen Schlesinger and Stephen Kinzer, *Bitter Fruit: The Untold Story of the American Coup in Guatemala* (Garden City, N.Y., 1983).

21. The real problem, however, is whether the mere existence of "great power" embodied in a state does not automatically conduce to an imperial policy. If so, the tortured attempts to seem noninterventionist when in fact inherently interventionist may profitably be discarded, and one may discuss instead under what forms intervention should take place.

22. PPS 4, July 23, 1947, *PPSP*, I, 67.

23. *Russia, the Atom, and the West*, p. 74.

24. See his exchange with Bohlen, who was much more sensitive to the politics of change: PPS minutes, Jan. 24, 1950, *FRUS*, 1950, III, 617–618. See also PPS 30, June 4, 1948, *PPSP*, II, 246–254; Address, Oct. 14, 1949, GFKP, Box 17.

25. PPS 23, Feb. 24, 1948, *PPSP*, II, 105–106. See also PPS minutes, June 3, 1949, PPS Files, Box 27: here Kennan was considering whether common colonialism would give German youth some idealistic outlet together with the rest of Europe. Curious as this idea may now seem, it was in a way nothing other than an example of midwestern progressivism circa 1912.

26. Minutes of Combined Meeting, Sept. 13, 1949, *FRUS*, 1949, I, 520.

27. John Saville, "Ernest Bevin and the Cold War, 1945–1951," *Socialist Register* (London, 1984). Bevin suggested in 1938 that there should be a pooling of colonies, which then would be attached to a European commonwealth. A. de Micheli of the Italian employers' association Confindustria proposed somewhat similarly after the war to send surplus Italians to Africa with American capital. See van der Pijl, *Making of NATO*, p. 165.

28. Address, Oct. 14, 1949, GFKP, Box 17; Press talk, Jan. 28, 1947, GFKP, Box 16; Address, Oct. 14, 1949, GFKP, Box 17; PPS 30, June 4, 1948, *PPSP*, II, 246–254. On French Indochina, see also GFK to Secretary, Aug. 21, 1950, *FRUS*, 1950, VII, 623. He considered the French situation "hopeless" and warned

against what he prophetically saw as a tendency for the United States to become the guarantor of French interests which could not in fact be guaranteed. In regard to the Italian colonies, he had been in favor of restoring them after the war. "Lend-Lease Aid to Russia," summer 1945, GFKP, Box 25.

29. A classic example of this dallying was PPS 25, March 22, 1948, *PPSP*, II, 142–149, another of the efforts produced during Kennan's absence in Japan. Written by Henry Villard and concerning the subject of French North Africa, it took the position that the United States should support French responsibility in the area and avoid disruption of their empire while at the same time persuading them that there ought to be "gradual evolution of dependent peoples toward self-government in accordance with their training and capacity to manage their own affairs" (p. 147).

30. Press talk, Jan. 28, 1947, GFKP, Box 16.

31. PPS 23, Feb. 24, 1948, *PPSP*, II, 126.

32. Introduction to PPS meeting, June 5, 1949, GFKP, Box 27.

33. This theme—the United States is not a finished civilization and ought to do less—became prominent in 1949 when Kennan was also increasingly alienated from the course of official policy. See e.g. Address outline, Feb. 16, 1949, GFKP, Box 17. On anticolonialism, see Address, Oct. 14, 1949, GFKP, Box 17. I infer that he attributed the cause of the newfound American dominance to the war.

34. The notion of a British-American-Canadian bloc went back at least to PPS 4 (July 23, 1947, *PPSP*, I, 55) and came to the forefront in his last-ditch attempts during 1949 to create a more variegated Western system based on a continental and a maritime center. It caused a sharp conflict with Bohlen, by then stationed in Paris and, like the French at that time, firmly in favor of British attachment to the Continent. See the exchange of letters Oct. 6, 12, 29, Nov. 7, 17, 1949, GFKP, Box 28, and the verbal debate, PPS minutes, Jan. 24, 1950, *FRUS*, 1950, III, 617–618. See also his memorandum for Acheson and Webb, Aug. 22, 1949, Bland Files, and *Memoirs*, I, 452–462 and passim. Not only did he consider Britain's connection with the United States inherently more natural; he also thought a continental union without Britain the best way to absorb Germany, a view that was probably correct but by then irrelevant. Eventually, of course, he would find a kindred spirit in General de Gaulle.

35. Memorandum for Secretary, Jan. 22, 1952, GFKP, Box 24. The *Times* of London took a more relaxed view of the incident, if we can judge from the rather limited news space (e.g. Jan. 11, 1952) devoted to it. But six months later diplomatic relations between the two countries had been severed.

36. Memorandum for Secretary, Jan. 22, 1952, GFKP, Box 24.

37. Ibid.

38. NEA [Near Eastern Affairs], Feb. 22, 1952, "Some Comments on the Kennan Enclosure," Bland Files. Ironically, Britain and (especially) France *favored* African nationalism in the form of states based on the colonial boundaries of administration—which mostly had nothing to do with popular homogeneity—over various indigenous attempts at *regional* pan-African association. Basil Davidson to the author in conversation, Los Angeles, Dec. 1987.

39. GFK to Bohlen, April 3, 1952, Bland Files.

40. Kermit Roosevelt, *Countercoup: The Struggle for Control of Iran* (New York, 1979), is a lively account of the CIA operation in Iran by the person who engineered it.

41. Address, Aug. 6, 1953, GFKP, Box 24.

42. "Comments on Ideology and Reality in the Soviet System," in *Proceedings of the American Philosophical Society*, Jan. 21, 1955.

43. Address, Oct. 17, 1956, GFKP, Box 19. He had a good point here about the Civil War, for why should the southern states not have been allowed to secede if they had entered the covenant on the basis of state sovereignty?

44. In the very same speech in which he castigated the "fanatical and childish passion of native nationalism" in Asia, he lauded the toughness of the rebellious Tito and speculated further that the Chinese would go the same way. See also Minutes of the Under-Secretary's meetings, Aug. 31, 1949, RG 59, NA, where he argued for encouraging Eastern European nationalism. To call Tito's assertion of independent power an expression of nationalism is perhaps, as Kennan has pointed out (letter to the author, Nov. 15, 1985), incorrect, since Yugoslavia is a multiethnic state and Tito himself was not of a single nationality. With that qualification, however, I still think the establishment of a Yugoslav *state* identity in opposition to both East and West must be seen in terms of the admittedly indistinct concept of nationalism.

45. Address, Oct. 17, 1956, GFKP, Box 19.

46. This is a note attached in Dec. 1973 to Address, GFKP, Box 19.

47. See Melvyn P. Leffler, "From the Truman Doctrine to the Carter Doctrine: Lessons and Dilemmas of the Cold War," *Diplomatic History*, 7 (Fall 1983).

48. For a representative statement on the Vietnam War, see Testimony, U.S. Congress, Senate Committee on Foreign Relations, *Supplemental Foreign Assistance Fiscal Year 1966—Vietnam*, Hearings, 89th Cong., 2d sess. (Jan.–Feb. 1966), Feb. 10, 1966.

49. GFK to Hamilton Fish Armstrong, July 25, 1970, Armstrong Papers, Box 34, Mudd Library, Princeton University, Princeton, N.J. The hostility to names, as distinct from the reality they are meant to express, comes from Gibbon. See Address, n.d., Lippmann Papers, Box 81, File 1202, Yale University Library, New Haven, Conn. His clearest historicist statements on colonialism were otherwise made in the late 1950s: "The erection of the edifice of modern colonialism was not a moral act or a series of moral acts, but the response to obvious historical conditions and necessities." "World Problems in a Christian Perspective," in *American History: Recent Interpretations*, vol. 2, ed. Abraham S. Eisenstadt (New York, 1962), p. 468. See also the Reith Lectures: "The establishment of the colonial relationship did not represent a moral action on somebody's part; it represented a natural and inevitable response to certain demands and stimuli of the age. It was simply a stage of history." *Russia, the Atom, and the West*, p. 74. In this respect he was actually at one with Marx and Engels.

50. "Hazardous Courses in Southern Africa," *Foreign Affairs*, 49 (Jan. 1971); GFK to Hamilton Fish Armstrong, July 25, 1970, Armstrong Papers, Box 34, Mudd Library, Princeton University, Princeton, N.J.

51. GFK et al., *South Africa: Three Visitors' Reports* (Pasadena, 1971), p. 7.

52. "Hazardous Courses," p. 220.
53. *South Africa*, p. 6.
54. *Chicago Tribune*, May 9, 1976. See also *New York Times*, May 2, 1976.
55. *Chicago Tribune*, May 9, 1976.

6. The Importance of Being Realistic

1. Diary note, Aug. 4, 1944, *Memoirs*, I, 218–219; PPS 23, Feb. 24, 1948, *PPSP*, II, 124–125. As he wrote in 1938, "Perfection does not exist in nature." "The Prerequisites," 1938, GFKP, Box 25. To work for perfection on the assumption that it could be accomplished was thus fundamentally unnatural.

2. *Russia and the West*, p. 372: "Power, like sex, may be concealed and outwardly ignored, and in our society it often is; but neither in the one case nor the other does this concealment save us from the destruction of our innocence or from the confrontation with the dilemmas these necessities imply."

3. He does speak of American "expansionism" in a handwritten note I found in the Ford Foundation Archives. Memorandum to unknown, Dec. 1950, Ford Foundation Archives, New York, GEN 51: A. Weinberg.

4. Address, Dec. 21, 1948, GFKP, Box 17.

5. This account is a synthesis of a great number of texts and is therefore suspiciously coherent. If taken with a grain of salt, it may nevertheless serve as a decent beginning (and partial summary). The basic documents used are PPS 23, Feb. 24, 1948, *PPSP*, II, 103–134; Address, June 4, 1948, GFKP, Box 17; Address, Dec. 21, 1948, GFKP, Box 17; Oral comments to Acheson, Jan. 3, 1949, Bland Files; Address, Feb. 14, 1949, GFKP, Box 17; Address, Aug. 30, 1949, GFKP, Box 17; Address, Dec. 21, 1949, GFKP, Box 17; Diary notes on alliances, Sept. 30, 1950, GFKP, Box 26; and above all *American Diplomacy, 1900–1950* (Chicago, 1951).

6. Address, Dec. 21, 1949, GFKP, Box 17.

7. Address, Aug. 30, 1948, GFKP, Box 17.

8. *American Diplomacy*, p. 59.

9. "Foreign Policy and the Professional Diplomat," *The Wilson Quarterly*, 1 (Winter 1977).

10. Address, Dec. 21, 1948, GFKP, Box 17.

11. "History and Diplomacy as Viewed by a Diplomatist," *The Review of Politics*, 18 (April 1956), pp. 171–172.

12. Ibid, p. 175.

13. Memorandum, May 5, 1942, GFKP, Box 23.

14. "Education for Statesmanship," *Foreign Service Journal*, 30 (May 1953). Since this was from a speech to Princeton alumni the reference to the honor code should be judged accordingly.

15. GFK to Russell, Oct. 11, 1950, GFKP, Box 28.

16. Ibid.

17. I have primarily Wilhelm Dilthey in mind. Understanding in his sense involves a fundamental "identification" on the part of the understanding subject with the world of the object to be understood. *Verstehen* is wholly different from the knowledge produced by the natural sciences; it is a reconstruction of embodied

meanings through "imaginative projection." See Stuart Hall, "On Historical Traces of Ideology," *Cultural Studies*, no. 9 (n.d.).

18. Address, May 11, 1965, GFKP, Box 21.

19. This is an extrapolation, since the question was not posed to Kennan in these terms; but see Address, Dec. 21, 1948, GFKP, Box 17, for a statement that comes close to my distillation. He assumed the existence of a "real interrelationship of forces" behind the conduct of foreign policy (Address, May 9, 1947, GFKP, Box 17) and believed that in the best of all worlds foreign policy would be run by diplomats or at any rate a caste of master strategists; thus it seems reasonable to induce that these people would concern themselves with adjustments in this balance or "interrelationship of forces."

20. Balance of power was a concept of diplomacy rooted in the nineteenth century, though it had actually been theorized as early as the 1730s by Jean Rousset. On that, and on Burke and Gibbon, see F. H. Hinsley's excellent *Power and the Pursuit of Peace* (Cambridge, 1963), pp. 160–164.

21. Kennan had been much taken with the British concept of European power balances during his time in Lisbon and the renewal of the Anglo-Portuguese alliance. I think his interest in land versus sea power stems from this period too; see GFK to Secstate, Oct. 5, 1943, DSF 841.34553B/4.

22. "Some Fundamentals of Russian-American Relations," 1938, GFKP, Box 16; and, for example, "Russia's International Position," winter 1945, *Memoirs*, I, 544.

23. C. Dewitt Poole, "The Balance of Power," *Life*, Sept. 22, 1947. Poole blamed the USSR for the incipient cold war on the grounds that it opposed the balance of power, not an enlightening accusation.

24. See n. 21. His clearest account of the traditional British view is otherwise to be found in *American Diplomacy*, pp. 10–11. Harold Nicolson, in his amusing *Curzon*, enumerates (p. 49) the three traditional British principles of foreign policy as (a) command of the seas, (b) maintaining the balance of power in Europe, and (c) defense of the imperial frontiers and communications, all of which was to be achieved without war and at minimum cost in manpower and money. Curzon, by the way, was an expert at the art of diplomacy as Kennan was to conceive of it.

25. PPS 23, Feb. 24, 1948, *PPSP*, II, 124–125; GFK to Jessup and Rusk, Sept. 8, 1949, PPS Files, Box 13; Address, Dec. 21, 1948, GFKP, Box 17. His remarks to Jessup and Rusk on the probable return of Japan as the power of natural dominance in Manchuria were soon thoroughly disproved.

26. Address, Dec. 18, 1952, GFKP, Box 18. See also GFK to Jessup and Rusk, Sept. 8, 1949, PPS Files, Box 13. The West was in fact implementing a somewhat similar balancing act: in both the Philippines and Malaya the occupation powers reinstalled the prewar administrations that had been collaborating with the Japanese. See John W. Barton, *International Relations: A General Theory* (Cambridge, 1965), p. 177.

27. Address, Feb. 20, 1947, GFKP, Box 17.

28. GFK to Jessup, April 9, 1953, Bland Files. A similar view is expressed in GFK to Toynbee, April 17, 1952, GFKP, Box 29.

29. Interview, *Foreign Policy*, 7 (summer 1972).

30. By 1815 the balance of power had come to have two related meanings:

the earlier notion of resistance against any one power of hegemony and the later idea of a system of basically equal but acquisitive states tied together by common expediency. Hinsley, *Power and the Pursuit of Peace*, p. 195. On various versions of the concept, see also Inis L. Claude, Jr., *Power and International Relations* (New York, 1962), pp. 13–20. The distinction here is between an equilibrium and a nonequilibrium model. Morgenthau, Claude points out, uses the concept in at least four different ways (pp. 25–37).

31. It is, however, a stylized version of the nineteenth-century system, which was complex. See Stanley Hoffmann's admirable introduction to his *Contemporary Theory*, in which he also poses the problem of mechanical metaphors. See further Barton, *International Relations*, pp. 57–58, 147; and Claude, *Power*, pp. 91–92.

32. Address, Dec. 18, 1952, GFKP, Box 18.

33. See Claude, *Power*, pp. 56, 66. An example of the use of the vacuum metaphor is in Robert W. Tucker, "America in Decline: The Foreign Policy of 'Maturity,'" *Foreign Affairs*, 58 (July 1980), which argues that the (putatively) emerging power vacuum in the Persian Gulf must *necessarily* be filled sooner or later by one of the two superpowers.

34. See Anthony Wilden, *System and Structure* (London, 1972), pp. 313, 332, for a cybernetic argument of this kind. Models of equilibrium systems tend to view any disturbances as external to the system; if one nation persistently tries to change the given, the whole theory becomes fairly pointless. A disturbance (or, in cybernetic terms, noise) should be seen as a necessary tension of the system, not as an intrusion, for the system is not a Newtonian harmony of objects and forces (pp. 402–403).

35. On the Soviet concept, see Stephanson, "On Soviet Foreign Policy."

36. He complains in *Memoirs*, I, 308–309, of the dearth of American writing on foreign policy and war (as opposed to foreign policy and peace), a lack that greatly hampered him when he began lecturing at the National War College in 1946. He mentions *Makers of Modern Strategy*, a collection of essays edited by E. M. Earle (Princeton, 1943) as the only real guide readily available. Earle's book discussed, rather superficially, all the "greats" in the field (e.g. Machiavelli and Clausewitz). The complaint was no doubt legitimate, but Clausewitz was available in English, and besides, Kennan was a talented polyglot by no means confined to reading what had been published in the United States. Yet there is no sign that he really studied Clausewitz. As far as national interest is concerned, he seems not to have read Friedrich Meinecke's classic *Der Idee der Staatsräson*, published in English as *Machiavellianism* (New York, 1965)—a peculiar translation of the title—of whose existence he must have been aware since he had read Charles Beard's American gloss on it, *The Idea of National Interest* (New York, 1934). See Note on Beard, Annex 4, GFKP, Box 26. The only reason I can imagine for this neglect is that he liked to think things out for himself, and when he studied others he studied literature or history,˙not philosophical writings. Still, Meinecke's great work was a conceptual history.

37. Minutes of the External Relations Project, Sept. 24, 1951, GFKP, Box 26, File 1-E-2, Annex 2; hereafter cited as Project.

38. This historical sketch, drastically simplified, is based mainly on Meinecke, *Machiavellianism*, and Albert O. Hirschman, *The Passions and the Interests* (Princeton, 1977), which despite, or because of, its impressionistic methodology

is a very suggestive book. For Bolingbroke, see his "Remarks on the History of England," in *The Works of Lord Bolingbroke* (1844; reprint, New York, 1967), I, 292–456. Referring to the Houses of Lancaster and York, for example, he states (p. 330): "The national interest was sunk, to the shame of the nation, in the particular interest of two families." In the 1980s the concept of national interest in the United States has taken on a flavor of hard-line assertiveness by becoming the name of a journal that expresses neoconservative views on foreign policy.

39. For a recent critique of realism from this viewpoint (or something fairly close to it), see Charles R. Beitz, *Political Theory and International Relations* (Princeton, 1979), esp. pp. 42–46. He stresses that the interdependent aspect sharply limits the analytical value of the concept.

40. Raymond Aron, in his massive *Peace and War* (New York, 1966), p. 599, points to the crusading anti-idealist aspect of Morgenthau's argument.

41. For this debate, initiated by his blistering attack on all kinds of idealism, see Morgenthau's contribution (originally from 1945) to Hoffmann's *Contemporary Theory*; his article "The Mainsprings of American Foreign Policy: The National Interest vs. Moral Abstractions," *American Political Science Review*, 44 (Dec. 1950); and "Another 'Great Debate': The National Interest of the United States," ibid., 46 (Dec. 1952); Robert W. Tucker, "Professor Morgenthau's Theory of Political 'Realism,'" ibid., 46 (March 1952); Arthur M. Schlesinger, Jr., "Policy and National Interest," *Partisan Review*, 19 (Nov.–Dec. 1951). Tucker's response was especially sharp. For later comments, see Aron, *Peace and War*, pp. 91–93; Barton, *International Relations*, pp. 17–18, 33.

42. "I can conceive of this study, as indeed of the formulation of foreign policy generally, only in terms of national interest. That must be the point of departure." Handwritten note, Project, n.d., [1950?]. Materials emanating from the project—which receives minimal attention in *Memoirs*, II, 9—can be found in GFKP, Box 26. He began to think about the project in September 1950 and continued to work with it in various forms until he became ambassador in the spring of 1952. A good deal consists of undated, handwritten notes, some of which I think were actually written in the autumn of 1950, though the project only got under way more systematically a year later. Most of the ensuing discussion of national interest is based on these materials. The idea of exploring the underlying assumptions of foreign policy had been brewing for some time: "The fact of the matter is that this operation cannot be unified and given real purpose or direction unless a firm theoretical groundwork has been laid to back up whatever policy is pursued." Diary note, Nov. 22, 1949, *Memoirs*, I, 468.

43. This is from a part of project called "Notes for Essays," written and typed in spring 1952. The remark about the United Nations is on p. 44.

44. Morgenthau's German roots may have been of significance too.

45. The concept of national interest is inadequate, as Jonathan Knight has pointed out, since "it purports to explain everything and therefore explains very little." Yet, his ensuing assertion ("Kennan maintains that American diplomacy can be analyzed basically in terms of the single decision-maker, namely, the statesman; he also maintains that there is an identifiable and objective national interest and a single criterion by which foreign policy can be judged") seems to me quite wrong. My reasons will become clear. J. Knight, "George Frost Kennan and the Study of American Foreign Policy: Some Critical Comments," *The West-*

ern Political Quarterly, 1 (March 1967). Aron makes a somewhat similar argument about national interest in *Peace and War*, p. 93, though his own enormous theorization of international relations as a "praxology" is more impressive as a sometimes brilliant critique than as a novelty.

46. Project notes, n.d., [1950?]. The following account is mainly based on this note and "Notes for Essays," p. 1, spring 1952.

47. "Notes for Essays," spring 1952, p. 37.

48. Ibid., p. 42.

49. Project notes, n.d., [1950?].

50. *American Diplomacy*, p. 5.

51. Such as, notoriously, Lenin's. Lenin was known for his indomitable capacity to subordinate everything to a single objective. The position of interest in the marxist canon has yet to be properly assessed, but it is obviously of great importance. If one lays bare what is considered a "true interest" of a specific social group and then finds a discrepancy between it and the ideological attitudes of that group, it is easy to go on and call the latter false while appointing oneself the supreme arbiter of the real interest. See Göran Therborn, *The Ideology of Power and the Power of Ideology* (London, 1980), pp. 4–5. This is perhaps the place to explain the absence of references to Jürgen Habermas and his epigones. Few contemporary thinkers have made more of interests than Habermas, whose philosophical system is in fact built on the derivation of "true interests" in a situation of value-free communication. Habermas's reasoning fails to excite me: I can fathom neither his generally Kantian assumptions nor the specific postulation of value-free communication. A good exposition of Habermas's standpoint can be found in Raymond Geuss, *The Idea of a Critical Theory* (Cambridge, Mass., 1981).

52. "Notes for Essays," spring 1952, p. 46.

53. *Realities of American Foreign Policy* (Princeton, 1954), p. 43.

54. Unused outline, 1954–55, GFKP, Box 26.

55. See Louis Althusser's essay on Rousseau in *Politics and History* (London, 1977), chap. 5. It may be added that for Rousseau the General Will is not equal to the will of all: while the former, being derived from the original social contract and the accumulated wisdom of historical society, is by definition always right, the latter is not inherently so. See A. J. Polan, *Lenin and the End of Politics* (London, 1984), p. 72.

56. "Notes for Essays," spring 1952, p. 132.

57. Project notes, n.d., [1950?].

58. *American Diplomacy*, p. 64.

59. These quotes are from Project notes, n.d., [1950?]. See also "Notes for Essays," pt. 1.

60. Project notes, n.d., [1950?].

61. "Notes for Essays," spring 1952, pp. 7–8; Project notes, n.d., [1950?].

62. "Notes for Essays," spring 1952, p. 25.

63. Address, May 29, 1953, GFKP, Box 18.

64. "Notes for Essays," spring 1952, p. 30.

65. Unused outline, 1954–55, GFKP, Box 26.

66. This tendency had become increasingly prominent by 1949. See e.g. Address, Feb. 16, 1949, GFKP, Box 17.

67. "Lectures on Foreign Policy," *The Illinois Law Review*, 45 (Jan.–Feb.

1951). It is the second of these, "The National Interest of the United States," that is under discussion here.

68. "Notes for Essays," spring 1952, pp. 12ff., 32ff. He does not take a position on what is expendable, but his general view was of course that the United States was trying to do too much.

69. Address, April 17, 1950, GFKP, Box 18.

70. See e.g. this Project note, n.d.: "With regard to nationalism: can one not say that all forms of identification that acquire emotional power are invidious in proportion to the crudeness and absurdness of the criterion or symbol? This modern popular-nationalism, based on language, would be exceeded in artificiality and viciousness by race-feeling, based on color. Is Gibbon not perhaps right that compared with such dangerous and irrelevant distinctions 'the superiority of birth' is both 'the plainest and the least invidious'?" And: "Modern nationalism was probably the result of the extension of education to classes lacking inherited property & status." "Further Talk with Bob B.," 1951–52, Project. See also my discussion of Third World nationalism.

71. "History and Diplomacy as Viewed by a Diplomatist," *The Review of Politics*, 18 (April 1956). At the same time he recognized that the diplomat, for better or worse, is the servant of this national state.

72. Quoted in Hans Georg Gadamer, *Truth and Method* (New York, 1975), p. 182.

73. See Kennan's collection *The Nuclear Delusion* (New York, 1982).

74. See "Lectures on Foreign Policy," *The Illinois Law Review*, 45 (Jan.–Feb. 1951). All quotations are from this article.

75. The concept is used in his monumental and continuous historical investigation of the causes of the First World War. One central problem he poses is whether the Franco-Russian alliance was really based on "well-considered and compelling national interest" or on simple "self-interest, prejudice, and intrigue." *The Decline of Bismarck's European Order* (Princeton, 1979), p. 10. See also *Russia and the West*, p. 367.

76. "Notes for Essays," 1951–52, p. 132.

77. Ibid.

78. Address, Aug. 30, 1949, GFKP, Box 17.

79. I am influenced here by Michel de Certau's exceptionally interesting essay "On the Oppositional Practices of Everyday Life," *Social Text*, 3 (Fall 1980). De Certau's concept is in turn derived from Dietrich von Bülow, the Prussian general and military theorist of the Napoleonic era. Von Bülow saw strategy as movement outside the vision of the enemy and tactics as movement within it. Raymond Aron, in his work on Clausewitz, criticizes von Bülow's concept on the same grounds that his subject did, namely that war cannot be reduced to a question of movement: the range of vision is altogether too concrete a starting point for a definition. Aron, *Clausewitz*, pp. 43–44. This may well be. Clausewitz's method is far more dialectical, as Aron rightly points out. That said, de Certau's appropriation of von Bülow remains intriguing and useful.

80. In PPS 15, Nov. 13, 1947, *PPSP*, I, 141, Kennan still thought this would be achieved. Instead policy conflicts ensued, from which resulted his negative strategic concept.

81. Introduction to meeting, June 5–6, 1949, PPS Files, Box 27: "Now

one thing that stands out in any consideration of objectives of U.S. foreign policy is that these cannot exist in the finite sense of goals susceptible of achievement at any given time or distance; they can exist only in terms of direction. We have not to decide really what we are going to achieve in foreign affairs. We have to decide what we are going to work toward." Contrast NSC 68: "The assault on free institutions is world-wide now, and in the context of the present polarization of power a defeat of free institutions anywhere is a defeat everywhere." NSC 68, April 14, 1950, in Etzold and Gaddis, *Containment*, p. 389.

82. "America's Administrative Response to Its World Problems," in *The American Style: Essays in Value and Performance*, ed. E. E. Morison (New York, 1958), p. 139.

83. Marcel Detienne and Jean-Pierre Vernant, *Cunning Intelligence in Greek Culture and Society* (Atlantic Highlands, N.J., 1978), pp. 3–4. This is a most stimulating work. See also de Certau, "On the Oppositional Practices."

84. Detienne and Vernant, *Cunning Intelligence*, pp. 312–318. See also Hans Georg Gadamer, "Planning for the Future," in *Conditions of the World Order*, ed. Stanley Hoffman (New York, 1970).

85. De Certau, "On the Oppositional Practices."

86. On the enormous and complex subject of Kant's aesthetics, see e.g. Lucien Goldmann, *Immanuel Kant* (London, 1971), pp. 182–185. Kant distinguishes an art from a science by referring to the analogy of geometry and surveying, and art from handicraft, less convincingly, by pointing out that the latter requires labor and drudgery. Immanuel Kant, *The Critique of Judgement*, trans. J. C. Meredith (1928; reprint, Oxford, 1980), p. 163. The reference to the acrobat is on p. 163 (par. 43) and n. See also de Certau, "On the Oppositional Practices."

87. See Gadamer, *Truth and Method*, pp. 33–39, on the subjectivization of taste. Kennan's organicism will be explored in Part III.

88. Ibid., pp. 16–17. On the element of distance in aesthetics, see also Pierre Bourdieu, *Distinction: A Social Critique of the Judgment of Taste* (Cambridge, Mass., 1984), p. 5.

89. *From Prague*, p. 85. More about style in Part III.

90. "Diplomacy as a Profession," *Foreign Service Journal*, 38 (May 1961), 23.

91. Diary note, Aug. 4, 1944, *Memoirs*, I, 219.

92. "Lectures on Foreign Policy," *Illinois Law Review* (Jan.–Feb. 1951), 738. Italics added.

93. "Observations," in Graebner, *Ideas and Diplomacy*, p. 825.

94. "Lectures on Foreign Policy," p. 731.

95. This analysis is based on Alexander Atkinson, *Social Order and the General Theory of Strategy* (London, 1981). As evidenced by the dictum "Political power grows out of the barrel of a gun," Mao was of course at the same time also convinced that power is sanctioned by violence. Judging from his famous lectures "On Protracted War" from 1938, Mao had read Clausewitz; it is interesting that the footnotes, probably added later by the editors, credit Lenin with the most obvious Clausewitzian quote (on war and politics). See Mao Zedong, *Selected Works* (Beijing, 1967), II, 152–153, 192, n. 19.

96. Mao Zedong, quoted in Atkinson, *Social Order*, p. 56.

97. Address, May 16, 1949, GFKP, Box 17.

98. On commerce and peace, see Aron, *Peace and War*, p. 253; and Hirschman, *The Passions*, pp. 60–61. Kennan made the distinction between sea and land power several times, beginning in a way with his wartime analyses of the Anglo-Portuguese alliance and then implicitly throughout his approaches to the Soviet Union and Germany; but he became very explicit about it in Address, Feb. 10, 1950, GFKP, Box 18. On the Junkers, see p. 313n21.

99. This goes back to Montesquieu. As Hirschman, *The Passions*, p. 60, quotes him: "It is almost a general rule that wherever the ways of man are gentle there is commerce; and whenever there is commerce, there the ways of men are gentle."

100. In the aforementioned note on American expansionism (see n. 3) Kennan elaborates on which areas of expansion "lasted" within the Union and which did not. He remarks: "Hawaii lasted—but perhaps only because the native population died out progressively, like the Indians of the west—the victims of an innocent and unintentional sort of genocide." Memorandum to unknown, Dec. 1950, Ford Foundation Archives, New York, GEN 51: A. Weinberg. Genocide it certainly was, though scarcely innocent or unintentional.

101. See Otto Hintze's lecture "Military Organization and the Organization of the State," in *The Historical Essays of Otto Hintze*, ed. F. Gilbert (New York, 1975); and Anderson, *Lineages*, pp. 134–135.

102. David Calleo, "Early American Views," in Freedman, *The Troubled Alliance*.

103. Miscamble, "Kennan," p. 186. Nitze's ensuing career from NSC 68 to the Committee on the Present Danger to his perhaps final destination as the key figure in Ronald Reagan's arms control agreements with Moscow is an ironic story, to say the least. On his early career, see Sanders, *Peddlers*.

104. *Memoirs*, I, 458–462.

105. This was one part of the Project plan.

106. See *American Diplomacy*, p. 65.

107. On his lack of bureaucratic acumen, see Bland, *Policy Planner*, p. 244.

108. This implies, in other words, a notion of something complete and immediate, readily available for inspection. Kennan is in good company, for the theoretical conflict between Being and Becoming can be traced back to classical Greek philosophy. In his early career he tended to stress historical eternities, whereas the struggle against legalistic formalism, in all probability, was what led him later on to emphasize process and change—in a way nonidentity.

109. Aron, among many others, has pointed to the reality of the inherently ideological nature of foreign policy in this epoch. See "The Quest," in Hoffmann, *Contemporary Theory*. Words and statements are not always free-floating, nonmaterial vapors but part of institutionally embodied structures.

110. See Wayne Hudson, *The Marxist Philosophy of Ernst Bloch* (New York, 1982), pp. 51–54. The anticipatory utopian impulse is in every respect real. On politics and calculation, see also Regis Debray, *Critique of Political Reason* (London, 1983), pp. 163–166.

111. "All utterances of the government of a great state, including collective statements of resolutions with which it may associate itself, are commitments. The fewer such commitments, the better." GFK to Acheson, Nov. 14, 1949, GFKP, Box 24.

Introduction to Part III

1. See Karl Mannheim, *Essays on Sociology and Social Psychology*, ed. P. Kecskemeti (New York, 1953), pp. 116–119, for a characterization of the position based on natural law. The epithet is taken from Henry Steele Commager, *The Empire of Reason* (New York, 1977), where he argues, somewhat exaggeratedly, that the United States was the fulfillment of the European Enlightenment.

2. Edmund Burke, *Reflections on the Revolution in France* (New York, 1983). While condemning the Gallic upheaval in the most venomous terms, Burke had found the American predecessor neither incomprehensible nor unnatural; but then again the French Revolution was both bloodier and, in its European effects, more radical. His view was ultimately not incoherent. Just as he considered the revolution of 1688 a restoration of ancient, time-honored rights, so he argued that the colonials were making a bid to have their proper English privileges respected. Thus he was also late in comprehending the revolutionary character of the developments. See Elliot R. Barkan's introduction to Edmund Burke, *On the American Revolution*, ed. E. R. Barkan (New York, 1966). The French upheaval, by contrast, was for Burke a rash gesture *against* every established product of organic growth, truly radical in the sense of uprooting (deracinating) the social tree—"tree" being a metaphor for the well-settled, naturally growing society of continuity that he had used twenty years before the French events. See Isaac Kramnick, *The Rage of Edmund Burke* (New York, 1977), p. 4. Otherwise Burke, Anglo-Irish upstart and a notoriously complex figure, combined an attachment to the free-market economy with laments over the loss of precapitalist values: "But the age of chivalry is gone.—That of sophisters, oeconomists, and calculators, has succeeded; and the glory of Europe is extinguished for ever. Never, never more, shall we behold that generous loyalty to rank and sex, that proud submission, that dignified obedience, that subordination of the heart, which kept alive, even in servitude itself, the spirit of an exalted freedom." *Reflections*, p. 170. He scorned, accordingly, "this new conquering empire of light and reason" (p. 171). See too Mannheim, *Essays*, pp. 134–138.

3. Mannheim, *Essays*, pp. 117–118, 170.

4. Address, NATO, Paris, Dec. 12, 1951, GFKP, Box 18. The argument was part of his disdain for universalist assumptions in American foreign policy (e.g. the UN and spreading U.S. democracy).

5. What unified Burke's argument from the 1750s to the 1790s was in fact his absolute dislike for abstract reason. Kramnick, *The Rage*, p. 21. For T. S. Eliot the elite was setting an example not by argument but through "the nervous system," as Terry Eagleton has pointed out in *Criticism and Ideology* (London, 1976), p. 147. See also Eliot's essay "The Class and the Elite," in his *Notes towards the Definition of Culture* (New York, 1949). On conservative antiabstraction generally, see Clinton Rossiter, *Conservatism in America*, rev. 2d ed. (New York, 1962), p. 46.

6. Friedrich Schiller, *Essays, Aesthetical and Philosophical* (London, 1884), pp. 27, 35.

7. Ferdinand Tönnies, *Community and Society* (1887; reprint New York, 1963), esp. pp. 35–44, 64–67; MacIntyre, *After Virtue*, p. 82; and Max Weber, *The Protestant Ethic and the Spirit of Capitalism* (New York, 1958), chap. 2.

8. See Mannheim, *Essays*, p. 88. The most important stratum of this kind, the southern plantation owners, were integrated into the world market and then eventually extinguished through the Civil War as a traditional slaveholding class.

9. Quoted in Myron Q. Hale, "American Conservatism: Conventionalism, Historicism, Functionalism" (Ph.D. diss., Columbia University, 1958), p. 152 n. 188. The idea of a military type of school for proper inculcation of values would, as we have witnessed, also suggest itself to Kennan, who had been educated at one.

10. Alexis de Tocqueville, *Democracy in America*, 2 vols. (New York, 1945), I, 275.

11. Ibid., II, 239.

12. I am referring here to the proto Jacksonian individualism characteristic of the American right today, as epitomized by Ronald Reagan. It is a very great distance between Reagan and, say, John Adams, or for that matter John C. Calhoun. Organicist conservatives such as Peter Viereck (who supported the New Deal) are difficult to find. Viereck's essay "The Philosophical 'New Conservatism,'" in Daniel Bell, *The Radical Right*, rev. ed. (New York, 1964), is worth reading against the backdrop of the 1980s.

13. Address, Oxford, May 13, 1958, GFKP, Box 19; *Memoirs*, I, 77.

14. See Dominick Lacapra's stimulating remarks in "Rethinking Intellectual History and Reading Texts," *History and Theory*, 19 (1980); and Kramnick, *The Rage*, for a (perhaps too psychological) treatment of Burke's ambivalences.

7. No Exit

1. "A Conversation with George F. Kennan," interview by George Urban, *Encounter*, 47 (1976), 43. This is the most revealing and important interview Kennan has ever given. It is reproduced with a series of comments and interventions by others in GFK et al., *Encounters with Kennan* (London, 1979).

2. GFK to his children, April 15, 1961, GFKP, Box 20.

3. This biographical sketch is based on ibid.; *Memoirs*, I, 6–8; GFK to his children, Feb. 1942, GFKP, Box 28. The aristocratic element was primarily represented by White Russian émigrés, with whom, for example, he lived in Berlin around 1930. Later he was to become very friendly with certain Prussian aristocrats such as Helmuth von Moltke (though he was relatively liberal).

4. Kennan had read Spengler's *Untergang des Abendlandes* in the 1920s. *Memoirs*, I, 19. On the "pathology of cultural criticism" in the interbellum years, see Fritz Stern, *The Politics of Despair* (New York, 1965); the quotation is from p. 1. The full extent of Kennan's alienation will become evident shortly. A diplomatic contemporary has remarked that Kennan expressed a wish at the time to be "de-Americanized." C. Ben Wright, off-the-record interview, Oct. 3, 1970, Bland Files.

5. GFK, enclosure to 808, DSF 853.00/1064, Feb. 4, 1943; "Fair Day, Adieu," pt. 2, chap. 1.

6. Address (unused), Feb. 10, 1953, B. Nelson Papers, Butler Library, Columbia University, New York. The father–son reference originated in personal experience: Kossuth Kennan was fifty-two when his son was born and had little

to say to him. See "A Conversation with Kennan," interview by Melvin J. Lasky, *Encounter*, 14 (1960).

7. "The Prerequisites," 1938, unused ms., GFKP, Box 26. Unless otherwise noted, all quotations are from this partly handwritten manuscript.

8. "Fair Day, Adieu," pt. 2, chap. 1, pp. 1, 18–19.

9. Projected disintegration along the lines of the quoted passage was an image curiously reminiscent of the Comintern position of the early 1930s, of which the Weimar Republic seemed to offer both example and proof: incipient fascism was assumed to be the sign of a tottering system, and the question was thus merely which group would take over.

10. Kennan considered Plato's *Republic* a favorite. Brooks Atkinson, "America's Global Planner," *New York Times Magazine*, July 13, 1947. The parallels between the proposals seem too close to be merely coincidental.

11. See "Fair Day, Adieu," pt. 1, and the introduction to Chapter 2 of this book.

12. "Progressive" reform has been copiously debated, going back, at least, to Richard Hofstadter's classic *Age of Reform* (New York, 1955). For a later contribution, which argues that urban machines were not in fact simply corrupt but also the source of reform, see John D. Buenker, *Urban Liberalism and Progressive Reform* (New York, 1973).

13. James L. Gearity, "The First Brain Trust: Academics, Reform, and the Wisconsin Idea" (Ph.D. diss., University of Minnesota, 1979), p. 41. On the German influence, see p. 244.

14. C. Ben Wright, interview with Mrs. Eugene Hotchkiss (Jeanette Kennan), Sept. 26, 1970, Bland Files.

15. Kossuth K. Kennan, *Income Taxation: Methods and Results in Various Countries* (Milwaukee, 1910), p. 307.

16. "Fair Day, Adieu," pt. 2, chap. 1, p. 32.

17. Address (unused), Feb. 10, 1953, B. Nelson Papers, Butler Library, Columbia University, New York.

18. As Evelyn Waugh wrote of a fellow conservative: "He has a liking for all long-living, slow-moving things, such as elephants, tortoises and clergymen." Kennan thought society was suffering from "hypermetabolism" (see n. 31), an organic metaphor he actually shared with Marx: "Labour is, first of all, a process between man and nature, a process by which man, through his own actions, mediates, regulates and controls the metabolism between himself and nature." *Capital* (London, 1976), I, 283.

19. Address (unused), Feb. 10, 1953, B. Nelson Papers, Butler Library, Columbia University, New York.

20. *Democracy and the Student Left* (London, 1968), p. 12. He was taking his chief inspiration here, it seems, from Dostoyevski.

21. "The Challenge of Freedom," *The New Leader*, Dec. 26, 1955.

22. "A Conversation," *Encounter* (1976), 23.

23. "The Challenge of Freedom."

24. "Conversation with George Kennan," in *Conversations with Eric Sevareid: Interviews with Notable Americans* (Washington, D.C., 1976), 89–90. The interview dates from 1975.

25. *Democracy and the Student Left*, p. 145.

26. Address, Oxford, May 13, 1958, GFKP, Box 19; "A Proposal for Western Survival," *The New Leader*, Nov. 16, 1959.

27. Address, Aug. 1, 1947, GFKP, Box 17.

28. "The Challenge of Freedom."

29. Theodor Adorno, *Prisms* (New York, 1967), pp. 67, 117.

30. Address, Feb. 20, 1947, GFKP, Box 17.

31. See e.g. his remarks regarding the need for cabinet coordination, Address, Oct. 1, 1946 (Rhode Island), GFKP, Box 16. Also: "In a healthy good-humoured democratic atmosphere, permeated by a spirit of compromise and give and take and by the basic belief that all human groups or classes which accept the laws of society are entitled to sympathy and respect . . ." Address, Oct. 22, 1946, GFKP, Box 16. The notion of established classes is itself foreign to democratic theory.

32. GFK to Hooker, Oct. 17, 1949, GFKP, Box 23.

33. "World Problems," in Eisenstadt, *American History*, pp. 467–468.

34. Draft letter to Harper, Sept. 27, 1950, GFKP, Box 26, File 1-E-2, Annex 3.

35. *Democracy and the Student Left*, p. 206.

36. On Gibbon, see David P. Jordan, *Gibbon and His Roman Empire* (Urbana, Ill., 1971), esp. pp. 75–80; and Lionel Gossman, *The Empire Unpossess'd* (Cambridge, 1981). On Kennan's attachment to the eighteenth century, see "A Conversation," *Encounter*, 1976.

37. Project notes, 1951–52, GFKP, Box 26, File 1-E-2, Annex 4. He quotes Madison's No. 10 of *The Federalist* here. The original impetus probably came from Beard, however. See C. Ben Wright, interview with Charles Bohlen, Sept. 29, 1970, Bland Files.

38. See John R. Howe, *The Changing Political Thought of John Adams* (Princeton, 1966). Adams, preeminently concerned with stability and order, originally rejected the monarchical element for obvious reasons; but once the revolution lost actuality, he began to favor a hereditary presidency. Above all, he was a firm believer in the necessity of balance to keep the human passions under proper control.

39. Kennan expressed sympathy for the Hamiltonian-Whig-Federalist view of government. "Further Talk with Bob B.," External Project Notes, 1951–52, GFKP, Box 26, File 1-E-2, Annex 4. But he seems not to have noticed his agrarian affinities with Jefferson.

40. *Memoirs*, II, 88.

41. Controversy emanated primarily from his Pittsburgh address of May 3, 1956 (*The New Leader*, June 18, 1956), where he made what became a notorious statement about the "finality" of the transformation of Eastern Europe, meaning that the best that could be hoped for was gradual evolution toward something less repelling; this ran absolutely counter to the common American notion of rollback (i.e. revolutionary change) in this region. On the election, see GFK to Bowles, Nov. 9, 1956, Chester Bowles Papers, Box 141, Yale University Library, New Haven, Conn. Oddly, *Memoirs*, II, makes no mention of his Stevenson campaign in New Jersey.

42. Address, Oxford, May 13, 1958, GFKP, Box 19.

43. "The Confusion of Ends and Means," in Samuel Hendel, ed., *The Soviet Crucible* (Princeton, 1963), p. 639. This stemmed from a speech given in Sept.

1959. He underscored that, however relative, the distinction between American democracy and Soviet authoritarianism was of great importance. For a similar statement, see "A Conversation," *Encounter*, 1960.

44. "Further Talk with Bob B."

45. *Democracy and the Student Left*, p. 207.

46. "A Different Approach to the World: An Interview," interview with Martin Agronsky, *The New York Review of Books*, Jan. 20, 1977.

47. "Morality and Foreign Policy," *Foreign Affairs*, 64 (Winter 1985–86), 209.

48. "A Conversation," *Encounter* (1976), III.

49. Address, Oxford, May 13, 1958, GFKP, Box 19; *Russia, the Atom, and the West*, p. 103 (the reference is from the undelivered seventh lecture in the Reith series of 1957); *Democracy and the Student Left*, p. 207; "Totalitarianism in the Modern World," *Totalitarianism*, ed. C. F. Friedrich (New York, 1964) (speech originally given on March 6, 1953); "A Conversation," *Encounter*, 1976; GFK to Frank [Altschul?], March 23, 1964, GFKP, Box 31.

50. Roland Barthes, *Mythologies* (New York, 1972), p. 153. It is unclear whether he is also referring to the bourgeoisie.

51. Outline for seminar, April 25, 1960, GFKP, Box 20. Also: "Many people have been spoiled by easy jobs and high wages and have neglected their homes and children. Family life has suffered. Juvenile delinquency has grown enormously. In many instances unscrupulous people have taken advantage of the country's need for industrial labor to exploit public funds and to bring pressure on political circles in Washington." Remarks at Lisbon, 1944, GFKP, Box 16. What he had in mind was no doubt the strike by John L. Lewis's United Mine Workers. If we may judge from the few times he mentions them, he seems to have considered strikes, at least sizable ones, examples of "insufficient social discipline." "A Proposal," *The New Leader*, Nov. 16, 1959, p. 15. Here he was probably referring to the steel strike of 1959.

52. Address, May 2, 1947, GFKP, Box 17; Despatch, Oct. 20, 1952, GFKP, Box 24; Address, Jan. 28, 1947, GFKP, Box 16; Address, Feb. 20, 1947, GFKP, Box 17; and *Realities*, p. 115.

53. Address, Oxford, May 13, 1958, GFKP, Box 19.

54. Outline, July 7, 1960, GFKP, Box 20.

55. From 1957, *Russia, the Atom, and the West*, pp. 112–113: "We are rapidly becoming a highly conservative welfare state, psychologically sufficient unto ourselves, largely committed . . . to the maintenance of overemployment in the name of social security, to a creeping inflation which we seem to have no serious intention of combating, to a growing dependence on the resources of others, and to the cultivation of a comfortable life at home."

56. Quoted in Rossiter, *Conservatism*, p. 21.

8. Utopian Containment

1. On romanticism I am essentially following Robert Sayre and Michael Löwy, "Figures of Romantic Anti-Capitalism," *New German Critique*, 32 (1984).

2. The ensuing sketch, a very simplified one, is drawn mainly from Eagleton, *Criticism and Ideology*; Jameson, *The Political Unconscious* and *Fables of Aggression:*

Wyndham Lewis, the Modernist as Fascist (Berkeley, 1981); Raymond Williams, *Culture and Society* (New York, 1960); Patrick Brantlinger, *Bread and Circuses*, (1983; reprint, Ithaca, N.Y., 1985); and Lucien Goldmann, *The Hidden God* (London, 1964).

3. Eagleton, *Criticism*, p. 158.

4. Quoted in Williams, *Culture*, p. 215.

5. On Leavis, see Francis Mulhern, *The Moment of "Scrutiny"* (London, 1979).

6. The salient notion of tradition is itself questionable. What is popularly projected as tradition is often historical construction of comparatively recent provenance, for example the pageantry of the British court or the "ancient" costumes of the Scottish Highlanders. See Eric Hobsbawm and Terence Ranger, eds., *The Invention of Tradition* (Cambridge, 1983), particularly Hugh Trevor-Roper, "The Invention of Tradition: The Highland Tradition of Scotland."

7. "Why Do I Hope?" *University: A Princeton Quarterly*, 29 (Summer 1966); "A Conversation," *Encounter* (1976), 12.

8. "Runo: An Island Relic of Medieval Sweden," *Canadian Geographical Journal*, II, (Nov. 1935), 264. Curiously, this article is not included in Kennan's official bibliography. There is mention elsewhere of two other articles from the 1930s, of which one is on Chekhov; but I have been unable to trace them.

9. "Fair Day, Adieu," pt. 2, chap. 1, p. 19; GFK to Frank [Altschul?], March 23, 1964, GFKP, Box 31; C. Ben Wright, interview with Mrs. Eugene Hotchkiss, Sept. 26, 1970, Bland Files.

10. "Fair Day, Adieu," pt. 2, chap. 1, is perhaps the best early example of this vision.

11. "A Conversation," *Encounter* (1976), 11–12.

12. Diary note, Feb. 19, 1950, *Memoirs*, II, 67.

13. "A Conversation," *Encounter* (1960), 52.

14. "A Conversation," *Encounter* (1976), 13.

15. GFK to Hooker, Oct. 17, 1949, GFKP, Box 23.

16. "The Experience of Writing History," in *The Craft of American History*, ed. A. S. Eisenstadt, vol. 2 (New York, 1966), p. 278; Address, Dec. 21, 1949, GFKP, Box 17; Address (unused), Feb. 10, 1953, B. Nelson Papers, Butler Library, Columbia University, New York; *Colloques de Rheinfelden par Raymond Aron, George Kennan, Robert Oppenheimer, et autres* (Paris, 1960), p. 239, my translation. Various versions of this colloquium were published. Of those I found, however, only the French contained the question-and-answer period. In the GFKP there is a draft address for this occasion, which, though not apparently used in that form, provides an excellent summary of his conservative ecologist position: in favor of the small scale generally, against natural devastation and technological growth, for state control of the media for the protection of the people. Unused paper on industrial society, Sept. 1959, GFKP, Box 26.

17. GFK to Hooker, Oct. 17, 1949, GFKP, Box 23; GFK, Address, June 1950, GFKP, Box 18; *Realities*, p. 115.

18. *Realities*, p. 115.

19. However, on occasion he would sound a more hopeful note, denying that things would necessarily lead to "decadence." *Russia, the Atom, and the West*, p. 113.

20. GFK to Lerner, Jan. 25, 1955, Box 4, Max Lerner Papers, Yale University Library, New Haven, Conn.

21. "Urbanization," External Affairs Project, 1951–52, GFKP, Box 26, File 1-E-2, Annex 4.

22. GFK to Frank [Altschul?], March 23, 1964, GFKP, Box 31.

23. "Fair Day, Adieu," pt. 2, chap. 1, pp. 19–20. Again, as with the case of the city, one discerns a distinctly libidinal aspect to his description of "the never-ending stream of sleek dark cars [flowing] quietly in and out of the little community in twilight" (p. 20). Some additional quotes on automotive evil: "These mechanical legs have a deleterious effect on man himself, drugging him into a sort of paralysis of the faculty of reflection and distorting his emotional makeup while they are in use." Diary note, Nov. 4, 1951, *Memoirs*, II, 81. And: "It is not absolutely essential that one to two tons of machinery, developing two or three hundred horsepower, should be employed to haul the individual American body around the streets and highways of our country." Address, Oct. 17, 1956, GFKP, Box 19.

24. "Fair Day, Adieu," pt. 2, chap. 1, p. 20.

25. Jean-Paul Sartre, *Critique of Dialectical Reason* (London, 1982), pp. 256–318; Fredric Jameson, *Marxism and Form* (Princeton, 1971), pp. 247–248.

26. GFK to Frank [Altschul?], March 23, 1964, GFKP, Box 31. I have found no sign in Kennan's subsequent execration of student militance in the 1960s that he ever read Marcuse's quintessentially "sixtyish" book, wherein he might have found some congenial arguments. In fact the whole Frankfurt School, with its marked pessimism and disdain for mass culture, television, and advertising, would have made interesting reading for him, Max Horkheimer and Theodor Adorno, *The Dialectic of Enlightenment* (1944; reprint, New York, 1969), in particular.

27. *New York Times*, Op-Ed page, Oct. 28, 1970. Advertising had been a bête noire of his for a long time. Consider for example this almost claustrophobic passage from "Fair Day, Adieu," pt. 2, chap. 1, pp. 20–21: "The advertising was the worst. It was as impossible to escape from advertisements as from the air itself. Indoors, outdoors, from printed pages, from the ether, from the screen, the words of advertisers and purveyors poured out like bullets and sought their mark on the consciousness of the individual." On "spectatoritis," see Address, Feb. 14, 1949, GFKP, Box 17.

28. "Fair Day, Adieu," pt. 2, chap. 1, pp. 21–22.

29. *Democracy and the Student Left*, p. 231.

30. "How Stands Our Pursuit of Happiness?" *The New Leader*, June 20, 1955, p. 17.

31. *The Cloud of Danger* (New York, 1977), pp. 19–22, includes a succinct statement along these lines; see also "More Controls Ahead," in *The Endless Crisis: A Confrontation on America in the Seventies*, ed. F. Duchene (New York, 1970), p. 83; and *Democracy and the Student Left*, esp. pp. 229–230. The allusion to cancer is in GFK to Frank, March 23, 1964, GFKP, Box 31.

32. Testimony, U.S. Congress, Senate Committee on Foreign Relations, *Informal Meeting with George Kennan*, Hearing, 86th Cong., 1st sess., May 12, 1959.

33. "Credo of a Civil Servant," *Princeton Alumni Weekly*, Feb. 2, 1954.

34. Address, Oxford, May 13, 1958, GFKP, Box 19.

35. "More Controls Ahead," in Duchene, *The Endless Crisis*, p. 82.

36. See Fredric Jameson's "Reification and Utopia," *Social Text*, 1 (Fall 1979), for a penetrating analysis of the utopian dimension of mass culture. See also Herbert Marcuse's essay from the 1930s, "The Affirmative Character of Culture," in *Negations* (Boston, 1968).

37. "A Conversation," *Encounter* (1976), 13.

38. Adorno, *Prisms*, p. 24. Adorno and the Frankfurt School (including Marcuse) were much concerned with the culture industry, at times coming perilously close to precisely the sort of thing Adorno criticizes here.

39. Ibid., p. 20.

40. Address, May 7, 1953, GFKP, Box 18. On the same occasion (lecturing members of the Century Club in New York) he attacked the "fantastic internal security arrangements, which no one dares to question," and "the extremism and intolerance and vindictiveness" from which they stemmed.

41. Remarkably Mr. Davies showed little bitterness about these events when I interviewed him (Asheville, N.C., April 26–27, 1981). His viewpoint on China during the disputed period was in fact that of a conservative realist, a position that with some mutations was eventually put into political effect decades later through the good offices of Richard M. Nixon, a man who had first made his political fortune by witch-hunting. When reminded of this monumental irony Mr. Davies made a sound which I interpreted as a chuckle.

42. On Davies, see for example Kennan's letter to the *New York Times*, Dec. 12, 1953, and the correspondence in GFKP, Box 28. When Davies's security clearance was finally restored in the late 1960s (a formality but not without symbolic force), Kennan again wrote to the *Times* (Jan. 22, 1969) to publicize the event and demonstrate that injustices committed had not been forgotten. In Oppenheimer's case, see his testimony in U.S. Atomic Energy Commission, *In the Matter of J. Robert Oppenheimer: Transcripts and Hearings before Personal Security Board and Texts of Principal Documents and Letters* (1954; reprint, Cambridge, Mass., 1971). On his view of McCarthyism more generally, see *Memoirs*, II, 220–228.

43. "Fair Day, Adieu," pt. 2, chap. 1, pp. 14–15; "Report to Mr. Russell of Summer 1946 Lecture Tour," Aug. 23, 1946, GFKP, Box 16; *New York Times Magazine*, Feb. 27, 1951. It should be added that this last message was not really about communists and teaching but, on the contrary, the necessity of allowing a variety of ideas to be aired: "It would be a serious situation indeed where we would have to conclude that sound teachings would not stand the competition of one or two challenging voices, however misguided we might think them to be." As I have said, however, there were exceptions to this tolerance and openness.

44. "The Climate of the Current Investigations of Communism—Effect on the Colleges and the Liberal Arts," *Vital Speeches of the Day*, June 15, 1953 (originally delivered at Notre Dame, it was widely disseminated and reprinted); "We have seen our public life debauched . . ." in Graebner, *Ideas and Diplomacy* (from an address at Radcliffe, June 16, 1954). *Berufsverbot* was the West German law forbidding radicals to hold teaching jobs in the 1970s.

45. "We have seen our public life debauched . . . ," in Graebner, *Ideas and Diplomacy*, pp. 768–769.

46. *New York Times Magazine*, Feb. 27, 1951.

47. *Realities*, p. 118.

48. GFK to Chamberlain, June 21, 1950, GFKP, Box 28; "Further Talk with Bob B." A quote from the first source: "The attitudes and methods of which we have been the witnesses in past weeks and months are ones which have in them the seeds of an American totalitarianism. Does the danger of penetration from *international* totalitarianism really seem so great that you are prepared to accept a sort of *national* totalitarianism to combat it?" This was written when Kennan was still at the State Department and Acheson initialed it "No objections." His view here should be contrasted with that of *Memoirs*, II, 220, where the notion of incipient American fascism (i.e. one type of totalitarianism) in connection with McCarthyism is imputed to the Europeans and then in turn disputed: "McCarthy had no police forces. The American courts remained almost totally unaffected." Yet it is obvious that not just the Europeans but Kennan himself had very serious concerns at the time about some form of American right-wing totalitarianism.

49. "Totalitarianism in the Modern World," in Friedrich, *Totalitarianism*, p. 29.

50. GFK to Bohlen, Aug. 21, 1952; *Memoirs*, II, 274–275; "The Ethics of Anti-Communism," *University: A Princeton Quarterly*, 24 (Spring 1965). The most trying moments occurred during his ambassadorship to Yugoslavia, the problem being Washington, not Belgrade. At times he seemed to be serving as Tito's ambassador on Capitol Hill.

51. *The Value of a St. John's Education*, June 4, 1960 (private printing). This was a speech given at the military academy where he had spent the years between ages thirteen and seventeen. One imagines it as a fairly harsh milieu. In retrospect he liked it: "We learned to dress neatly and how to keep a room in order. We were *not* allowed to run around looking like hoboes or lumberjacks. We were not permitted to work at being sloppy."

52. *Russia, the Atom, and the West*, p. 110.

53. *Wall Street Journal*, July 16, 1968. This passage suggests some irate colonel (ret.), writing to the London *Times* to complain about "today's youth" and their regrettable habits. It is, however, perhaps not very far either, in form and content, from what leading lights within the French Communist party thought and said about the students of May 1968.

54. *Democracy and the Student Left*, p. 170,

55. This was *Democracy and the Student Left*. The comparison about the Civil War is on p. 19. It was a great exaggeration, no doubt, but even if the two events are basically incomparable, the 1960s were probably the period of greatest domestic disturbance in *political* terms since the Civil War.

56. Ibid., pp. 218, 17.

57. Ibid., p. 20, 223.

58. Ibid., pp. 9, 211, 223–224, 228–238; *Rand Daily Mail* (Johannesburg), May 7, 1970.

59. *Democracy*, pp. 216–217.

60. *Rand Daily Mail*, May 7, 1970.

61. "More Controls Ahead," in Duchene, *The Endless Crisis*, p. 87. Lillian Hellman took issue with Kennan on this public occasion, characterizing, pretty fairly in my view, the students as follows: "Some of them are fools, and many of

them, I think, will be sellouts. But most of them are a better generation in knowledge and spirit than we were." Kennan, typically backtracking somewhat when confronted with unalterable force, changed tone, still finding it hard to see anything positive in these people but agreeing, contrary to earlier arguments, that "there should be student councils, whose views should be listened to and taken into account." Ibid., pp. 87–92.

62. *Democracy and the Student Left*, p. 151; italics added.

63. Ibid., pp. 150–151.

64. See Chapter 5.

65. "The Sources of Soviet Conduct," p. 567. The theme of radicals as failed, frustrated intellectuals was particularly evident in the late 1940s, but Kennan's ambivalence about these "neurotic" rejectionists was seldom far from the surface. Assessing the Russian Revolution in the 1960s, for example, he actually deplored the loss of so "many brilliant youths" to revolutionary activity under tsarism. "The Russian Revolution—Fifty Years After," *Foreign Affairs*, 46 (Oct. 1967), 3. Mention has also been made earlier of his intermittently high regard for the original Bolshevik leadership. Perhaps the best expression of his contradictory attitude on that topic is his remarks on Trotsky: the "unscrupulous" revolutionary as contrasted with "the man who faces inward—to the immediate personal entourage, to the small circle of recognized political intimates, and, above all, to the loneliness of self: the personal conscience, the intimations of beauty, the premonitions of death." "Introduction to Translation of the Trotsky Diary," Nov. 1954, GFKP, Box 26. This introduction was never published.

66. GFK to Hooker, Oct. 17, 1949, GFKP, Box 23. His view of the Chinese communists contradicted this. Here he also espoused the auxiliary thesis that there was a kind of mutation of the human species (between 5 and 15 percent) who would invariably be Quislings, looking to foreign governments for outlets for their frustration.

67. In outlining *ressentiment*, I am following Fredric Jameson, *Fables*, pp. 116–132, and *Political Unconscious*, pp. 201–202.

68. *Rand Daily Mail*, May 7, 1970. I owe the comparison with Lippmann to Ronald Steel, his biographer.

69. The eminent columnist had more room to take a detached view and was perhaps personally less inclined to become incensed. As Kennan wrote of himself: "I fear I am a person who rouses himself to intellectual activity only when he is stung. The more outraged I become at the preposterousness of the things other people say, the better I do." GFK to Kallin, June 29, 1957, GFKP, Box 31. His self-assessment is not altogether off the mark: he did tend to be reactive and at his polemical best when angry. In that sense he became too angry in the 1968–1971 period.

70. *Democracy and the Student Left*, pp. 204; 211; 193, 211.

71. *Memoirs*, II, 88; *Democracy and the Student Left*, p. 207; Address, May 13, GFKP, Box 19.

72. *Democracy and the Student Left*, pp. 228, 238; *Wall Street Journal*, July 16, 1968.

73. Prudence is inscribed, I think, in the Aristotelian doctrine of the mean, i.e. for every virtue there are two vices. As regards Burke: "The first of all virtues, prudence." *Reflections*, p. 153.

74. *Democracy and the Student Left*, p. 236.

75. Unused preface to *Memoirs*, II.

76. On Thompson's oddly parallel trajectory from a romantic starting point, strongly influenced by the nineteenth-century British marxist William Morris, see Perry Anderson, *Arguments within British Marxism* (London, 1980), though Anderson would probably disagree with the use of the term *romantic*.

77. Public television documentary, Oct. 13, 1982; "Beyond the Shadow of the Atom," *Congressional Record*, Dec. 7, 1981. As indicated, he has defended the movement against red-baiting: "I can think of nothing more contemptible than this effort to pin a Communist label on a movement which is actually motivated by nothing other than a deep concern for the security of this country and this civilization in the face of a volume of weaponry quite capable of putting an end to both." Address, Union Theological Seminary, New York, Oct. 27, 1982 (press release).

78. "Beyond the Shadow of the Atom,"

79. Address, Oct. 27, 1982 (author's notes).

80. Address, May 31, 1948, GFKP, Box 17. The Roman reference betrays the Gibbonesque source.

81. "Fair Day, Adieu," pt. 2, chap. 1, p. 25.

82. See Chapter 3.

83. *Memoirs*, II, 5; for an example of lay preaching, see Sermon, April 15, 1962, GFKP, Box 20; "Foreign Policy and Christian Conscience," *The Atlantic Monthly*, 203 (May 1959), (probably his most important statement on the subject during the 1950s); "A Proposal for Western Survival," *The New Leader*, Nov. 16, 1959. .

84. Sermon, Belgrade, Oct. 1, 1961, GFKP, Box 20.

85. Calvin is quoted in Sheldon Wolin, *Politics and Vision* (Boston, 1960), p. 186. See chap. 6 of the same work on Calvinism, order, and political theory generally.

86. Ernst Troeltsch, *The Social Teachings of the Christian Churches* (London, 1931), pp. 589, 607. I have drawn heavily here on chap. 7 of this important work. The "intramundane asceticism" of Calvinism contrasts with the traditional Catholic practice of consigning asceticism to monasteries, i.e. to the "extramundane." It also differs from the tragic vision of Jansenistic Catholicism, in itself largely a dialectical response to the Reformation. While sharing the concept of a hidden God, in the abstract at once present and absent, the Jansenist is both more detached from the world (though he accepts being wholly in it) and less compromising toward it. See Goldmann's eminent work on Pascal et al., *The Hidden God*. Apart from the works of Wolin and Troeltsch, this sketch is influenced by Michael Walzer, *The Revolution of the Saints* (New York, 1976), pp. 22–47. Like every such condensation, mine is a simplification, perhaps in this case excessively so.

87. "Reflections: Streets Once Really Seen or Seen in Dreams," *The New Yorker*, April 29, 1974.

88. "A Conversation," *Encounter* (1960), 55; GFK to Oppenheimer, Nov. 16, 1962, GFKP, Box 31. Primordial talent and inclination no doubt induced part of his aesthetic orientation. Despite a childhood milieu deprived of music

(and visual arts), he became a proficient musician (and his half-brother a musicologist). See "The Arts in American Society," *Cultural Affairs*, 15 (May 1971) (statement originally made in June 1965).

89. *Memoirs*, I, won both a National Book Award and a Pulitzer Prize.

90. "Opening Address," *Proceedings of the American Academy of Arts and Letters–National Institute of Arts and Letters*, 2d ser., vol. 19 (New York, 1969).

91. Gossman, *The Empire Unpossess'd*, pp. 74–75.

92. Arriving on the Riviera with his wife in the 1930s Kennan was immediately disgusted and hurried north to Norway as quickly as possible. He comments: "The world had become too big, too bewildering for us." "Fair Day, Adieu," pt. 1, p. 46.

93. See Eagleton, *Criticism*, p. 145.

94. "The Confusion of Ends and Means," in Hendel, *The Soviet Crucible*.

95. This will be recognized as Claude Lévi-Strauss's theory of myth, though it is used here filtered through Fredric Jameson's reading. See Jameson, *The Political Unconscious*, pp. 77–80, and passim.

96. See ibid., pp. 82–83, 166–169, 254–257; and A. J. Greimas and J. Courtes, *Semiotics and Language* (Bloomington, Ind., 1979), pp. 308–311, for expositions of the semiotic rectangle.

97. "The Arts in American Society" is a good example.

Appendix A

1. *Russia and the West*, a historical account that follows the trajectory of his own views rather faithfully, is a good example. A more startling one is the sudden reiteration in 1953 of his idea that the United States "should never have established *de jure* diplomatic relations with the Soviet Government." GFK to McGeorge Bundy, Feb. 2, 1953, Lippmann Papers, Box 81, File 120, Yale University Library, New Haven, Conn.

2. *Russia and the West*, p. 295. See also "Observations" (1956) in Graebner, *Ideas and Diplomacy*.

3. "Totalitarianism in the Modern World," in *Totalitarianism*, ed. Carl J. Friedrich (New York, 1964) (address originally given in 1953). He excused the atheoretical approach by mentioning his own encounters with totalitarianism (Nazi Germany, Stalinist Russia). Hannah Arendt may have been in the audience, thus perhaps inhibiting theoretical effusiveness.

4. See e.g. GFK to Chamberlain, June 21, 1950, GFKP, Box 28. He had raised the specter of an internal "totalitarian beast" earlier in the sense of a dormant but ever-present weakness or temptation. Address, March 28, 1947, GFKP, Box 17.

5. On the metaphor of crusts, see Address, Jan. 21, 1950, GFKP, Box 18. Sometimes he would dilute the theoretical meaning of the concept even further by inserting his old comparison between Stalinism and Old Muscovy in the totalitarian framework. See Address, Jan. 15, 1948, GFKP, Box 17; and "Russia and the United States" (Stamford, Conn., 1950). On the impossibility of revolt, see Press conference, April 1, 1952, GFKP, Box 18. He continued to argue this

after abandoning the totalitarian theme. See *On Dealing*, p. 11. For earlier references to this theme, see GFK to Secstate, July 8, 1949, PPS Files, Box 23; Address, Dec. 12, 1949, GFKP, Box 18; and Press conference, Aug. 22, 1950, GFKP, Box 18. For the instability point, see Lecture draft (unused), Feb. 10, 1953, B. Nelson Papers, cataloged correspondence, Butler Library, Columbia University, New York; and "America and the Russian Future," *Foreign Affairs*, 29 (April 1951), 366, where he argues that no system "based on the evil and weakness in man's nature" could achieve "genuine stability."

6. For the old developmental theme, see Address, May 2, 1947, GFKP, Box 17; on Soviet change, see Press conference, April 1, 1952, GFKP, Box 18.

7. GFK to Lerner, Jan. 25, 1955, Max Lerner Papers, Box 4, "Kennan," Yale University Library, New Haven, Conn.; "Observations," in Graebner, *Ideas and Diplomacy*; "World Problems" (from an address given in Jan. 1959), in Eisenstadt, *American History*; *Colloques de Rheinfelden par Raymond Aron, George Kennan, Robert Oppenheimer et autres*, Sept. 20, 1959; and in somewhat different form "Confusion of Ends and Means," in Hendel, *The Soviet Crucible; On Dealing*, pp. 14–16.

8. "World Problems," in Eisenstadt, *American History*, p. 467.

9. Unused conclusion to *The Decision to Intervene*, Jan. 1957, GFKP, Box 26; *Colloques*. He remains convinced (and now Gorbachev is agreeing) that the systems face similar difficulties of industrial life. The systems themselves, however, have not converged: they are as separate today as ever.

10. Testimony, U.S. Congress, Senate Committee on Foreign Relations, *East-West Trade*, Hearings, 89th Cong., 1st sess., pt. 2, Feb. 26, 1965; Testimony, U.S. Congress, Senate Committee on Foreign Relations, *The Communist World in 1967*, Hearings, 90th Cong., 1st sess., Jan. 30, 1967.

11. *Washington Post*, Oct. 18, 1964; "The Russian Revolution—Fifty Years After"; Testimony, U.S. Congress, Senate Committee on Foreign Relations, *Exchanges of U.S.-U.S.S.R. Officials*, Hearings, 91st Cong., 2d sess., Feb. 6, 1970.

12. "Mr. X Reconsiders: A Current Assessment of Soviet-American Relations," *Encounter*, 50 (March 1978), 11; *Washington Post*, Dec. 18, 1974; "Are All Russians 8 Feet Tall?" *Military Review*, no. 5 (May 1977); *Cloud of Danger*, pp. 180–182.

13. "America's Unstable Soviet Policy," *Atlantic Monthly*, 250 (Nov. 1982); Testimony, U.S. Congress, Senate, Committee on Foreign Relations, *United States Relations with Communist Countries*, Hearings, 93d Cong., 2d sess., Aug. 20, 1974. His view of Khrushchev was not always (relatively speaking) favorable. In the late 1950s he found him more "erratic" than the more predictable Stalin "Points for New Leader Meeting," draft notes, Sept. 25, 1958, GFKP, Box 19. On Gorbachev, see "The Gorbachev Prospect," *New York Review of Books*, Jan. 21, 1988.

14. His ambassadorial experience is depicted in *Memoirs*, II, 111–167. For the position he was about to propound, see "Draft Statement for London Conference," Sept. 23, 1952, GFKP, Box 26. *Pravda* attacked him ferociously, and another organ compared him to Hitler and Goebbels—on account of his realist lack of ethics! *New York Times*, Sept. 27 and Dec. 25, 1952. This was not the first time Moscow misread Kennan. In early 1950 he wrote a fairly (by the standards of the time) conciliatory article which was then excerpted in the State

Department *Bulletin* in a way that made it sound more hawkish. The Soviet chargé d'affaires in Belgrade was thus prompted to ask the American ambassador whether this article was not conclusive proof that the United States wanted to obliterate the Soviet Union. See Allen to Secstate, Feb. 25, 1950, *FRUS*, 1950, IV, 1376.

15. GFK to Matthews, July 15, 1952, GFKP, Box 24.

16. Ibid. The alleged absence of internal contradiction has indeed been a major obstacle for Soviet cultural production since the rise of Stalin.

17. GFK to Director of Central Intelligence, May 12, 1953, Allen Dulles Papers, Box 58, Mudd Library, Princeton University, Princeton, N.J.; *The Value of a St. John's Education*. In more recent years, however, he has pointed to social problems such as alcoholism (see e.g. *The Cloud of Danger*, p. 183).

18. On paper, at least, Soviet positions at the time seemed closer (if not close) to Kennan's in the sense that they aspired to more compromise than the American one. On atomic weapons the Soviet policy has certainly been much closer to Kennan's views since 1950.

19. "The Soviet Union and the Atlantic Pact," as reproduced in *Memoirs*, II, app.

20. GFK to Bowles, Oct. 16, 1955, GFKP, Box 31. On the great-power theme, see also *On Dealing*, pp. 16–17. It is particularly interesting since he maintained that neither Stalin nor his successors had any interest in offensive wars.

21. "Observations," p. 826.

22. GFK to Altschul, Jan. 5, 1950, GFKP, Box 31. This did not prevent him from making the occasional "ideological" reading. Address, May 11, 1959, GFKP, Box 19.

23. See n. 12. Yet he was of course aware too of the competition in the Third World and the (more serious) arms race. See "The Russian Revolution," *Foreign Affairs*, 46 (Oct. 1967).

24. "Two Views of the Soviet Problem," *The New Yorker*, Nov. 2, 1981, p. 55.

25. *New York Post*, Oct. 6, 1959. This was stated in retrospect, but it was still in line with his view that the Soviet Union was justly worried that members leaving the Warsaw Pact would join NATO. See Testimony, U.S. Congress, Senate Subcommittee of the Committee on Foreign Relations, *Control and Reduction of Armaments*, Hearings, 85th Cong., 1st sess., pt. 2, Jan. 9, 1957.

26. C. Ben Wright, interview with Charles Bohlen, Sept. 29, 1970, Washington, D.C., Bland Files. I extrapolate here from the fact that Kennan is said to have been outraged, and that he had stated only three years earlier that the Soviet Union would allow more freedom to Eastern European countries as long as they did not cut ties with the Warsaw Pact or renounced marxism in toto, neither of which the Dubcek regime did. See "American Involvement," in *The Viet-Nam Reader*, ed. Marcus G. Raskin and Bernard B. Fall (New York, 1965), p. 26 (from congressional testimony, March 11, 1965).

27. *New York Times*, Jan. 5, 6, 1982.

28. Thus he also took a detached view of the Soviet invasion of Afghanistan, "a crude, bungled operation, an obvious mistake" but also not fundamentally infringing on American interests, "particularly if it be considered that the alter-

native might have been the growing influence of a Khomeini type of violently anti-American Moslem fanaticism in that part of the world." "America's Unstable Soviet Policy," p. 79.

29. "The Future of Soviet Communism," *The New Leader*, June 18, 1956.

30. "Is Détente Worth Saving?" *Saturday Review*, March 6, 1976; "Are All Russians 8 Feet Tall?"; Interview, *New York Review of Books*, Jan. 20, 1977.

31. A partial enumeration of his variously stated depictions of the Soviet view of war and other means in the 1950s: (1) the Russians wish to avoid war because it is risky (GFK to Secstate, Aug. 8, 1950, *FRUS*, 1950, I, 365); (2) war is very "low" on their "list of means of achieving their objectives." (Address, Feb. 7, 1952, GFKP, Box 18); (3) war is not part of the Soviet marxist scheme (Press Conference, April 1, 1952, GFKP, Box 18); (4) they do not desire war now, but "if circumstances were favorable, I can conceive of no iniquity that they should not inflict with a cold delight on the entire western coalition, and ourselves in particular" ("Draft Statement for London Conference," Sept. 23, 1952, GFKP, Box 18); (5) they wish "to tear down every other form of authority and influence in the world" and "in this effort, they use every device that comes to hand" (GFK to Anisimov, Jan. 14, 1957, GFKP, Box 31); (6) "I have never thought that the Soviet Government wanted a general world war at any time since 1945 or that it would have been inclined, for any rational political reason, to inaugurate such a war," though some people seem to think "that if the Russians gain the slightest edge on us in the capacity to wreak massive destruction at long range, they will immediately use it, regardless of our capacity for retaliation." (*Russia, the Atom, and the West*, p. 51); and (7) nuclear weapons do not easily fit into the marxist way of thought ("Russia, the Atom, and the West, 1959," *The Listener*, Oct. 29, 1959).

32. It was in means and methods that he saw the greatest change since Stalin. Improvement here was pivotal in his reclassification of the regime; see "Confusion," in Hendel, *The Soviet Crucible*. The retrogression during Brezhnev's regime did not cause him to revert to the "any means" position.

33. "Two Views of the Soviet Problem."

34. "Re Stalin Article Published in BOLSHEVIK," Oct. 20, 1952, GFKP, Box 24. This interesting piece is one of the few places where Kennan dissects the content of Soviet marxism in any detail. It indicates that, with more application, he could have become a penetrating analyst in this area. See also Address, Feb. 26, 1964, GFKP, Box 21; "Boris Ivanovich Nicolaevsky, 1887–1966," *Slavic Review*, 25 (June 1966).

35. In the mid-1960s he thought communism was relevant only to industrializing countries, and thus the USSR had left it behind, objectively speaking, while the PRC had not. In his words, "History tends to iron out in the course of time all the great extremes." Testimony, Feb. 25, 1965, pp. 8, 36–37 (see n. 10).

36. *Russia, the Atom, and the West*, pp. 21–23. Exasperated, he once declared all basic concepts of Soviet marxism designations for nonexistent things, such as the proletariat: "Concepts and expressions have to be invented which actually have no reality." Address, May 11, 1959, GFKP, Box 20. This was an unprofitable line of argument.

37. An example is his analysis of a Soviet statement denying that peaceful

coexistence meant the end of the class struggle. He interpreted this as a way of placating the Chinese, as though it was not in fact perfectly coherent with what Moscow had argued for a long time. "Comments on Moscow Statement of December 6, 1960," Dec. 8, 1960, GFKP, Box 20.

38. GFK to Sullivan, FBI, Dec. 13, 1963, GFKP, Box 31; Address, New York, Oct. 27, 1982 (author's notes).

39. GFK to Matthews, June 6, 1952, GFKP, Box 24.

40. "America's Unstable Soviet Policy" (referring to communist parties in Stalin's times as "instruments"). In 1965 he said, "The old idea of revolution, as Lenin conceived it coming in Western Europe, has really gone." "American Involvement," in Raskin and Fall, *The Viet-Nam Reader*, p. 25. His interest in communist parties was by then chiefly with reference to the Vietnam war.

41. Seminar notes, April 27, 1969, GFKP, Box 22; "American Involvement."

42. *Realities of American Foreign Policy*, pp. 86–88; Testimony, U.S. Congress, House Committee on Foreign Affairs, Draft Report, *Foreign Policy and Mutual Security*, and Hearings, Oct. 11, 1956.

43. "Meet the Press," NBC, Nov. 5, 1967; "An Historian of Potsdam and His Readers," *American Slavic and East European Review*, 20 (April 1961). The latter, a review of Herbert Feis's *Between War and Peace*, is typical of a Kennan stung into action by a work that by implication could be construed as a critique of his position circa 1945. The passage should therefore be taken with a grain of salt.

44. GFK to Matthews, Aug. 8, 1952, GFKP, Box 28.

45. This was his basic point in the disengagement controversy of the 1950s (see Part II). See e.g. Testimony, Jan. 9, 1957 (see n. 25).

46. *Russia, the Atom, and the West*, p. 24.

47. Address, Dec. 14, 1960, GFKP, Box 20. Kennan's views, incidentally, were too controversial for him to be brought into the Kennedy administration, and it was in part only after Adlai Stevenson had quietly interceded that he was offered the diplomatic post to Yugoslavia. Adlai Stevenson Papers, Box 832, "Kennan," Mudd Library, Princeton University, Princeton, N.J.

48. See *Memoirs*, II, 269–315, for a lively account of these absurdities.

49. Congressional testimony, March 11, 1965, in Raskin and Fall, *The Viet-Nam Reader*.

50. Testimony, Aug. 20, 1974 (see n. 13); "America's Love-Hate Affair with China," *The Observer*, Feb. 20, 1972; "A Fresh Look at Our China Policy," *New York Times Magazine*, Nov. 22, 1964.

51. See his collection *The Nuclear Delusion* (New York, 1982).

52. "The United States and the Soviet Union, 1917–1976," *Foreign Affairs*, 54 (July 1976), 682.

Appendix B

1. The ensuing delineation is my own, but the distinction between theory and ideology is inspired by Louis Althusser's partly similar distinction between science and ideology in *For Marx* (London, 1969); the actual definition of ideology comes from Fredric Jameson's reworking, in "Postmodernism, or the Cultural Logic of Late Capitalism," *New Left Review*, 146 (1984), of Althusser's own

reworking of Jacques Lacan's psychoanalytical and Claude Lévi-Strauss's structuralist writings; the term "discursive formation" comes from Michel Foucault, *The Archaeology of Knowledge* (New York, 1972), although my use of it has a different meaning.

2. Herbert Marcuse, *Soviet Marxism*, remains the outstanding work here.

3. Smith, "Russian History." This antiheretical notion of truth was actually a product of surviving medieval Catholicism, not of Byzantine influence (see Chapter 2, n. 61). Readers of Swedish might also see Kristian Gerner, *Arvet från det Förflutna* (Stockholm, 1980), pp. 22–23.

4. Leonid Brezhnev's following claim was thus more than an obligatory invocation: "For more than half a century the Soviet Union's foreign policy has been based on Lenin's ideas and precepts. Written into the decisions of our Party and of the higher organs of the Soviet State they remain the immutable, principled foundation of all the Soviet Union's actions in the international arena." Farther along he confirms: "Imperialism is moving exactly in the direction foreseen by Lenin." Leonid Brezhnev, *On the Policy of the Soviet Union and the International Situation* (New York, 1973), pp. 47, 54. Lenin himself would have been surprised to see his theory become canonical law; he subtitled his most ambitious elaboration of it "A Popular Outline," and a popular outline it certainly was. V. I. Lenin, "Imperialism: The Highest Stage of Capitalism," in *Collected Works*, vol. 22 (Moscow, 1964). Moreover, much of his concept originated with other theorists such as Hilferding, Bukharin, and Hobson.

5. I have explored this idea in greater detail in Stephanson, "On Soviet Foreign Policy."

6. R. Rotermundt and U. Schmiederer, "Social Structure and Foreign Policy in the Soviet Union," in *Soviet Foreign Policy: Its Social and Economic Conditions*, ed. Egbert Jahn (London, 1978); Michael Löwy, "Marx and Engels: Cosmopolites," *Critique*, 3 (n.d.). See also Lenin, *Collected Works*, XXII, 147. A nation like Libya, however, that happens to be relatively marginal and is also a purveyor of very desirable commodities can get away with antisystemic behavior for a considerable time.

7. Jane Degras, *Soviet Documents on Foreign Policy*, vol. 2 (London, 1961), pp. 512–513; Cláudin, *The Communist Movement*, pp. 115–116. I owe the vertical-horizontal imagery to Kubálková and Cruickshank, *Marxism-Leninism*.

8. The Comintern, as quoted in Claudin, *The Communist Movement*, p. 192. He refers to a statement from 1935, but the definition was actually adopted by the Comintern executive in 1933 and employed during ultraleft and Popular Front periods alike. It is still operative. For a trenchant critique of the Comintern position on fascism, see Poulantzas, *Fascism and Dictatorship*, chap. 3.

9. See Anders Stephanson, "The CPUSA Conception of the Rooseveltian State, 1933–1939," *Radical History Review*, 19 (1979).

10. Moshe Lewin, "The Social Background of Stalinism," in Tucker, *Stalinism*.

11. Feher et al., *Dictatorship*, pp. 199–200. Interesting marxist theory survived in somewhat esoteric forms such as the literary criticism of Mikhail Bakhtin. But the area of possible discussion had shrunk enormously.

12. The characterization of religion is taken from Richard K. Fenn, *Liturgies and Trials* (Oxford, 1982). See also Marcuse, *Soviet Marxism*, pp. 72–73.

13. For two summaries of this ideology, see Alec Nove, *Stalinism*, pp. 179–180; and Fehér et al., *Dictatorship*, p. 200. One might also quote Roy Medvedev, *All Stalin's Men* (Oxford, 1983), p. 62, on the importance of this discourse: "No one can hold an important post in any social or state organization if he does not adhere to the Party ideology of Marxism-Leninism. The foundations of Marxism-Leninism are taught in all schools and institutions of further education, regardless of their type. No higher degree, be it in physics, mathematics, astronomy, literature or law, is awarded before the candidate has sat a preliminary examination in marxist philosophy."

14. Stephanson, "On Soviet Foreign Policy."

15. The exact constellations in the internal conflicts are still unclear. In this respect McCagg's *Stalin Embattled* is more suggestive than definitive.

16. Andrei Zhdanov, "The International Situation," in U.S. Congress, *The Strategy and Tactics of World Communism*, p. 215.

17. Ibid., pp. 216, 220, 230, 229, 219.

18. Claudin, *The Communist Movement*, p. 582. On the peace policy, see Shulman, *Stalin's Foreign Policy*, p. 80, and passim.

19. On peaceful coexistence, see Kubálková and Cruickshank, *Marxism-Leninism*, pp. 202–210. For an example of Soviet reasoning, see P. Timofeyev, "Inter-State Relations and Social Contradictions," *International Affairs* (Moscow), Feb. 1960. Détente was interpreted in a similar manner.

20. Kubálková and Cruickshank, *Marxism-Leninism*, pp. 204–208.

21. Spriano, *Stalin*, chap. 11.

Bibliographic Sources

Given the focus on text as opposed to context in the present work, only two archival sources proved of extensive use: the George F. Kennan Papers at Mudd Library, Princeton University, Princeton, N.J., and the various collections in the National Archives in Washington, D.C. Materials in other libraries yielded surprisingly little with regard to works authored by Kennan. His own papers were by far the most important collection. They contain a wealth of major documents and are particularly useful in that they include an enormous number of unpublished addresses. I imagine, however, that Kennan, an irrepressible writer, maintains a large collection of more private papers, letters, and diaries outside this collection. His unpublished biography of Anton Chekhov, an opus of potentially great interest, is unfortunately not available. While the collection offers a fairly complete set of the major diplomatic writings, there is a marked absence of the less important materials from that domain. A crucial guide, "Bibliography of Published Writings and Unpublished Addresses and Lectures of George Frost Kennan" (May 1974), with supplement, was procured through Kennan's Princeton office.

The National Archives is a decent complement here, although the central records of interest were not always available or open. For example, the records of the Division of Eastern European Affairs, where Kennan spent 1937–38 and which was abolished in the latter year, had to a large extent been reappropriated by the State Department, at least during the period of my various visits. A significant number of the otherwise valuable Policy Planning Staff files (1947–1950) had been shipped back to the same destination. Requests under the Freedom of Information Act, often a costly shot in the dark, did not always remedy this lack. The highly intriguing records of the National Security Council are generally unavailable and must be obtained through the same unreliable method. Finally, documents pertaining to the Soviet Union since 1950 have as of this writing remained closed—contrary to previous practice—because of the schism between the Reagan administration and the National Archives regarding principles of declassification, thus very largely eliminating sources for Kennan's ambassadorial effort in Moscow during 1952.

The PPS files themselves are sometimes spotty and at any rate not very forthcoming. Minutes of meetings, disappointingly, often state in a single line what was discussed and nothing more. Notably, Kennan's personal PPS file contains almost nothing of value: most of its content was probably transferred into his papers at Princeton. Worth mentioning are the records of the Moscow embassy of the 1940s, which are kept at the Suitland, Md., branch of the NA outside Washington: they harbor some important despatches not published in the *Foreign Relations* series. However, records of the Moscow embassy up to 1941 were destroyed in that year, purposely, I believe, when it looked as if the city would fall to the Germans.

Kennan's published materials are in his papers, but most research libraries would carry the publications in which they appeared. His personal bibliography lists them meticulously. As regards other published documents, the *Foreign Relations* series was of obvious assistance: numerous memoranda and despatches by Kennan are reproduced there in whole or in part. Also invaluable was the recently published collection of PPS studies that appeared during Kennan's tenure. Marred only by the exclusion of his secret addendum to PPS 4 (central in the formulation of the Marshall Plan), this excellent compilation (*The State Department Policy Planning Staff Papers*, vols. 1–3, New York, 1983) has not been given the attention it deserves. T. H. Etzold and J. L. Gaddis, *Containment: Documents on American Policy and Strategy, 1945–1950*, was useful as well.

The myriad of memoirs by more or less important figures around Kennan were of slim value for my purposes. But his own *Memoirs* (vols. 1 and 2) were of the utmost importance, both as a primary source in their own right and as an analytical (if obviously partial) account against which mine by necessity had to be measured. Interspersed throughout these fine *Memoirs*, surely among the most outstanding of their kind in American literary history, are also a number of illuminating and extensive excerpts from his otherwise unavailable diaries.

With regard to relevant secondary works, my notes contain extensive comments. The following will thus be brief and narrow in scope. Aside from various minor collaborative editions of essays, much of the published work on Kennan specifically has taken the form of articles, of which there are too many to allow any critical survey here, though some have been of indisputable import for the way in which my work was conceived. Jonathan Knight's early "George Frost Kennan and the Study of American Foreign Policy," *The Western Political Quarterly*, no. 1 (March 1967), should be mentioned, as well as the exchange between John Lewis Gaddis and Eduard M. Mark in *Foreign Affairs* (July 1977 and January 1978). Otherwise there are only two published monographs of note: Jürgen Reiss's short but competent summary of containment, *George Kennans Politik der Eindämmung* (Berlin, 1957); and Barton M. Gellman, *Contending with Kennan* (New York, 1984). The latter, which grew out of a senior thesis at Princeton, is perceptive but understandably limited in terms of depth of research and range of subjects. The problem of the Soviet Union is for instance excluded. *The Wise Men: Six Friends and the World They Made* (New York, 1986) by Walter Isaacson and Evan Thomas is of biographical interest but too popular in tone, content, and method to be of fundamental importance.

Among the unpublished works, three should be recognized for their undeniable value. C. Ben Wright's extensive examination of the early Kennan, "George F. Kennan: Scholar-Diplomat, 1926–1946" (diss., University of Wisconsin, 1972), is a very good historical account, particularly useful with regard to the Portuguese interlude in 1943. William D. Miscamble, "George F. Kennan: The Policy Planning Staff and American Foreign Policy, 1947–1950" (diss., University of Notre Dame, 1980), covers its ground with admirable thoroughness. What it lacks, perhaps because of the approach, is a certain analytical depth. Larry Bland has written a long and interesting unpublished essay (generally unavailable) based on primary sources, mainly with reference to the same period as Miscamble.

All in all, however, Kennan's *Memoirs* remain the only full-scale account in the field.

A list of primary sources follows, as well as a list of unpublished secondary sources.

Unpublished primary sources

Archives and manuscript collections

Butler Library, Columbia University, New York: Jacques Barzun, Lewis
    Galantiere, Philip Mosely, Benjamin Nelson, Eugene Nickerson (pa-
    pers); Dean Acheson, Joseph Ballantine, Joseph Barnes, Prescott
    Bush, Harold Dodds, Bela Fabian, Harry W. Hill, Sol M. Linowitz,
    Walter Lippmann, Norman Ness, Dewitt C. Poole, Norman Ramsey,

Edward E. Rice, Morris Rosenthal, George Sansom, John Sharon, Delmar T. Spivey, Arthur Stevens, Henry A. Wallace (oral histories).

Council on Foreign Relations, New York: Records of Groups, Records of Meetings.

Ford Foundation Archives, New York: Grant project archives; oral history of George F. Kennan.

National Archives, Washington, D.C., Diplomatic Branch: Department of State Decimal File, Daily and Weekly Summaries of the Department of State, Records of Charles E. Bohlen, Records of the Office of European Affairs (Matthews-Hickerson Files), Records of the Office of Eastern European Affairs, Records of the Policy Planning Staff, Records of the Executive Secretariat, Records of Interdepartmental Committees, European Advisory Commission Records.

National Archives, Washington, D.C., Military Branch: National Security Council Documents, Office of Strategic Studies.

National Archives, Suitland, Md.: Department of State, Russia, Moscow post records.

Mudd Library, Princeton University, Princeton, N.J.: Hamilton Fish Armstrong, Allen Dulles, John Foster Dulles, Louis Fischer, James V. Forrestal, George F. Kennan, Arthur Krock, Adlai Stevenson (papers); Charles Bohlen, George F. Kennan (Dulles oral histories).

Public Records Office, Kew Gardens, London: Foreign Office files.

John F. Kennedy Library, Boston, Mass.: Photocopy of George F. Kennan oral history.

Franklin D. Roosevelt Library, Hyde Park, New York: Harry L. Hopkins, R. Walton More, Franklin D. Roosevelt (papers); Adolf Berle (Official File, president's secretary's file).

Dwight D. Eisenhower Library, Abilene, Kans.: John Foster Dulles, C. D. Jackson, Dwight D. Eisenhower (prepresidential) (photocopies of papers).

Harry S. Truman Library, Independence, Mo.: Dean G. Acheson, George V. Allen, Eben A. Ayers, Myron L. Black, Ralph Block, William L. Clayton, Clark M. Clifford, Matthew J. Connelly, Jonathan Daniels, George M. Elsey, Thomas K. Finletter, A. Robert Ginsburg, Stanton Griffis, S. Everett Gleas, Paul G. Hoffman, Joseph Jones, Charles P. Kindleberger, David D. Lloyd, John F. Melby, Edward G. Miller, Charles S. Murphy, Frank Pace, Jr., Sumner T. Pike, William M. Rigdon, John W. Snyder, Stephan F. Spingarn, Sydney W. Souer, Harry S. Truman (Central Files, postpresidential files, President's Official files, president's secretary's files), James E. Webb (papers); Theodore Achilles, George E. Allen, Eben A. Ayers, Robert W. Barnett, David E. Bell, Ralph Block, Merwin L. Bohan, Niles W. Bond, Winthrop G. Brown, David K. E. Bruce, Matthew J. Connelly,

Paul C. Daniels, William H. Draper, Elbridge Durbrow, Michael J. Dux, George M. Elsey, Thomas K. Finletter, Loy W. Henderson, Paul G. Hoffman, John D. Hickerson, Benjamin M. Hulley, Alexis U. Johnson, John Wesley Jones, Perry Laukhoff, Marx Leva, Edwin A. Locke, Jr., Geoffrey W. Lewis, John Maktos, Thomas C. Mann, Edward S. Mason, Elbert G. Mathews, Clifford C. Matlock, H. Freeman Matthews, Livingston Merchant, Charles S. Murphy, Frank Pace, Jr., Graham J. Parsons, James R. Riddleberger, Francis Russell, Charles E. Saltzman, Durward Sandifer, Joseph Satterthwaite, John W. Snyder, Philip D. Sprouse, John L. Sullivan, Willard L. Thorp, Philip H. Trezise, Harry H. Vaughan, Fletcher Warren, Fraser Wilkins, Evan M. Wilson, Edwin M. Wright, Arthur N. Young, John P. Young (oral histories); Charles Bohlen, Hugh Gaitskell, W. Averell Harriman, George F. Kennan, George C. Marshall, Francis Wilcox (interviews re Marshall Plan).

Yale University Library, New Haven, Conn.: Chester Bowles, Arthur Bliss Lane, Max Lerner, Walter Lippmann (papers).

Other: Papers pertaining to GFK and the PPS provided by Dr. Larry Bland.

Personal interviews

John Paton Davies, Asheville N.C., April 26–27, 1981; Sir Frank Roberts, London, Nov. 1984; Sir William Hayter, Oxfordshire, Nov. 1984.

Letters to the author

George F. Kennan, Nov. 15, 1985; Douglas Wheeler, April 1982.

Published primary sources

Published writings by and interviews with George F. Kennan

"Runo: An Island Relic of Medieval Sweden." *Canadian Geographical Journal* 11 (Nov. 1935).

"Report: The Internment and Repatriation of the American Official Group in Germany, 1941–42." *The American Foreign Service Journal* 19 (Aug. and Sept. 1942).

"University Education and the Public Service." *American Foreign Service Journal* 24 (May 1947).

["Mr. X"]. "The Sources of Soviet Conduct." *Foreign Affairs* 25 (July 1947).

"The United States and the United Nations." *Vital Speeches*, Nov. 15, 1948.

"The International Situation." *The Department of State Bulletin*, Sept. 5, 1949.

"Foreign Aid in the Framework of National Policy." *Proceedings of the Academy of Political Science* 23 (Jan. 1950).

"Germany–Soviet Union." *Review of Documents on German Foreign Policy, III. The American Foreign Service Journal* 27 (Feb. 1950).

"Is War with Russia Inevitable?" *The Reader's Digest* 56 (March 1950).

"Current Problems in the Conduct of Foreign Policy." *The Department of State Bulletin*, May 15, 1950.

"Russia and the United States." Stamford, Conn., 1950. (Private printing.)

"The Situation in the Far East." *University of Chicago Round Table*, Aug. 27, 1950.

American Diplomacy, 1900–1950, Chicago, 1951.

"Lectures on Foreign Policy." *The Illinois Law Review* 45 (Jan.–Feb. 1951).

"Let Peace Not Die of Neglect." *New York Times Magazine*, Feb. 25, 1951.

"America and the Russian Future." *Foreign Affairs* 29 (April 1951).

"Where Do You Stand on Communism?" *New York Times Magazine*, May 27, 1951.

Statement by Ambassador George F. Kennan. *The Department of State Bulletin*, April 21, 1952.

"American–Soviet Relations." *Vital Speeches*, Feb. 15, 1953.

"Education for Statesmanship." *Foreign Service Journal* 30 (June 1953).

"The Climate of the Current Investigations of Communism: Effect on the Colleges and the Liberal Arts." *Vital Speeches of the Day*, June 15, 1953.

"Did Stalin's Death Change Anything?" Review of *Russia: What Next?* by Isaac Deutscher. *The Reporter*, July 7, 1953.

"Russia and the West." *The New Leader*, Aug. 14, 1953.

Realities of American Foreign Policy. Princeton, 1954.

"Credo of a Civil Servant." *Princeton Alumni Weekly*, Feb. 2, 1954.

"Das Amerikanische Volk und die auswärtige Politik." *Europa-Archiv*, Feb. 20, 1954.

"Amerika und Russland von Brest Litowsk bis Potsdam." *Osteuropa*, 4 (Oct. 1954).

"Das amerikanisch-russische Verhältnis." *Aussenpolitik* 5 (Oct. 1954).

"For the Defense of Europe: A New Approach." *New York Times Magazine*, Sept. 12, 1954.

"Comments on Ideology and Reality in the Soviet System." In *Proceedings of the American Philosophical Society*, Jan. 21, 1955.

"How Stands Our Pursuit of Happiness?" *The New Leader*, June 20, 1955.

"The Future of Our Professional Diplomacy." *Foreign Affairs* 33 (July 1955).

"The Challenge of Freedom." *The New Leader*, Dec. 26, 1955.

Russia Leaves the War. Princeton, 1956.

"History and Diplomacy as Viewed by a Diplomatist." *The Review of Politics* 18 (April 1956).

"The Future of Soviet Communism." *The New Leader*, June 18, 1956.

"Breach in the Grand Alliance." Letter to the editor. *Washington Post and Times-Herald*, Nov. 3, 1956.

"The Soviet Will Never Recover." Interview by Joseph Alsop. *Saturday Evening Post*, Nov. 24, 1956.

"The Awards: A Talk with George Kennan." Interview by Maurice Dolbier. *New York Herald Tribune Book Review*, March 17, 1957.

The Decision to Intervene. Princeton, 1958.

Russia, the Atom, and the West. New York, 1958.

Introduction. *Siberia and the Exile System*. Chicago, 1958.

"America's Administrative Response to Its World Problems." In *The American Style: Essays in Value and Performance*, ed. E. E. Morison. New York, 1958.

"Ein Brief George Kennans." Letter to the editor. *Neue Züricher Zeitung*, Feb. 1, 1958.

"Below the Summit." Letter to the editor. *Time*, June 23, 1958.

Letter to the Editor. *The National Review Bulletin*, Dec. 27, 1958.

"Walter Lippmann, 'The Republic,' and the Russian Revolution." In *Walter Lippmann and His Times*, ed. Marquis Childs and James Reston. New York, 1959.

"History as Literature." *Encounter* 12 (April 1959).

"Foreign Policy and Christian Conscience." *The Atlantic Monthly* 203 (May 1959).

"Berlin and the Geneva Meeting." *The New Leader*, May 11, 1959.

"Tribute to General Marshall." *New York Times*, May 22, 1959.

"Our Aid to Russia: A Forgotten Chapter." *New York Times Magazine*, July 19, 1959.

"Russia, the Atom, and the West, 1959." *The Listener*, Oct. 29, 1959.

"A Proposal for Western Survival." *The New Leader*, Nov. 16, 1959.

"Disengagement Revisited." *Foreign Affairs* 37 (Jan. 1959).

"Peaceful Co-Existence: A Western View." *Foreign Affairs* 38 (Jan. 1960).

Russia and the West under Lenin and Stalin. New York, 1960.

Soviet Foreign Policy, 1917–1941. Princeton, 1960.

"American Troops in Russia: Aid for the Czecho-Slovaks?" In *American Intervention in the Russian Civil War*, ed. B. M. Unterberger. Lexington, Mass., 1960.

Colloques de Rheinfelden par Raymond Aron, George Kennan, Robert Oppenheimer et autres. 1959. Reprint. Paris, 1960.

"Soviet Historiography and America's Role in the Intervention." *The American Historical Review* 65 (Jan. 1960).

"A Commentary." *Washington Post and Times Herald*, Jan. 10, 1960.

"A Conversation with Kennan." Interview by Melvin J. Lasky. *Encounter* 14 (March 1960).

"The Value of a St. John's Education." June 4, 1960. Private printing.

"That Candles May Be Brought . . ." *Encounter* 16 (Feb. 1961).

"An Historian of Potsdam and His Readers." Review of *Between War and Peace* by Herbert Feis. *American Slavic and East European Review* 20 (April 1961).

"Lenin und der politische Terror." Letter to the editor, *Der Monat* 139 (April 1960).

"Diplomacy as a Profession." *Foreign Service Journal* 38 (May 1961).

"World Problems in Christian Perspective." 1959. In *American History: Recent Interpretations*, ed. Abraham S. Eisenstadt. Vol 2. New York, 1962.

"Contemporary Perspectives." In *Russian Foreign Policy: Essays in Historical Perspective*, ed. Ivo J. Lederer. New Haven, 1962.

"Policy on Yugoslavia." Letter to the editor, *New York Times*, June 23, 1962.

"U.S. Shouldn't Slam Door on Yugoslavia." *Washington Post and Times Herald*, July 8, 1962.

"The Confusion of Ends and Means." In *The Soviet Crucible*, ed. Samuel Hendel. 1959. 2d ed. Princeton, 1963.

"Can We Deal with Moscow?" *The Saturday Evening Post*, Oct. 5, 1963.

"Kennan Backs Sales to Tito." Letter to the editor. *New York Times*, Oct. 16, 1963.

"Our Foreign Policy is Paralyzed." Interview with J. Robert Moskin. *Look*, Nov. 19, 1963.

"Sein Tod is nicht allein Amerikas Tragodie." *Tages-Anzeiger* (Zürich), Nov. 30, 1963.

On Dealing with the Communist World. New York, 1964.

"Totalitarianism in the Modern World." March 1953. In *Totalitarianism*, ed. Carl J. Friedrich. New York, 1964.

"George F. Kennan's Observations on the New Soviet Leadership, August 1956." In *Ideas and Diplomacy*, ed. Norman A. Graebner. New York, 1964.

"We Have Seen Our Public Life Debauched." 1954. In *Ideas and Diplomacy*, ed. Norman A. Graebner. New York, 1964.

"How the 1914 War Started in Russia." *The Listener*, July 9, 1964.

"Japanese Security and American Policy." *Foreign Affairs* 43 (Oct. 1964).

"The Price We Paid for War." *The Atlantic Monthly* 214 (Oct. 1964).

"A Triumph for Mao." *Sunday Times* (London), Oct. 18, 1964.

"A Fresh Look at Our China Policy." *New York Times Magazine*, Nov. 22, 1964.

"The Ethics of Anti-Communism." *University: A Princeton Quarterly* 24 (Spring 1965).

"American Involvement." In *The Viet-Nam Reader*, ed. Marcus G. Raskin and Bernard B. Fall. New York, 1965.

"For a New Act of Faith." In *Pacem in Terris: Peace on Earth*, ed. E. Reed. New York, 1965.

Introduction. Boris I. Nicolaevsky. *Power and the Soviet Elite: "The Letter of An Old Bolshevik" and Other Essays*, ed. J. D. Zagorio. New York, 1965.

"China Policy. Comments on Stanley Spector's review of three books on China in the last issue of *The Correspondent*." *The Correspondent* 33 (Winter 1965).

"A Policy for the Far East: An Exchange between G. F. Kennan and A. J. Muste." *Liberation* 10 (April 1965).

"An Authority on Communism Says We're Letting This One Area Disbalance Whole Policy." *Washington Post*, Dec. 12, 1965.

"The Experience of Writing History." 1960. In *The Craft of American History*, ed. A. S. Eisenstadt. Vol. 2. New York, 1966.

"Boris Ivanovich Nicolaevsky, 1887–1966." *Slavic Review* 25 (June 1966).

"Why Do I Hope?" *University: A Princeton Quarterly* 29 (Summer 1966).

"Kennan Urges War Policy of Moderation." Letter to the editor. *New York Times*, Sept. 25, 1966.

Memoirs, 1925–1950. Boston, 1967.

"Oppenheimer." *Encounter* 28 (April 1967).

"The Russian Revolution—Fifty Years After." *Foreign Affairs* 46 (Oct. 1967).

From Prague after Munich. Princeton, 1968.

Democracy and the Student Left. London, 1968.

Foreword. Edward M. Kennedy. *Decision for a Decade*. Garden City, N.Y., 1968.

"The Breakdown of the Tsarist Autocracy." In *Revolutionary Russia*, ed. Richard Pipes. Cambridge, Mass., 1968.

"The Soviet Union, 1917–1939." In *The New Cambridge Modern History: The Shifting Balance of World Forces, 1898–1945*. 2d ed. Cambridge, 1968.

"Introducing Eugene McCarthy." *New York Review of Books*, April 11, 1968.

"America after Vietnam." *Wall Street Journal*, July 25, 1968.

"Excerpts from a Draft Letter Written at Some Time during the First Months of 1945." *Slavic Review* 27 (Sept. 1968).

Review of *The Young Stalin: The Early Years of an Elusive Revolutionary*, by Edward Ellis Smith. *The American Historical Review* 74 (Oct. 1968).

"The Purges Unpurged." Review of *The Great Terror*, by Robert Conquest. *New York Times Book Review*, Oct. 27, 1968.

"The Contemporary Literary Scene in Russia." Panel discussion. Jan. 1968. In *Proceedings of the American Academy of Arts and Letters–National Institute of Arts and Letters*, 2d ser. Vol. 19. New York, 1969.

"The Relation of Religion to Government." *The Princeton Seminary Bulletin* 62 (Winter 1969).

"Justice for Davies." Letter to the editor. *New York Times*, Jan. 22, 1969.

Review of *Vospominiia Sovetskogo Posla: Voina, 1939–1943*, by I. M. Maisky. *Slavic Review* 28 (March 1969).

"Remembering for the Russians." Review of *The Siege of Leningrad*, by Harrison Salisbury. *Times Literary Supplement*, Aug. 14, 1969.

"Kennan Urges Speedy Withdrawal." Interview by Israel Shenker. *New York Times*, Nov. 10, 1969.

"Opening Address." In *Proceedings of the American Academy of Arts and Letters–National Institute of Arts and Letters*, 2d ser. Vol. 19. New York, 1969.

"Weltkonflikte und Weltpolizisten," *Die Zeit* 45 (Nov. 7, 1969).

"More Controls Ahead." Dec. 1968. In *The Endless Crisis: A Confrontation on America in the Seventies*, ed. F. Duchene. New York, 1970.

"To Prevent a World Wasteland." *Foreign Affairs* 48 (April 1970).

"An Interview with George F. Kennan." John F. Cambell. *Foreign Service Journal* 47 (Aug. 1970).

"Con III Is Not the Answer." *New York Times*, Oct. 28, 1970.

The Marquis de Custine and His "Russia in 1839." Princeton, 1971.

Introduction to Charles W. Thayer. *Russia*. Rev. ed. New York, 1971.

GFK et al. *South Africa: Three Visitors' Reports*. Pasadena, 1971.

"Hazardous Courses in Southern Africa." *Foreign Affairs* 49 (Jan. 1971).

"A Note on Russian Foreign Policy." *Encounter* 36 (Feb. 1971).

"Dead Souls." Review of *Khrushchev Remembers*, by N. S. Khrushchev. *New York Review of Books*, Feb. 25, 1971.

"The Arts in American Society." June 1965. *Cultural Affairs* 15 (May 1971).

"The Historiography of the Early Political Career of Stalin." *Proceedings of the American Philosophical Society* 115 (June 1971).

Memoirs, 1950–1963. Boston, 1972.

Foreword to Louis Fischer. *The Road to Yalta: Soviet Foreign Relations 1941–1945*. New York, 1972.

Introduction to *For the President: Personal and Secret Correspondence Between Franklin D. Roosevelt and William C. Bullitt*, ed. O. H. Bullitt. Boston, 1972.

GFK et al. "Research in Contemporary Events for the Writing of History." In *Proceedings of the American Academy of Arts and Letters–National Institute of Arts and Letters*, 2d ser. Vol. 22. New York, 1972.

"Commemorative Tribute to the Late Rev. Reinhold Niebuhr." In *Proceedings of the American Academy of Arts and Letters–National Institute of Arts and Letters*, 2d ser. Vol. 22. New York, 1972.

"America's Love-Hate Affair with China." *The Observer*, Feb. 20, 1972.

"X Plus 25." Interview. *Foreign Policy* 7 (Summer 1972).

Interview by Ingegerd Galtung. *Morgenbladet* (Oslo), Sept. 15, 1972.

"After the Cold War: American Foreign Policy in the 1970s." *Foreign Affairs* 51 (Oct. 1972).

"Dokumentation: Aus dem Kadermaterial der illegalen KPD, 1945." *Vierteljahrshefte für Zeitgeschichte 1972*, 20 (Oct. 1972).

"What We've Lost in Vietnam." *Washington Post*, Jan. 14, 1973.

"Noble Man." Review of *Helmuth von Moltke: A Leader against Hitler*, by Michael Balfour and Julian Frisby. *New York Review of Books*, March 22, 1973.

"Hamilton Fish Armstrong, 1893–1973." *Foreign Affairs* 51 (July 1973).

"Double Standards over Mozambique." Letter to the editor. *Times* (London), July 25, 1973.

Interview by Ingegerd Galtung. *Morgenbladet* (Oslo), Aug. 18, 20, 1973.

"U.S.-Soviet Trade: Favored Is No Favor." Letter to the editor. *New York Times*, Sept. 25, 1973.

"Detente, Diplomatic Opportunity . . . " *Washington Post*, Oct. 8, 1973.

"And Thank You Very Much." *New York Times*, Dec. 2, 1973.

"Europe's Problems, Europe's Choices." *Foreign Policy* 14 (Spring 1974).

"Between Earth and Hell." Review of *Gulag Archipelago*, by Aleksandr Solzhenitsyn. *New York Review of Books*, March 21, 1974.

"Cold-Warrior Eyes Age of Detente: George Kennan Speaks Out, Maps New Career at 70." Interview by Steve Neal, *Philadelphia Inquirer*, April 21, 1974.

"Streets Once Really Seen or Seen in Dreams." *The New Yorker*, April 29, 1974.

"The Legacy of Woodrow Wilson." *Princeton Alumni Weekly*, Oct. 21, 1974.

Review of *St. Petersburg and Moscow: Tsarist and Soviet Foreign Policy, 1814–1974*, by Barbara Jelavich. *Slavic Review* 34 (June 1975).

"The United States and the Soviet Union, 1917–1976." *Foreign Affairs* 54 (July 1976).

"Conversation with George Kennan." 1975. In *Conversations with Eric Sevareid: Interviews with Notable Americans.* Washington, D.C., 1976.

"Is Détente Worth Saving?" *Saturday Review*, March 6, 1976.

"George F. Kennan Replies." C. Ben. Wright. *Slavic Review* 35 (March 1976).

"The United States and the Soviet Union, 1917–1976." *Foreign Affairs* 54 (July 1976).

"A Conversation with George F. Kennan." Interview by George Urban. *Encounter* 47 (Sept. 1976).

The Cloud of Danger. New York, 1977.

Commemorative Tribute to the Late Walter Lippmann. *Proceedings of the American Academy and Institute of Arts and Letters*, 2d ser. Vol. 27. New York, 1977.

"Foreign Policy and the Professional Diplomat." *The Wilson Quarterly* 1 (Winter 1977).

"A Different Approach to the World: An Interview." Interview with Martin Agronsky. *New York Review of Books*, Jan. 20, 1977.

"Are All Russians 8 Feet Tall?" *Military Review* 5 (May 1977).

"Russen und Amerikaner: Warum sie sich fürchten." *Die Zeit*, July 1, 1977.

GFK et al. *Decline of the West?* Washington, D.C., 1978.

"Mr. X Reconsiders: A Current Assessment of Soviet American Relations." *Encounter* 50 (March 1978).

"George Kennan on Containment Reconsidered." *Foreign Affairs* 56 (April 1978).

"Begegnungen mit Deutschland." *Frankfurter Allgemeine Zeitung*, June 3, 1978.

"Some Thoughts on Stalin's Foreign Policy." *Slavic Review* 36 (July 1978).

"A Last Warning: Reply to My Critics." *Encounter* 51 (July 1978).

The Decline of Bismarck's European Order. Princeton, 1979.

GFK et al. *Encounters with Kennan.* London, 1979.

"Two Views of the Soviet Problem." *The New Yorker*, Nov. 2, 1981.

"Beyond the Shadow of the Atom." *Congressional Record*, Dec. 7, 1981.

The Nuclear Delusion. New York, 1982.

"America's Unstable Soviet Policy." *Atlantic Monthly* 250 (Nov. 1982).

"Morality and Foreign Policy." *Foreign Affairs* 65 (Winter 1985–86).

"The Gorbachev Prospect." *New York Review of Books*, Jan. 21, 1988.

Published government testimonies by George F. Kennan

Testimony. U.S. Congress. House. Committee on Foreign Affairs. Draft Report. *Foreign Policy and Mutual Security*, and Hearings, Oct. 11, 1956.

Testimony. U.S. Congress. Senate. Subcommittee of the Committee on Foreign Relations. *Control and Reduction of Armaments*. Hearings. 85th Cong., 1st sess., pt. 2, Jan. 9, 1957.

Testimony. U.S. Congress. Senate. Subcommittee of the Committee on Foreign Relations. *Disarmament and Foreign Policy*. Hearings. 86th Cong., 1st sess., Feb. 4, 1959.

Testimony. U.S. Congress. Senate. Committee on Foreign Relations. *Informal Meeting with George F. Kennan*. Hearing. 86th Cong., 1st sess., May 12, 1959.

Testimony. U.S. Congress. Senate. Subcommittee on National Policy Machinery of the Committee on Government Operations. *Organizing for National Security, the Policy Planning Staff, and the National Security Council*. Hearings. 86th Cong., 2d sess., pt. 6, 1960.

Memorandum. U.S. Congress. Senate. Subcommittee on National Security Staffing and Operations of the Committee on Government Operations. *Administration of National Security*. Hearings. 88th Cong., 1st sess., pt. 5, Dec. 11, 1963. Memorandum published Nov. 3, 1963.

Testimony. U.S. Congress. Senate. Committee on Foreign Relations. *East-West Trade*. Hearings, 89th Cong., 1st sess., pt. 2, Feb. 26, 1965.

Testimony. U.S. Congress. House. *Sino-Soviet Conflict*, Report and Hearings. 89th Cong., 1st sess., March 11, 1965. In *The Viet-Nam Reader*, ed. Marcus G. Raskin and Bernard B. Fall. New York, 1965.

Testimony. U.S. Congress. Senate. Committee on Foreign Relations. *Supplemental Foreign Assistance Fiscal Year 1966—Vietnam*. Hearings. 89th Cong., 2d sess. (Jan.–Feb. 1966), Feb. 10, 1966.

Testimony. U.S. Congress. Senate. Committee on Foreign Relations. *The Communist World in 1967*. Hearings. 90th Cong., 1st sess., Jan. 30, 1967.

Testimony. U.S. Congress. Senate. Committee on Foreign Relations. *Exchanges of U.S.-U.S.S.R. Officials*. Hearings. 91st Cong., 2d sess., Feb. 6, 1970.

Testimony. U.S. Congress. House. Subcommittee on Europe of the Committee on Foreign Affairs. *United States Relations with Europe in the Decade of the 1970s*. Hearings. 91st Cong., 2d sess., March 11, 1970.

Testimony. U.S. Congress. Senate. Committee on Foreign Relations.

United States Relations with Communist Countries. Hearings. 93d Cong., 2d sess., Aug. 20, 1974.

Statement. U.S. Congress. House of Representatives. Subcommittee on Europe and the Middle East of the Committee on International Relations. *The Soviet Union: Internal Dynamics of Foreign Policy, Present and Future.* Hearings. 95th Cong., 1st sess., Sept. 27, 1977.

Statement. U.S. Congress. Senate. Committee on Foreign Relations. *Perceptions: Relations between the United States and the Soviet Union.* 1978. Statement from Sept. 25, 1978.

Unpublished secondary sources

Beck, Kent Moore. "American Liberalism and the Cold War Consensus: Policies and Policymakers of the Moderate Democratic Left, 1945–1953." Dissertation, University of California, Irvine, 1977.

Bland, Larry. "Policy Planner." Unpublished manuscript, n.d.

Denman, Dorothy I. "The Riddle of Containment: As Reflected in the Advice and Dissent of George F. Kennan." Dissertation, University of Miami, 1975.

Gearity, James L. "The First Brain Trust: Academics, Reform, and the Wisconsin Idea." Dissertation, University of Minnesota, 1979.

Goldstein, Joshua S., and John Freeman. "Containment Theory and Reality: The Strategic Triangle, 1948–1978." APSA paper, 1987.

Green, James Frederick. The Political Thought of George F. Kennan: A Study of the Development and Interrelations of American and Soviet Foreign Policies." Dissertation, The American University, 1972.

Hale, Myron Q. "American Conservatism: Conventionalism, Historicism, Functionalism." Dissertation, Columbia University, 1958.

Hanson, Betty Crump. "American Diplomatic Reporting from the Soviet Union, 1934–41." Dissertation, Columbia University, 1966.

Mark, Eduard M. "The Interpretation of Soviet Foreign Policy in the United States, 1928–1947." Dissertation, University of Connecticut, 1978.

Miscamble, Wilson D. "George F. Kennan. The Policy Planning Staff and American Foreign Policy, 1947–1950." Dissertation, University of Notre Dame, 1980.

Newman, Parley W. "The Origins of the North Atlantic Treaty: A Study in Organization and Politics." Dissertation, Columbia University, 1977.

Powers, Richard James. "Kennan against Himself? From Containment to Disengagement." Dissertation, Claremont Graduate School and University Center, 1967.

Sand, George W. "Clifford and Truman: A Study in Foreign Policy and National Security." Dissertation, St. Louis University, 1973.

West, Cornel. "Marxism, Historicism, Ethics." Dissertation, Princeton University, 1980.

Wright, C. Ben. "George F. Kennan. Scholar-Diplomat: 1926–1946." Dissertation, University of Wisconsin, 1972.

Yurechko, John J. "From Containment to Counteroffensive: Soviet Vulnerabilities and American Policy Planning, 1946–1953." Dissertation, University of California, Berkeley, 1980.

Index

Acheson, Dean, 114, 149, 152, 204, 239
Adams, Brooks, 93, 212
Adams, John, 226
Adenauer, Konrad, 124, 126
Adorno, Theodor, 223–224, 237–238
Advertising, 236
Aestheticism, 199–202, 251–255
Afghanistan, 351n28
Africa: relations with European federation, 139; recolonization of, 166
Albania, 77
Alliance(s): military necessity vs. political compatibility in, 34–37; and parallel interests, 42; as vehicle of containment policy, 137–144, 146, 147–148, 150–151; realist critique of, 139–140; and rollback policy, 151; balance-of-power alternative to, 183; antifascist, 269–270, 271; anti-American, 271
Allied Control Council, 122, 124, 125, 126, 144
American Academy of Arts and Letters, 251
American Communist party, 87, 239
American Diplomacy (Kennan), 191
American Revolution, 211
Anderson, Perry, 283n14
Angola, colonialism in, 172–173
Anti-Americanism, 271; in Third World, 158, 160, 161, 162, 164
Anticommunism: and relations with Third World nations, 162–165; in domestic

politics, 238–240, 242. *See also* Containment
Anti-Semitism, in Foreign Service, 6
Apartheid, 173–174
Aristocracy: and German reconstruction, 120; in organic society, 222–223
Aristotle, 198, 246, 298n34
Armenians, 33
Arms control, 273
Arms race, 156, 194, 247–248, 264–265
Aron, Raymond, 153
Athens, ancient, 77
Atlantic Charter, 36–37
Atomic weapons, 149, 247–248, 249, 265
Austria, 21, 101, 124, 131, 133, 147, 155, 156, 284n16; social security law, 24, 220; authoritarianism in, 24–25, 219; postwar reconstruction of, 38, 123; political neutrality of, 41
Austro-Hungarian (Hapsburg) empire, 25, 27, 170; as model for European order, 117–118
Authoritarianism: benevolent efficiency of, 24–26; benefits to American society, 216, 217–221, 224–225, 227; popular sanctioning of, 225. *See also* Fascism
Automobiles, 234–236, 237

Backer, John H., 318n58
Balance of power, 13; and European reconstruction, 137, 138; as principle of diplomacy, 182–185